CADOGANguides

BAVARIA

'Beer is sometimes served in a Maß – a challenging litre-tankard.
Whether you are gulping down a Maß in a rowdy beer tent, or sipping
it in a smoky cellar, or drinking alongside the huge copper vats in a
local Brauerei, or sailing down the River Isar propped up against your
own barrel (a popular Bavarian springtime activity), your encounters
with beer in Germany may well number among the most memorable
moments of your visit.'

Rodney Bolt

About the Guide

The **full-colour introduction** gives the author's overview of the region, together with suggested **itineraries** and a regional **'where to go' map** and **feature** to help you plan your trip.

Illuminating and entertaining **cultural chapters** on local history, culture, food, wine and everyday life give you a rich flavour of the region.

Planning Your Trip starts with the basics of when to go, getting there and getting around, coupled with other useful information, including a section for disabled travellers. The **Practical A–Z** deals with all the **essential information** and **contact details** that you may need while you are away.

The **regional chapters** are arranged in a loose touring order, with plenty of public transport and driving information. The author's top **'Don't Miss'** ⭐ **sights** are highlighted at the start of each chapter.

A **language and pronunciation guide**, a **glossary** of cultural terms, ideas for **further reading** and a comprehensive **index** can be found at the end of the book.

Although everything listed in this guide is **personally recommended**, our author inevitably has his own favourite places to eat and stay. Whenever you see this **Authors' Choice** ⭐ icon beside a listing, you will know that it is a little bit out of the ordinary.

Restaurant Price Guide (*see also* p.65)

Expensive	€€€	€50+
Moderate	€€	€30–50
Inexpensive	€	– €30

Hotel Price Guide (see also p.61)

Luxury	€€€€€	€250+
Expensive	€€€	€150–249
Moderate	€€	€100–149
Inexpensive	€	– €100

About the Author

Rodney Bolt grew up in Africa, was educated at Cambridge University and now lives in Amsterdam. He has travelled throughout Europe and has lived and worked in Greece, the Netherlands and Germany. He has written Cadogan Guides to the Netherlands, Amsterdam and Madeira, and won travel-writing prizes from Germany and the USA.

4th Edition published 2010

01 INTRODUCING BAVARIA

Top: Old Town Hall,
Bamburg

Above: Munich City Hall

Of all the tribes of Germany, none is fiercer about its singularity and independence than the Bavarians. A race of romantics whose national hero is a fantastical, dreamy 19th-century king, and who dismiss countrymen north of the border as spiritless *Saupreissen* (swinish Prussians), Bavarians often express their loyalties in a descending scale: 'Bavaria first, Europe second and Germany third'. The state capital, Munich, is twinned with Edinburgh in Scotland, and, like the Scots, many Bavarians cherish ideas of national independence, though without quite the same degree of seriousness.

North Germans regard the southerners as rumbustious hedonists, pushy and uncouth. Foreigners expect (and often find) fat, lederhosen-clad men with feathers in their hats, munching sausages and guzzling giant-sized measures of beer. The truth is that Bavaria packs between its borders a variety of spectacle and style that beats anywhere else in Germany. You'll find sleepy bucolic villages, chic highlife, cornerstones of European culture and (many say) the tastiest cooking in the land. In Munich you can plunge into arguably the country's best art collection, and its most Bacchanalian festival. Bayreuth and Oberammergau stage two of the most famous arts events in the world.

You can swarm down the Romantische Straße with millions of foreign tourists and jostle with jetsetters in Alpine ski resorts, or you can wander into a tiny village where life potters on in much the same way as it has done for centuries and head off into the un-spoiled backwoods of the Bavarian Forest, along the Czech border.

Above:
Munich's modern skyline

Opposite:
Bayern Church with the
Alps in the background

Some argue that the Bavarians are not one tribe, but three; ethnic nitpickers can dig out as many as seven. Augsburg in the west, for instance, is still very much in placid Swabian territory; and Franconia (the northern part of the Land) was only integrated into Bavaria in 1805. Locals here can insist that they are not really Bavarian at all, and look to Nürnberg as their capital.

Bavaria is fervently Roman Catholic. This means lots of holidays and festivals, but also a staunch, sometimes alarming conservatism. But as a visitor to Bavaria you're more likely to be swept up by good cheer than politics. Take the advice of the favourite Bavarian saying: *Mir san mir* ('we are us', take us as we are). Soon the local greeting, *Grüß Gott*, will trip easily off your tongue. You may even end up peppering your conversation with near pious expressions such as *Vergelt's Gott* (thank you, or literally 'May God reward you for this'), or find yourself linking arms with your neighbours in a beer garden and swaying to the sound of an oompah band.

Bavaria Fact Box

- **Land area:** 70, 458 sq km (27,200 sq miles)
- **Population:** 12.5 million
- **Major cities:** Munich (population 1.3 million); Nuremberg (500,000) and Augsburg (263,000) are the three major cities, followed by Regensburg, Wurtzburg, Ingolstadt, Furth and Erlangen
- **Religion:** overwhelmingly Roman Catholic
- **Internal borders:** Bavaria borders on the German lander of Baden Wurttemberg, Hesse, Thuringia and Saxony
- **International borders:** Bavaria borders on Austria (south and east); Czech Republic (east) and Switzerland (Lake Constance)

01 Introduction

Where to Go

Because cultural and religious boundaries do not always conform to the administrative ones, this guide is not divided into chapters devoted to each of the seven *Bezirke* (districts), but is structured around regions that have a common outlook or historical traditions, or which visitors are likely to tackle as a single piece.

The first section focuses on the city of **Munich**, Bavaria's compact and cosmopolitan capital; but it also takes in the low-lying hinterland and attractive river of the Altmühl to the north, and the historic towns of the Inn-Salzachgau to the east.

South of Munich lie the **Bavarian Alps**, with their sparkling lakes, mountains galore and clusters of Baroque churches and chapels. This is the stamping ground of the most rural and conservative Bavarians, who wear local *Tracht* (costume) with pride. The route runs from the Alpine scenery of the upper Bavarian Alps in the east to the undulating pre-Alpine pastures and cosy towns of the Allgäu, as far as Lindau on Lake Constance (Bodensee).

Next comes Germany's most popular theme road, the **Romantic Road**, all 343km of it, travelling – as most people do – from north to south, with diversions sideways into forests and along the Danube.

The section on **Eastern Bavaria** begins with the Italianate cities of Regensburg and Passau on the Danube. The route moves eastward into the less accessible (but delightful) regions of the Bavarian and Upper Palatinate Forests, which is Bavaria at its sylvan best, luring hikers and bikers into its unspoilt, lonely wilderness.

Finally, across the top of the state stretches **Franconia**, Bavaria's largest region. Franconia is a mixed bag, with Nürnberg (Germany's unofficial capital in the Middle Ages), Bayreuth (home to the Wagner Festival) and Bamberg (a Baroque gem) thrown in with the rocky gorges of Franconian Switzerland and misty pine forests.

Above: Lindau Lighthouse

Below: Historic Old Town Hall, Regensburg

Right: A view on the way up to the Zugspitze in Garmisch-Partenkirchen

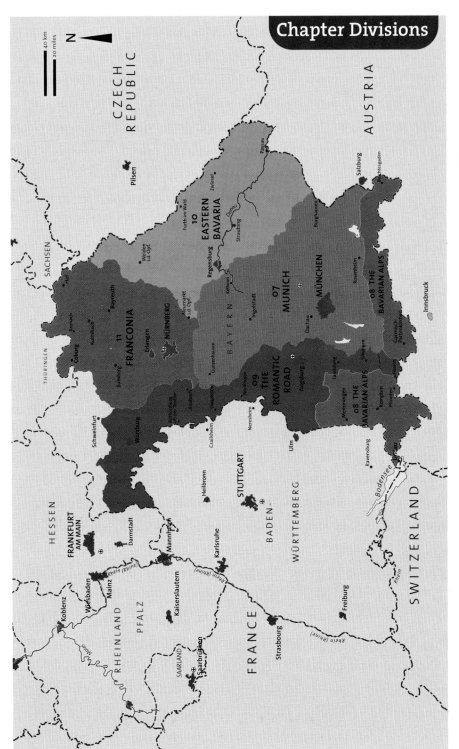

Chapter Divisions

Bavarian Palaces

From grim medieval strongholds which conceal labyrinths of echoing, tapestry-hung halls to fanciful confections fit for a fairy prince, Bavaria is rich in stately grandeur.

- The rambling **Residenz** complex was the home of the Wittelsbachs until 1918 and is still one of the most attractive royal palaces in the world, p.79
- The gorgeous Baroque palace of **Schloss Nymphenburg**, on the outskirts of Munich, was the summer residence of the Electors of Bavaria and stands amid formal gardens adorned with faux-classical statuary, p.86
- It's not technically a palace, but Munich's **Altes Rathaus**, dominating the east side of the Marienplatz, is a superb example of Bavarian Gothic architecture, p.75
- **Neuschwanstein**, built for the eccentric King Ludwig II, is the ultimate in fairytale castles, p.173
- **The Kaiserburg**, dominating Nurnberg's medieval Altstadt, is a massive fortress founded more than 1,000 years ago and embellished over the centuries, p.202

Above:Nymphenburg castle, Munich

Right: The 'Residenz', the former royal palace in Munich

Opposite: Neuschwanstein Castle

Museums and Galleries

Bavaria's museums and art galleries display an astonishing eclectisism and span thousands of years of the region's history, from the prehistoric era to the quirks of 19th century monarchs and the works of some of Europe's greatest artists.

- The **Germanisches Nationalmuseum** in Nürnberg houses an enormous collection of German art and artefacts within the walls of a 14th century Carthusian monastery, p.207
- Munich's **Alte Pinakothek** contains an incomparable array of works by early German masters, a vast Rubens collection and paintings by Botticelli, Durer and Lippi, p.81
- The **Neue Pinakothek** houses some stunning 19th and 20th century works by Goya, Turner, Van Gogh, Gauguin and a stellar collection of 19th century German painters, p.83
- Regensburg's **Diözesanmuseum St Ulrich** is a 12th century chapel with a fine collection of religious paintings and sculptures from the Middle Ages, p.182

Top: The Alte Pinakothek, Munich

Above: Germanisches Nationalmuseum, Nürnberg

Churches and Cathedrals

The onion-dome churches which dominate almost every town and village in Bavaria are perhaps the most potent icon of this devoutly Catholic region, while grandiose cathedrals – some of them begun more than 1,000 years ago – are at the heart of the old quarter of each Bavarian city.

- **Regensburg's giant Dom** (Cathedral) is the finest Gothic church in southern Germany, looming over the low red rooftops of the old town, p.180
- The twin onion-domed towers of the **Frauenkirche** (Church of Our Lady) are Munich's best-known landmark. The Gothic cathedral is the seat of the archbishopric of Munich and Friesing, p.78
- Work on **Augsburg's Dom** (Cathedral) began in 1060 and it represents several centuries of changing religious architectural styles, p.168
- **St Stephan's Cathedral**, atop Passau's historic centre, is an elaborate 17th-century Baroque confection whose ornate white stucco interior houses the largest pipe organ in the world, p.191

Tops: Sculptures and paintings decorating the interior of Passau Cathedral

Above: Munich's Frauenkirche

Above:
Spring landscape near
Garmisch-Partenkirchen

The Great Outdoors

In summer, Bavaria offers superb walking in rolling countryside or energetic hiking amid Alpine scenery, watersports on lakes and rivers, and even yachting on Europe's third-largest lake. In winter, ski slopes beckon.

- **Garmisch-Partenkirchen**, at the foot of the Wetterstein range in the Bavarian Alps, is Germany's leading ski resort in winter and a base for mountain walking in summer. Above it (reached by cable car) is Germany's highest summit, the Zugspitze, p.125
- The pretty town of **Lindau** is Bavaria's gateway to the 'inland sea' of **Lake Constance** (Bodensee), with steamer trips on the lake, watersports and yachts and sailboats for hire, p.134
- The **Frankische Schweiz** ('Franconian Switzerland') between Baberg, Bayreuth and Nürnberg, is a region of deep valleys, lush meadows and fruit orchards interspersed with deep gorges and rocky crags, p.227
- The **Upper Palatinate Forest** and the **Bavarian Forest** offer more than 500km of waymarked walking trails through pristine woodland and mountain meadows, p.194

Right:Zugspitze
Below: Lindau Harbour,
Lake Constance

Itinerary 1: The Romantic Road

Realistically, you need a car to cover the 343 km of Germany's 'Romantic Road' at leisure. The route is well signposted, and is best followed from north to south.

Opposite: Cathedral of St Ulrich, Augsburg

Below: Cobbled alleyway in the ancient town of Rothenburg ob der Tauber

Day 1 Spend a full day among **Wurzburg**'s alternately dreamy palaces and grim fortresses, visit the spectacular Residenz, then spend the evening sipping wine in a cosy weinstube.

Day 2 Roam for a day through the **Pflulben and Iphofen vineyards**, pausing at the Iphofen Vinothek to taste vintages from more than 20 local winemakers.

Day 3 Miraculously unscathed, **Miltenberg** is by far the most romantic town on this romantic road. Spend a day wandering its well preserved streets of half-timbered houses along the banks of the River Main.

Bottom: Half-timbered houses in Miltenberg

Day 4 For many, the meticulously reconstructed medieval architecture of **Rothenburg ob der Tauber** constitutes what the Romantic Road is all about.

Day 5 Plan to spend at least one day in **Augsburg**, a city with a history that spans at least 2,000 years. Start at the elegant Rathaus with its magnificent Goldener Saal, then walk to the Dom. Don't miss the Fuggerpalast, home since the 16th century to the dynasty who invented modern investment banking.

Day 6 Nothing could be a more romantic finale to a tour of the Romantic Road than Ludgwig II's ridiculously charming lakeside castle at **Neuschwanstein**. Poor Ludwig only stayed six months in his designer dream-home; the rest of his reign was spent in the nearby ancestral fortress of **Hohenschwangau**. You will need a full day to make the most of both of these.

Itinerary 2: A weekend in Munich

Bavaria's capital, evocative of the eccentric Wittelsbachs, offers you an eclectic mix of high culture and simple pleasures. It makes Germany's best beer and sausages, is the venue for a month-long celebration of both, and is home to some of Europe's finest museums and art galleries.

Day 1 Buy a day ticket for all of the superb collections in the **Pinakothek complex** and devote a day to old masters in the Alte Pinakothek, 19th and 20th century stars in the Neue Pinakothek, and superb modern art by Matisse, Picasso and Max Beckmann in the Pinakothek der Moderne.

Day 2 Get to the **Marienplatz** by 11am to watch the miniature figures of the famous Neues Rathaus glockenspiel go through their mechanical dance . Then for a change of cultural pace, head out of the centre to the uber-kitsch **Schloss Nymphenburg**, summer residence of the Electors of Bavaria, with its lavish salons and formal gardens adorned with faux-classical statuary. Return to the centre via a stroll through the **Englischer Garten**, winding up back at the Marienplatz for an evening of beer, sausages and merriment at the famous Munchner Hofbrauhaus.

Above: Englischer Garten, Munich

Below: Munich Siegestor (Victory Gate)

CONTENTS

Contents

History

02

Beginnings

As with Scotland and Brittany, the first glimmers of a Bavarian history are seen through a Celtic twilight. **Celtic** tribes first settled the lands of modern Bavaria around 800 BC. By 400 BC the deft iron-workers had become Europe's dominant culture. They left behind some 200 *Keltenschanzen* (barrows) chock-full of fine pottery, gold jewellery and decorated weapons, as well as a string of place and river names still in use today. By 200 BC Germanic tribes migrating south from Jutland and northern Polish regions had come up against Roman armies marching north. In 113 BC two of these tribes, the **Cimbri** and the **Teutones**, had the effrontery to defeat a Roman army in the Alps. In turn, they and their kind were very nearly annihilated by the great Roman general **Marius**.

The Romans

By 15 BC Roman armies had forced their way into the land between the Alps, Dolomites and the Danube, securing Rome's northern frontier and garnering the riches of Celtic iron and salt mines in the process. They divided the southern part into the provinces of **Raetia** and **Noricum**, but the defeat of two Roman legions by **Arminius**, chief of the *Cherusci*, in the Teutoburg Forest in AD 9 foiled any more expansionist moves across the Danube. The fortified settlements that the Romans built along the banks of the river behind the ramparts of their imperial border formed the foundation blocks of many a present-day Bavarian town. **Kempten** (*Kambodounon*), **Regensburg** (*Radasbona*), **Passau** (*Batavis*) and **Augsburg** (*Augusta Vindelicorum*) were important outposts of the empire, and there are Roman ruins throughout the land south of the Danube.

For the next two hundred years the Romans kept an uneasy peace with the tribes across the Danube. It was at this time that the Roman historians **Strabo** and **Tacitus** first began to mention one Germanic tribe, the *Baiuvarii*, establishing for posterity the name of the Bavarians. The Latin probably comes from a Celtic word meaning 'those from Boihaemum', modern-day Bohemia. Recent research suggests this tribe descended from the Celtic *Boier*. The *Baiuvarii* seem to have belonged to non-Roman *Germania*, a vague, uncharted territory that covered much of eastern Europe.

After about AD 488 and after constant battering, the Roman defences finally gave in, and the *Baiuvarii* swept across the waters from the north and east to establish lands for themselves south of the Danube.

Tribal Duchy

In the chaos of the collapsing Roman Empire, the Franks, under **King Clovis** (*c.* 466–511), emerged as the most powerful tribe in northern Europe. Clovis established the Christian **Merovingian** dynasty, which ruled over nearly all of France and the Low Countries, as well as most of western and southern Germany, for more than two and a half centuries. The Merovingians claimed the land north of the river Danube (roughly approximating to modern-day Franconia) as royal crown land in the early 8th century. South of the Danube they installed the Burgundian **Agilolfing** family to rule over the mix of invading Germanic tribes and the remaining Celts and Romans. The family stayed from about 555 to 788, establishing their main seat at Regensburg. Later, though, they began to get uppity, befriending the Lombards (in present-day Italy) and Christianizing the Slavs to the south in an attempt to secure their own power base. They failed to establish more than a transitory presence in what is now known as Austria, but succeeded mightily in displeasing their Merovingian overlords. In AD 788 the last of the Agilolfing dukes, **Tassilo III**, was deposed by Charlemagne and the Bavarian duchy was absorbed into the **Carolingian** Empire.

Charlemagne's empire collapsed after the death of his successor, Louis the Pious, in AD 840, and was partitioned into three separate kingdoms. Bavaria came under the suzerainty of **Louis the German**, king of the eastern Franks, becoming part of what was later referred to as the **Holy Roman Empire of the German Nations**, though it retained its own dukes. Louis appointed as margrave **Luitpold**, who founded the **Schyren** dynasty and slowly set about consolidating his power base. But he was unable to check incursions by marauding bands of Slavs. At the **Battle of Pressburg** in AD 907, the Magyars of Hungary inflicted a disastrous defeat on Luitpold, who was slain in the conflict. Two years later, his son **Arnulf** quashed the belligerent eastern tribes and drove them out of the land, but when, in AD 937, he made a bid to assert his own independence, Emperor Otto I clipped his wings and reduced him to ruling over his ancestral margravate. From then on Bavaria became a battleground for the **Welf** and **Staufian** dynasties, reflecting the power games played by these two rival families elsewhere in Germany. Eventually, in 1158, **Emperor Frederick I Barbarossa** gave the duchy to his cousin **Henry the Lion**, the powerful Saxon duke who had founded Munich (*see* p.72). But Henry the Lion overreached himself and upset his imperial cousin by refusing him military help. Barbarossa retaliated in 1180 by handing Bavaria over to the Count Palatine **Otto of Wittelsbach**, a descendant of the margraves of Schyren. Thus began a dynasty that was to last, unbroken, until 1918.

The Wittelsbachs

By the time the first Wittelsbach came to power, Bavaria covered the lands between the Bohemian Forest in the north, the rivers Inn and Lech to the east and west, and the Alps to the south. The focus of the Wittelsbach power, however, was their extensive ancestral domains around Kelheim, the home town of the early Wittelsbachs.

The real founder of the dynasty was Otto's son, **Duke Ludwig**. He took a leading part in the affairs of the Holy Roman Empire and, through astute politics, inheritance, feudal acquisitions and force, extended his domains. Towns, monasteries and abbeys founded by him, such as Cham, Landau, Landshut and Straubing, played an important role in the colonization of the country and soon became centres of cultural life. Duke Ludwig also won control of the **Palatinate of the Rhine** in 1214, and secured succession to the **County of Bogen** by marrying the widowed countess, adding the white and blue diamonds of its coat of arms to that of his own family (blue and white are still Bavaria's national colours). His bright career came to a sudden end in 1231 when he fell victim to a crazed assassin on the bridge at Kelheim.

The affairs of the duchy were quickly put back on the straight and narrow by Ludwig's son, **Otto II (the Illustrious)**, who, in an effort to put his father's murder behind him, decided to relocate his residence to the newly founded **Landshut**. Duke

Otto set about expanding his territory even further, though he relied on purchase rather than conquest, picking up small patches of land that were strategically useful to the defence of his expanding borders. On his death in 1253 the Wittelsbachs fell to bickering over the family fortune. Personal rifts between Otto's sons led to territorial divisions that for the next 250 years, nurtured by family feuds and petty squabbles, sapped the power of the dynasty and all but undid their earlier successes. By the late 14th century, the family's various branches had fragmented into a cluster of **four separate duchies** (Landshut, Straubing, Ingolstadt, Munich). The prosperous Landshut branch outshone everyone else in wealth and aspirations. In 1475 they found a way to flaunt their superior status, hosting the extravagant **Landshut Wedding** between Duke Georg and Jadwiga, daughter of the king of Poland.

Meanwhile, the new **merchant class** was steadily building up its wealth and power – both in the Franconian towns such as Nürnberg, and in towns such as Augsburg and Regensburg on the busy southern trade routes. The most powerful trading towns became **Free Imperial Cities**, responsible only to the emperor. Outside these civic strongholds, however, Bavaria was backward, chaotic and violent. Neighbouring states encroached upon its borders, and the lesser nobles fought each other for land and ignored the authority of the dukes. At the time, the **Landtag**, an assembly of representatives from all the *Land*'s estates instituted at the beginning of the 14th century, oversaw much of the day-to-day administrative and financial affairs of state. It maintained a veneer of stability and gradually began to acquire political clout.

Consolidation and the Electorate

This state of affairs lasted until 1506, when **Duke Albrecht IV (the Wise)** of the Munich branch of the Wittelsbachs made the first tentative steps to re-establish a unified Bavarian duchy under his rule. Albrecht put the brakes on further fragmentation of territory by introducing a system of inheritance through primogeniture into the Bavarian domains, and elevated Munich to his capital.

Under his son, **Duke Wilhelm IV**, the **Reformation** began to have an impact on Bavaria – but the Wittelsbachs were fervent Catholics, and under Dukes Albrecht V and Wilhelm V the **Counter-Reformation** gathered momentum. The religious movement had political consequences as the neighbouring princes of the Palatinate – the Rhineland, Baden, Württemberg and Hesse – somewhat forcefully espoused Protestantism. Despite the **Peace of Augsburg** of 1555, which preached religious tolerance and *cuius regio, eius religio* (the principle that subjects assumed their monarch's faith), Bavaria's Protestants were subjected to increasing persecution. Teaming up with the equally devout Catholic Habsburgs, the Wittelsbach dukes began forcibly to convert Bavaria to Catholicism by pursuing a ruthless crusade against all heretics and purging the land of Protestant communities, save in the Free Imperial City of Regensburg.

By 1609 Germany had split into a **Protestant Union** led by the Palatinate and a **Catholic League**, founded by the Wittelsbach **Duke Maximilian I,** which centred on Bavaria. Bigotry and persecution were rife, and in 1618 the situation erupted into one of the most pointless and destructive conflicts Europe has known – the **Thirty**

Years' War. France, Spain, Denmark and Sweden were sucked into the fray. For three decades, armies plundered and pillaged the land, swapping sides at will and losing any sense of what they were fighting for (apart from self-gain). Eventually the armies of King Gustav Adolphus of Sweden swept across Bavaria to defeat the notoriously cruel **Johann Tilly**, reformer of the Bavarian forces and military champion of the Catholic armies. Both Augsburg and Munich were briefly occupied by the Swedes in 1632.

Bavaria needed some 40 years to recover from the social and economic deprivation that the war brought about, but the Wittelsbachs were amply rewarded for their pains. Duke Maximilian had gained the Upper Palatinate and was given the hereditary title of **Elector**, putting him on a par with the much older grandees who had formal powers to mint their own coinage, build fortresses, extract tolls and operate their own legislature and judiciary. The Wittelsbachs now set about the task of restoring a battered Bavaria, finding in the exuberant, sensuous **Baroque style** the perfect antidote to sober Protestantism. Towns, castles, churches and monasteries were rebuilt, often by the best architects and artists the movement had to offer.

But once again the Wittelsbachs hawkishly began to eye land other than their own. Neighbouring states began to get twitchy. Splits emerged with Austria, an erstwhile ally, when Bavaria challenged her authority by making claims against Habsburg territories. In 1701 the pugnacious Habsburg Leopold I openly turned against his wealthy northern neighbour and unleashed the **War of the Spanish Succession**, which again brought havoc to the Bavarian lands. In 1704 Prince Eugene of Savoy and the Duke of Marlborough led a coalition of Habsburg and British troops to victory over the French and Bavarians at the **Battle of Blenheim** (for which Marlborough received the Bavarian town of Mindelheim in the Allgäu as a reward). For ten years, despite popular unrest, Bavaria was under the control of the Habsburg Emperors.

Thirty-five years on, and again the Wittelsbachs found themselves at the receiving end of a devastating war, again under Austrian occupation. The young, fastidious **Maximilian III Joseph** withdrew from the **War of the Austrian Succession** by making peace with Austria, renouncing many hereditary titles, and concentrating instead on vital reforms at home. More of a thinker than a warrior, he set up the Munich-based **Academy for the Arts and Sciences** and oversaw the abolition of the increasingly conniving Jesuit order in Bavaria. It was left to **Frederick the Great of Prussia**, a brilliant military strategist, to halt Austrian inroads into Bavaria during the 1778 **War of the Bavarian Succession** and ensure the territory of the Wittelsbach Electors.

The Kingdom of Bavaria

Following successive waves of Imperial Austrian and French Revolutionary occupations across the region in the late 1790s, **Elector Maximilian IV Joseph** (King Maximilian I Joseph from 1806) decided to throw in his lot with **Napoleon**. He was one of the few princes in Germany to switch his allegiance. Napoleon remembered his friends, and in 1805 Bavaria was doubled in size by the **Treaty of Pressburg**, acquiring, at the expense of Austria, approximately the boundaries it now has. The largest chunks it gained were most of the secular and ecclesiastical principalities of

Franconia to the north and several Swabian territories to the east. The treaty also elevated the Bavarian duchy to the status of a **kingdom**. Although the fledgling monarchy was drawn into Napoleon's expansionist activities, the internal stability it enjoyed under the Emperor's wing proved good ground for laying the foundations of a modern state: by 1808 serfdom was abolished, universal taxation and equality before law were established, municipal governments were strengthened and the secularization of various monasteries was pushed forward, regardless of the vigorous objections of Bavaria's Church establishment.

After some 30,000 Bavarian troops were casualties of Napoleon's futile Russian campaign, King Maximilian I once again changed his foreign policy and between 1813 and 1815 became an ally of the **Germanic Confederation**. This switch ensured that Bavaria emerged politically and territorially virtually unscathed from the **Congress of Vienna** in 1815, becoming the third largest German state after Austria and Prussia.

The Bavarian Kingdom is still recalled as Bavaria's **Golden Age**. On Maximilian's death in 1825, his son **Ludwig I** took over the helm of state and introduced further, much needed administrative and religious reforms. During his brief rule Bavaria's international prestige soared and this led to a blossoming of Bavarian nationalism. Ludwig was committed to the promotion of commerce and the arts. It is him we have to thank for many of Munich's most graceful neoclassical buildings, put up under the guidance of his court architect **Leo von Klenze**. Yet, in 1848, Ludwig was forced to abdicate following the waves of popular unrest (now known as the **1848 Revolts**), but also as a result of a scandalous affair with a dancer, Lola Montez (*see* p.174). Ludwig's son **Maximilian II** carried on the good work, forging alliances with Saxony, Hanover and Württemberg, chiefly to establish a strong third force to put a check on the growing power of Austria and Prussia. There was no love lost between Bavaria and the wily Prussian **Prince Otto von Bismarck**, and Maximilian subsequently tended to support Austria against Prussia.

In 1832, seeking a mutually acceptable candidate for the vacant throne of newly independent **Greece**, Britain, France and Russia agreed on Otto, second son of Ludwig I, who was duly crowned **Otho I**. He made gallant efforts to modernize his new kingdom, but his entourage of Bavarian courtiers, soldiers and carpet-baggers grew increasingly unpopular and in 1862 he was deposed. Nevertheless, his legacy endures: Greece adopted the blue and white banner colours of Bavaria as its national flag, Bavarians created the country's first modern beer and wine brands (Fix and Achaia Clauss), and many of Athens's neoclassical official buildings date from his reign.

In 1864 the famed **Ludwig II** (*see* pp.174–5) became king of Bavaria, also showing reluctance towards Bismarck's attempts to incorporate his kingdom into a German state under Prussian leadership. However, in the **Seven Weeks' War** (1866) Prussian victory over the Austrian armies dislodged Austria as a main player on the German field, and established Prussia in its place. This left Bavaria the final stumbling block on the road to a united Germany. Shrewdly, Bismarck didn't punish Bavaria for siding with Austria. Rather, Ludwig II was forced to assent to a '**defensive alliance**' under Prussian domination. It needed another carefully engineered, victorious war with France, the **Franco-Prussian War** (1870–71), in which Bavarian troops fought side by side with the Prussians, finally to coax Bavaria into a greater German Reich. With Germany under Prussian dominance, Bavaria was now a monarchy in name only, though under the **German Constitution of 1871** it was granted a greater degree of independence than other German states.

The Weimar Republic and the Nazis

Germany's defeat in the **First World War** spelt an ignominious end to Bavaria's Golden Age. On 7 November 1918 Kurt Eisner, the leader of the Independent Socialists in Bavaria, deposed Ludwig III, the last of the Wittelsbachs, and proclaimed Bavaria a **republic**, bringing the 738-year-old dynasty to a close. What followed was a short-lived Soviet-style republic, with revolutionary councils spearheading some Bolshevik-inspired '**Red Terror**' in the streets of Munich. By May 1919, however, the left-wing uprising had been quelled by units of the infamous **Freikorps**, volunteers comprising mainly ex-officers and right-wing extremists, who relished the task of stamping out any opposition to the government in a ruthless '**White Terror**'. Under the new Bavarian constitution of August 1919 Bavaria became a parliamentary state in the **Weimar Republic**. The Weimar years were a tumultuous period of political unrest throughout Germany. Munich quickly turned into a hotbed of reactionary movements, with unsuccessful right-wing coups in 1920 and 1921.

It is perhaps no coincidence that ex-Austrian **Adolf Hitler** (1889–1945) centred so much of his activity on Munich, later calling the city 'the Capital of our Movement'. In 1919 he joined the Munich-based German Workers' Party, whose assets amounted to a resounding 7.50 Marks (about £2) at the time and whose membership didn't even reach three figures. But Hitler went to work immediately. In 1920 he renamed the party the **National Socialist German Workers' Party** (NSDAP); members were soon to be referred to as **Nazis**. He adopted the ancient good-luck symbol, the swastika, and established the brown-shirted **SA**, short for *Sturmabteilung* (stormtroopers), a group of armed heavies that lined the walls at meetings and beat up opponents.

In 1923 Hitler had enough confidence in his private army to make a grab at power himself. Backed by some 600 followers he staged the **Munich Beer Hall Putsch**, storming into a beer hall, firing into the air and capturing the Bavarian state leaders. The next day he held a mass demonstration, but the police turned out in force and opened fire, and Hitler and his cronies were arrested. He was tried for high treason and sentenced to five years' imprisonment at **Landsberg Prison** – though he was released after only nine months, having used his time to dictate his manifesto *Mein Kampf* (*My Struggle*).

When Hitler finally came to power in 1933, bringing an end to the Weimar Republic, Bavaria was already a bastion of Nazism. Nürnberg was the scene of the *Reichsparteitage*, the stage-managed Nazi Party Conventions, and in 1935 provided the platform for the declaration of the *Nürnberger Rassengesetze* or Racial Purity Laws, the anti-semitic legislation that provided the framework for the Holocaust. **Dachau** was the site of the first of the concentration camps that swallowed up the scapegoats for all of Germany's ills – the Jews, Communists and other dissenters, gypsies and homosexuals. Even the sleepy, picture-postcard Alpine resort of

Berchtesgaden was blackened by Nazi connotations: the **Eagle's Nest**, perched awesomely on the Kehlstein mountain, became Hitler's personal mountain retreat.

Despite all these unsavoury associations with the Third Reich, Bavarians, fired perhaps by their sense of Bavarian rather than German nationalism, put up some resistance against being incorporated into the over-centralized Nazi nation state. But the Nazis had quickly established party control over every institution in the state, including the police, universities and professional associations. Munich University was one of the few places where resistance flickered on. In the course of 1942 and 1943, a clandestine circle of friends, calling themselves the **White Rose Society**, printed and circulated a number of underground pamphlets on the university premises. When they were finally caught, they were tried for 'civil disobedience' and executed.

During the **Second World War**, Bavarian labour and industry fuelled Hitler's war effort – notably at Augsburg, where the famous Messerschmidts were made. Bavaria offered safe locations well behind Germany's air defences, but from mid-1944 British and American planes **carpet-bombed** Bavarian cities night and day, reducing the region to ash and rubble. In March 1945 the first US troops rumbled through Bavaria, crushing last-ditch resistance and liberating the desolate concentration camps before marching on the capital.

A Free State in Post-War Germany

After the war, Bavaria became part of the **US zone of occupation**. The Palatinate was merged into the new *Land* of Rhineland-Palatinate and the island of Lindau became part of Baden Württenberg (though it later reverted to Bavaria). The rest of the state remained intact. Because of its indelible associations with the Nazis, Nürnberg was chosen by the Allies for their **war crimes trials**. In Bavaria, as elsewhere in Germany, the Allies began a desperate search for leaders untainted by Nazi affiliations to take control of a new federal state and put the region back on its feet. But more pressing needs were occupying the minds of the war-torn populace: not only did they have to struggle with the rebuilding of their land and industry, they also had to find new homes and employment for literally thousands of displaced refugees, as Bavaria was flooded with German-speaking people expelled from the Sudetenland, now in the Czech Republic. In 1946 a constituent assembly gave the new **Federal Land of Bavaria** its post-war constitution. However, Bavarian bloody-mindedness and separatism again reared its head when the majority of Bavarians refused to ratify the **Basic Law**, the constitution of the Federal Republic (the only federal state in Germany to do so). As a result, Bavaria was declared a **Free State** with its own constitution. Since its inception, the State government has been firmly under the control of the right-wing **Christian Social Union** (CSU).

The 1990 **reunification** of East and West Germany came as something of a mixed blessing to Bavaria. On the one hand, northern Bavaria, notably Franconia, found itself again in the centre of a unified Germany, with all the political and economic gains that were expected from the union. On the other hand, Bavaria stood to see a diminishment of its status. However, after twenty years, the novelty of reunification has worn off, and Bavaria's remarkable prosperity has made its inhabitants feel more complacent about the role of their state within an enlarged Germany.

The Arts and Culture

03

Art and Architecture

The princelings, archbishops, kings, dukes and electors who parcelled up Germany into states, then ran their domains with all the pomp and splendour they could muster, left a trail of grand palaces, beautiful churches and rich art collections right across the country, particularly in Bavaria. Wealthy burghers in the merchant towns joined in with competitive zeal, and the result is a prodigious, widespread artistic heritage. Local princes kept a tight hold on their collections, so Germany's treasures haven't all filtered down to one capital city or been carried off to foreign museums. The fierce sense of *Heimat* (local history) and, in the 19th century, a growing Romantic nationalism meant that local works of art stayed put, so small-town museums still come up with big-time surprises.

The petty rulers and their protégés were conservative, however, and took a while to get to grips with new ideas. Artists practised anonymity long after their colleagues in other countries were signing works, and so are known to us by the names of their major achievements (such as the 'Master of the St Bartholomew Altarpiece'). The Gothic style arrived later and stayed on longer than elsewhere in Europe, and the first shoots of the Renaissance in Germany appeared nearly a century after Italy was already blossoming. Of course you can see French, Italian and Dutch influences at work, especially in border regions, but schools and movements usually centred on one or two of the tiny states, developing a distinctive style, though often with little international recognition or impact.

German art has, however, had at least two Golden Ages – one in the **16th century**, with Cranach, Dürer, Grünewald and Holbein as the stars, and another early last century, when the **German Expressionists** developed a powerful individual style, and the **Bauhaus** group (quite literally) changed the shape of 20th-century architecture.

Early Days

Apart from a few Roman buildings, such as the remains at Trier, Germany's earliest surviving architecture dates back to the **Carolingian Period** (9th century). **Charlemagne** saw himself as a direct successor to the Caesars, and energetically set about imitating things Roman. He imported southern building techniques and design for his huge palace chapel at Aachen, and established the prototype for what was later to develop into the Romanesque style (*see* below). The secluded upper floor – from which the emperor could watch the goings-on at the high altar without being seen by the masses below – became the basis for later *Doppelkirchen* ('double churches') throughout Germany.

Although he himself could barely read, Charlemagne was an enthusiastic collector of books, and imported whole libraries from Italy and Byzantium. The lavish illustrations in these tomes must have astonished the hitherto rather inept northern painters, who were stimulated into a frenzy of **manuscript illumination** – much of it deft, vibrant and extraordinarily sophisticated. Germany's first acknowledged great painter, known as the **Master of the *Registrum Gregorii***, was an illuminator – you can see his *Codex Egberti* in Trier. Charlemagne also commissioned the renowned scholar Alcuin of York to renovate the alphabet, which had collapsed into an illegible scrawl through centuries of semiliterate scribes copying out the pages of the Bible. The letters on this page are descended from the alphabet worked out by Alcuin and his followers at Tours in France.

Charlemagne's empire survived him by a mere 30 years: plundering Vikings and Magyars plunged the land into desolation and confusion. But a new dynasty of German emperors, the **Ottonians**, emerged in the mid-10th century and managed to salvage Carolingian culture. During the Ottonian period there were even greater advances in manuscript illumination and architecture.

Romanesque Art

Between the 10th and the 12th centuries medieval Europe stopped looking back at Imperial Rome, and began to explore new directions for itself. **Church-building** became an obsession, even (wrote Raoul Glaber, an 11th-century monk) when congregations were 'not in the least need... It was as if the whole earth, having cast off the old...were clothing itself in the white robe of the church'. 19th-century historians called the style that emerged '**Romanesque**', in the belief that it mimicked Roman monumental building and was just a flawed step on the way to Gothic perfection. They were wrong – Romanesque architecture has a spirit all of its own.

The new generation was determined to build in **stone**, remembering the earlier destruction of wooden-roofed buildings as barbarians had burned their way through the land. Enterprising masons came up with groin vaults that supported daringly large stone ceilings. The churches they put up were solid, blocky masses of geometric shapes – rectangles, cubes, cylinders and semicircular arches. Less successful Romanesque churches are heavy and ponderous, but the best ones are sublime. The rhythmic patterns of rounded arches and columns have a soothing, meditative effect – a purity and simplicity closer to Islamic than to later Christian architecture. Decorative elements are confined to repetitive carving on the columns and around portals, some chunky relief work and sculpture, and **frescoes**. Fresco cycles – picture-bibles for an illiterate congregation – developed into a major art form in Romanesque churches. The achievements of the 11th and early 12th centuries were Germany's first and, until the 20th century, last major contributions to international architecture.

The Gothic Period

Renaissance critics, who revered classical antiquity, first used '**Gothic**' as a derisive label for a style they thought violated the standards of Greece and Rome, and so simply must have come from the nasty, barbaric Goths. 'May he who invented it be cursed,' wrote one outraged historian. The exuberant, decorative style does seem cheerfully to ignore most good and true classical norms, but it has its roots in a change of mood that was permeating Europe. The insecurities of rural, feudal life were disappearing, and a middle class of wealthy merchants and professionals, safe in their walled towns, could keep the aristocracy in check. 'The air of the city is the breath of freedom', went the slogan. Soaring Gothic cathedrals expressed this new confidence. They were images on earth of the Heavenly Jerusalem, often (in Germany at least) paid for by public subscription rather than aristocratic largesse. Burghers proudly called these new churches towering over their towns *opus modernum* (modern work). The attitude to women was changing too. The heroes of earlier ballads waxed rhapsodic about their swords; those of the Gothic *minnesingers* (lyric poets and musicians) swooned over their ladies. This was the time of gallant knights and courtly love. The church eased its restrictions on representing women in art, and the **cult of the Virgin Mary** burgeoned all over Europe. Romanesque painting and carving had dwelt on severe themes such as the Last Judgement. Gothic favoured gentler subjects, often centring on the Madonna.

Gothic Architecture

The pointed arches, flying buttresses, high towers and delicate tracery that characterize Gothic architecture are not merely decorative, but are the result of complicated new building ideas. **Pointed arches** led to a lighter and far more flexible system of vaulting, opening up possibilities for a more varied ground plan and much bigger windows. **Buttresses** helped carry the weight of the supporting masonry, so cathedrals could shoot up to impressive heights. **Filigreed stonework** gave support, yet also helped architects to realize their ambitions of building almost diaphanous structures. **Stained glass** flourished as an art form.

New Gothic styles had begun to appear in France around 1140, but nearly a century passed before they took hold in Germany. But soon German builders were imitating Gallic flair, and by 1250 they had embarked on their supreme achievement, the cathedral at **Cologne**. In contrast to this, many German builders favoured the more sober *Hallenkirche* ('hall church' – a church with nave and aisles of the same height, often with a flat roof), which had its origins in the design of monasteries for the austere Cistercian order. The *Liebfrauenkirche* in Munich is one of the most famous.

Gothic Sculpture

Early Gothic stone-carving, especially in Thuringia and Saxony, was in the aptly named *Zackenstil* ('jagged style'), where hard, angular lines of cloth covered the scarcely perceptible anatomy of the figures. Soon French influence was felt here. In around 1300 masons began to carve in the so-called **Soft Style** – soft, flowing robes, draped over perfectly moulded limbs and bodies: they were obviously working from live models. Along with this move towards naturalism came far more subtle characterization. Intense, anguished facial expressions became a speciality, and the *Man of Sorrows* was a favourite subject. Christ's face on crucifixes began to show real suffering. **Portraiture** began to emerge as an art form, and patrons often appeared in works they had commissioned. **Tilman Riemenschneider** (1460–1531), arguably the greatest sculptor of the late Gothic period, worked mainly in wood. His restless, flamboyant carvings crop up all over, but especially around his native Würzburg. The other great woodcarver of the period was **Veit Stoss** (*c.* 1447–1533), a talented old rascal (*see* p.207) who spent most of his life in Nürnberg turning out exquisite, realistic masterpieces.

Gothic Panel Painting

When artists began to paint on wooden panels (in Germany around 1300), art became portable and saleable, and styles began to spread more quickly. Early painters were seen as craftsmen, trained and controlled by powerful guilds. The guild got them commissions and made sure that the work was well paid. It was only later, during the Gothic period and the early Renaissance, that artists began to emerge as individuals and personally sign their work.

Most early panel paintings were intended as **altarpieces**. Initially, the pictures were quite static. Backgrounds were of gold leaf or covered in ornament, and figures related to each other with stylized gestures. Later, the **Soft Style** (which is also known as the International Style) took over here too. Painters created little scenes; people talked to each other, and there was far more realism and a stronger narrative element than before. **Master Bertram** (c. 1345–1415), a Hamburg painter and the first German artist we know by name, liked to paint narrative cycles on small panels that he would group around a sculpture. **Conrad von Soest** (active c. 1394–1422) did appealing, brightly coloured pieces with fine attention to detail. **Conrad Witz** (c. 1400–46) did much to move German painting towards a greater sense of realism, though his work is very much in a blunt, sculptural 'hard' style. It was **Jan Joest** of Kalkar (c. 1455–1519) and **Hans Pleydendurff** (c. 1420–72) who were most influenced by Dutch naturalism. Pleydendurff's panels especially show a richness of colour and careful composition reminiscent of the Flemish painter Dirk Bouts. Pleydendurff was the first German to paint landscapes into the background of his works. Painters of the **Danube School** based in Passau and Salzburg refined this technique towards the end of the 15th century, filling out their panels with lush Danube country scenes.

Artists working in the south, such as Conrad Witz (who spent much of his life in Switzerland) and the Tyrolean **Michael Pacher** (c. 1435–98) came under Italian influence. Pacher painted with hard, bright colours. A harsh light shines on his subjects, casting strong, clear shadows. Painters in Cologne, on the other hand, followed the trends in the neighbouring Netherlands. In the 15th century they

The Cologne School

The first to paint in the softer, more realistic Cologne style was the **Master of St Veronica** (c. 1420). He is named after a painting (now in the Alte Pinakothek in Munich) of St Veronica holding up the Sudarium (a cloth she had offered to Christ on the road to Golgotha to wipe the sweat from his brow, and which was handed back with the Lord's face miraculously imprinted upon it). The large-scale image of Christ's countenance and Veronica's features are said to have sent Goethe into raptures.

The supreme artist of the school, if not of the entire German Soft Style, was **Stefan Lochner** (c. 1410–51). He paints with loving detail and subtle shading, often with a glowing ethereal quality. (You can see many of his paintings in the Alte Pinakothek.) Later artists of the Cologne School, such as the **Master of the Life of the Virgin** (active c. 1460–85) and the **Master of the St Ursula Legend** (active c. 1490–1505), developed a more narrative style and filled their panels with anecdotal detail. The School's last great practitioner was also its most idiosyncratic. The **Master of the St Bartholomew Altarpiece** (active c. 1470–1510) handles colour in a more sophisticated way than even Lochner, but includes quirky details. In the St Bartholomew altarpiece his fashionably dressed, bejewelled women look like anything but the saints they are meant to depict. Behind them, a brocade backdrop recalls the gold backgrounds of earlier paintings; over the top you can see a more modern, dreamy landscape.

developed such a distinctive style that later art historians have grouped them together as the **Cologne School** (*see* box, previous page).

The Renaissance

Architecturally, Germany was immersed in the Gothic until well into the 16th century, though in sculpture and painting new forces were already stirring in the late 1400s. At the beginning of the 16th century this new energy burst into a brief but brilliant Golden Age of German painting. But, by 1528, with the death of the main exponents, Dürer and Grünewald, the force seemed spent. The exact reason for the sudden decline is not clear – though the religious wars that racked the land and the rise of Protestantism no doubt played a part.

Painting and Graphics

The new movement was triggered by a conscious desire to copy what was going on in **Italy**. Wealthy south German merchants had close contact with Venice, and Germany's humanists were in touch with scholars in Florence. Italian engravings circulated throughout northern Europe and led to a corresponding German interest in **graphic arts**. The most skilled and adventurous German engraver was **Martin Schongauer** (*c.* 1450–91). His subtle metal-engraving technique became a standard, and his blending of realism with delightful innovation, and choice of exotic subjects, have led art historians to call him the father of the German Renaissance.

The name that overshadows all others of the period is Nürnberg artist **Albrecht Dürer** (1471–1528). He is Germany's complete Renaissance Man: an artist, scientist, mathematician and thinker; the 'Leonardo of the North'. He worked with tremendous energy and was the first artist outside Italy to become internationally famous in his own time. Many say he was best at engraving – the versatility, luminosity and power of his woodcuts have never been surpassed. His best work is in Munich and Nürnberg.

Matthias Gothardt-Neithardt, known as **Grünewald** (*c.* 1480–1528), another artist of highly original genius, worked for the archbishops of Mainz as court painter, architect and hydraulic engineer before fleeing Germany in 1525, having been on the wrong side in the ill-fated Peasants' Revolt. Unlike Dürer, he was largely forgotten until recent years. His reputation rests mainly on an enormous polyptych, the *Isenheim Altarpiece* (1510–15), which many regard as the supreme achievement of German art.

Albrecht Altdorfer (*c.* 1480–1538) was the kingpin of the **Danube School** (*see* p.31), which continued to flourish into the Renaissance, and is credited with the first landscape in Western art painted for its own sake. He was a talented and unorthodox colourist, especially when it came to light and atmospheric effects, and had a penchant for depicting fantastic buildings (he was also an architect). His most important work is the enormous *Battle of Issus* (1529, in the Alte Pinakothek). At least half the canvas is taken up by a dramatic landscape that gives the onlooker a god's-eye view across the Alps to Cyprus and Egypt.

Lucas Cranach the Elder (1472–1553), another artist of the Danube School, is best known for his later works. These are usually on humanist rather than religious themes (mythology, history and portraits) and feature nudes painted with disarming, almost naïve charm. A strain of humorous, rather wicked eroticism runs through his paintings. In the latter part of his life, in answer to a summons from the Elector of Saxony, he settled in Wittenberg. Here he became a friend of Luther, and established a workshop that churned out paintings at an alarming rate. His son **Lucas Cranach the Younger** (1515–86) carried on the work, but without much original flair. The period's quirkiest painter was **Hans Baldung** (1484–1545), known as **Grien** because he always wore green clothes. He studied under Dürer, from whom he learnt his fine colouring technique. His choice of subject matter and even his treatment of conventional themes is delightfully (almost wilfully) bizarre. You can easily spot his works, which are scattered throughout Germany: if your eye is caught by an odd painting of an evil-looking cupid or a weird woman, it's sure to be by Baldung.

Augsburg, seat of the Habsburg court and home to the powerful Fugger family (*see* p.170), was an influential centre of the Renaissance in Germany. The most notable artists to rise from this milieu were **Hans Burgkmair** (1473–1531), a master of opulent Italianate decoration, and **Hans Holbein the Younger** (1497–1543), best known for his firm, faultless portraits. When Holbein upped sticks for England in 1531, he left the German Renaissance in its dying throes. While it lasted, it was primarily a boom in painting and graphics. Developments in **architecture** came later and were more episodic. In Augsburg **Elias Holl** (1573–1646) took Italian models to heart, and put up buildings that have little of Germany about them. Most survivors of the period are civil or domestic buildings – ornate Rathäuser or high-gabled merchants' houses decorated with scrolls, obelisks and statues.

Baroque and Rococo

There is no clear dividing line between Renaissance and Baroque. The Renaissance was an age of innovation and discovery, but its images were relatively static. **Baroque art** moves – artists tested the new ground that their predecessors had laid out, took a few shaky steps, then ran riot. Art historian Helen Gardner described the era as 'spacious and dynamic, brilliant and colorful, theatrical and passionate, sensual and ecstatic, opulent and extravagant, versatile and *virtuoso*'. Façades were sinuous and irregular; interiors writhed with twisted pillars, horseshoe vaulting and stucco. The dome, oval and circle became the underlying shapes of design. Bumps were gilded, and flat surfaces covered in bright painting. Witty *trompe l'œil* abounded, often combined with clever 3D stucco trickery. Stained glass was banished and churches flooded with light – often from hidden sources, throwing up contrasting patterns of shade. Enthusiasm for the Virgin and the saints was redoubled, and altarpieces became monumental. Later, as Baroque broke into the lighter, airier and even more fantastic **rococo**, stuccowork became less intense but even more irregular, with asymmetrical cartouches and cake-icing licks of dazzling plaster aplenty.

Early Baroque painting in Germany is fairly unremarkable: the glory days were in the late 17th and early 18th centuries, as late Baroque became rococo. After about 1660 churches were exuberantly rebuilt; most abbots and bishops couldn't resist a show of triumph and commissioned top, fashionable architects. Today Germany's most spectacular Baroque and rococo art is to be seen here. The responsibility for

The Big Names in Architecture

Balthasar Neumann (1687–1753) was the era's supremo. He started work in Würzburg as a bellfounder, took up architecture as a hobby and was soon snapped up by the powerful Schönborn family to build churches and palaces throughout Germany. His complicated designs have such energy and intricate detail, and there is such a flowing pulse between space and massive structure, that at least one art critic likens them to a Bach fugue, as 'frozen music'. Grand, sweeping staircases were a speciality (you can see a fine example in Würzburg), and his churches can be breathtaking – the Vierzehnheiligenkirche near Bamberg is one of the best.

The **Asam Brothers** – sculptor Egid Quirin Asam (1692–1750) and painter Cosmas Damian Asam (1686–1739) – formed a team, first to decorate existing churches, later to undertake entire projects of their own (such as the Asamkirche in Munich). The brothers studied in Rome and were never seduced from their stately, southern high Baroque style into the frivolities of rococo. Cosmas Asam became particularly well known for his tricks with perspective and vast dome paintings of the open heavens.

The rococo period was dominated by two other siblings, architect **Dominikus Zimmerman** (1685–1766) and fresco-painter **Johann Baptist Zimmerman** (1680–1785). Together they worked on the Wieskirche in 1750 (see p.173), often called Germany's supreme achievement in the style. Johann Baptist also worked with another great architect of the time, the Belgian **François de Cuvilliés** (1695–1767), on the Munich Residenz and Schloß Nymphenburg. The diminutive Cuvilliés was originally employed by Elector Maximilian Emmanuel as a court jester, and only began working as an architect in his thirties. His theatre in the Munich Residenz and the Amalienburg in the Nymphenburg park are rococo at its most delightful.

most of the best work lies with a brilliant few who seldom restricted themselves to one skill but designed, painted frescoes and often did the stuccowork too.

Neoclassicism

Frederick the Great's Berlin became the focus for growing moves towards a more restrained neoclassicism, which later became fashionable in Munich and around Mainz and Cologne. Neoclassicism was a more stringent and academic revival of Greek and Roman architecture: buildings became plainer, with simple pediments and colonnaded porticoes in front of the entrances. Interiors were muted, with the odd rococo flourish, or decorated in Greek and Roman styles. German architects favoured colder Doric styles, and the desire for symmetry became obsessive. The leading architect of the day was **Karl-Friedrich Schinkel** (1781–1841). Neoclassical **painting** tended to be skilful but cold, or subject to nationalistic fervour. One painter who did introduce some warmth into his canvases was **Johann Heinrich Wilhelm Tischbein** (1751–1829), the youngest of a dynasty of neoclassical artists. His idyllic landscapes were a source of great inspiration to Goethe, whose portrait Tischbein painted.

The 19th Century

We desire to surrender our whole being, that it may be filled with the perfect bliss of one glorious emotion.

Goethe's Romantic hero, Werther

Eighteenth-century gallants thought it in bad taste to be 'original' or 'enthusiastic' (read 'eccentric' or 'sincere'). Stony, sober neoclassicism vanquished the artifice and frivolity of rococo and banished emotion from polite society. Yet, almost at the same time, after 1750, another quite different mood was filtering through Europe. It became quite fashionable to swoon, languish in unrequited love and weep. This was done with gusto by the heroes and heroines of a new literary phenomenon that was sweeping the continent: the novel (*Roman* in German). German critics were the first to call this flowering of sensibility '**Romantic**' and to distinguish what they saw as peculiarly 'modern' traits in the arts from the old values of neoclassicism.

In Germany the Romantic movement, which reached its peak in the first half of the 19th century, was felt primarily in music and literature, and to a lesser extent in painting. In architecture neoclassicism held out until around 1830, when it was routed by **neo-Gothic**. Many great Gothic cathedrals (Cologne, for example) received their finishing touches in the 1800s, seven centuries after they had been started. For the Romantics the Gothic style epitomized their dreamy ideal of Old Germany. Fake Gothic (and some classical) 'ruins' popped up in the grounds of grand homes all over the country. In Bavaria King Ludwig II outdid everyone with his series of fairytale castles (*see* p.119 and pp.173–6).

Romantic Painting

In **Caspar David Friedrich** (1774–1840) you can see Romantic painting in its very essence. He is perhaps the one 19th-century German painter whose works are widely popular and familiar outside his own country. His highly original pictures of mist-shrouded Gothic ruins, winter-blasted landscapes and violent, windswept seas hauntingly reveal the Romantic obsession with death and isolation, and prints of these adorn the walls of sensitive and suicidal youth throughout the western world.

Few other German artists of the time can match Friedrich's stature. The architect **Karl-Friedrich Schinkel**, who took to painting to earn extra money, managed to slip easily into a more Romantic style and came up with spectacular architectural fantasies. **Philipp Otto Runge** (1777–1810) is best known for portraits of chubby-cheeked children, but at the time of his early death was collaborating with Goethe on a project involving vast paintings, poetry and music with which he hoped to recover the lost harmony of the universe. Only studies of the paintings, *The Times of Day*, remain. **Anselm Feuerbach** (1829–80), rather neglected outside Germany, painted big, Italianate canvases and is at his best with powerful, brooding portraits of women. The Swiss-born **Arnold Böcklin** painted delightful, fey pictures on mythological or fairy-tale themes. **Hans Thoma** (1839–1924) could come up with sensitive, moving paintings, but often lapsed into gooey sentimentality.

In an abandoned monastery in Rome **Johann Friedrich Overbeck** (1789–1869) founded the **Nazarene Brotherhood**, a group of German artists who painted detailed, idealistic, rather enchanted canvases in a style later taken up by the Pre-Raphaelites in England. Overbeck lived in Italy, but other painters, including **Peter von Cornelius** (1783–1867) and **Wilhelm von Schadow** (1788–1862), returned to Germany, where their activity centred on the **Düsseldorf Academy**. Here the style of the school degenerated into vast, pompous historical paintings. The painters were popular, however, and their frescoes are emblazoned on the walls of public buildings across the country.

Other 19th-century Painters

During the 19th century, Munich and Berlin became centres of the arts, each developing avant-garde groups that rebelled against powerful, conservative institutions such as the Düsseldorf Academy. In Berlin painters formed the **Secession movement**, headed by **Max Liebermann** (1847–1935), but it was in the Schwabing quarter of Munich that the most adventurous artists gathered (see p.81). At the centre of the Munich movement was **Franz von Stuck** (1863–1928), a highly individual artist whose dark, mysterious paintings seem an odd mixture of Pre-Raphaelite style and Expressionist violence.

Portraiture was in popular demand, and obliging artists such as **Franz von Lenbach** (1863–1904) moved in the highest society, making themselves very rich. **Realism** returned as a style later in the century. **Adolf von Menzel** (1815–1905) was one of the first painters to capture scenes from the newly industrialized cities on canvas, while **Wilhelm Liebl** (1844–1900) is especially renowned for his studies of Bavarian peasants, painted from life.

Jugendstil

Towards the end of the 19th century a reaction set in against the blunt, hard shapes that were the aesthetic by-product of industrialization. Influenced by the flowing lines of Japanese prints, and by William Morris's intricate, interwoven designs and radical views, a new style emerged, centred mainly in Paris and Vienna. The French called this ornamental style of graceful, serpentine lines and organic forms **Art Nouveau**. In Germany it was known as *Jugendstil*, named after the journal that promoted it, *Jugend* (Youth; *Stil*: style). Architecture, sculpture, painting and especially the applied arts were swept up into an enormously popular movement that lasted until the First World War. German furniture-makers and glass-blowers excelled themselves, and exquisite examples of their work crop up in museums all over the country. Look out for jewellery by **Patriz Huber**, glassware by **Peter Behrens** and stylish household goods by **Joseph M. Olbrich**.

20th–21st Century

It was France that led European painting into the 20th century. Germany lagged rather sorrowfully behind. **Impressionism** hardly made a mark east of the Rhine, but when the Fauves (led by Henri Matisse) hit Paris in 1905, German artists began to stir again, turning out intense, savage canvases, lashed with vigorous brushwork, blazing with clashing colours and strongly expressive of personal feeling. The movement, known as **Expressionism**, also affected literature (especially drama) and film, and produced the first German art for centuries to make an impact on the outside world. Some of the painters who come under the Expressionist umbrella were also part of simultaneous movements, such as the anarchic Berlin **Dadaists**, the **Neue Sachlichkeit** and the **Bauhaus** school (see pp.37–8).

German Expressionist Painters

Although the Expressionist movement was ignited by the Fauves, it burned on solid German fuel. The strong colour, hard line, emotional subject matter and even the otherworldly overtones are direct descendants of earlier German painting and engraving. The Expressionists organized themselves into two schools: *Die Brücke* (The Bridge, uniting nature and emotion) and *Der Blaue Reiter* (The Blue Rider, after a picture by Kandinsky).

Die Brücke was founded in Dresden in 1905 by three disgruntled architecture students who had taken to painting – **Ernst Ludwig Kirchner** (1880–1938), **Erich Heckel** (1883–1970) and **Karl Schmidt-Rottluff** (1884–1976). They revived the woodcut as an art form and put such emphasis on colour that it became as much a component of their paintings as the subject itself. Soon after it was founded the group moved from Dresden to Berlin, left off painting gaudy landscapes and turned to scenes from city life. They broke up to follow their individual careers in 1913, Kirchner having the most sustained success.

Der Blaue Reiter was formed in 1911 by two artists scorned by the powerful Munich establishment – **Wassily Kandinsky** (1866–1944) and **Franz Marc** (1880–1916). Later they were joined by (amongst others) **August Macke** (1887–1914) and the Swiss painter **Paul Klee** (1879–1940), and *Der Blaue Reiter* became a more loosely knit group, aimed at promoting Modernism in all the arts. Colour, line and shape became more important than subject matter – a brave and imaginative step that set painting well on the way to pure abstraction.

Many of Germany's most renowned Expressionists, however, belonged to neither school. The most individualistic of these (though he was for a time a member of *Die Brücke*) was **Emil Hansen** (1867–1956), known as 'Nolde' after his birthplace. His distorted, violent canvases are very much reminiscent of Grünewald, or the Flemish painter Hieronymus Bosch. **George Grosz** (1893–1959) was a prominent member of the anarchic Berlin Dadaists (*see* p.38), and is best known for the savage, indignant caricature-like drawings with which he lambasted capitalist society, the decadent Weimar Republic in particular. **Käthe Kollwitz** (1867–1945), one of the leading women artists of the 20th century, took the woodcut and engraving to heights not reached since Dürer. Her heart-wrenching black and white images are usually powerful, poignant cries against the horrors of war. **Ernst Barlach** (1870–1938) produced haunting sculptures with sharp, smoothly planed lines that show medieval influence. **Max Beckmann** (1884–1950) was an independently minded painter who bridged the gap to *Neue Sachlichkeit* (*see* p.38). His bitter paintings of distorted figures accentuated by hard, black lines reflect the horrors of the First World War and of Nazi oppression in the Second.

Bauhaus

In 1906 the Belgian *Jugendstil* designer **Henry van de Velde** (1863–1957) started a School of Arts and Crafts in Weimar. When he left Germany at the outbreak of the First World War he recommended a young architect, **Walter Gropius** (1883–1969), as his successor. In 1919 Gropius took over the directorship, changed the name of the school to *Das Staatliche Bauhaus Weimar*, redesigned the curriculum and in 1925 moved the whole caboodle to a sparkling new building in Dessau. The new **Bauhaus**, which immediately attracted artists such as Kandinsky and Klee as teachers, was rooted in the Arts and Crafts tradition of the previous century in that it offered a broad range of disciplines, from architecture to drama and basket-weaving. However, it set itself squarely in post-war Germany and, unlike the Arts and Crafts movement in Britain, it was prepared to exploit modern mass-production techniques to solve problems in areas such as housing and urban planning. Bauhaus wanted to unite art and technology and had two main aims – to work '*am Bau*' (hands-on, rather than theoretically), and to come up with inventive but practical prototypes for industry.

Around 1911 both **Le Corbusier** (1887–1965) and **Frank Lloyd Wright** (1867–1959) were using the new invention of prestressed concrete to revolutionize building design, and had become leading exponents of the **International Style**, a 'machine-age' architecture of clean, straight lines, open-plan interiors and no decoration at all. The Dessau Bauhaus not only fitted into this climate, but firmly established the principles of the International Style. Indeed, Gropius designed the skeleton of concrete slabs held up by steel pillars that was to be the heart of Le Corbusier's buildings, and which still forms the basic structure of much of 20th-century architecture. Buildings designed by Gropius and other Bauhaus architects, such as the superbly imaginative **Ludwig Mies van der Rohe** (1886– 1969), designer of New York's Seagram Building, became touchstones of modern architecture.

Neue Sachlichkeit

Neue Sachlichkeit is usually translated into English as 'New Objectivity' – a loose term which is really only comprehensible when you take 'objectivity' to mean neutrality, or 'matter-of-factness'. The name describes a small trend that grew up in opposition to Expressionism around 1923. *Neue Sachlichkeit* artists painted with a ruthless realism, often with a harsh, almost sadistic touch and an acid left-wing political comment. Though many of the painters in this new movement had come through a period of Expressionism, they now renounced what they regarded as Expressionism's emotional excess and lack of control. George Grosz and Max Beckmann were both associated with the style for a time, but its most famous practitioner was **Otto Dix** (1891–1969). His meticulous and at times rather vicious pictures show grotesque, larger-than-life characters and dwell on human suffering and the decadence of city life.

Oddly, *Neue Sachlichkeit* and Bauhaus had little to do with each other, though the no-frills, tidy approach characteristic of both schools has led to the work of some later Bauhaus artists being given a *Neue Sachlichkeit* label. Later work spills over into complete abstraction with the work of **Willi Baumeister** (1889–1955) and **Oskar Schlemmer** (1888–1943), a mercurial artist who flits between styles and schools. He is perhaps most famous for the ballets he designed for students at the Bauhaus.

The Dadaists

The zany, irreverent, nihilistic Dada movement (which was based mainly in Zürich, Barcelona and New York) had its followers in Germany too. Dada art was intentionally disruptive and ephemeral. **Kurt Schwitters** (1887–1948), however, did contribute some more lasting works. He made collages from rubbish and scrap paper, which he called *Merz Pictures*. (*Merz* is a syllable from the German word for 'commercial', and caught Schwitters' attention one day when he was cutting up newspapers.)

After the War

In 1937 the Nazis had held an exhibition of *Entartete Kunst* ('Degenerate Art') in Munich. Most of the prominent artists of the day were featured, and their work was later banned or destroyed. It is not surprising that after this, and the horrors of the Second World War, German artists wanted to start afresh. In 1957 **Heinz Mack** (b. 1931), **Günther Uecker** (b. 1930) and **Otto Piene** (b. 1928) formed **ZERO**. Their aim was to strip away all the elements by which art was traditionally defined and reduce it to pure absolutes – space and colour. Their anti-individualist manifesto had an influence all over Europe by the 1960s.

Other German artists, working in more individual ways, have also made a mark on the international scene. **Georg Baselitz** (b. 1938) is the most easily recognizable, as he hangs his bright, energetic, rather primitive paintings upside down in an attempt to redefine the way we see things. **Sigmar Polke** (b. 1941) began by painting abstract designs onto boards, blankets and odd bits of cloth, but has recently become intrigued by colour, producing thinly coated pastel-shaded panels. **Anselm Kiefer** (b. 1945) wants to counter the power of American culture by appealing to the traditions of Old Europe. He works on a monumental scale employing good, old-fashioned painterly skills in new ways. His vast paintings would seem to hark back to the styles of the Renaissance, but are filled with modern surprises such as tacked on bits of paper and the odd hole in the canvas. **A.R. Penck** (b. 1939) paints giant stick figures interspersed with symbols from different epochs – from mythological signs to technical designs.

The movement of art over the past few decades – away from painting and towards installation, performance and constructed sculpture – is seen by many to have its origins in the work of **Joseph Beuys** (1921–85). Beuys has been called the father of the European avant-garde. His piles of fat and felt and esoteric statements on man and nature are to be found all over Germany, and are imitated in art colleges around the world. His 'action art' – walks or water journeys, planting oak trees in Kassel – has become the core of much recent ecologically focused work. The work of **Gerhard Richter** (b. 1932) is more accessible and is becoming increasingly popular. He begins with photographs, blows them up and then lightly stylizes them, frequently in shades of grey and blue paint. **Jörg Immendorf** (b. 1945) is best known for his grotesque carvings, and nightmarish paintings that would seem to owe a debt to Otto Dix. Like Dix, he takes his politics seriously and his works often carry an overt political message.

The destruction wrought by Allied bombers led to a building boom in the 1950s and 1960s. Much of the work was hurried, functional and ugly. The trend towards **Brutalism** – an austere style that had its origins in the Bauhaus and is characterized by its emphasis on the building materials (especially bare concrete) and unconcealed service pipes – did little to improve the situation. The one area where there was interesting innovation was in **church architecture**, and more recently inventive designs for shiny glass hotels, office blocks, museum buildings and concert halls have been popping up in cities all over Germany, including Bavaria, assisted by healthy federal budgets.

Literature: a Chronology of Bavarian Writing

The Middle Ages

Not counting a fragment of the nine lines of the 8th-century *Wessobrunn Prayer*, the beginning of German literature in Bavaria is usually seen as the *Abrogans*, a glossary of German words from medieval Latin dating from *c*. AD 765, preserved in the Bavarian State Library in Munich. Later, Bavarian monasteries spawned a rich heritage of religious lectionaries and sacred poetry. In 1050 a monk in the Tegernsee abbey eulogized the adventures of a Christian knight in the *Ruodlieblied* (only fragments of which still exist). In the 12th century the abbey was the source of the **mystery plays** that became the bedrock of popular Christian instruction. Close contact with French culture, during long marches to the Holy Land in the 12th century, fired crusaders with an enthusiasm for ballads and narrative poems and led to the evolution of the *Minnesang* (*see* 'Music' opposite). At the same time writers began to record sagas and anthologies from Germany's rich oral tradition. One of these, the *Carmina Burana*, originates from the abbey at Benediktbeuren around 1250.

c. **1250: Wernher der Gartenaere** A Franciscan friar most famed for his tale *Meier Helmbrecht*, about a farmer's son who left his village to lead the life of a wanderer.

1477–1534: Aventinus Innkeeper's son who took the name of his Bavarian birthplace (Abensberg) and became a bestselling author of his time. His Latin textbooks and *Bavarian Chronicle* of 1522 led to a flourishing of early printed books in Bavaria.

Jesuit Plays

In the 17th century the Catholic Wittelsbachs took it upon themselves to champion the cause of the Counter-Reformation through a number of mystery and morality plays produced under the aegis of the Jesuit order. The plays set the Virgin and saints firmly back on their pedestals and led to a burgeoning of religious drama that has survived to this day in the form of rural **passion plays**, such as at Oberammergau.

1578–1639: Jacob Bidermann A professor of rhetoric at Munich, Bidermann developed a kind of educational drama that served to teach morality and the transience of human greatness – as in his illuminating play *Cenodoxus, Doctor of Paris* (1609).

The Golden Age

The heyday of Bavarian literature was during Bavaria's Golden Age, in the second half of the 19th century, when Munich came to play a major role in the intellectual life of a recently united Germany. The triumph of nationalism and the growth-pains of the Industrial Revolution led to the emergence of much politically inspired literature. Stylistically, apart from the odd experimenter, writers tended to favour a more earthy, naturalistic approach, in reaction to the Romanticism of the previous decades.

1830–1914: Paul von Heyse Poet and poet laureate of King Maximilian II. With fellow lyricist **Emanuel von Geibel** (1815–84) he presided over a literary circle known as the *Tafelrunde* (Round Table). He received the Nobel Prize for literature in 1911.

1855–1920: Ludwig Ganghofer Having spent most of his adult life as a dramatist in Vienna, Ganghofer returned to Munich to compile an anthology of Bavarian folk tales inspired by local oral culture.

1867–1921: Ludwig Thoma A lawyer from Dachau turned writer, known for his politically charged articles in the satirical periodical *Simplicissimus*. He later upset his fellow Bavarians with wry yarns about incestuous, small-minded village life.

1881–1920: Lena Christ Bavaria's most illustrious female novelist wrote two doleful psychological novellas, *Rumpelhanni* and *Erinnerungen einer Überflüssigen* (*Recollections of an Unwanted Person*) based on her own humiliating childhood memories (she was an illegitimate child). She later committed suicide in Munich.

1882–1948: Karl Valentin Bavaria's answer to Charlie Chaplin. A performing comedian and humorist, the lanky Valentin drew heavily on his experience on the Variety stage. His quirky sketches were an inspiration to German Surrealists (*see* p.76).

1894–1967: Oskar Maria Graf In his *Bayerisches Dekameron*, a collection of erotic tales, and his novel *Wir sind Gefangen* (*We are Prisoners*), Graf, a politically active socialist, captures a strong sense of ambivalence and duality.

Music

Germany has produced some of the world's greatest composers. (Many – such as Mozart – were, in fact, Austrian, but this is a pedantic quibble.) For centuries the cities of Vienna and Leipzig were the twin vortices of European music, and in each major period German musicians have been among the great movers and shakers in their field. Even the briefest of overviews of the development of German music leaves you wondering if there was anyone of note left who *wasn't* German.

Beginnings

Discounting ancient military horns, whose chief function was to make a stirring racket, we can trace the beginnings of German music back to the early Middle Ages, and to two main sources – the Church and the court. The first manuscripts of **ecclesiastical music** (such as the *Carmina Burana*) date back to the 12th century, and as early as the 11th century wandering troubadours entertained courtiers. These minstrels developed a form of lyrical ballad known as the ***Minnesang*** (from the German for 'love song'). Most famous of all *Minnesingers* was **Walther von der Vogelweide** (1170–1228) – some of his songs have survived, and devotees still decorate his grave in Würzburg with flowers (*see* p.147). By the 15th and 16th centuries the *Minnesingers* had organized themselves into guilds, and were recognized as master craftsmen – local supremos being granted the title of *Meistersinger* (mastersinger). The inventiveness and spontaneity that had characterized the *Minnesang*, however, was strangled by rigid and complicated rules enforced by the guilds. Top-ranking *Meistersinger* of all time was **Hans Sachs** (1494–1576), a Nürnberg cobbler who produced some 6,000 works. In the 19th century Richard Wagner – who, like his Romantic contemporaries, was fascinated by Germany's medieval past – celebrated Sachs and his colleagues in the opera *The Mastersingers of Nürnberg*.

Early Music and the Baroque Period

For a long time court and church music developed alongside each other. In churches the part song flourished, and led to the growth of **masses** and **motets**. The earthier, more popular hymns that came into fashion in Protestant churches during the Reformation manifested in Roman Catholic church music too, developing into **chorales** and **cantatas**. After the banquet and around the hearth the movement was more towards instrumental and dance music. The main domestic instrument was the **lute**, though later small **orchestras** were formed, and from the 15th century onwards independent instrumental forms such as the **sonata** and the **concerto** began to emerge. Also around this time, the **organ** became a solo instrument in churches.

The Thirty Years' War put a stop to most cultural activity across the whole country. The Germany that emerged after the war was a very different place. Old feudal structures had been severely shaken, and local merchants were becoming more powerful. When a musical revival came, it happened in town orchestras, choirs, student *Collegia Musica* and opera houses.

Two rival musicians emerged during this period – **Georg Philipp Telemann** (1681–1767) and **Johann Sebastian Bach** (1685–1750). At the time Telemann was considered the superior of the two; Bach's work as a composer was all but forgotten after his death and was only acknowledged in the 19th century when his great works – such as the *Brandenburg Concertos* and the *St Matthew Passion* – were rediscovered. Another innovative composer of the time, an early master of opera and oratorio, was **Georg Friedrich Händel** (1685–1759). Händel eventually settled in England, where he composed the famous *Messiah* (1741), it is said, in three weeks.

The Classical Period

The second half of the 18th century saw the blossoming of new musical genres. Many of these new forms, as well as older ones such as the sonata and concerto, were given their classical shape by composers **Joseph Haydn** (1732–1809) and the man many consider to be the greatest musical genius of all time, **Wolfgang Amadeus Mozart** (1756–91). Mozart also took German opera to a new peak, while **Ludwig van Beethoven** (1770–1827) is usually considered to be the most powerful exponent of the symphony. He gave the three dominant forms of this period (the **symphony**, the **string quartet** and the **piano sonata**) dramatic new expression; his tremendous, moody later symphonies set the tone for the 19th century's Romantic movement.

Romantic and 19th-Century Music

The success of the French Revolution seemed to inspire artists to a celebration of humanity's freedom and power, which was accompanied by a loosening of classical restraints on form. Early 19th-century instrumental music such as that by **Felix Mendelssohn-Bartholdy** (1809–47) and **Robert Schumann** (1810–56) was still bound by classical structure, but the final operas of **Carl Maria von Weber** (1786–1826), and music by **Anton Bruckner** (1824–96) and **Johannes Brahms** (1833–97) aligned German music with the Romantic movement that swept the country.

The grand master of the Romantic opera was undoubtedly **Richard Wagner** (1813–83). Wagner drew on heroic tales from German mythology, wrote his own libretti and involved himself in all aspects of staging. He wanted his 'musical dramas' to be spiritually uplifting *Gesamtkunstwerke* (total works of art), and brought a new psychological density to opera. Musically, his approach was also revolutionary – especially in his use of the *leitmotif*, a recurring theme used to depict a character or evoke an idea or a change in psychological state. Wagner's name is closely associated with Bavaria, through the passionate patronage of King Ludwig II, and through Bayreuth, which Wagner made his home and which stages the famous Wagner Festival every year.

Two further developments occurred in the 19th century that are still felt today. The German *lied* (solo voice and piano), which had had its foundations in song cycles by **Franz Schubert** (1797–1828), became an independent form that was to keep its popularity with composers into the 20th century. Also, people began to make a clearer distinction between serious and light music, though the latter had perfectly respectable champions in German-born **Jacques Offenbach** (1819–80) (best known as the composer of *Orpheus in the Underworld*, the music used for the can-can) and in the father and son whose name is synonymous with the waltz: **Johann Strauss Senior** (1804–49) and **Junior** (1825–99).

Into the 20th Century

Gustav Mahler (1860–1911), who carried the torch for the symphonic form, and **Richard Strauss** (1873–1946), whose operas such as *Salome* and *Der Rosenkavalier* are very much constructed on groundwork laid out by Wagner, move German music into contemporary times. In the 20th century Germany had its share of inventive, though traditionally orientated, composers such as **Paul Hindemith** (1895–1963) and **Carl Orff** (1895–1982), whose energetic *Carmina Burana* is one of the most widely listened to of all modern 'serious' compositions. More adventurous experimenters include **Arnold Schönberg** (1874–1951), whose **twelve-tone system** completely redefined musical frontiers, and the Cologne-based **Karlheinz Stockhausen** (b.1928), whose performances continue to delight and perplex.

Cinema

Thanks to the patronage of the Wittelsbachs and Munich-based financiers at the beginning of the 20th century, cinema quickly developed into a respected art form in Bavaria. As early as the 1920s film-makers from around the world came to Munich, the centre of the region's film industry, lured by excellent studios and technical equipment. The then-unknown **Alfred Hitchcock** made an appearance in 1925 with his *The Pleasure Garden*, and *Mountain Eagle* was to follow a year later. Even in the bleak years of the Second World War a series of insipid, escapist movies were shot here, most notably under the talented direction of **Helmut Käutner**, who had started his career as an actor and comedian.

Following the post-war division of Germany, Munich's studios benefited greatly from the fact that their main rivals around Berlin remained off-limits for West German film-makers, and they soon became the centre of the revival of German art cinema. In 1959 the **Bavaria Film Studios** (*see* 'Bavaria-Filmstadt', pp.87–8), which had begun production in 1920, were reorganized at Geiselgasteig on the southern edge of town. Here the young German directors tended to work as *auteurs*, often producing the film and writing the screenplay as well, giving the work a distinctive personal imprint. The 1970s were the heyday of this **new German cinema**, with the big three directors (**Fassbinder, Wenders** and **Herzog**) producing a string of Munich-based, award-winning films and commercial successes.

As a consequence, Munich became known as the 'Los Angeles of the Isar Valley', and increasingly drew international film-makers into its orbit. As early as 1957 **Stanley Kubrick** filmed the interior sets for *Paths of Glory* at the Bavaria Studios. Actors of the calibre of Dirk Bogarde, Gregory Peck and Kirk Douglas (for Richard Fleischer's *The Vikings*) worked here. In 1971 **Bob Fosse** made a name for himself with the production of *Cabaret*, and the **Monty Python** team also filmed here. By the late 1970s Munich had spawned a new generation of German directors, fascinated with recent Hollywood successes. **Wolfgang Petersen** shot to fame in 1981 with his epic wartime drama *Das Boot* (*The Boat*), one of the costliest film productions ever attempted in Germany and filmed almost entirely at the Bavaria Studios. Worldwide successes continued with the productions of *The NeverEnding Story* (1983), *Enemy Mine* (1985), Jean-Jacques Annaud's *The Name of the Rose* (1986), Joseph Vilsmaier's *Stalingrad* (1993), *Asterix and Obelix Take On Caesar* (1999), Tom Tykwer's *Perfume: The Story of a Murderer* (2006), and Uli Edel's *Last Exit to Brooklyn* (1989) and *The Baader Meinhof Complex* (2008). In the past ten years the Studios have concentrated more on television.

Food and Drink

04

Bavarian Cuisine

Eating is a serious business in Bavaria. There are strong local culinary traditions and tremendous variation between regions. Franconia has one of the best reputations for food in all Germany. People eat out frequently and plentifully, feeding is the focal activity of most fairs, and drinking the *raison d'être* of many Bavarian festivals.

Basic German cookery is a meat-and-one-veg affair, and in Bavaria the essential pattern is no different. Potatoes and cabbage (the latter boiled, pickled as *Sauerkraut*, or cooked with apples to make *Apfelrotkohl*) are the favourite vegetables. 'Meat' almost invariably means pork. The Germans get through 50kg of it per head each year, and eat every conceivable part of the pig, cooked in all imaginable ways. Nowadays, especially in newer restaurants, the heavy, fatty meat dishes are offered together with a contrasting array of well-prepared fresh salads and a more imaginative selection of vegetables.

Vegetarians will have a difficult time. Pork appears without warning – a sausage floating in bean soup, or bacon mixed in with a side dish of potatoes. Often the only 'vegetarian meal' on the menu involves fish. Until recently 'salads' meant pickles, or meat and tinned vegetables smothered in mayonnaise. (This is still true in some traditional eateries.) In the larger cities you will find specialist vegetarian restaurants, while the mainstream ones will also offer more of a choice to vegetarians. Keep an eye open also for *Reformladen* (health food shops), and *Naturcafés*, which sell wholefood (but again not necessarily purely vegetarian) fare.

The prospect of such hearty, meat-based grub might be daunting, but Bavarian dishes are often subtle and delicious. Standards are high and portions generous. ('It looked an infamous mess,' remarked one 18th-century traveller of the meal set before him in Nürnberg, 'but tasted better than passable.')

Soups range from clear broths populated by plump dumplings to purée-thick mixtures of potatoes or beans. An ideal autumnal tummy-warmer is an *Eintopf* ('one pot'), a cross between a soup and a stew, containing anything the cooks could lay their hands on. (*Eintopf* on the main part of the menu means casserole.) You can have extra sausages chopped into it if you wish. Another favourite, adapted from the Hungarian original, is a thick, peppery *Gulaschsuppe*.

Sausages come in all colours and thicknesses. Most are made with pork. White ones (*Weißwurst*) are popular south of Frankfurt (the River Main is nicknamed the 'Weißwurst equator'), and contain veal and brains. Black ones are made with blood. The most popular of all is the *Bratwurst* (literally 'grilled sausage', though often it is deep-fried), which is served with a bread roll and a dollop of mild mustard. Some of Germany's most celebrated sausages come from Nürnberg, where they are cooked over wood grills. You'll find sausages at fast-food stalls, in beer halls and in taverns. Bavaria even has specialized *Wurstküchen* (sausage kitchens) that can boast Michelin ratings.

Apart from sausages, fairly ubiquitous pork dishes are *Schweinshaxen* (huge knuckles of pork that look as if they belong on a medieval banqueting table) and *Schweinebraten* (roast pork, often sprinkled with ground coriander). **Veal**, **chicken** and **game** (especially **venison**, **boar** and **hare**) make their way on to many menus.

Venison is often cooked in fruity sauces and served with wild mushrooms, or simmered in a mouthwatering stew. **Goose** and **turkey** are common, even out of the festive season. **Beef** makes its appearance mainly as steak. **Lamb** is more of a rarity, confined mainly to Turkish and Middle Eastern restaurants. Bavaria's lakes provide an abundance of **fish**: the favourites are **carp**, **salmon**, **trout** and **perch**. Fish is cooked with delicacy and flair, though it is usually more expensive than other items on the menu.

Potato dumplings (*Knödel*), or light, crinkly **noodles** (*Spätzle*) in Bavarian Swabia, come with almost everything. Dumplings may also be made from stale bread (*Semmelknödel*) or with liver (*Leberknödel*). A variation on the noodles is Swabian *Maultasche*, a sort of giant ravioli.

Desserts are fairly run-of-the-mill, though *Bayerische Creme* (a sweet sauce best served with a tangy mush of various red fruits and berries) makes an invigorating palate cleanser. *Dampfnudeln* (steamed dumpling, smothered in sweet, fruity sauce) is a meal in itself. You can also indulge your sweet tooth by joining in the great pastime of *Kaffee und Kuchen* (coffee and cake) – the German equivalent of English afternoon tea. *Kaffee und Kuchen* can be the end point of a Sunday afternoon excursion, the excuse for a good gossip in the local café, or a genteel means of whiling away the morning. *Apfelkuchen* (apple pie) is a reliable standard and *Hefeteignudeln* or *Ausgezogene* (sweetened yeast pastries) can be found all over the region – but you are more likely to be tempted by the splendid, calorie-charged creations of a local baker supremo.

Meals

Breakfast, in all but the stingiest of hotels, involves coffee and fruit juice, cold meats, cheeses (including *Quark* – curd cheese a little like yoghurt), jams, fruit and a bewildering variety of **breads**. German bread is one of the great pluses of the cuisine. Even small local bakeries are cornucopias of 30 or so different varieties – ranging from damp, heavy *Schwarzbrot* (black bread) and healthy multigrain loaves to crusty white rolls. The famous *Pumpernickel* – a rich, black rye bread – is by no means the only *Schwarzbrot*. You can get variations with hazelnuts and all sorts of other additions. Brown breads can be made with combinations of three, four or six different types of grain, and are often pepped up by the addition of sunflower seeds, onion or spices. A sandwich made with a good, grainy brown loaf can keep you going all day.

Lunch is still the main meal of the day for most Bavarian families (though it doesn't preclude eating out at night). The **evening meal** usually takes the form of a light supper (*Abendbrot*), similar in style to breakfast but with salads and sometimes a soup. Late afternoon or evening entertaining may take place over cakes and wine.

Eating Out

For a quick snack or takeaway there is the ubiquitous *Imbiß*. There are two main categories of *Imbiß*: traditional (mainly sausages) and foreign (mainly Turkish doner kebabs or Italian pizzas) – though sometimes there are inspired regional variations, such as stalls serving fried forest mushrooms or delicate noodle dishes. In an *Imbiß* you usually order at the counter, pay on delivery and eat standing up, or at one of a scattering of plastic tables. Sausages, hamburgers and meatballs are the usual fare, though some *Imbisse* are more sophisticated and offer modest meals. *Halbes Hähnchen* (spit-roast chicken, unceremoniously hacked in two) is usually good value.

Another place for a quick lunch or snack is the **Stehcafé** ('standing café'). These are usually attached to bakeries or butchers, or found in stations or busy shopping areas. You buy your food at the counter then eat standing at elbow-high tables nearby. It is perfectly acceptable to get your bread roll at one shop, your cream cake at another and polish them off in a third which sells coffee. Often a number of establishments will share tables so you can do just that.

At the other end of the scale are classy **restaurants**, good enough to rival any in the world. Often, though, you end up paying well over the odds for food that isn't particularly special. Bavarians seem best at cooking variations of their own cuisine, rather than imitating others. Recently, though, a **New German Cuisine** has emerged. This blends traditional ingredients and techniques with a lighter, French-influenced approach – subtle sauces and imaginative combinations of flavours – with delicious results.

For a tasty, good-value meal, by far the best option is to head for a *Gaststätte*, *Gasthaus*, *Brauhaus* or *Wirtschaft* – inns that serve *gutbürgerliche Küche* (good solid cooking). Standards are higher than you would expect in similar establishments in Britain or the USA: food is often simple, portions are generous and you will rarely eat a bad meal.

You can join in the ritual of *Kaffee und Kuchen* in a café or **Konditorei** (cake shop) – some are quite trendy, others the realm of redoubtable old ladies in severe hats. A *Konditorei* will usually have a better selection of cakes, and often hand-made chocolates too. The usual practice is to choose your cake at the counter, tell the attendant, then order your coffee from the waitress at your table. She will then bring everything together.

Drinking

The distinction between restaurants and bars is less rigidly drawn in Germany than in most English-speaking countries. At a **café**, **Weinstube** (wine bar) or **Bierstube**, you can also usually get good, freshly cooked food. Nobody complains, though, if you want only a beer or a cup of tea.

Bars that are mainly for drinking are called **Bierkeller** or **Bierstadel**. Even here, people seldom stand and drink, as they do in an English pub. If there is no table free, it is perfectly acceptable to join a table of strangers. You might even end up chatting to each other for the rest of the evening. Regulars will have a private table – a *Stammtisch* – in one corner of the pub. Sometimes this is marked by a small sign. Even if it isn't, you'll soon be told if you sit at the *Stammtisch* by mistake.

Beer

Germany's annual beer consumption averages 150 litres a head for every man, woman and child in the country (more than their consumption of milk, wine and soft drinks). Tourists do their bit to add to the statistics, but there can be little doubt that beer is Germany's favourite drink. It has over a third of the world's breweries – more than half of them in Bavaria. The beer-drinking reputation of Bavaria is enhanced by the massive Munich **Oktoberfest**, but this is by no means the only big beer-drinking beano: there are spring and autumn beer festivals in virtually every town in Bavaria. Even in the wine-producing northern part of Bavaria beer is seen not as just a drink, but as part of the German way of life, with all the associated tradition. Beer and *Abendbrot* (snacks) is an evening pastime and it is still common to see colourful horse-drawn drays delivering wooden barrels of beer to pubs around town.

Controversies centred on beer can incite fervent passion. In the 19th century rioters stormed and sacked breweries in Munich when the government tried to raise a tax on beer. Today even the most devoted European federalist will bridle if you mention the *Reinheitsgebot* (Purity Law), legislation which dates back to 1516, but which was first put forward in Bavaria as early as 1487. Its strict regulation of standards of beer production (which preclude the use of any chemicals) were rigidly adhered to for centuries, but recently EU bureaucrats ruled that the law amounted to an illegal restriction on trade. Beer from other countries is full of preservatives – foam stabilizers, enzymes, and additives such as formalin and tannin – and so could not be imported to Germany. The German government was forced to back down, but feeling still runs high. Over 95 per cent of the populace believed that the *Reinheitsgebot* should have been maintained – and all Bavarian breweries still obey its strictures. Beer is at the heart of a more recent dispute, pitting Bavaria against Berlin. Bavarians were incensed when the *Bundesverwaltungsgericht* (Federal Administration Tribunal) in Berlin decided that, in accordance with federal noise-protection laws, beer gardens adjacent to residential neighbourhoods would have to sell the last glass of beer by 9.30pm and close by 10pm. Twenty thousand protesters proclaimed a 'First Beergarden Revolt'. The Bavarian government passed a 'special ordinance' to allow for a later closing that was rejected by the Berlin court, inspiring a 'Second Beergarden Revolt'. At the time of writing, the outcome is still uncertain. (The ruling only applies to beer gardens in residential neighbourhoods; others close as late as 1am).

Much of the beer brewed in Bavaria is aimed primarily at the home market. Sampling a region's or a town's beer is as crucial a part of a visit as tasting the local cuisine. Many towns have excellent local breweries, with a **Brauhaus** (drinking tavern) on the premises – often a good place for a hearty meal and rousing evening. Bamberg is known for a smoky beer that gets its taste from beechwood burned during the brewing process. In Neustadt (near Coburg) the beer also gets a fine, smoky flavour after hot stones are plunged into the brew to caramelize the malt. Munich is one of the top European beer-producing cities. It offers a wide range of brews from light lagers to various *Bocks*, the strongest beer type. Kulmbach (near Bayreuth) comes up with the strongest beer in the world, at 22 per cent proof.

Beer in Bavaria is either bottom-fermented (the process most common in other countries, whereby beer is made with yeast that has sunk to the bottom of the fermentation tank) or top-fermented (an age-old process, recently revived, made with yeast from the top of the tank). Top-fermented beer tends to have more body and be more characterful than beer made by the easier, more modern method – though *Pils*, a bottom-fermented beer high in hop content, is the most popular brew.

Beer is sometimes served in a *Maß* – a challenging litre-tankard. Whether you are gulping down a *Maß* in a rowdy beer tent, or sipping it in a smoky cellar, or drinking alongside the huge copper vats in a local *Brauerei*, or sailing down the River Isar propped up against your own barrel (a popular Bavarian springtime activity, *see* p.85), your encounters with beer in Germany may well number among the most memorable moments of your visit.

Wine

Don't be put off by the sickly-sweet German wines that are generally offered in Britain or the United States. Many German wines are dry and delicious. The same applies to the wines of Bavaria, which because of climatic conditions are produced mainly in Franconia, in a small but outstanding belt of land that runs between Frankfurt (in Hesse) and Nürnberg. The leading grape in Bavaria is Müller-Thurgau, alas, which all too often produces bland wines. Traminer, however, makes a tangy, spicy wine, while Silvaner is milder and more full-bodied. The fruity Bacchus and Scheurebe are other varieties worth looking out for. Whites feature more strongly than reds because red-wine grapes don't ripen easily in northern climates. All Franconian varieties are sold in traditional flagon-shaped bottles called *Bocksbeutel*.

Tafelwein is basic plonk, **Landwein** is just a step up from that (like the French *vin de pays*). Better quality wines are labelled **Qualitätswein**, and *really* good wines will have an additional *Prädikat* or *Kabinett* (grower's reserve) on the label. Better quality wines may also be labelled according to the timing and manner of the harvest. *Spätlese* (late-picked) wines are full and juicy, while for *Auslese* (specially selected) brands the grapes are picked separately to produce a rich, ripe, honey-sweet nectar. (Wines are discussed in more detail in the chapter on **Franconia** and the section on **Würzburg**.) In addition to bottled wine, restaurants often sell half- and quarter-litre carafes of a wide selection of wines – not just the house plonk. It is also acceptable practice for people eating together to order their own glasses or mini-carafes to go with a meal. In summer many prefer a refreshing *Schorle* – wine with mineral water or soda.

Warmth and Spirit

Even in the humblest *Imbiß* **coffee** is likely to be freshly brewed and filtered. Cafés and restaurants will also offer espresso and cappuccino. **Tea** is usually taken black. Herb and fruit teas are becoming popular, and some cafés have long 'tea menus'.

In the winter, street-side stalls pop up selling *Glühwein* (hot, spicy mulled wine) and *Feuerbohle* (a similar brew that has had a rum-soaked sugar cone melted over it). Common **spirits** include *Schnapps* (often drunk with beer as a chaser). There is also a wide range of sticky, fruity liqueurs, such as **Obstler** and the gentian-based **Enzian**.

German Menu Reader

Local Dishes

Aal eel – popular in the north; served smoked or *grün*, cooked in creamy herb sauce
Ausgezogene flaky pastry dessert with a sweet soft centre
Bauernfrühstück literally 'peasant breakfast' – ham, egg and potatoes – or any large, hot breakfast
Bayerische creme vanilla-flavoured whipped cream served with raspberry or strawberry purée
blaue Zipfel pork sausages in spiced vinegar
Bohnensuppe thick bean soup
Brägenwurst sausage made with brains
Braunkohl kale
Bratwurst grilled sausage (usually pork)
Dampfnudeln sweet steamed dumplings
Eintopf/Topf stew, casserole or thick soup
Flädlesuppe soup with strips of pancake in it
Forelle trout
Gaisburger Marsch thick beef soup with noodles and potatoes
Grünkohl cabbage
Gulaschsuppe thick, peppery beef soup
halbes Hähnchen half a chicken (grilled)
Hopfensprossen steamed hop-shoots, tasting like asparagus; available only in spring
Kasseler Rippchen pickled loin of pork (named after a Berlin butcher who was called Kassel)
Leberkäs Bavarian-style meat loaf
Leberknödel liver dumplings
Lebkuchen traditional spicy gingerbread, made with honey and nuts
Maultaschen giant ravioli, stuffed with meat and usually spinach too
Mettwurst pork and beef sausages
Mehlpüt pear and butter sauce dessert
Nürnberger Bratwurst grilled pork sausage about the size of your little finger
Obaazta a blend of Camembert and butter, bound with egg yolk; called *Gerupfter* in Franconia
Pfefferpotthast spicy boiled beef
Pumpernickel dark rye bread
Reiberdatschi potato cakes
Sauerkraut pickled cabbage
Schlachtplatte platter of various meats, usually including blood sausage and offal
Schweinshaxe roast knuckle of pork
Schweinepfeffer jugged pork
Semmelknödeln bread dumplings
Spargel asparagus
Spätzle noodles
Speckkuchen substantial bacon quiche
Tellerfleisch minced beef preparation served with horseradish sauce; also known as *Tafelspitz* and *Ochsenbrust*

Weißwurst veal and pork sausage, sometimes with brain
Zünger pig's tongue
Zwiebelbraten beef in brown onion sauce

Useful Words

Frühstuck; Brotzeit breakfast
Mittagessen; Vesper (in rural Bavaria) lunch
Abendessen dinner
Abendbrot supper

Speisekarte menu
guten Appetit bon appétit
Tasse cup
Kännchen pot (e.g. of coffee)
Glas glass
Flasche bottle
Salz/Pfeffer salt/pepper
Senf mustard
Milch/Zucker milk/sugar
Brot/Butter bread/butter
belegtes Brötchen filled roll
hausgemacht home-made

Art à la
frisch fresh
gekocht boiled
gedämpft steamed
gebacken baked
gebraten roasted
geräuchert smoked
gefüllt stuffed
Vorspeise starters
Suppe soup
Hauptgericht main course

Fleisch Meat

Wurst sausage
Schinken ham
Aufschnitt cold cuts
Schweinefleisch pork
Schweineshaxe knuckle of pork
Speck bacon
Rindfleisch beef
Lammfleisch lamb
Kalbfleisch veal
Ochsenschwanz oxtail
Hase hare
Kaninchen rabbit
Leber liver
Wild game
Hirsch, Reh venison
Hackfleisch minced (ground) beef
Steak steak
Boulette meatball
Kotelett, Schnitzel chop
Geflügel poultry
Huhn, Hähnchen chicken
Ente duck
Truthahn, Puter turkey
Gans goose

Fische Fish

Forelle trout
Karpfen carp
Lachs salmon
Schellfisch haddock
Zander perch
Hecht pike
Kabeljau cod
Seezunge sole
Butt flounder
Scholle plaice
Hering, Matjes herring
Thunfisch tuna
Hummer lobster
Garnelen prawns
Muscheln mussels
Venusmuscheln clams
Tintenfisch squid
Aal eel

Gemüse Vegetables

Salat salad
Tomaten tomatoes
Gurke cucumber
Paprika peppers/capsicums
Zwiebeln onions
Knoblauch garlic
Schnittlauch chives
Kräuter herbs
Pellkartoffeln jacket potatoes
Kartoffelbrei mashed potatoes
Pommes frites chips
Salzkartoffeln boiled potatoes
Reis rice
Bohnen beans
Kohl/Rotkohl (red) cabbage
Pilze, Champignons mushrooms
Mais maize
Erbsen peas
Blumenkohl cauliflower

Spinat spinach
Lauch leeks
Linsen lentils
Kichererbsen chickpeas
Knödel, Klösse dumplings
Spargel asparagus
Aubergine aubergine

Nachtisch Dessert

Torte/Kuchen tart/cake
Eis ice-cream
Sahne cream
Schlagsahne whipped cream
Nüße nuts
Mandeln almonds
Schokolade chocolate
Käse cheese

Obst Fruit

Apfel apple
Apfelsine, Orange orange
Zitrone lemon
Pampelmuse grapefruit
Banane banana
Ananas pineapple
Birne pear
Kirsche cherry
Pfirsich peach
Pflaume plum
Trauben grapes
Rosinen raisins
Himbeere raspberry
Erdbeere strawberry
Johannisbeere redcurrant

Getränke Drinks

Wasser water
Mineralwasser mineral water
Saft fruit juice
Bier beer
Rotwein/Weißwein red/white wine
Brandwein brandy

Planning
Your Trip

05

When to Go

Climate

Bavaria is in the Central European Temperate Zone, but that does not mean that it has a uniform climate. In fact there is a considerable climatic difference between regions. The south has cold but bracing winters, but in the north the winters are damp and soggy.

Spring comes to Lindau on Lake Constance (the Bodensee) at the beginning of May, a good six weeks earlier than to the heart of the Allgäu Alps, just a few kilometres away. Around this time you can still ski in the Alps, then nip down to Lake Constance for an invigorating first swim of the season. A good summer can seem positively Mediterranean, with long scorching days and sultry nights throughout Bavaria. Misty autumn is the perfect time to visit forest areas, which dissolve into shades of gold, and wine-growing regions, where you can soak in the infectious energy of the harvest, then sit in taverns drinking the cloudy grape juice.

Festivals

The Bavarian calendar is crammed with festivals, from the formal national and religious holidays to riotous local romps, usually with pagan roots. The most important festival in Germany is **Christmas** (*Weinachten*), a time of candlelight and gingerbread, relaxed chats over *Glühwein* (mulled wine) around the fire and magical markets. Christmas decorations are less tacky and festivities less forced than in most parts of the English-speaking world. *Fasching* is essentially a southern, Roman Catholic form of carnival, but it is beginning to catch on in the Protestant areas of Franconia as well. Festivities include costume parades, feasts, and general clowning about and hilarity.

Local festivals are listed under the separate towns, but below is an overview.

Calendar of Events

January–February

Fasching (**Shrovetide carnival**) Traditional festivities; begins in early January and runs up to Shrove Tuesday (*Faschingsdienstag*). All over the region, particularly in Munich, Bavarian Swabia and Franconia.

Hornschlittenrennen Sledge-racing in the Bavarian and Allgäu Alps, during *Fasching*.

March–April

Palmsonntag (**Palm Sunday**) Aside from the religious festival, a tradition that's similar to April Fool's Day: if you're last out of bed you're nicknamed the *Palmesel*, a lazy palm donkey.

Starkbierzeit (**Strong Beer Season**) At the end of *Fasching*, where strong Lent beer is drunk. All regions.

March–September

Schäfertanz (**Shepherd's Dance**) One Sunday each month between Easter and September, in Rothenburg.

May–June

Fronleichnam (**Corpus Christi**) Street processions, all around the region.

Maibaumaufstellen (**Raising of the Maypole**) This turns into a competitive sport between towns, with tall and elaborately decorated poles (blue and white stripes, ribbons and carvings). Traditionally, towns might steal their neighbours' poles and hold them to ransoms of beer and food, which is then shared among all.

Pfingsten (**Whitsun**) Festivals throughout Bavaria, including mass horseback rides from Kötzting, St Englmar and Ochsenfurt (all in the Bavarian Forest); beer festivals; and the mayor's wine-quaffing and fancy dress in Rothenburg.

Sonnwendfeiern (**Midsummer festivals**): bonfires on the eve of the summer solstice; all over the region.

May–November

Bavarian Olympics This is Bavaria's equivalent of Scotland's Highland Games. The competitors traipse all over Upper Bavaria to take part in the various rounds throughout the summer, and you can watch beery men dust off their old *lederhosen* and impress spectators with fierce contests of finger-wrestling, tree-stump-sawing, beer-*stein*-lifting or snuff-sniffing. All this takes place against a bacchanalian backdrop and to the sounds of many an oompah band. The **Bavarian Tourist Board** (Leopoldstraße 146, 80804 München, t (089) 2123 970, *www.bayern.by*) holds listings of the individual annual competitions.

Weinfeste **(Wine Festivals)** Over a hundred wine festivals are held in Franconian towns and villages each year, with an elected Wine Queen.

July–August

Further Drachenstich **(Slaying of the Dragon in Furth)** At Furth im Wald in August, a huge historical procession on the theme of one of Germany's oldest folk plays, *Drachenstich*.

Kinderzeche Dinkelsbühl This is a re-enactment of an event during the Thirty Years' War in the 17th century, where the children of Dinkelsbühl saved their medieval city from destruction. Those taking part in the procession are rewarded with sweets.

Ritterspiele in Kaltenberg **(Kaltenberg Knights' Tournament)** The world's largest medieval tournament which draws around 1,200 visitors and includes a jousting display performed by professional stuntmen, a market, entertainment, handicrafts and lots to eat and drink.

September–October

Summer and Harvest Festivals In the wine-growing regions.

Viehscheid or *Almabtrieb* **(transhumance)** Cows, wearing bells and headdresses, are driven downhill from alpine pastures (*see* **The Bavarian Alps**, p.133).

Oktoberfest Around six million people come to Munich for the October beer festival, which is the largest in the world. Held from mid-September to the first Sunday in October. *See* pp.88–9; and *www.oktoberfest.de*.

November–December

Christkindlmarkt **(Christmas Markets)** Ever popular places to find *Glühwein*, *lebkuchen* (ginger cake) and gifts. From the last week in November until two or three days before Christmas Eve; regionwide, and especially good in Nürnberg, Munich and Rothenburg.

National Holidays

See p.67.

Tourist Information

There is a comprehensive network of tourist offices in Bavaria – even small villages are likely to have one. Most are located in or near the main railway station, or on the market square. Ask for the *Verkehrsamt*, or simply Tourist Information (for the *Kurverwaltung* at spas). Most offer **room reservation** services with local hotels (for a booking fee of €3–5), and can also help you find accommodation in private homes (*see* 'Where to Stay', p.61).

For information about Bavaria before you leave, contact the **Bavarian Tourist Office** in Munich (Leopoldstraße 146, Munich, **t** +49 89 2123 970, *www.bayern.by*), or one of the branches of the **German National Tourist Office** (*www.cometogermany.com*), below.

Canada: 480 University Avenue, Suite 1410, Toronto, ON, M5G 1V2, **t** (416) 968 1685.

Irish Republic: no office; contact UK address instead or call **t** 1 800 484 480.

UK: 18 Conduit Street, London W1A 3TN, **t** (020) 7317 0908.

USA: 122 East 42nd Street, 52nd floor, New York, NY 10168-0072, **t** (212) 661 7200.

Embassies and Consulates

Abroad

Canada: 1 Waverley Street, Ottawa, Ontario K2P 0T8, **t** (613) 232 1101, *www.ottawa.diplo.de*.

Republic of Ireland: 31 Trimelston Avenue, Booterstown, Blackrock, Co. Dublin, **t** (01) 269 3011, *www.dublin.diplo.de*.

UK: 23 Belgrave Square, London SW1X 8PZ, **t** (020) 7824 1300, *www.london.diplo.de*.

USA: 4645 Reservoir Road NW, Washington, **t** (202) 298 8140, *www.washington.diplo.de*.

In Munich

Canada: Tal 29, **t** (089) 2199 570, *munic@international.gc.ca*.

Irish Republic: Denninger Straße 15, **t** (089) 2080 5990.

UK: Bürkleinstraße 10, **t** (089) 211090, *info.munich@fco.gov.uk*.

USA: Königinstraße 5, **t** (089) 28880, *munich.usconsulate.gov*.

Entry Formalities

Passports and Visas

European Union and US citizens, Canadians, Australians and New Zealanders do not need visas to visit Germany; a valid **passport** will do. If you are arriving by road from another EU country you are likely to find border posts unstaffed, or to be waved through without a second glance.

If you intend to stay for any longer than 90 days, you should pay a visit to the local *Einwohnermeldeamt* (registration office) to register your address.

Customs Regulations and Currency Restrictions

Since the dissolution of internal borders in the EU there are no restrictions on the quantities of alcohol, tobacco and perfume that can be taken across EU borders, provided it has been bought duty-paid (i.e. not in a duty-free shop) within the EU and is for personal use only. American citizens may take up to 100 cigars and 200 cigarettes back into the USA. You may also take in 1 litre of spirits or 2 litres of wine, 50g of perfume and 250ml of eau de toilette. Most states restrict the import of alcohol, and the laws of the state in which you arrive override Federal law – so it's worth checking up on this before you leave.

You can bring or take any amount of money in or out of Germany – but you must declare sums of cash exceeding €12,500.

Disabled Travellers

Travellers with disabilities will find themselves well catered for in Bavaria. Buses can be a problem, but many of the newer trams have lowered steps. Train stations that are not fully converted for wheelchairs have eagle-eyed attendants to help (look for someone with a *Bahnhofsmission* armband).

In Germany, **Touristik Union International** (TUI, Karl-Wiechert-Allee 23, Hannover, t (0511) 567 2294, *www.tui.de*) has a list of hotels, and provides advice and assistance on travel.

Münich has official **international sign language guides** for groups of up to 15

Disability Organizations

In the UK and Ireland

Tourism for All, c/o Vitalise, Shap Road Industrial Estate, Shap Road, Kendal, Cumbria LA9 6NZ, t 0845 124 9971, *www.tourismforall.org.uk*. Information on accommodation, transport, equipment hire, services, tour operators and contacts.

Irish Wheelchair Association, Blackheath Drive, Clontarf, Dublin 3, t (01) 818 6400, *www.iwa.ie*. This publishes travel advice guides.

RADAR, 12 City Forum, 250 City Rd, London, EC1V 8AF, t (020) 7250 3222, *www.radar.org.uk*. Information and books.

RNIB (Royal National Institute of the Blind), 105 Judd St, London WC1H 9NE, t 0303 123 9999, *www.rnib.org.uk*. The mobility unit has a 'Plane Easy' audio-tape with advice for visually impaired flyers, and also advises on finding accommodation abroad.

In the USA and Canada

American Foundation for the Blind, 11 Penn Plaza, Suite 300, New York, NY 10001, t (212) 502 7600, *www.afb.org*. Info for visually impaired travellers.

Federation for the Handicapped, 211 West 14th St, New York, NY 10011, t (212) 747 4262. Organizes summer tours for members.

SATH (Society for Accessible Travel and Hospitality), 347 5th Ave, Suite 610, New York, NY 10016, t (212) 447 7284, *www.sath.org*. Travel and access information. The website has good links and a list of online publications.

Internet Sites

Access-Able Travel Source, *www.access-able.com*. Information for older and disabled travellers.

Access Ability, *www.access-ability.org/travel. html*. Information on travel agencies.

Emerging Horizons, *www.emerginghorizons. com*. An online newsletter for disabled travellers.

people, price €103 per group, for 2hrs. Book through *gaestefuhrungen@muenchen.de*.

See box, above, for a list of disability organizations.

Insurance and EHIC Cards

EU nationals are entitled to free medical care in Germany; you need a European Health Insurance or **EHIC card** (see *www.dh.gov.uk/travellers* or pick up a form at a post office).

Citizens of other countries have no such privileges. All travellers are advised to take out some form of **travel insurance**. Many travel insurance packages include not only medical cover, but lost luggage, theft and ticket cancellation. For further information for US citizens, visit the Bureau of Consular Affairs, *www.travel.state.gov/medical.*

If you are involved in a motor accident, scratch somebody's car with your shopping trolley or knock over something in a shop, you could find yourself involved in a costly court action. The Germans are a litigious bunch, and losers in court have to pay the opponent's legal costs as well. If you are staying in Germany for any length of time, or doing much bicycling, take out **personal liability insurance** (*Haftpflichtversicherung*). In Germany nearly everybody does this, and policies are cheap (around €45 a year). Most travel insurance also includes cover for third-party liabilities.

Money

The Reichs Doller of Germany is worth foure shillings foure pence, and the silver Gulden is accounted three shillings and foure pence English. Twenty Misen silver Groshes, 32 Lubecke shillings, 45 Embden stivers, foure Copstocks and a halfe, 55 groates, 36 Maria grosh, 18 spitz-grosh, 18 Batz, make a Reichs Doller. Two seslings make a Lubecke shilling: foure Drier a silver grosh: two dreyhellers a Drier: two schwerd grosh a schneberger: foure creitzers a batz: foure pfennig a creitzer.
A travel guide of 1617

Since January 2002, Germany, like much of continental Europe, has been using the single European currency: the **euro** (€). Banknotes come in seven denominations: €500, €200, €100, €50, €20, €10 and €5. The eight denominations of coins include 1, 2 5, 10, 20 and 50 **cents**, plus €1 and €2 coins. There are 100 cents to 1 euro. Some Germans still reckon in the old currency, and prices are sometimes marked in both euros and Deutschmarks.

Most hotels, restaurants and larger stores accept **credit cards**. Cash is available from **ATMs** in all major cities and towns, using a Maestro or Cirrus credit or debit card. **Prepaid cash cards** such as those available from Caxton Fx (*www.caxtonfx.com*) are a very safe and cost-effective way of carrying spending money. However, petrol stations, larger hotels and upmarket restaurants will take plastic. **Traveller's cheques** in dollars, sterling or euros are the safest way to carry your money; banks will give you the best rates for changing them.

Getting There

By Air

Bavaria's main international airport is **Munich**, with flights from London and several UK regional airports. There are also flights from the UK to **Nürnberg**. You can also fly to Friedrichshafen, on Lake Constance, just across the border between Bavaria and neighbouring Wurttemberg. Travellers to the southeast and the Bavarian Alps should also consider flying to **Salzburg** in Austria, just minutes from the border (there are no border formalities between Austria and Germany).

From the UK and Ireland

There are flights to Munich from Belfast, Birmingham, Dublin, Edinburgh, London Gatwick, London Heathrow, London Stansted, and Manchester. Prices vary wildly, depending entirely on supply and demand, so shop around. With so-called 'no-frills' airlines, beware of a bewildering array of extra charges for everything from luggage to check-in. Note that Memmingen, which Ryanair calls 'Munich West', is actually around 100km west of the city.

From the USA and Canada

Lufthansa is the best option for flights from North America, with services direct to Munich from San Francisco, Los Angeles, Chicago, Boston, Washington, New York and Charlotte, and an even wider choice of flights from North America to Frankfurt. Some of these may be operated in conjunction with Lufthansa's airline partners in the Star Alliance consortium. Frankfurt, Germany's busiest international airport, is only around 30km beyond Bavaria's northwest border. With a much wider choice of flights, it may be a more useful gateway to Bavaria for visi-

Airline Carriers

UK and Ireland

Aer Lingus, t (Ireland) 0818 365 000, **t** (UK) 0871 718 5000, *www.aerlingus.com*. Belfast, Cork, Dublin and London Gatwick to Munich.

Air Berlin, t 0871 5000 737, *www.airberlin.com*. Stansted to Munich.

BMI, t 0870 607 0555, *www.flybmi.com*. London Heathrow, Birmingham and Manchester to Munich.

British Airways, t 0844 493 0787, *www.ba.com*. Heathrow to Munich; London Gatwick to Salzburg; Birmingham to Frankfurt and Stuttgart; Manchester to Stuttgart.

easyJet, t 0871 750 0100, *www.easyjet.com*. Edinburgh, Manchester, Gatwick and Stansted to Munich.

Flybe, t 0871 700 2000, *www.flybe.com*. Exeter and Southampton to Salzburg.

Lufthansa, t 0871 945 9747, *www.lufthansa.com*. Birmingham to Munich and Frankfurt; Dublin to Frankfurt.

Ryanair, *www.ryanair.com*. Dublin, Edinburgh and Stansted to Memmingen; Dublin and Stansted to Salzburg; Stansted to Friedrichhafen.

USA and Canada

Air Canada, t 1 888 247 2662, *www.aircanada.com*. Frankfurt and Munich from Toronto.

American Airlines, t 1 800 433 7300, *www.aa.com*. Frankfurt from Dallas and Chicago.

Delta Air Lines, t 1 800 241 4141, *www.delta.com*. Munich from Atlanta; Frankfurt from New York JFK, Cincinnati and Atlanta.

Lufthansa, USA **t** 1 800 645 3880, Canada **t** 1 800 563 5954, *www.lufthansa.com*. Munich from Boston, Charlotte, Chicago, Los Angeles, New York, San Francisco and Washington DC.

United Airlines, t 1 800 247 3663, *www.unitedairlines.com*. Frankfurt from Washington and Chicago.

tors from North America, Australia and New Zealand. Travellers from North America can also look for connecting flights to Munich via London with British Airways or Dublin with Aer Lingus.

By Train

Journey time to Munich from London St Pancras International takes around 9hrs 30 minutes, travelling by Eurostar to Brussels, then to Cologne by high-speed Thalys train to connect with the German high-speed ICE network.

From 2010, an ever faster high-speed line will shave 30 minutes off the journey time between Brussels and Cologne. In real, door-to-door terms, this is about five hours longer than going by air, but if you break the journey with a one-night stopover in Cologne (one of Germany's pleasantest cities) going by rail can be one of the most enjoyable and stress-free ways of getting to Bavaria.

Eurostar, t 08705 186 186, *www.eurostar.com*.

Rail Europe, t 08708 371 371, US **t** 1 877 257 2887, Canada **t** 1 800 361 RAIL, *www.raileurope.co.uk*, *www.raileurope.com*.

By Coach

Coach travel is the slowest and most uncomfortable option, and is not necessarily cheaper than flying. Special-offer fares with **Eurolines**, which runs coaches two to five times weekly from London to Munich, start at around £33 each way, while the cheapest air fares can be less than £20. The coach takes up to 24 hours, against about 2hrs 30 minutes by air.

Eurolines, t 08717 818 179, *www.eurolines.com*.

By Car (via Ferry)

Car and passenger ferries link the UK with a number of ports that are within one day's drive of Bavaria's borders. Almost all of the six- to nine-hour journey is on motorways, making for fairly stress-free driving. If you own a performance car, you can probably shave some more time off that journey by making the most of the long stretches of *Autobahn* that have no maximum speed limit.

The most convenient mainland ports for onward travel are Calais and Dunkirk in northern France; Zeebrugge in Belgium; and IJmuiden, near Amsterdam, in the Netherlands.

Ferry companies include:

P&O Ferries, t 08716 645 645, *www.poferries.com*. Dover to Calais and overnight Hull to Zeebrugge.

Seafrance, t 0871 663 2546, *www.seafrance.com*. Dover to Calais.

Norfolk Line, t 0844 499 0077, *www.norfolkline.co.uk*. Dover to Zeebrugge and overnight from Rosyth to Zeebrugge.

LD Ferries, t 0906 75 33 451, *www.ldline.co.uk*. Dover to Boulogne.

DFDS, t 0871 522 9955, *www.dfds.co.uk*. Newcastle to IJmuiden.

Fares vary widely. The least popular sailings (midweek, off-season and with late-night or very early-morning departures) can cost less than half as much as a standard return. A return trip with P&O between Dover and Calais for a standard car and up to nine passengers can cost as little as £60 return or as much as £150.

By Car (via Eurotunnel)

With up to three car-carrying trains every hour between Dover and Coquelles, near Calais, and a journey time of around 20 minutes, Eurotunnel is the quickest way of crossing the Channel. Fares start at £53 per car for a standard single trip.

Eurotunnel, t 08705 35 35 35, *www.eurotunnel.com*.

Bavaria is about 500km from the Channel ports, and you can travel by motorway all the way. **UK drivers** taking their own car need to take valid driver's licences, insurance certificates, and all relevant vehicle documents, including registration documents and MoT test certificate. Also fit stickers to deflect your headlights. You must carry a warning triangle in Germany.

Getting Around

By Train

German Rail (**Deutsche Bundesbahn**, *www.bahn.de*) can whizz you around Bavaria with speed and awesome efficiency. For longer journeys, the **InterCityExpress** (ICE) reaches speeds of up to 250kph while you recline in sleek, air-conditioned carriages. Unless you

are travelling on a German Rail Pass (*see* below) you will need to pay a surcharge for this speed and comfort. You also need to pay one (€4) for the next notch down, the **InterCity** (IC) and **EuroCity** (EC) (international) express trains. If you're not in a hurry, you'll find these just as good as the ICE. For journeys between smaller centres there are the **InterRegio** trains, or you can meander about on the local **D-Zug** (normal service) or **E-Zug** (slow) trains. **Ticket** (*Fahrkarte*) prices are based on the distance travelled, so a return journey is no cheaper than two singles.

A **Freedom/Euro Domino Pass** (2nd class adult pass for 3 days £138, 5 days £168, 8 days £300; youth pass (under 26) for 3 days £104, 5 days £126, 8 days £160) is available only to non-residents of Germany, and should be bought before you leave (German Rail offices and some travel agents supply them). With this you can travel on any service. It also allows you to travel on bus services run by German Rail and on local S-Bahn trains.

DER Travel Service Ltd, UK **t** (020) 7290 1104, *www.dertravel.co.uk*.

German Rail DER Tours Inc., 9501 W. Devon Av, Rosemont, IL 60018–4832, **t** (847) 692 6300.

Rail Europe, UK **t** 0870 837 1371, US **t** 1 877 257 2887, Canada **t** 1 800 361 RAIL, *www.raileurope.com, www.raileurope.co.uk*.

By Car

During the 1930s Germany built the world's first motorways. Today the *Autobahn* network is still one of the most extensive and best-maintained in Europe – and there are no charges. Regional roads ('B' roads) and country routes are also impressive. On non-*Autobahn* roads outside built-up areas there are **speed limits** of 80–100kph; in towns the limit is 50kph.

If you have a serious **accident** in Germany you must wait until the police arrive. Failure to do this can result in prosecution. In the case of a minor accident, swap insurance details and look for a witness.

If your car **breaks down**, move it to the side of the road and place your warning triangle a few metres behind it. The German motoring organization, the **ADAC**, will give you free help if you break down on a main road.

However, you will have to pay for parts and towing. Call them on the orange emergency telephones by asking for *Strassenwachthilfe*, or on **t** (0180) 222 22 22 (dial **t** 222 222 if you are using a mobile). If you are a member of the AA or RAC in Britain, you should make enquiries about reciprocal deals before you leave. If you take your car to a garage to be repaired, you are legally required to leave the registration documents with it.

In Germany you **drive on the right** and overtake on the left. As in the UK, cars already travelling around a roundabout have right of way. Be especially careful in cities with **trams**: they always have right of way, even crossing roundabouts or junctions. Often they travel up and down the centre of wide roads; stops are on the pavement and tram-users must cross the traffic to reach it. When a tram stops in such places, cars are not allowed to overtake, and must leave clear access to the doors . Sometimes there is a line on the street coinciding with the back of the tram to show you where to stop.

In many of the larger cities and historical towns, the centre is closed to cars. There are usually ample **car parks** around the periphery, which are well signposted. **Park and Ride** facilities (marked 'P+R') are usually farther out, but are cheaper (or even free), with public transport connections to the centre. **Street parking** is either metered or on the 'pay and display' system. Sometimes parking is free but subject to a time limit; this is indicated by a blue 'P' sign with a dial symbol, and you must indicate your arrival time (buy cardboard clocks from petrol stations).

The major **car hire** firms – Avis, Budget and Hertz – have branches all over Bavaria. Easycar (*www.easycar.com*) offers very competitive rates online.

The cheapest way of all to get around Bavaria is by using **Mitfahrzentralen**, *www.mifaz.de* (lift agencies). For a small fee the agency will put you in touch with a motorist who is driving to your destination; all you pay is a contribution to the petrol cost. Drivers have to leave their address and registration number at the *Mitfahrzentrale*, and you usually meet at the agency itself, so the system is quite safe.

By Bus

There is no national German bus network – with such an efficient rail service there is little need for one. German Rail itself runs buses to many areas not served by trains. Otherwise, local buses can be useful for visiting more out-of-the-way sights and ?travelling between villages.

By Boat

Much of Bavaria can be visited by boat, and several trips are among the most romantic river journeys in Germany. Local cruise liners and ferries make a slow but delightful travel alternative, and sometimes afford the best views of all. Particularly recommended are the routes along the easternmost stretch of the **Danube** (*see* p.193) and along the **Altmühl Valley** (*see* p.113).

Bicycling and Hiking

The Bavarians are enthusiastic walkers and cyclists, and both are well catered for. Often a bike is the most sensible, convenient and economical means of transport in a town. Most towns, especially in the west, have well-laid-out **cycle paths**. You will also find cycle paths by regional roads, and crisscrossing the countryside between villages.

Commercial **bicycle hire** firms are listed under the separate 'Getting Around' sections for each city. Most will require a deposit.

To take your **bicycle on a train** you will have to buy a ticket for it (*Fahrradkarte*) and put it in the luggage van yourself. InterCity, EuroCity and some local trains don't allow bicycles, so check first.

Country areas are webbed with well-marked **hiking trails**. Few of them are very arduous, and over weekends and holidays they swarm with healthy marchers (many of whom really do wear knee breeches and bright woollen socks). Even the longer trails are liberally punctuated by shelters, villages and inns, so there is rarely any danger of starving, or of dying a lonely death on a mountainside. Nevertheless, carry an adequate **map** (the local tourist office can generally oblige), as signposting sometimes isn't clear.

Urban Transport

Trams and **buses** make up the backbone of public transport in many Bavarian cities. When you have the choice, you'll find trams the quicker and more frequent of the two. Munich has an **U-Bahn** (*Untergrundbahn*, underground railway) which also runs overground, while an **S-Bahn** (*Stadtbahn*, town railway) is a suburban railway.

Tickets are usually dispensed by machines at stations and stops, and are valid on all forms of public transport (subject to zones). Rail passes and Deutsche Bundesbahn (DB) tickets are also valid on S-Bahns only. Single journeys can be expensive, but a day pass (*Tageskarte* or *24-Stunden-Karte*), which offers unlimited travel on whatever the city has to offer, is always good value. Whatever form of ticket you buy, you must **validate** it by sticking it in the franking machines on trams and buses and at the entrance to platforms.

Where to Stay

Eighteenth-century travellers through southern Germany complained of having to undress in front of the landlord and share their quarters with cows and hogs. A travel guide of the time advised visitors to push furniture against the door at night and to make an extravagant display of their firearms before retiring. Today, life in Bavaria's inns and hotels could hardly be more different. Standards are uniformly high: you are unlikely to have to share your room, the beds will be spotless and comfortable, and the only accusation you might level is one of dullness.

Hotels

German hotels are graded on a scale of nearly 80 classifications, which is ironic since standards are pretty even (apart from at the luxury end of the market). In the broad bracket of moderately priced hotels, you will find rustic ones (with wooden beams and folksy knick-knacks), others stuck in a 1970s time warp and smart new ones with plastic-coated furniture. An en suite bathroom or shower is standard, except at the lower end of the market. You are also likely to find a TV and phone in the room. Service is usually

Hotel Price Ranges

Categories are based on a standard double room with WC and bath or shower, where appropriate, in high season (summer in some places and winter in ski resorts).

luxury	€€€€€	€250 +
expensive	€€€€	€150–249
moderate	€€€	€100–149
inexpensive	€	– €100

?efficient and often friendly. Most of the hotels mentioned in this book have been chosen because they offer something exceptional, in atmosphere, location or service.

Pensions and Private Rooms

Inexpensive alternatives to hotels are pensions (which also keep high standards) and private rooms. The latter are a good bet in country areas. Look out for signs advertising *Fremdenzimmer* or *Zimmer frei*. Local tourist offices carry lists of people offering rooms, and the staff can often make a reservation for you.

Youth Hostels

The first youth hostel (*Jugendherberge*) in the world opened in Germany, and youth hostels in Bavaria still provide cheap and reliable dormitory accommodation for all people under the age of 27. Most are members of the **International Youth Hostel Association** (see *www.jugendherberge.de* – some will take online reservations). Bear in mind that to use IYHA hostels it is necessary to become a **member**. You can sign up at the first one you visit, but it's cheaper to join at a branch in your own country. Many hostels close in winter.

Farm Holidays

For a fraction of the normal cost of an overnight stop (as little as €30 per person for bed and breakfast) you can take your pick from around 1,500 rustic dwellings that form part of the farm holidays scheme. The houses range from the characteristic sloping-roofed farmhouses of traditional Allgäu farms to the tiered farmsteads of the Franconian heights. You'll get a taste of Bavarian farm life, meet local people, and you might even pick up a

Specialist Tour Operators

In the UK

Holt's Battlefield Tours, t (01293) 455300, *www.battletours.co.uk*. Military history tours of Munich, Nürnberg and Berchtesgaden.

Martin Randall Travel, t (020) 8742 3355, *www.martinrandall.com*. Architecture, art, ?history and music.

Page & Moy Ltd, t 0870 832 7000, *www.pagemoy.co.uk*. Cultural guided tours.

Peter Deilmann River Cruises, t (020) 7436 2931, *www.deilmann-cruises.com*.

In the USA

For a complete list of US tour operators to Germany, contact the **German National Tourist Office**, 122 East 42nd Street, 52nd Floor, New York, NY 10168–0072, **t** (212) 661 7200, *www.visits-to-germany.com*.

Gerhard's Bicycle Odysseys, PO Box 757, Portland, OR 977207, **t** (503) 223 2402.

Travcoa, t 1 800 992 2003, *www.travcoa.com*. Medieval castles and towns.

Viva Tours, 192 Nepperhan Avenue, Yonkers, NY 10701, **t** (914) 423 4640. Bayreuth.

few tips on Bavarian cooking; but you generally do need to book ahead at the individual farm, and to stay for at least three nights. Contact the following agency:

Landesverband 'Urlaub auf dem Bauernhof in Bayern' e.V., Kaiser-Ludwig-Platz 2, D-80336 Munich, **t** (089) 534312, *www.farmholidays.de*.

Camping

Camping is a pleasure during Bavaria's sunny summers, and it's also a good way to meet locals, as Bavarians are keen campers in their own countryside. Bavaria has around 420 sites, around 70 of which are open in winter. Many of them are beside lakes or rivers, but there are also well-appointed sites on the outskirts of Munich and other cities. For information and reservations, visit *www.camping-in-bayern.de*.

Practical A–Z

06

Conversions: Imperial–Metric

Length (multiply by)
Inches to centimetres: 2.54
Centimetres to inches: 0.39
Feet to metres: 0.3
Metres to feet: 3.28
Yards to metres: 0.91
Metres to yards: 1.09
Miles to kilometres: 1.61
Kilometres to miles: 0.62

Area (multiply by)
Inches square to centimetres square: 6.45
Centimetres square to inches square: 0.15
Feet square to metres square: 0.09
Metres square to feet square: 10.76
Miles square to kilometres square: 2.59
Kilometres square to miles square: 0.39
Acres to hectares: 0.40
Hectares to acres: 2.47

Weight (multiply by)
Ounces to grams: 28.35
Grammes to ounces: 0.035
Pounds to kilograms: 0.45
Kilograms to pounds: 2.2
Stones to kilograms: 6.35
Kilograms to stones: 0.16
Tons (UK) to kilograms: 1,016
Kilograms to tons (UK): 0.0009
1 UK ton (2,240lbs) = 1.12 US tonnes (2,000lbs)

°C	°F
40	104
35	95
30	86
25	77
20	68
15	59
10	50
5	41
-0	32
-5	23
-10	14
-15	5

Volume (multiply by)
Pints (UK) to litres: 0.57
Litres to pints (UK): 1.76
Quarts (UK) to litres: 1.13
Litres to quarts (UK): 0.88
Gallons (UK) to litres: 4.55
Litres to gallons (UK): 0.22
1 UK pint/quart/gallon =
  1.2 US pints/quarts/
  gallons

Temperature
Celsius to Fahrenheit:
multiply by 1.8 then
add 32

Fahrenheit to Celsius:
subtract 32 then multiply
by 0.55

Germany Information

Time Differences
Country: + 1hr GMT; + 6hrs EST
Daylight saving from last weekend in March
to end of October

Dialling Codes
Germany country code 49
To Germany from: UK, Ireland, New Zealand 00
/ USA, Canada 011 / Australia 0011 then dial 49
and the number, dropping the initial zero
From Germany to: UK 00 44; Ireland 00 353;
USA, Canada 001; Australia 00 61; New Zealand
00 64 then the number without the initial zero
Operator: 03
Directory enquiries/assistance: 11837

Emergency Numbers
Police: 110
Ambulance: 112
Fire: 112
Car breakdown: (0180) 222 22 22 (ring 222 222 if
using a mobile)

Embassy Numbers in Germany
UK: (089) 211090; **Ireland** (089) 2080 5990;
USA: (089) 28880; **Canada** (089) 2199 570.

Shoe Sizes

Europe	UK	USA
35	2½ / 3	4
36	3 / 3½	4½ / 5
37	4	5½ / 6
38	5	6½
39	5½ / 6	7 / 7½
40	6 / 6½	8 / 8½
41	7	9 / 9½
42	8	9½ / 10
43	9	10½
44	9½ / 10	11
45	10½	12
46	11	12½ / 13

Women's Clothing

Europe	UK	USA
34	6	2
36	8	4
38	10	6
40	12	8
42	14	10
44	16	12

Children

The Germans are the first to talk anxiously about the nation's *Kinderfeindlichkeit* (antipathy to children). In public, children are generally well disciplined – all part of civic duty, reinforced by public notices to remind parents of their responsibilities. A rabble of noisy foreign brats will be looked on very coolly. Before unification West Germany had the lowest birth rate in Europe and was in many respects a very adult-orientated society. Bavaria, too, followed this pattern.

That said, it is easier to find somewhere to eat and drink as a family in Bavaria than it might be, for example, in Britain, where attitudes to children are supposed to be more sympathetic. Children accompanied by adults are welcome in inns and cafés. Many city museums are especially aimed at younger visitors, with lots of hands-on exhibits.

Crime and the Police

Bavaria does not have a particularly bad crime problem. Provided you take the normal precautions, you shouldn't be troubled by petty theft. However, if you are robbed, then report the incident to the police immediately. This will plummet you into the usual morass of bureaucracy, but is essential if you are going to make any insurance claims.

You are required to have some form of **identification** with you at all times (preferably a passport). If you are found to be without one, you may be subject to prosecution.

If you end up on the wrong side of the law, get in touch with your **consulate** (*see* p.55) – though in drug-related offences you are unlikely to receive much sympathy. Possession of illegal drugs is an offence for which the penalty is a prison sentence or deportation.

Eating Out

See **Food and Drink**, pp.45–52, for a description of Bavarian specialities and a menu reader.

Restaurant Price Categories

Restaurants are priced for a three-course meal for one with a glass of wine. In cafés and inns most main dishes, often with vegetables or salad, are under €15. In general, prices are reasonable by European standards.

expensive	€€€	€50+
moderate	€€	€30–50
inexpensive	€	– €30

Electricity

The supply in Germany is **220 volts**, so UK appliances (which require 240 volts) will work. North American equipment will need a **transformer**. Plugs are of the two-pronged kind that are standard in much of continental Europe. **Adaptors** are available from electrical suppliers in Germany, and can be found in most travel and specialist electrical shops.

Etiquette

Germany is still a very formal society, ?especially in the world of business. Work colleagues – even of the younger generation – still tend to use *Herr* (Mr) and *Frau* (Mrs/Ms) instead of first names, and often use the formal *Sie* rather than the *du* form of 'you'. This can be the case even among people who have worked in the same office for decades. Leaping the chasm between *Sie* and *du* is a tricky exercise, even for Germans themselves. Generally the rule is always to use *Sie* with a stranger or new acquaintance, until you mutually agree not to. The older or more senior person will suggest this first. The transition is often made quite formally – and is sometimes even marked with a toast. Younger people meeting in informal situations – such as bars or discos – usually use *du*, but the borders can be hazy.

If someone has a title, use it when addressing him or her: *Herr Professor*, *Frau Doktor*, for example. Women get lumbered with their husband's title as well. Gone are the days, however, when you would even call your baker *Herr Bäcker* – though you will still hear older people summoning a waiter with *Herr Ober!* ('Mr Waiter').

The Gay Scene

Conservative Roman Catholic Bavaria has mixed feelings towards the gay scene ('gay': *schwul*). The main centre of gay and lesbian life is Munich, where the atmosphere is busy and friendly. Elsewhere, especially in rural areas, attitudes can be intolerant. In 1987, this intolerance was codified in a law making AIDS-testing mandatory for anyone 'suspected of being HIV positive'. Later, another even more draconian law found its way onto the Bavarian statute book allowing the police to arrest and hold indefinitely anyone with the HIV virus suspected of not 'behaving properly'.

Münchner AIDS-Hilfe, Lindwurmstraße 7, t (089) 5446 470, *www.muenchner-aidshilfe.de*.

Sub Info Laden, Müllerstraße 38, Munich, t (089) 2603 056, *www.subonline.org*. For information on Bavaria's gay scene.

Health and Emergencies

Ambulance or **Fire Brigade**: t 112
Police: t 110

Other emergency numbers are listed by city, in each gazetteer chapter of this book.

Prescription drugs can be bought from an *Apotheke* (pharmacy). A list of duty emergency pharmacies, which stay open after normal working hours, is posted on the door of all *Apotheken*. They may look closed, but ring the doorbell and the pharmacist will emerge from an inner recess to serve you through a hatch.

Internet

Internet **access** is available at cafés in larger towns. Many hotels and business centres offer access, sometimes from your room. If you're bringing a **laptop**, remember you'll still need an adaptor to plug it into an electrical socket when necessary.

Maps

The German motoring organization, the **ADAC**, offers excellent route maps (free to members, or a minimal charge). They also publish a simplified tourist map of Bavaria.

Even more useful is the detailed 37-part **Generalkarte** series – clear, individual maps covering the whole of Germany in sections and printed in detail. The handiest and most up-to-date city maps are published by **Falk**.

If you want to buy a map before you leave, look for one published by any of the above or **Kümmerly & Frey**. The best source of specialist hiking and cycling maps will be the tourist office in the relevant region.

Complete Traveler, 199 Madison Ave, New York, t (0212) 685 9007, *www.complete trav.com*.

Stanfords, 12–14 Long Acre, London WC2 9LP, t (020) 7836 1321, *www.stanfords.co.uk*.

Media

Newspapers in Germany tend to be regional rather than national, in focus and distribution. The main respectable exception is the Munich-based *Süddeutsche Zeitung*, which is read all over Germany, as are the *Frankfurter Allgemeine Zeitung* (popular with the business community), its liberal counterpart the *Frankfurter Rundschau*, and the left-wing Berlin paper the *Tageszeitung*, known as the *Taz*. The bestselling papers are the right-wing *Die Welt* and the notorious, sleazy, sensationalist *Bild Zeitung*.

The three most prominent **magazines** are the leftish *Der Spiegel*, the Munich-based *Focus* and the right-of-centre weekly *Die Zeit*, all of which include serious and informative reportage. In most cities and larger towns, leading British and American newspapers are on sale on the day of publication, usually from railway station newsagents.

You can get the **BBC World Service** on 604 kHz MW and on 90.2 FM in the Munich area, and Radio 4 on 198 LW.

Museums

Bavaria has an extraordinary array of high-quality museums. For centuries Bavaria was a loose amalgamation of independent political entities. Each ruler built up an art collection, and most collections have stayed put, so that even the smaller towns can have museums of a high standard. Opening hours vary, but many museums are closed on a Monday.

National Holidays

1 Jan (*Neujahr*)
6 Jan Epiphany (*Heilige Drei Könige*)
Good Friday (*Karfreitag*)
Easter Monday (*Ostermontag*)
1 May (*Maifeiertag*)
Ascension Day (*Christi Himmelfahrt*)
Whit Monday (*Pfingstmontag*)
Corpus Christi (*Fronleichnahm*)
15 Aug Assumption (Mariä Himmelfahrt)
3 Oct Day of German Unity (*Tag der Deutschen Einheit*)
1 Nov All Saints Day (*Allerheiligen*)
Christmas Day (*Erster Weihnachtstag*)
Boxing Day (*Zweiter Weihnachtstag*)

Smaller museums may close for lunch; opening hours in winter may be shorter. In some towns, museums stay open until 8pm on a Wednesday or a Thursday night.

Bavaria has three museums that rank among the best in Germany:

Alte Pinakothek, in Munich, p.81: one of the world's great art galleries, with an outstanding collection of German masters.

Germanisches Nationalmuseum, in Nürnberg, p.207: a shrine to the artefacts of German civilization throughout the ages.

Deutsches Museum, in Munich, p.85: the country's top technological museum.

Opening Hours

Germany used to have the most irritating and inconvenient **shopping hours** in Europe, with a notorious six o'clock rush for provisions and a law forbidding bakers to light their ovens on Sundays. A 1996 law improved the situation somewhat by allowing shops to remain open weekdays until 8pm and, early in 2004, as part of an initiative to help boost the German economy, Saturday opening hours were extended until 8pm. Department stores and grocery shops in larger cities keep these hours, but smaller shops still close at 6pm.

Except in the very centre of the largest cities, most shops and businesses take a **lunch hour.**

Banks are generally open Mon–Fri 9am–12.30pm and 1.30–3.30pm. On Thursdays some remain open until 5pm; all are shut on Saturdays and Sundays. Banks with extended hours and commercial **Bureaux de Change** can be found near railway stations and airports.

Post Offices

Post offices are open Mon–Fri 8–6 and Sat 8 or 9–12 noon. Some cities have extended or 24-hour services – usually at the post office nearest the station. You can send **telegrams** from a post office or by phoning t 1131. Different counters have different functions (look at the sign above the clerk's head), though most sell **stamps** (*Briefmarken*) and accept parcels (*Pakete*). You can also change money at a post office. Larger post offices operate a Poste Restante service – letters should be marked *Postlagernde Sendungen*.

Sports and Activities

There is an old local joke that when two Germans meet they shake hands; when three meet they form a society. This certainly holds true for Bavaria in the field of sport. Every third inhabitant is a member of a **sports club**. Public sports facilities are good – but you are likely to find courts, fields or lanes reserved for organized club activities. **Football** is by far the most popular spectator sport, and ?thousands attend matches in season.

Summer Sports

The Bavarians are outdoor folk. Most towns, even in colder parts of the region, will have an **open-air swimming pool** (*Freibad*) that opens for the summer months. Many of the rivers and most of the lakes are clean enough to swim in, and **water sports** – especially **windsurfing** – are becoming increasingly popular.

Hiking (*Wandern*) and **cycling** (*Radfahren*) are two great national enthusiasms and are practised with vigour. Marked hiking trails abound, especially in mountain resorts.

Some 22 local operators offer unusual **river trips**: on massive log **rafts** similar to those used in the Middle Ages. Jaunts range from hair-raising rapid-shooting to more leisurely cruises on 18-log rafts, complete with barrels of beer, oompah bands and 60 passengers:

Hölzl Floßfahrten, Mittenmühlweg 23, Ingolstadt, **t** (0841) 33700, *www.hoelzl-top-events.de*.

Isar-Floßfahrt, Theresienhöhe 14, Munich, **t** (089) 8712 399, *www.isarflossfahrt.de*.

Winter Sports

Bavaria has some of the best **skiing** in Germany. The Bavarian Alps offer the best resorts (*see* p.129), but smaller ranges such as the Franconian Forest are also popular (and generally cheaper).

The upland areas around **Garmisch-Partenkirchen** and **Berchtesgaden** in the Upper Bavarian Alps and **Oberstdorf** in the Allgäu Alps are punctuated with lifts and runs. High season normally runs from mid-December to mid-January. Local tourist offices provide information on regional skiing and lifts. **Ski passes** for *Abfahrt* (downhill skiing) aren't cheap (between €20 and €30 for an adult), but many resorts grant discounts to guests at local hotels and ?guesthouses. There are graded slopes for skiers of all levels as well as carefully prepared *Loipen* (tracks) for *Langlauf* (cross-country skiing), especially around Berchtesgaden and Oberstdorf.

Telephones

Operator: t 03
Directory Enquiries/Assistance: t 11837

Most **public telephones** operate on the prepaid debit **phonecard** system. You can buy a card (*Telefonkarte*) from a post office for €6 or €25, and it is a good idea to carry one. You can call abroad from most public telephones, and you can **receive calls** on those that display a picture of a bell on the booth. For cheaper rates try calling between 8pm and 6am or at weekends. Another way to pay low rates when calling abroad is to use an **international call card**, available in €10, €15, €35 and €50 units.

If you wish to take your **mobile/cell phone** with you to Germany, your service provider will tell you whether it's compatible with the German system. Signal coverage is excellent for most networks.

International dialling codes: Australia: **t** 00 61; Irish Republic: **t** 00 353; New Zealand: **t** 00 64; UK: **t** 00 44; USA and Canada: **t** 00 1.

Tipping

Tips are included in restaurant bills, but it is customary to round up the amount to the nearest euro, or to the nearest five if the bill is large. Tips for exceptionally good service never go amiss. Taxi drivers and hairdressers also appreciate an extra few euros or cents.

Munich

*Bavarians see Munich (München)
as Germany's 'secret capital'.
Berliners call it the* Millionendorf, *a
big provincial village. Ludwig I
proclaimed it 'Athens on the Isar';
tourist brochures say 'Weltstadt mit
Herz', 'the metropolis with a heart'.
Munich can't decide if she is a
sophisticated courtier or a boisterous
village wench. Her architectural
wardrobe is a resplendent array of
royal castoffs, but one whiff of hops
and she's dancing on the table.
  Here is German high society, one of
the world's great opera houses,
transcendent art – and the
Oktoberfest, the world's beeriest
beano. Munich is fast-moving, high-
powered and modern, yet everyone
seems exuberant and relaxed.
Businessmen shed their pinstripes
and sunbathe by the Isar; in smart
cafés, wealthy Schikimikis (beautiful
people) show off designer clothes,
while in cellars and beer gardens
jolly families in real* lederhosen *and
feathered hats swill beer.
  The Berliners are right. Munich is
parochial. That's what makes it so
enticing.*

07

Don't miss

⭐ **Gothicry and
glockenspiel**
Marienplatz **p.74**

⭐ **The best of the
wurst**
Münchner Hofbräuhaus
p.75

⭐ **The legacy of
the Wittelsbachs**
The Residenz **p.79**

⭐ **Old Masters
and modern
masterpieces**
Museum Quarter **p.81**

⭐ **Rococo and
Baroque**
Schloß Nymphenburg
p.86

See map overleaf

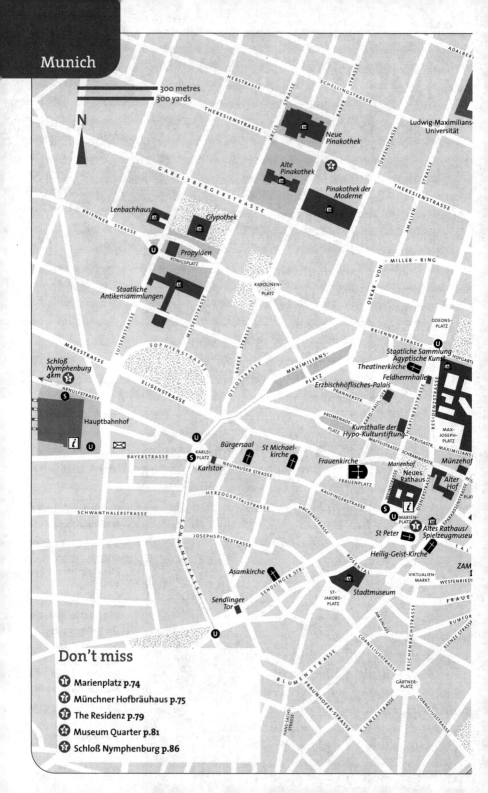

Munich

300 metres
300 yards

N

HEBSTRASSE

THERESIENSTRASSE

SCHELLINGSTRASSE

BARER STRASSE

ARCIS STRASSE

Ludwig-Maximilians-Universität

ADALBER

Neue Pinakothek

GABELSBERGERSTRASSE

Alte Pinakothek ⭐

Lenbachhaus

BRIENNER STRASSE

Glypothek

Pinakothek der Moderne

TÜRKENSTRASSE

THERESIENSTRASSE

AMALIEN STRASSE

Propyläen

KÖNIGSPLATZ

KAROLINEN-PLATZ

- MILLER - RING

OSKAR VON

Staatliche Antikensammlungen

MEISERSTRASSE

LUISENSTRASSE

MARSSTRASSE

SOPHIENSTRASSE

OTTO-STRASSE

BARER STRASSE

MAXIMILIANS-

BRIENNER STRASSE

ODEONS-PLATZ

Staatliche Sammlung Agyptische Kunst

HOFGARTE

Schloß Nymphenburg 4km ⭐

ARNULFSTRASSE

ELISENSTRASSE

PLATZ

Theatinerkirche

Feldherrnhalle

Erzbischhöfliches-Palais

PRANNERSTR.

RESIDENZSTRASSE

THEATINERSTRASSE

KARD-FAULHA

Hauptbahnhof

PROMENADE

PLATZ

Kunsthalle der Hypo-Kulturstiftung

KARD-FAULHA

PERUSASTR.

MAFFEISTRASSE

MAX-JOSEPH-PLATZ

MAXIMILIANS

Münzehof

BAYERSTRASSE

KARLS-PLATZ

Bürgersaal

St Michaelskirche

Frauenkirche

SCHRAMMERSTR.

WEINSTRASSE

Marienhof

Neues Rathaus

DIENERSTRASSE

Alter Hof

PFIS

Karlstor

NEUHAUSER STRASSE

FRAUENPLATZ

KAUFINGERSTRASSE

SPARKASSENSTRASSE

PLAT

HERZOGSPITALSTRASSE

HACKENSTRASSE

MARIEN-PLATZ

St Peter

Altes Rathaus/Spielzeugmuseu

SCHWANTHALERSTRASSE

JOSEPHSPITALSTRASSE

SONNENSTRASSE

Heilig-Geist-Kirche

TAL

ZAM

ROSENTAL

Asamkirche

SENDLINGER STR.

ST-JAKOBS-PLATZ

Stadtmuseum

VIKTUALIEN-MARKT

WESTENRIEDI

Sendlinger Tor

AM EINLASS

REICHENBACHSTRASSE

FRAUE

RUMFOR

KLENZE STRA

CORNELIUSSTRASSE

GÄRTNER-PLATZ

BLUMENSTRASSE

FRAUNHOFER-STRASSE

HANS-SACHS-STRASSE

KLENZESTRASSE

CORNELIUSSTRASSE

Don't miss

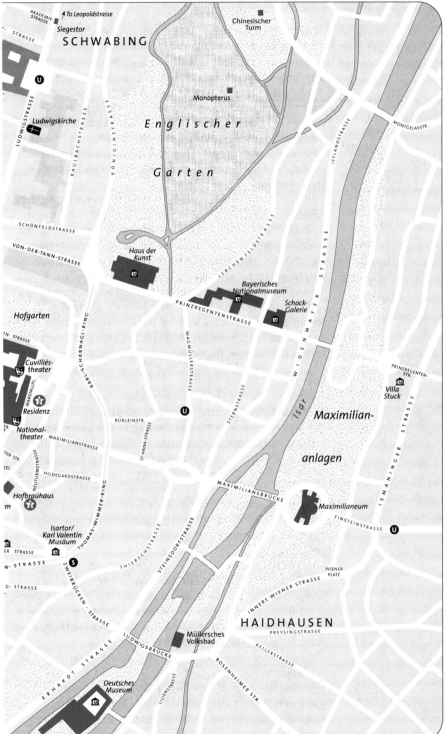

AKADEMIE-
STRASSE
To Leopoldstrasse

Siegestor

SCHWABING

Chinesischer
Turm

STRASSE

LUDWIGSTRASSE

Ludwigskirche

KAULBACHSTRASSE

KÖNIGINSTRASSE

Monopterus

Englischer

Garten

MONTGELASTR.

SCHÖNFELDSTRASSE

VON-DER-TANN-STRASSE

Haus der
Kunst

LERCHENFELDSTRASSE

IFFLANDSTRASSE

WIDENMAYER STRASSE

Bayerisches
Nationalmuseum

Schack-
Galerie

PRINZREGENTENSTRASSE

Hofgarten

EN- STRASSE

Cuvilliés-
theater

MARSTALLPL.

Residenz

National-
theater

MAXIMILIANSTRASSE

WAGMÜLLERSTRASSE

STERNSTRASSE

BÜRLEINSTR.

ST-ANNA-STRASSE

KARL-SCHARNAGL-RING

Isar

Maximilian-

anlagen

PRINZREGENTEN-
STR.

Villa
Stuck

ISMANINGER STRASSE

-TER- STR.

TZL

HILDEGARDSTRASSE

NEUTURMSTRASSE

Hofbräuhaus

Isartor/
Karl Valentin
Musäum

THOMAS-WIMMER-RING

THIERSCHSTRASSE

STEINSDORFSTRASSE

MAXIMILIANSBRÜCKE

Maximilianeum

EINSTEINSTRASSE

ER- STRASSE

N- STRASSE

D- STRASSE

ZWEIBRÜCKEN- STRASSE

WIENER
PLATZ

INNERE WIENER STRASSE

HAIDHAUSEN

PREYSINGSTRASSE

Müllersches
Volksbad

KELLERSTRASSE

ROSENHEIMER STR.

ERHARDT STRASSE

LUDWIGSBRÜCKE

LILIENSTRASSE

Deutsches
Museum

Der Deutsche Himmel. (The German heaven.)
Thomas Wolfe

Voilà une capitale.
Charles de Gaulle, on his first visit

Most Germans dream of living in Munich. Polls show that, if they had to move, this is the city most would choose, even despite the smugness of the locals (Munich is simply the best in everything and *Zugereiste*, newcomers, remain so for decades) and the *Föhn*. The *Föhn* is a warm wind that blows off the Alps, clearing the sky and causing headaches and bolshy bad temper in otherwise cheery *Münchners*. (Even the *Föhn* avoids *Zugereiste*: you have to live here for five or so years before you feel its effect.) So if you're bouncing around with other happy visitors on an apparently perfect day, don't be surprised by growling barmen and snappy shop assistants.

Apart from the style, conviviality and architecture, what attracts people most to Munich is its setting and size. In the time that it takes other city-dwellers to get to work, *Münchners* can be in the Alps. The city itself is compact and manageable. In the centre, on the left bank, is the **Altstadt**, a heart of swish streets and rollicking *Brauhäuser*. To the north is the erstwhile bohemian quarter of **Schwabing**, now tamed and gentrified, the main museum complex and the vast **Englischer Garten**. To the west is the **Schloß Nymphenburg**. Across the River Isar and to the south you'll find the quirkier corners, pockets of immigrants and artists, and the biggest technical museum in the world.

History

In 1158 Emperor Frederick I Barbarossa was asked to settle a dispute between his uncle, Bishop Otto von Freising, and his cousin, Henry the Lion. Otto had controlled a very profitable toll bridge across the Isar, directly on the lucrative salt route. With his customary leonine ferocity, Henry simply burnt the bridge down, and built his own further along the river. He called the settlement that sprang up 'Munichen', after the monks of a nearby church. Barbarossa decided in favour of his cousin; but in 1180 Henry fell from grace for refusing him military help and power was handed over to the Wittelsbach family, who ruled Bavaria continuously until 1918.

At first the capital of the region was Regensburg. The first Wittelsbach to set up home in Munich was Duke Ludwig the Severe, who built a suitably plain Residenz in 1255. By the beginning of the 16th century Munich was capital and the official family seat.

The salt trade boomed, and Munich got fat. Even the Thirty Years' War left the town relatively undiminished. King Gustavus Adolphus of Sweden called it 'the golden saddle on a scraggy nag'. In the 18th century, Baroque style blossomed here as hardly anywhere else north of Italy. Then, in 1806, Napoleon made Bavaria a kingdom. The first king, Ludwig I, with his penchant for neoclassical architecture, set about creating his Athens of the

Getting to and from Munich Airport and the Hauptbahnhof

Munich's new airport is **Franz Josef Strauß Airport**, t (089) 97500, *www.munich-airport.com*. Lines S1 and S8 on the **S-Bahn** go to the Hauptbahnhof, Marienplatz and Östbahnhof in 40–45mins, for only €9. The **Airport Bus** also goes to the Hauptbahnhof (Arnulfstraße entrance; 45mins, €9). Both services leave every 20mins.

The **Hauptbahnhof** (main-line railway station), just west of the city centre, locks into the extensive metro system. Munich is a hub of rail travel, and Europe's fastest trains speed you all over Germany and across its borders. For information, **t** (0180) 5996 633.

Getting to and around Munich

By Public Transport

The fast, efficient **buses**, **S-Bahn** (trams) and **U-Bahn** (metro) trains cover the city between 5am and 1am. Tickets cost from €2.30 for one zone to €9.20 for four or more zones. A single ticket costs €2.30, but it may be more cost-effective to buy a *Tageskarte* (day ticket), which is €5 for the central zone, €10 for the entire metropolitan area. This entitles two adults, three children and a dog to unlimited travel from 9am one day to 4am the next. There is no expiry date on a *Streifenkarte* (strip ticket; €11 for 10 strips). Two strips are valid for a one-zone trip, with appropriate hops and changes, for two hours in any one direction.

Streifenkarten and single tickets must be validated at the beginning of each journey, and *Tageskarten* should be stamped before you set out on your first journey. Validating punches are found on buses and trams and at the entrance to stations. You can **buy tickets** from dispensing machines at the stops, from tobacconists and newsagents with a white 'K' in the window, or on buses and trams.

The Munich Tourist Office sells a **City Tour Card** that allows free travel on all public transport inside Munich (blue area of the fare zones) and to the Flugwerft and the palaces of Oberschleissheim (both on line S1); plus reductions (25–50%) on city sightseeing tours, bicycle hire and admission to castles, museums and the zoo. It costs €6.50 for a day, €16 for 3 days, or €23.50 for a Partner 3-Day Card, which is valid for up to five adults, with two children (aged 6–14) counting as one adult.

Bus, U-bahn and S-Bahn Information, t (089) 4142 4344, *www.mvv-muenchen.de*.

By Car or Taxi

Munich is a major node on Germany's *Autobahn* system, though the Munich–Berlin route barely copes with post-unification traffic. Pedestrians rule in the middle of town and, though some parking is available, it's better to use one of the car parks south of the centre, or around the Bahnhof, and rely on public transport.

The following **car rental** companies are found at the Mietwagenzentrum (Rental Car Centre), upstairs in the Hauptbahnhof, as well as at the airport:

Avis, t (089) 5502 251, *www.avis.com*.
Europcar, t (089) 5501 341, *www.europcar.com*.
Hertz, t (089) 5502 256, *www.hertz.com*.
Budget, t (089) 5502 447, *www.budget.com*
Sixt, t (0180) 5252 525, *www.e-sixt.de*.
Mitfahrzentrale, Lämmerstraße 4, t (089) 19440, *www.mitfahrcentrale.de*.

Licensed **taxis** abide by a fixed fare plan: the basic charge is €2.50; thereafter, you pay per kilometre according to a grading system (€1.45 per km, dropping to €1.30 per km after 5km and to €1.20 per km after 10km). There are additional charges for large pieces of luggage (50 cents each), ordering by phone (€1) and for animals (50 cents each).

Taxizentrale München, t (089) 21610, or t (089) 19410.
Isarfunk Taxizentrale, t (089) 450540.

By Bicycle

Many railway stations rent bicycles; ask at the parcels counter in the Hauptbahnhof.
Mike's Bikes, Bräuhausstraße 10, t (089) 2554 3988/3987, *www.mikesbiketours.com*. Located near Marienplatz, Mike's is convenient if you want to cycle through the Englischer Garten or along the Isar. Their cycle tours depart daily from the Altes Rathaus, at 11.20am and 3.50pm (€22, including bike rental).
Radius Touristik, near track 32 in the Hauptbahnhof, t (089) 596113, *www.radiustours.com*. Rents out bikes for €3 per hour or €14 per day. They also offer guided cycle tours.

North, but a love affair with the Spanish dancer Lola Montez caused a scandal that eventually led to his abdication. Ludwig's son, Maximilian II, also had the building bug, and Munich grew even grander. The next king, Ludwig II, brought Wagner to Munich (*see* p.174), but hated the capital and spent most of his time in the mountains, dressing up and building fantastical castles.

In the 1900s, under Prince Regent Luitpold, Munich became one of the centres of European intellectual life. *Jugendstil* germinated here, and during the first part of the century, in smoky cafés in the Schwabing district, you could have met the likes of Trotsky and Thomas Mann, the painters Marc, Kandinsky and Klee, or the playwright Bertolt Brecht.

Hitler put an end to this Golden Age. In 1919 he set up the Nazi party headquarters in Munich, and though his 1923 putsch failed (*see* p.25), he made Munich the 'Capital of our Movement'. Near here Chamberlain signed the 1938 agreement for 'peace in our time'. Within months war was declared. Munich was home to one of the very few groups to actively oppose the Nazis and the war, the White Rose, but its six members (all students) were executed in 1943. Allied bombing destroyed 40 per cent of the city centre, but most of the Baroque buildings (and, alas, some Nazi monstrosities) survived. Restoration work was careful and sensitive, and there are few high-rise blocks or ugly concrete sprawls.

Munich still has a flourishing artistic life. It has more theatres than any other German city and is the centre of the German film industry (*see* pp.43–4). Fassbinder lived and worked here. Nearly a fifth of the city's population are scholars or students, and there is a busy publishing industry. Above the bohemian undercurrent lies a glossy layer of prosperous bankers and hi-tech industrialists. The twinkle in Munich's social sheen is still the Wittelsbach family, an unofficial local royalty. Bavarians still address the Duke of Bavaria as 'Your Royal Highness', and the Wittelsbach parties at Schloß Nymphenburg are the highlight of the Munich social calendar.

Marienplatz and the Southern Altstadt

⭐ Marienplatz   **Marienplatz** has been the centre of Munich since the town began. It started life as a corn market, then became a public execution site and jousting arena. In 1315 Emperor Ludwig the Bavarian affably decreed that the square should never be built on, so that it would remain 'all the more jolly, attractive and leisurely for gentlemen, citizens and friends'. And so it has – though today it is a touch more frenetic than leisurely. There is no motor traffic in 'Munich's parlour' (as locals call it), just two types of people: those crisscrossing the square with purpose, and those sitting about in white metal chairs, chatting sociably or cricking their necks to look up at the pinnacles of the neo-Gothic **Neues Rathaus**, which fills the entire northern edge of Marienplatz. This was built between 1867 and 1909 to supersede the graceful, real Gothic Altes Rathaus (built in 1475, on the east side of the square; its modest tower has a small Toy Museum, *see* 'Munich's Other Museums', p.87). The tower of the 19th-century upstart is a full 80m high, and sports an elaborate **glockenspiel**. Every day, carved figures re-enact the wedding of the 16th-century Duke Wilhelm V and Renata von Lothringen: at a few minutes past the hour (marked with reckless lack of synchronization by all the bells of the city), the glockenspiel creaks and jangles into life. The carillon hammers out a haphazard, tinny tune as trumpeters, banner-waving citizens and jousting knights jerk past the impassive couple. Below them, figures revolve in the *Schäfflertanz* (coopers' dance) – a joyful jig from 1517 that celebrated the end of the plague. Finally, a cockerel pops out and crows thinly, and it's all over.

Just beyond the Altes Rathaus, on Platzl, the famous **Münchner Hofbräuhaus** (Court Brewery) roars and trumpets its way well into the night (*see* p.94). Nearby is **Alter Hof** (Old Court), built up from the sparse ruins of Ludwig the Severe's 13th-century Residenz, but requiring quite a feat of imagination to endow it with any medieval atmosphere.

Just off the southeast corner of Marienplatz, looking loftily out over the town, is **St Peter's**, Munich's oldest church. First records appear in 1169, though most of the present structure was built between the 15th and 17th centuries. The church is no architectural stunner, but locals love it. They call it *Alter Peter* (Old Peter) and come in their hundreds for weddings and Sunday services – after which, in good Munich fashion, they file out for a quick drink in one of the surrounding bars. Visitors can clamber up the tower for a fine view over the city.

South of St Peter's, the **Viktualienmarkt** (produce market) sprawls between ancient chestnut trees. The wooden stalls are piled high daily with bright fruit and flowers, choice cuts of game, exotica such as banana leaves and dried worms, and more types of sausage than you could imagine. As you thread between the barrels of wine, piles of eggs and Winnie-the-Pooh honeypots, you get whiffs of fresh bread, tangy spices, cheeses and ground coffee. Everything is under the control of women vendors, renowned for their earthy wit, but notoriously grumpy if you handle their wares. The little alleys around the market are lined with long-established family food shops, and are great fun to explore. The Viktualien-markt is also a favourite lunch spot: in good weather people sit in its midst, drinking beer under the chestnut trees, or duck off into one of the many surrounding *Gaststätte* (*see* 'Eating Out in Munich', p.92).

Neues Rathaus
glockenspiel
*at 11am; May–Oct also
at noon and 5pm*

② Münchner
Hofbräuhaus

East of the market, in Westenriederstraße, are Munich's quirkiest museums. Seven are under one roof at ZAM (Das Zentrum für Außergewöhnliche Museen, the Centre for Unusual Museums). The **Corkscrew Museum** and the **Padlock Museum** are cabinet-sized and merit a quick glance; the others are more intriguing. Two millennia of potties fill the **Chamber Pot Museum**: Roman ones with dumpy handles, Chinese porcelain ones with lids, pompous Royal Doulton and nifty Art Deco ones, humble workers' potties and some that met very grand royal bottoms. The **Bourdalou Museum** features the delicate porcelain containers, shaped rather like gravy boats, that discreetly served the needs of 18th- and 19th-century society ladies trapped for long hours in toiletless courts. Children can skip off to the **Easter Bunny Museum** (where there are thousands of the creatures), but you'll probably want to join them in the **Pedal Car Museum**. Pedal cars hit the streets soon after the first horseless carriages. There are bone-shaking contraptions from the 1880s; flash mini-Bugattis, Buicks and Morgans; Noddy cars, pert French numbers and solid British bangers. The **Sisi Museum** is a shrine to one of Bavaria's heroines, Elisabeth ('Sisi'), the favourite cousin of Ludwig II, who married the Emperor of Austria (see right).

Westenriederstraße leads up to the Isartor, one of the three remaining medieval town gates. Here, in one of the towers, is an even odder collection, the **Karl Valentin Musäum**. Karl Valentin (1882–1948) was the German Charlie Chaplin and still has a cult following. His spindly statue in the Viktualienmarkt always has fresh flowers in its hand and little offerings about its feet. Brecht and Hermann Hesse were fans, but Valentin's humour can leave foreigners a little perplexed. His most famous joke is: 'Why does St Peter's have eight clocks?' 'So that eight people can tell the time at once.' The tower is chock-a-block with memorabilia, cartoons and jokey exhibits such as a melted snowman and a nest of unlaid eggs, but the labels are all in German.

Retreat back through the Viktualienmarkt and out of its western side for the more conventional **Stadtmuseum** in St-Jakobs-Platz, housed in a late-Gothic arsenal. The heart of the museum is an excellent local history collection, where you can see Erasmus Grasser's vibrant *Moriskentänzer* (*Morris Dancers*, 1485) carved for the Altes Rathaus ballroom. The turn of an ankle, a fold of cloth and the angle of the hands give the figures uncanny life and grace. These statues alone make a visit worthwhile, but the Stadtmuseum has other collections too. The **Museum of Musical Instruments** is of world renown, though unimaginatively presented. Look out for periodic concerts, when you can hear the instruments in use. The **Puppet Museum** has around 25,000 exhibits from all over the world, from life-size marionettes to quaint creatures cobbled together out of junk (again, rather

ZAM
open daily 10–6;
adm for the lot €4

Karl Valentin Musäum
www.valentin-museum.de; open Mon, Tues and Thurs 11–5.30, Fri–Sat 11–6, Sun 10–6, closed Wed; adm adults €2.99, children and students €1.99, under 6s free

Stadtmuseum
www.stadtmuseum-online.de; open Tues–Sun 10–6; adm €4

Elisabeth, Empress of Austria ('Sisi')

Sisi is the nation's most revered tragic royal, a sort of 19th-century Princess Di. She was born in 1837 in Munich to Duke Maximilian Joseph and his wife Ludovika, sister of the Grand Duchess of Austria. She was a plain child – with the looks of a peasant maid, her aunt said – but made up for it in sweetness, charm and good humour. By 16, the ugly duckling had grown into a graceful, fetching young woman, so much so that, when she met her cousin Emperor Franz Joseph of Austria one summer evening in the spa resort of Bad Ischl, he fell head over heels in love with her. The emperor was just seven years Sisi's senior. The match seemed ideal, and it wasn't long before an engagement was announced – despite Sisi's private misgivings, which she spelled out in her *Versbüchlein* of sorrowful poems.

Sisi's caution was justified. Her aunt and mother-in-law, the domineering Grand Duchess Sophie (perhaps the most politically powerful woman in Europe since Maria Theresa) developed an antagonism to the young bride and made her life at court unbearable. Her relationship with her new husband was also not a success. Sisi began to put herself through punishing fasts. Soon the 1.72m-high empress weighed just 50kg and had a waist measurement of 50cm. She developed fevers and coughs, which immediately disappeared once she was away from Vienna, her husband and her mother-in-law. Publicly, though, Sisi was wildly popular. She had blossomed into an exceptionally beautiful woman, was spirited and sympathetic, and spent her time visiting hospitals and old people's homes. When family pressure got too much for her, she would take herself off to Italy or Greece for 'rest cures' lasting months on end, until the emperor arrived to take her back home. But even these long absences didn't alienate her subjects, who continued to adore their nobly suffering empress.

In 1872 Grand Duchess Sophie died (Sisi nursed her through her final illness and was continually at her bedside), but this did not really ease Sisi's lot. In 1886 her cousin, and one of her closest friends, King Ludwig II of Bavaria, drowned mysteriously (*see* p.175). Then in 1889 her son, the Crown Prince Rudolph, and his mistress were found dead in an apparent joint suicide. From now on Sisi wore only black, and sank into a deep melancholy. When she was cautiously asked if she didn't feel a sense of rebellion against her fate, she replied coolly, '*Nein, ich bin von Stein*' ('No, I'm made of stone'). On 10 September 1898 while she was taking an evening walk, heavily veiled, she was fatally stabbed by an Italian anarchist who had mistaken her for someone else.

Like Ludwig, Sisi has a cult following today, especially in the gay community. The museum of her memorabilia in Munich has a shrine-like atmosphere, cafés have been named in her honour, and a popular TV series.

statically presented). As well as the expected shelves of historical equipment, the **Photography Museum** has some interesting old pictures of Munich. Ludwigomanes can delight in some rarely seen photographs of the eccentric king. Film buffs should keep an eye open for the daily programme of rare movies. The temporary exhibitions are usually superb.

Beyond the Stadtmuseum is Sendlinger Straße, leading to **Sendlinger Tor**, another medieval town gate. Halfway along the street is the florid rococo **Asamkirche** (1746), designed by the brothers Cosmas Damian and Egid Quirin Asam (*see* p.34), a high point of their long partnership. The third medieval gate, **Karlstor**, is to the north on Karlsplatz, a vast square with a modern fountain. Locals call Karlsplatz 'Stachus' – supposedly for one Eustachius Föderl, who had a beer garden here long ago. Even underground train-drivers say 'Stachus', to announce the stop.

Munich's busiest shopping precinct connects Karlsplatz and Marienplatz. In the midst of the pedestrian hubbub the

Liebfrauendom (or 'Frauenkirche') points two knobby towers skywards. The two steeples date from 1525; their tops look rather like beer mug lids, and have become something of a city symbol. The church itself is a huge but disappointingly plain Gothic hall, built between 1468 and 1494. It contains the oldest Wittelsbach vault, and a mysterious black footprint – reputedly that of the Devil – burned into the marble floor.

The more interesting Wittelsbachs (including 'mad' Ludwig II) are buried in **St Michael's**, farther along Neuhauser Straße. This church was built in 1583–97 for Duke Wilhelm V. In a niche on the Renaissance façade the Archangel Michael delivers the finishing blow to the forces of Evil (a satyr). The capacious white stucco interior is covered by a barrel vault, second in size only to St Peter's in Rome. Nearby is the **Bürgersaal**, an 18th-century oratory. The church itself is upstairs; at ground level there is a dimly lit hall, invariably with a handful of people lighting candles at the grave of Father Rupert Mayer. This popular priest was packed off to a concentration camp for his resistance to the Nazis, but his congregation created such an uproar that he was later released and kept under house arrest at Kloster Ettal (see p.123). He survived to preach a few more times at the Bürgersaal, but died in 1945.

The Northern Altstadt and the Residenz, and Schwabing

In the 19th century, three successive Wittelsbachs turned the patch north of Marienplatz into one of the most elegant suites of squares and boulevards in the world. It all began at the turn of the century, when King Maximilian I Joseph laid out Max-Josef-Platz and built the Opera House, raising the enormous sums by imposing a local beer tax. His son, King Ludwig I, returned from a seven-month tour of Italy and Greece so struck with classical architecture that he declared he would not rest 'until Munich looked like Athens' (a more comprehensible ambition in the 19th century than it would be today). By the time he died, he had done so much to achieve his aim that his son, King Maximilian II, wondered, 'Do you think I am allowed to build something different?' Max was not plagued by self-doubt for long, but hatched the graceful 'Maximilian style', and in 1851 built **Maximilianstraße**, now Munich's grandest shopping boulevard. Maximilianstraße sweeps away to the east of Max-Josef-Platz, over the Isar and up the opposite bank to the **Maximilianeum** – a striking pile of pale, glimmering stone, home to the Bavarian State Parliament. From the roof, an archangel loftily surveys the cream of Munich society gliding in and out of the classic boutiques and exclusive cafés. The **Vier Jahreszeiten**, one of the world's most prestigious hotels, stands among them with quiet composure.

The Residenz

⊗ The Residenz
*www.residenz-
muenchen.de; open
April–15 Oct daily 9–6;
16 Oct–Mar daily 10–4;
adm €6; note that
you'll need to buy
further tickets for
admission to other
museums in the
complex, or buy a
combined ticket
(Verbundeintritts-
karte, €11)*

Max-Josef-Platz is boxed in by the Doric colonnade of the Hauptpost (a 19th-century family palace), the imposing classical façade of the Opera House and the mighty Residenz – once the Wittelsbach family home, now a splendid museum. It is so large that guided tours manage only half at a time (you come back later for the other part). If you wander about in your own time, set aside at least half a day for the visit, and invest in the *Residenz Guidebook*, an exhaustive room-by-room guide, from the ticket office.

When the Swedes conquered Munich during the Thirty Years' War, King Gustav Adolf looked over the Residenz and sighed, 'If only it had wheels!' Luckily for *Münchners*, he could not take it back to Sweden with him, and left it pretty much intact. Today, the Residenz is considered one of the finest Renaissance palaces in Europe, though the buildings clustered around the seven inner courts date from the 16th to the 19th centuries, and are a jumble of Renaissance, rococo and neoclassical styles. After Second World War bomb damage, the complex had to be almost entirely rebuilt, but most of the sumptuous furniture was saved and is on display.

The oldest part is the **Antiquarium**, a cavernous barrel-vaulted hall, decorated with views of Bavaria, grotesques and grumpy *putti*. It was built in 1571 to house the Wittelsbachs' collection of antiquities. The Antiquarium leads off the **Grotto Court**, one side of which is a cavern of volcanic rock inset with mussel shells and chunks of crystal. Duke Wilhelm V built it in 1586 as a 'secret pleasure garden'. Other highlights on the ground floor are the **Nibelungen Halls**, left of the main entrance, decorated with glossy paintings of the Nibelung legends for Ludwig I between 1827 and 1867; the **Ancestral Gallery** on the northern side of Königsbauhof, a rococo corridor lined with (often imaginary) portraits of past Wittelsbachs; and a 17th-century **Court Chapel**. The rooms around the Grotto Court house a **porcelain** collection.

Most spectacular of all are the aptly named **Rich Rooms** on the upper floor – rococo extravaganzas designed by François de Cuvilliés (*see* box, p.80). They lead through to Duke Maximilian I's tiny **Secret Chapel** (*c.* 1615), an outrageous nook of marble and lapis lazuli, flecked with gold tendrils and coloured stone. In an adjoining room you can see the duke's impressive collection of reliquaries, including those containing the heads of John the Baptist and his mother.

Schatzkammer
*www.schloesser-
bayern.de; adm €5*

The **Schatzkammer** holds the Bavarian crown jewels, other crowns dating back to the year 1000 and a striking collection of

François de Cuvilliés

When Elector Maximilian III Joseph (1745–77) wanted a new palace theatre in 1750, he chose as architect the deputy head of his Office of Works, François de Cuvilliés. Cuvilliés, born in Belgium in 1695, had joined the elector's grandfather's court as a jester at the age of 11. Later, *le nain* became a cadet and made such a mark that, despite his small stature, he was promoted to the elector's own regiment in 1717. Here he proved especially clever at mathematics and the theory of fortification – so much so that the emperor paid for him to be sent to study court architecture at the *Académie Royale* in Paris (though Cuvilliés would have preferred to be drafted to the Hungarian front). When he arrived back in Germany in 1726, design commissions flowed in, including one to decorate the palace at Brühl near Cologne (1728, for Prince Bishop Clemens August, brother of the Elector of Bavaria), and for the Amalienburg in Nymphenburg Park (1734, *see* p.86). Cuvilliés, now approaching middle age, was at the forefront of the golden age of rococo just beginning in Bavaria. When Max III Joseph approached him to build the new Residenztheater he was at the zenith of his career and produced one of the most splendid interiors to be seen in Munich.

jewellery and precious objects – golden stags with coral antlers, carved rhino-horn drinking vessels, inlaid boxes. Look out for Duke Wilhelm V's private altar (1580), carved from ebony and laden with gold, enamel, precious stones and pearls; and the breathtaking statuette of *St George* (1590). He straddles an agate stallion draped with rubies and diamonds and slays an emerald dragon with a crystal sword. Under his bejewelled visor is a tiny painted face.

Altes Residenztheater
entrance off the Brunnenhof; adm €2

The **Altes Residenztheater** or Cuvilliés-Theater is a rococo triumph by erstwhile court jester François de Cuvilliés. Elector Maximilian Emmanuel spotted the Belgian dwarf's talent as a designer and sent him off to Paris to study. Cuvilliés returned to give rococo flair and flourish to buildings all over Germany. In 1943 all the boxwood panels of the plush, gilded interior were dismantled and safely stored. Later, after Allied bombs had burnt out the old building, a modern **Neues Residenztheater** was built within the walls; the old interior was reconstructed on this site.

Staatliche Münzsammlung
open Wed–Sun 10–5; adm €2.50

The Residenz also accommodates the **Staatliche Münzsammlung** (State Coin Collection), the largest and oldest of its kind in Germany. To the north of the palace is a stiffly formal **Hofgarten**, once the royal park.

The Hofgarten opens onto **Ludwigstraße**. At the start of the 19th century this was a vegetable garden: Ludwig I flattened it with a broad, grand avenue in a straight line from Odeonsplatz to the **Siegestor**, a triumphal arch built in 1850 to honour all Bavarian armies. Odeonsplatz is dominated by the **Feldherrnhalle** (1841), a pompous monument to Generals Tilly and von Wrede (of the Thirty Years' and Napoleonic Wars respectively). Sixteen Nazis were killed here in Hitler's 1923 putsch. The rococo façade and twirly-topped towers of the **Theatinerkirche** (designed by Cuvilliés in 1768) brightens the square, but the rest of Ludwigstraße is very much four-square and solid. Suitably, the stately buildings that line the street house such august institutions as the state archives and library, the government offices and the university.

Schwabing

Beyond the Siegestor the mood changes completely. Trees line the street, cafés spill onto the pavement, students and *Schikimikis* chatter under bright umbrellas or wander around trendy shops and galleries. This is **Schwabing**, no longer the hotbed of Bolsheviks and bohemians it was at the turn of the century, but still vibrant and fun to explore. It is one of the most fruitful areas in town for cafés, restaurants, fringe theatres and nightlife. The central axis is **Leopoldstraße**, with the glitzier cafés. The student bars, quirky shops and cheaper restaurants are mainly to the west of Leopoldstraße. Hopeful young artists ply their wares, and snack bars double as galleries. The east of Leopoldstraße, towards Wedekindplatz and Münchener Freiheit, is more the province of black clothes, sharp haircuts and pounding discos.

In its heyday Schwabing attracted artists, writers and thinkers from all over Germany. From around a *Stammtisch* in the Alte Simpl café came *Simplicissimus*, the leading satirical magazine of the time. Another local publication, *Jugend* (Youth), named *Jugendstil*, the German equivalent of Art Nouveau. Thomas Mann, Rainer Maria Rilke, Lovis Corinth and countless other artists lived and worked here. Even Lenin put in an appearance between 1900 and 1902. (There was a Bolshevik revolution in Munich in 1918, and for a few months Bavaria was a republic.) Some artists became famous and moved to grander parts of town; hopefuls, would-bes and property speculators moved in. Nowadays Schwabing is fashionable but expensive, and has lost its edge. The truly trendy are in Haidhausen (*see* 'Bars and Cafés in Munich', p.93).

The Museum Quarter

07 Munich | The Museum Quarter

⊕ **The Museum Quarter**

Munich has more museums than any other German city, and their quality puts even Berlin in the shade. The credit (or blame) for this lies with the pillaging Wittelsbachs. All around Bavaria and the Palatinate (which was ruled by a branch of the family), museum directors will sulkily reel off lists of treasures that went south to Munich.

Most of the important museums are north of the Altstadt. The Alte Pinakothek (14th–18th century), the Neue Pinakothek (18th–19th century), the Glypothek (classical sculpture), the Staatliche Antikensammlungen (Greek, Roman and Etruscan) and the Lenbachhaus (Munich painters from Gothic to contemporary) are west of Ludwigstraße. East, along Prinzregentstraße, are the Haus der Kunst (20th-century art), the Bayerisches Nationalmuseum (from the Middle Ages onwards), the Schack-Galerie (19th-century painting) and the Villa Stuck (*Jugendstil*).

Alte Pinakothek

Barer Straße,
www.pinakothek.de;
open Wed–Sun 10–6,
Tues 10–8, closed Mon;
adm €7; day ticket for
all three Pinakotheks
and Schack-Galerie €12

The **Alte Pinakothek** holds one of the world's top art collections. An incomparable array of early German Masters gives the clearest art history lesson you're ever likely to get; the few Italian paintings are pearls; and there is more Rubens than you can find in one spot anywhere else. Yet this is a quirky collection, reflecting the tastes of the Wittelsbachs who put it together over nearly 400 years. Elector Maximilian I (1597–1651) had a penchant for Dürer and tracked down pieces all over the country. His court artists imitated the master impeccably, and 'corrected' smaller paintings to a size more appropriate for the vast Residenz walls. Elector Maximilian Emmanuel, Governor of the Spanish Netherlands from 1692 to 1701, acquired many of the Flemish works. It took Brussels dealers, and the Bavarian treasury, some time to recover from one spending spree in which he allegedly got through 200,000 francs in half an hour. A century later, King Ludwig I brought crates of paintings back from his Italian journey. He also spent a fortune on contemporary art.

The Early German collection is in the lower floor left wing and overflows upstairs. The lower right wing has Renaissance and Baroque paintings from all countries. Upstairs, from left to right (after the Early German and Early Netherlandish rooms) you will find Italian, Flemish and Dutch works, and finally painting from France and Spain. Confusingly, room numbering begins afresh upstairs, and is a mixture of Roman and Arabic numerals.

Highlights of the **Early German** collection include *The Golden Age* (1530; **ground floor, Room IIa**) by Lucas Cranach the Elder. Cranach, one of the first German artists to paint nudes, fills an Eden-like garden with frolicking souls. Look out for Bernhard Strigel's realistic *Guard with a Crossbow* (1521; **ground floor, Room IIb**) and Wolf Huber's dramatic *Christ Taken Prisoner* (1530) hanging nearby. Jesus is set upon by a relentlessly ugly mob (one of whom seems intent on looking up the Saviour's robe). This dramatic realism was influenced by Netherlandish painters, and is used with powerful effect in the vividly coloured *Kaisheim Altar* (1502) by Holbein the Elder and *Crucifixion* (1450) by the Master of the Benediktbeueren Crucifixion, both in **Room III**.

The line between Flemish and German painting can be hard to draw. One of the leading artists of the late Gothic **Cologne School**, Bartholomew Bruyn, was Flemish. Bruyn's work, as well as more fine Cologne School painting (such as the 1420 *St Veronica* by the Master of St Veronica) is in Cabinets 1–3. To see the best Cologne School work (by Stefan Lochner, and the Masters of the Bartholomew Altarpiece and of the Life of the Virgin) go to **Room III upstairs**. South German painters were more under the influence of the Italians, as you can see from the harsh light and clear shadows of Michael Pacher's altarpiece in the same room.

Albrecht Dürer was the first European artist to paint self-portraits. In **Room II upstairs** is his *Self-Portrait with Fur-Trimmed Robe* (1500), which he inscribes with delightful self-assurance: 'Thus I, Albrecht Dürer of Nürnberg, painted myself in imperishable colours at the age of 28.' Room II is a treasure trove with many of Dürer's finest works, such as *The Four Apostles* (1526), and superb paintings by contemporaries. Look out for Hans Burgkmair's *Altarpiece of St John the Evangelist* (1518), populated by monkeys and colourful birds; Altdorfer's seething *Battle of Issus* (1529); and Matthias Grünewald's intricate *Saints Erasmus and Maurice* (1520).

The **Italian rooms** have Botticelli and Fra Filippo Lippi; Raphael, including his *Tempi Madonna* (1507), which King Ludwig I battled for 20 years to own; Leonardo's earliest known painting, the *Madonna with a Carnation* (1473); and superlative works by Titian and Tintoretto.

The vast Rubens collection fills the rooms at the heart of the upper floor. The 65 pieces on display range from hasty *modellos*, run off for his workshop, to an enormous *Last Judgement* (**Room VII**). Look out for *Drunken Silenus* (1616, Room VII), where a flabby Silenus (Bacchus's tutor) stumbles about in bleary intoxication, mocked by his retinue and goosed by a Moor. The **Flemish** and **Dutch** collections have Van Dyck, Rembrandt and the neglected Jan Steen.

After frothy French painting by François Boucher and Nicolas Lancret (**Room XII**), and the darker El Greco and Murillo (**Room XIII**), pop downstairs to see Pieter Breughel's *Land of Cockaigne* (1566). Three fat men sprawl on the ground in this Promised Land of Gluttons while around them are fences made of sausages and eggs that run about on little legs waiting to be eaten. Nearby is Jan Breughel's densely populated *Harbour Scene* (1598).

Neue Pinakothek
Barer Straße,
www.pinakothek.de;
open Thurs–Mon 10–6,
Wed 10–8, closed Tues;
adm €7, concs €5,
€1 on Sun

Across from the Alte Pinakothek is the shiny modern **Neue Pinakothek** – lean fare after the banquet of the Alte Pinakothek, but still worth a visit. The collection begins with artists such as Gainsborough, Goya and Turner, who broke with Baroque traditions and set the style for 19th-century painting, but the Germans get the strongest look-in. Look out for Arnold Böcklin's dreamy *Pan in the Reeds* (1859), Anselm Feuerbach's *Medea* (1870), the murky paintings of Hans von Marées and the translucent Greek and Italian landscapes of Ludwig I's court artists. There is a respectable range of French work, including Manet's *Breakfast in the Studio* (1868) and Degas' *Woman Ironing* (1869) – a change from the ballet dancers. You can also see a version of Van Gogh's *Sunflowers* and familiar works by Gauguin, Egon Schiele and Gustav Klimt.

Pinakothek der Moderne
www.pinakothek.de;
open Tues, Wed and
Fri–Sun 10–6, Thurs
10–8, closed Mon; adm
€10, concs €7, €1 on Sun

Architecturally, the star attraction of the Pinakothek complex is the **Pinakothek der Moderne**, a museum of 20th- and 21st-century

07 München | The Museum Quarter

art, architecture and design. At its core is the **Sammlung der Staatsgalerie Moderner Kunst** (State Gallery of Modern Art), a superb collection of modern art which includes work by Matisse, Picasso and German artists such as Max Beckmann.

Glyptothek
open Tues, Wed and Fri–Sun 10–5, Thurs 10–8, closed Mon; adm €3.50

Antikensammlungen
www.antike-am-koenigsplatz.mwn.de; open Thurs–Sun 10–5, Wed 10–8, closed Mon–Tues; adm €3; joint ticket for both museums €5

The Glyptothek and Antikensammlungen occupy two neoclassical piles on either side of an otherwise barren Königsplatz. Ludwig I commissioned the buildings to house his collection of antiquities. The Glypothek is the more interesting, with a pediment plundered from the Aphaia Temple in Aegina, the outrageously erotic Barberini Faun and fine Hellenistic statues. The chief attraction of the Antikensammlungen is the glittering array of Greek and Etruscan gold jewellery.

Lenbachhaus
www.lenbachhaus.de; Tues–Sun 10–6, closed Mon; adm €2, concs €1

Directly across Luisenstraße is the Lenbachhaus, the elegant, Italianate villa of the 'painter prince' Franz von Lenbach (1836–1904). Many rooms retain their original fittings, but most of the villa is now the Municipal Museum. The main reason for a visit is the extensive collection of Kandinsky and fellow members of the *Blaue Reiter*, such as Klee, Marc and Macke (*see* p.37). Ironically, the conventional, established von Lenbach was the group's greatest foe. Most of the works here were part of a hoard stashed away for years by Gabriele Münter, Kandinsky's jilted mistress. Russian-born Kandinsky had to leave Munich at the outbreak of the First World War, and left everything he owned in her charge. While he was away he married someone else. Gabriele gave him back his furniture, but kept the art. Well into her eighties, she handed the lost collection over to an astonished city council, who, in the search for somewhere large enough to display all the works, came up with the Lenbach villa. The museum often also holds good exhibitions of contemporary German work.

Haus der Kunst
www.hausderkunst.de; open Fri–Wed 10–8, Thurs 10–10; adm around €7–10 depending on exhibition

Bayerisches Nationalmuseum
www.bayerisches-nationalmuseum.de; open Tues, Wed and Fri–Sun 10–5, Thurs 10–8, closed Mon; adm €3, free on Sun

The Haus der Kunst, a nasty 1930s building on Prinzregentenstraße that still has swastikas carved into the stone above the doorways, is now used for exhibitions of avant-garde art that would have been cast into a bonfire by the Nazis. Almost next door is the sprawling Bayerisches Nationalmuseum. Its core is again a Wittels-bach collection, this time of art and artefacts from all around Europe. Highlights are sculptures by Tilman Riemenschneider (*see* p.30) and a collection of nativity scenes dating from the 17th to 19th centuries. Other divisions of the museum contain folk art and applied art, with especially good displays of porcelain and clocks.

Schack-Galerie
www.pinakothek.de; open Wed–Sun 10–5, closed Mon and Tues; adm €2.50, €1 on Sun

Farther down the street is the Schack-Galerie, a cosy museum worth a visit for its collection of 19th-century artists: Anselm Feuerbach, Arnold Böcklin, Franz von Lenbach and Moritz von Schwind, often unfairly ignored outside Germany.

Villa Stuck
Prinzregentenstraße 60; www.villastuck.de; open Wed–Sun 10–6, closed Mon and Tues; adm depends on exhibition

Over the river, past the Angel of Peace on her column and across Europaplatz, is a gem, Villa Stuck, home and studio of the painter Franz von Stuck (1863–1928), which holds changing exhibitions of his work and other 20th-century artists. Perhaps Stuck's greatest gift was for interior design: the villa is a monument to *Jugendstil*, with patterned floors, painted walls and stylish furniture.

The Englischer Garten and the Isar

The **Englischer Garten** is an enormous park from the late 18th century which stretches for over 5km along the Isar, north of Prinzregentenstraße. Icy brooks crisscross its broad meadows, and skip along through thick forests and past cultivated lawns. At times all you can hear is birdsong and splashing water – and you can't see the city at all. It is easy, indeed pleasant, to get lost. People stroll about, play ball games and sunbathe – completely naked in the grass around the Eisbach – but the Garten is most famous for its large, shady beer gardens. The idea for the park came from an American, Benjamin Thompson (inventor of the cast-iron stove), who was made Count Rumford by a grateful Elector Karl-Theodor, who loved the garden.

Japanese Teahouse
Japanese tea ceremonies held April–Oct every 2nd and 4th weekend in the month: Sat at 3, 4 and 5pm, Sun also at 2pm

Near the south entrance there is a **Japanese Teahouse** built in 1972. Farther into the park you'll find the **Monopteros**, a 19th-century temple with a fine view back over the city, and the **Chinesischer Turm**, a fragile Chinese pagoda in the middle of one of Bavaria's largest beer gardens (which has seating for 7,000).

South of the Englischer Garten, you can follow the **Isar** past grand 19th-century buildings and some very elegant old bridges. In summer the sandy banks are spread with sunbathers and, between Wolfratshausen and Thalkirchen, enormous log rafts float gently downstream, laden with revellers, beer barrels and sometimes even small bands and portaloos.

Deutsches Museum
www.deutsches-museum.de; open daily 9–5; adm €8.50

On Museumsinsel, just past the Ludwigsbrücke, is the **Deutsches Museum**, a gigantic science and technology museum where you'll have to walk over 16km to take in everything. There's a model of a bow drill from the fourth millennium BC and a space capsule; the first German submarine, the original *Puffing Billy* and a Wright Brothers' aeroplane. You can go down a coal mine or sit under the stars in the Zeiss Planetarium. There are sections on metallurgy, hydraulic engineering, carriages and bicycles, telecoms, new energy techniques, physics and photography – and that's just for starters. The Aeronautics and Space Travel exhibitions are the most interesting, but even Power Machinery comes up with intriguing surprises. You can clamber in and out of many exhibits, and even operate a few. Children love it. The museum shop is a treasure trove of models, toys for boffins and splendidly illustrated books, and they also sell a very necessary floor guide. The Deutsches Museum also has a separate aircraft section called **Flugwerft** in a hangar at Schleißheim, 13km north of Munich. Covering more than

Flugwerft
open daily 9–5; adm €6

7,000 square metres of glassed-in exhibition space, it displays some 50 original aircraft, from early reconstructed gliders and a Heinkel He III bomber to a post-war Starfighter jet and a full-size Europa Rocket.

Schloß Nymphenburg

⭐ Schloß Nymphenburg
tram 12, bus 41; open April–15 Oct daily 9–6, 16 Oct–31 Mar daily 10–4; adm €8 for Schloß, €10 including pavilions and Amalienburg

When, after ten years of hoping, the Electress Henriette Adelaide finally gave birth to a son in 1662, her husband celebrated by building her a small palace 5km to the west of the city. She called the Italianate villa *Castello delle Ninfe*. Later generations of Wittelsbachs added a succession of symmetrical wings, and, as Schloß Nymphenburg, it became their favourite summer residence.

The stately palace is set in acres of Versailles-style park. Inside, the rooms are suitably lavish – mainly rococo and high Baroque. In the notorious **Schönheitengalerie** (Gallery of Beauties) there are 36 portraits of women who took King Ludwig I's fancy between 1827 and 1850, including one of his scandalous mistress Lola Montez

Staatliche Porzellan-Manufaktur Nymphenburg

For most people, fine German porcelain *objets d'art* mean one thing – sought-after wares in the classic Meissen tradition. For those in the know, however, Wittelsbach patronage did as much for the craft as did the Wettins of Dresden. For over 230 years now the factory at Nymphenburg has been producing virtuoso pieces of porcelain, today identified by its green armorial trademark.

It was the last prince-elector of the ancestral line of the Wittelsbachs, Max III Joseph, who in 1747 founded the first porcelain manufactory at the diminutive Neudeck palace on the outskirts of Munich. Then in 1761 the workshops moved to the Schloßrondell to the east of Nymphenburg palace, where new premises, complete with their own mill and kiln (still used in the manufacturing process), had been built.

The factory had its first golden age when the services of the most talented artist ever employed here, Italian-born **Franz Anton Bustelli,** were secured in 1754. In less than nine years he sculpted about 150 rococo pieces, including the much-acclaimed set of 16 figurines from the *commedia dell'arte*. Meanwhile glittering dinner services painted by adroit floral and landscape artist Joseph Zächenberger were produced at the workshops. Bustelli's successor, **Dominikus Jakobus Auliczek,** is famed for a series of sculptures of the Greek gods and goddesses, and his Perl Service, which became the Wittelsbach household's dinner service (*Bayerisches Königs-Service*). In 1799 the Palatine Frankenthaler porcelain factory merged with the one at Nymphenburg, and in 1815 King Ludwig I made the factory a royal academy with a special emphasis on ceramic painting. The famous *Onyx Service*, based on paintings in the Alte Glyptothek, dates from this period. In 1888 the business magnate **Albert Bäuml** took over the management of the porcelain factory, introduced new techniques and concentrated on contemporary designs and reproductions of the factory's own 18th-century classic pieces. In 1975 control of the factory returned to descendants of the Wittelsbachs; it is now run by a family foundation.

Nearly 20,000 individual, hand-painted articles have been made at the Nymphenburg workshops and are now all over the world. Painstaking attention to detail ensures that only a very limited number of items is added to this total every year. Most of the finest pieces are still in Munich, in the collection of the Porzellan-Sammlung Bäuml in the Marstallmuseum at Schloß Nymphenburg (*see above*); the *Verkaufs- und Ausstellungspavillon* (shop and showroom) at Schloßrondell (*open Mon–Fri 8.30–12 and 12.30–5; adm free*); the Residenz (*see p.79*) and the Bayerisches Nationalmuseum (*see p.84*). The factory shop, at Odeonsplatz in Munich, offers fine reproductions and modern originals for sale.

(*see* p.174). (The king cherished his favourites, chatted to them during the sittings, and even selected husbands for a few.) The interiors of the **Amalienburg**, a hunting lodge behind the south wing of the palace, designed by Cuvilliés, surpass anything in the main building. Cuvilliés gives the dinky lodge the sumptuousness and splendour of a grand palace, but with a refined lightness of touch. He even manages a diminutive Hall of Mirrors without violating the boundaries of good taste.

Look out for the park's pavilions: the **Magdalenenklause** (1728), a 'ruined' hermitage retreat with a grotto; the **Pagodenburg** (1719), a chinoiserie party house; and the **Badenburg** (1721), a Baroque bathing house with submerged benches in the pool.

Munich's Other Museums

This is one city where you will never be at a loss for something to do on a rainy day.

Staatliches Museum Ägyptischer Kunst, Hofgartenstraße 1. Mummies, Coptic robes and artworks from the Wittelsbachs' Egyptian phase.

Staatliche Graphische Sammlung, Meiserstraße 10. An enormous selection of drawings, woodcuts and etchings. Particular strengths are the collections of 15th-century German woodcuts and graphics by German Expressionists.

Deutsches Jagdmuseum, Neuhauser Straße 53. Equipment, clothes and end products of huntin', shootin' and fishin'. This is the place to come to see the world's largest collection of fish-hooks.

Archäologische Staatssammlung, Lerchenfeldstraße 2. Bavarian household items, from prehistoric to early Middle Ages.

Staatliches Museum für Völkerkunde, Maximilianstraße 42. Ethnological museum with good Asian and Oriental collections.

Siemens Forum, Oscar-von-Miller-Ring 20. Hi-tech, hands-on electronics museum (which strangely makes no mention of Siemens' use of slave labour at Dachau during the Second World War).

BMW Museum, Petuelring 130. A massive PR job. Flash, modern exhibits rather than vintage oddities.

Spielzeugmuseum, Altes Rathaus. A towerful of cases crammed with toys from carved Futurist figures to Barbie dolls.

Bavaria-Filmstadt

The Bavaria-Filmstadt at Geiselgasteig, 10km south of Munich's Hauptbahnhof, provides riveting insights into a special-effect-laden chapter of Germany's film history. With 320,000 square

---

Staatliches Museum Ägyptischer Kunst
www.aegyptisches-museum-muenchen.de; open Tues 9–9, Wed–Fri 9–5, Sat–Sun 10–5; adm €5, concs €4

Staatliche Graphische Sammlung
t (089) 5591 490; open Tues–Wed 10–1 and 2–4.30, Thurs 10–1 and 2–6, Fri 10–12.30; adm free

Deutsches Jagdmuseum
open daily 9.30–5; adm €3.50

Archäologische Staatssammlung
open Tues, Wed and Fri–Sun 9–4, Thurs 10–8; adm €3

Staatliches Museum für Völkerkunde
open Tues–Sun 9.30–5.15; adm €3

Siemens Forum
www.siemens.de; open Mon–Fri 9–5; adm free

BMW Museum
www.bmw.museum.de; open summer daily 10–10; winter daily 10–8; adm €2

Spielzeugmuseum
open daily 10–5.30; adm €3, children €1, family €6

Bavaria-Filmstadt
U-Bahn line 1 or 2 to Silberhornstraße, then tram 25 to Bavaria-filmplatz; www.filmstadt.de; open Mar–Oct daily 9–4, Nov–Feb daily 10–3; adm adults €11, children €8, extra for stunt show; very busy – avoid visiting at weekends or holiday periods, and arrive first thing

Stunt show
variable times; 30mins; adm €7

metres of production area, the studios constitute the largest film-making and post production centre in Europe and Bavaria's answer to Hollywood (see 'Cinema', pp.43–4).

The first motion picture made here was shot in 1919 when the owner of the studios, Bavaria Film, staged a spectacle to commemorate their 75th anniversary. Alfred Hitchcock used the production facilities to set up his early films *The Pleasure Garden* (1925) and *The Mountain Eagle* (1926). Highlights of the long line of successes that have emerged from these studios include *The Great Escape* (1962), *Cabaret* (1971), Wolfgang Petersen's film *Das Boot* (1981), Jean-Jacques Annaud's *The Name of the Rose* (1986), Joseph Vilsmaier's *Stalingrad* (1993), and Uli Edel's *Last Exit to Brooklyn* (1989) and *The Baader Meinhof Complex* (2008).

You can tour some of the sets from these films (including Petersen's U-Boat); the live exhibition also includes a **stunt show**.

Tourist Information and Services in Munich

Munich's tourist information centres supply brochures and maps, and will book you a hotel room (15% deposit, no phone bookings). See also *www.muenchen-tourist.de*.

Useful Addresses and Telephone Numbers

Ambulance: t 1 92 22.

American Express: Promenadeplatz 6, **t** (089) 290900. Branches of most German banks can be found nearby.

EasyEverything, opposite the Hauptbahnhof, *www.easyeverything.com*. The largest Internet café in town.

Emergency Pharmacy Service: t (089) 594475.

EurAide, Room 3 at Track 11 in the Haupt-bahnhof, **t** (089) 3965, *www.euraide.de*. Travel agency offering services including English-language advice on rail travel, Romantic Road tour bus and Rhine cruise schedules. Will locate hotel rooms for €3 fee.

Police: t 110.

Post Office: Opposite the Hauptbahnhof. It has ranks of telephones and fax machines, and a good *bureau de change*. Open Mon–Fri 7am–8pm, Sat 8–4, Sun 9–3.

Festivals in Munich

Oktoberfest

The first thing about the *Oktoberfest* (*www.oktoberfest.de*) is that it takes place in September. In just over two weeks (mid-September to the first Sunday in October), revellers get through over five million litres of beer, half a million sausages, 650,000 chickens, 70,000 knuckles of pork and around 85 oxen. Most of the drinking is done in enormous beer tents on the Theresienwiese (the 'Wies'n', a vast fairground behind the Hauptbahnhof), under the towering statue of Bavaria. Those who have had their fill of beer and oompah bands spill out of the tents to whoop it up on the dodgems, big dippers and other stomach-churning rides in the surrounding funfair. The autumn air is pungent with roasting meat, spilt beer and toasted almonds.

During the *Oktoberfest* there are balls and parties all over town, and two spectacular parades. The **Opening Parade** of landlords and brewers starts at 11am on the first day. Landlords and their families ride to the fairground in ornate carriages or prettily decorated horse-drawn drays. Jostle with the crowds in Schwanthalerstraße, or get a better view from the grandstand in Sonnenstraße (tickets from the tourist office). On the first Sunday of the festival there is a two-hour-long procession of bands, coaches, decorated floats, people in traditional dress, thoroughbred horses, prize oxen and even the odd goat. The route goes from the Max II Denkmal, through the city centre to the fairground.

Rather wisely, there is no parking around the *Oktoberfest* grounds, so people are encouraged to use public transport. The U-Bahn to Theresien-wiese (Lines 4 and 5) is very crowded; Lines 3 and 6 to Goetheplatz or Poccistraße are easier going and deposit you a short walk from the southern end of the grounds.

Stadtgründungsfest

Munich's *Stadtgründungsfest* (City Anniversary, in mid-June) is a much smaller affair, but in many ways more fun. This is the festival the locals keep for themselves. From Marienplatz to Odeonsplatz and in the courtyards of the Rathaus you'll find food stalls, long beer tables and ad hoc cafés. Lots of people dress up in traditional *Tracht*, and even those who don't are prone to bouts of folk dancing. Aromas of pretzels, fresh chocolate, crispy pork and countless other local and foreign foods fill the air. Oompah bands, local choirs and visiting musicians keep up a steady beat. There is an intimate, birthday-party atmosphere, no uncomfortable crush and only a scattering of tourists.

Other Festivals

Flea-market fans should look out for the thrice-yearly *Auer Dult*, an outdoor fleamarket on Mariahilfplatz, for eight days at the end of April, July and October.

The *Christkindlmarkt* (Christmas market) is on Marienplatz from the end of November. Stalls sell gifts, kitsch and trivia, charming German handmade decorations and lots of *Glühwein* and food. Every evening at 5.30pm there's live Christmas music.

Munich has its own lively carnival tradition – here the celebration is called *Fasching*. High jinks last from mid-January to Shrove Tuesday, with rounds of costume balls and jolly doings at the Viktualienmarkt on the final day.

On the cultural side there is the *Münchner Opernfest*, an opera festival of world renown which takes place from mid-July until the beginning of August. Contact the tourist office or the Nationaltheater, t (089) 2185 1920, long before the event if you want a ticket. Special concerts are also held all over town during the festival.

Shopping in Munich

Along Maximilianstraße even the shops have crystal chandeliers. Here you'll find the Chanels, Cartiers and Cardins. In Schwabing, the rents are lower and the fashion shops trendier. Consumer-culture department-store shopping goes on in the pedestrian walkways of Neuhauser Straße and Kaufingerstraße, and along Sendlinger Straße.

Just behind the Rathaus, in Dienerstraße, is a 300-year-old delicatessen, Dallmayr (*www. dallmayr.de*), which still supplies the Wittelsbachs with teas and coffees from its wooden chests, sticky sausages from its racks and lobster and caviar from beneath its gushing fountain. (If money is tight, you can get your smoked wild boar and Riesling for less in the basement supermarkets of the Kaufhof stores on Marienplatz or Karlsplatz.) For even headier tastes and aromas try the Viktualienmarkt (*see* p.75). At Loden-Frey in Maffeistraße, you can buy Bavarian hats and *Lodentracht*, hardy green Alpine wear. Nearby, in the Wallach-Haus, a hand-made dirndl can be expensive, though you could run up your own from their selection of hand-printed textiles. The humbler Hans-Sachs-Straße (southeast of the Sendlinger Tor) is a quaint street of ethnic stores, second-hand shops, galleries and quirky clothes shops. Schellingstraße, north of the Neue Pinakothek, has two English bookshops (Anglia's, No.3; and Words Worth's, Schellingstraße 3).

Sports and Activities in Munich

Jogging, walking and cycling in the Englischer Garten is a favourite Munich activity. You could also join the locals for a swim in one of the

⭐ Charles Hotel >>

lakes or rivers in the park (they are quite clean enough). In colder weather try the beautifully restored **Mullersches Volksbad**, just across the Ludwigsbrücke (Rosenheimer Straße 1, **t** (089) 2361 343; *open Mon–Sat 9–6*): a graceful *Jugendstil* indoor swimming pool with mahogany cubicles, stuccoed ceilings, and a sauna and Turkish bath.

Olympiapark

Northwest of Schwabing, off the Georg-Brauchle-Ring (U-Bahn Line 3 or 8, S-Bahn Line 8) is the Olympiapark (*www.olympiapark-muenchen.de*) a vast sports complex created for the 1972 Olympic Games including a huge **swimming pool** (as well as five smaller pools), an **ice rink**, a **cycle track** and **tennis courts**. The buildings are set in landscaped parkland beside an artificial lake and are also used for concerts and festivals in the summer.

⭐ Vier Jahreszeiten >>

The park has a museum, **Olympic Spirit** (*open Fri–Sat 10–9, Sun 10–7; adm €10*), that uses virtual reality to subject visitors to the rigours of training (following five athletes from five different countries) or the responsibilities of judging. Through simulation, you can negotiate a white-water run in a kayak, ski the grand slalom or step up to the starting line with the world's fastest sprinters.

Where to Stay in Munich

ℹ️ Munich >

Munich

Hauptbahnhof
*Bahnhofplatz 2, **t** (089) 2330 300; open Mon–Sat 9–8, Sun 10–6*

Neues Rathaus
*Marienplatz, **t** (089) 2333 0272; open Mon–Fri 10–8, Sat 10–4*

Munich Tourist Office
*Head Office, **t** (089) 233 96500*

Tourist Call Centre
t *(089) 239 6500; open Mon–Fri 8–7, Sat 9–5*

Luxury (€€€€)

Bayerischer Hof, Promenadeplatz 2–6, **t** (089) 21200, *www.bayerischerhof.de*. Luxurious, glossy hotel, right in the centre of the city. Rooms are elegantly furnished in several styles. The restaurants offer French-fusion, traditional Bavarian and Pacific Rim cuisine, as well as your champagne breakfast; the six bars take you from the cool and sophisticated glass-topped **Falk Bar**, located in the hotel's famous *Spiegelsaal* (Mirrored Hall), to the more down-to-earth cocktails in **Trader Vic's**. There's a rooftop pool, sauna and solarium, as well as beauty and therapy treatments. The Hof even

has its own **theatre** (*www.komoedie-muenchen.de*), nightclub, ballroom and piano bar.

Charles Hotel, Sophienstraße 28, **t** (089) 544 55 50, *www.roccoforte collection.de*. One of the city's newer (and most luxurious) hotels, the Charles is in the old botanical gardens, close to Königsplatz in the heart of the old city. Within, its public areas are graced by paintings by the 19th-century artist Franz von Lenbach. The hotel is purpose-built, the facilities are state of the art, and the rooms are comfortable in the extreme.

Opera, St-Anna-Straße 10, **t** (089) 2104 940, *www.hotel-opera.de*. Hotel heaven in a side street off chic Maximilianstraße. The inner courtyard is shaded by palm trees and watched over by bronze busts of goddesses and heroes. Its 28 beds can only accommodate a lucky few, so book.

Vier Jahreszeiten Kempinski, Maximilianstraße 17, **t** (089) 21250, *www.kempinski-vierjahrezeiten.de*. From its classic wood-panelled lobby to the glass-walled, rooftop swimming pool, this is the Grand Duchess of the world's top hotels. An exalted guest list (the Windsors have been here), palatial period suites, smart modern rooms and award-winning restaurants come together with genuine warmth and discreet, impeccable attention to your every need. This is the one hotel in Germany to splash out on, even if your budget doesn't usually stretch so far.

Expensive (€€€)

Insel-Mühle, Von-Kahr-Straße 87, just beyond Schloß Nymphenburg, **t** (089) 81010, *www.inselmuehle-muenchen.de*. Converted 16th-century mill in a leafy spot by a stream, which is run with love and flair. Rooms are cosy, and most look over a small park.

Olympic, Hans-Sachs-Straße 4, **t** (089) 231890, *www.hotel-olympic.de*. Centrally located in a trendy street, just to the south of the Altstadt. It has a pretty little garden courtyard and most rooms get a peek. The owners give it a friendly, personal touch.

Sofitel Munich Bayerpost, Bayerstraße 12, **t** (089) 599 480, *www.sofitel.com*.

Although it is managed by a leading international chain, this large hotel (in a palatial listed building) is not lacking in style and character. Rooms are large and beautifully appointed, service is smooth, and facilities include a spa as well as bar, restaurant and bistro. It is less than 100 metres from the Hauptbahnhof.

Splendid Dollmann, Thierschstraße 49, **t** (089) 238080, *www.hotel-dollmann.de*. Sober 19th-century mansion with pastel colours, soft lighting and hushed guests. Situated near the Isar, in a peaceful street just off Maximilianstraße.

Moderate (€€)

Hotel Englischer Garten, Liebergesellstraße 8, **t** (089) 3839 410, *www.hotel englischergarten.de*. Idyllic pension on the northern side of the Englischer Garten. Avoid the annexe, where rooms are quite spartan.

Lex im Gartenhof, Briennerstraße 48, **t** (089) 597 673, *www.hotel-lex.de*. Comfortable, modern and affordable small hotel, conveniently close to the centre and to most of the city's major attractions.

Nymphenburg, Nymphenburger Straße 141, **t** (089) 1215 970, *www. hotel-nymphenburg.de*. Well-appointed rooms and a pocket-sized garden away from the bustle, on the road to Schloß Nymphenburg.

Uhland, Uhlandstraße 1, **t** (089) 54335 250, *www.hotel-uhland.de*. Neo-Renaissance villa in a residential neighbourhood near the Theresien-wiese Oktoberfest grounds. Each one of its 31 rooms is different. The friendly staff lend bicycles to guests.

Inexpensive (€)

Am Hauptbahnhof, Schillerstraße 18, **t** (089) 597 673 *www.pensionam hauptbahnhof-muenchen.de*. Clean and simple rooms at affordable rates in the centre of town.

Locarno, Bahnhofplatz 5, **t** (089) 545 042, *www.pensionlocarno.de*. This cheap and cheerful hotel has clean, bright but basic rooms (not all with en-suite facilities, but all with basin and hot water) and is right across the street from the main railway station.

Youth Hostels

Euro Youth Hotel, Senefeldstraße. 5, **t** (089) 599 0880 *www.euro-youth-hotel.de*. Probably the best value accommodation in the city centre, this is more like a hotel than a hostel, though it does offer dorm beds as well as single, double and family-size rooms. Your bed is made for you, and there are no charges for bedlinen.

Eating Out in Munich

Some of Munich's top restaurants offer affordable lunch menus that can cost as little as €14.

Expensive (€€€)

Brenner Grill Pasta Bar, Maximilianstraße 15, **t** (089) 4522 880. This 300-seat restaurant – divided into different sections for breakfast, pasta and gourmet Italian meals – is one of the most happening spots in Munich.

Dallmayr, Dienerstraße 14–15, **t** (089) 213510, *www.dallmayr.de*. A justly famous gourmet delicatessen and restaurant, specializing in smoked wild boar and Riesling.

Grüne Gans, Am Einlass 5, **t** (089) 266268. Private-dinner-party atmosphere in tiny restaurant, personally supervised by cooks Julius and Inge Stollberg. Delicious classic cuisine, without fuss or pretension. Dining *à la carte* is the more expensive option, but you can also eat for €18–25.

Halali, Schönfeldstraße 22, **t** (089) 285909. A rarity: rustic Bavarian décor that isn't kitsch, and a chef who experiments with local cuisine and comes up with wonders. Wild boar, venison and strange local mushrooms abound. Lunch for €17, dinner for €42.

Hunsingers Pacific, Maximiliansplatz 5, **t** (089) 5502 9741. The restaurant's theme is the Pacific Rim but many of the dishes are closer to Europe, such as French *bouillabaisse* or *cassoulet* of lamb. The fixed-price menus (€14 for lunch, €41 for dinner) are one of the city's top culinary bargains.

Tantris, Johann-Fichte Straße 7 (U-Bahn line 6, Dietlindenstraße), **t** (089) 3619 590, *www.tantris.de*. Munich's gourmet temple is located in an ugly concrete building and decked out in garish black and orange. But the soul of the place is Hans Haas, one of Germany's great chefs, honoured for over 25 years with multiple toques, points and stars. He aspires to perfection in everything he cooks, from lobster in truffle cream sauce to a humble apple turnover.

Moderate (€€)

Augustiner-Großgaststätten, Neuhauser Straße 25–27, t (089) 5519 9257. Quaintly decorated with seashells and hunting trophies. Devour mounds of *Weißwurst* (boiled veal sausages) and pretzels. *Weißwurst* is the south Bavarian speciality. They must be fresh (one of the ingredients is brain) and you shouldn't eat the skin.

Deutsche Eiche, Reichenbachstraße 13, t (089) 2311 660, *www.deutsche-eiche.com*. Cosy, old-fashioned *Gast-stätte* that was Fassbinder's local. Attracts an arty crowd; the matronly owner cooks splendid, simple meals – occasionally surprising you with duck or curry.

Haxnbauer, corner of Sparkassen-straße and Platzl, t (089) 2916 2100. Strictly for carnivores: enormous grilled knuckles of pork disappear with astonishing rapidity down the throats of the frailest customers.

Lowenbraukeller, Nymphenburgerstr 2, t (089) 547 266 90, *www.loewen braukeller.com*. The Lowenbraukeller rivals the Hofbrauhaus in size but (except during *Oktoberfest*) it is generally patronized more by local people than by foreign visitors, and regional food and beer are a bit cheaper than in its famous rival.

Lyra, Bazeillesstraße 5 (Haidhausen, S-Bahn Rosenheimerplatz), t (089) 486661. The Greek food (garlic-laced starters, succulent lamb, grilled fish) evokes a warmer climate and the live music adds to the temperature. It doesn't stop until 1am.

Paulaner im Tal, Tal 12, t (089) 219 9400, *www.paulaner-im-tal.de*. This tavern has been serving Bavarian traditional food for almost five centuries. It's popular with city-centre locals at lunchtime.

Weinhaus Neuner, Herzogspitalstraße 8, t (089) 2603 954, *www.weinhaus neuner.de*. On the left is a well-stocked wine bar, on the right is a busy restaurant serving tasty food. Mains for around €9–18.

Inexpensive (€)

Bratwurstherzl, Dreifaltigkeitsplatz 1, near the Heilig-Geist-Kirche, t (089) 295113, *www.bratwurst herzl.de*. Quick-stop beer-and-*Brotzeit* pub with mounds of delicious sausages, *Leberkäse* and *Obaazta* (a classic snack made with mature Camembert, peppers and spices).

Nürnberger Bratwurst Glöckl am Dom, Frauenplatz 9, t (089) 2919 450. Home of the grilled *Bratwurst*. You order them in pairs with sweet mustard and bread rolls, and eat them out under the trees beside the Frauenkirche in summer, or in the snug wood-panelled *Stüberl* in winter.

Riva Pizzeria, Tal 44, t (089) 220240, *www.rivabar.com*. The best pizza in Munich, cranked out of a wood-burning oven for the hungry hordes. Pasta and salads are also good. Always crowded, indoors and out.

Viktualienmarkt, Blumenstraße 7–11. This is the best place of all for a cheap snack. Try a *Wurstsemml* (roll with sliced sausage) or a *Schinkensemml* (with ham) direct from one of the butchers, or steaming soup from the **Münchner Suppenküche**. Lots of booths sell *Bratwurst* and *Weißwurst*, which you can take along to the beer garden. The *Ausgezogene* (heavy doughnuts, also called *Schmalznudeln*) at **Café Frischut** (Prälat-zistl-straße 8), on the market, are reputedly the best in town.

Bars and Cafés in Munich

Central

Café am Beethovenplatz, Goethestraße 51. This stately old 'concert-café' regales you with classical music while you tuck into your sticky pastries or cakes.

Café Glockenspiel, Marienplatz 28. Trendy *Münchners* meet at this posh

★ Lowenbraukeller >

★ Café am Beethovenplatz >>

★ Café Glockenspiel >>

café right in the city centre for coffee, cakes or drinks.

Café Kreuzkamm, Maffeistraße 4, *www.kreuzkamm.de*. A defeating array of cream cakes and *haute couture*. There's a flicker of excitement in the atmosphere, as if coffee-drinking were still a vice.

News Bar, Amalienstraße 55. It may once have been popular with media types, but News Bar is now a haven for students and other young *Münchners* on a budget, with a menu of affordable salads, soups and pizza.

Café Zweistein, Hans-Sachs-Straße 12. Intimate and elegant theatre-bar serving tasty food from the buffet. It's popular, so get there early to be sure of a table in the evening.

Zoozie'z, Wittelsbachstraße 15. Open for breakfast, lunch and dinner, this café-bar turns into a relatively low-key nightspot (catering to a 30-something audience) later in the evening.

Haidhausen and Farther Afield

Glance through the windows in Haidhausen and you'll see Bavarian kitsch, Turkish textiles and bright new canvases. Immigrants, artists and ageing Munich originals live side-by-side in one of the liveliest quarters in town. Between the Isar and the Ostbahnhof, in the streets around Wiener Platz and Max-Weber-Platz, and in the 'French Quarter' around Orleansplatz and Rosenheimer Platz, you'll find galleries, good restaurants, bars and cafés galore.

Café Wiener Platz, Innere Wiener Straße 48, *www.cafewienerplatz.de*. Nothing special to look at, but it has one of the warmest atmospheres of any café in the district. The crowd is a mixed bag of actors, students and local shopkeepers.

Café Freiheit, Leonrodstraße 20, *www.cafefreiheit.de*. This is currently Munich's 'in' café. Crowded, unpretentious and friendly, but subject to poisonous exhaust fumes from the hectic Mittleren Ring.

Ruffini, Orffstraße 22–24, *www.ruffini.de*. A quieter alternative, famed for its soups and Sunday breakfasts. Arrive early to get a seat.

Beer Halls and Beer Gardens in Munich

The entire population of Ingolstadt (all 110,000 of them) could descend on Munich in one swoop, and each find a seat in a beer garden. *Münchners* – with a little help from their visitors – get through prodigious quantities of beer annually (five million litres during the *Oktoberfest* alone). In great beer tents during festivals, out under the trees in the summer, and in noisy halls and cellars the whole year round good burghers, grannies, *Schikimikis* and punks rub shoulders and down hefty *Maße* (litre mugs) of beer. Clusters of tourists join in, curious as to whether the fat men in feathered hats are for real (they are), and all too often destined to become one of the *Bierleichen* (beer corpses) that litter the ground at the end of the evening.

You can get hearty helpings of Bavarian nosh in most beer gardens: sausages, roast pork and grilled fish are the standard fare, or it is perfectly acceptable to take your own picnic. Kick-off time is around 10am, and the hardy keep going to midnight and beyond. In bad weather you can usually retreat into an adjacent beer hall. What follows is a selection of watering holes to start you off.

A little knowledge of **local terminology** is also useful:

Maß (or *Helles*) A litre of conventional beer.

Dunkles Strong malt beer, popular at festivals.

Weißbier Beer made from wheat instead of barley, and served with a slice of lemon.

Radler-Maß A 50/50 lager and lemonade shandy.

Russn-Maß *Weißbier* shandy.

Isar-Maß Mixture of *Weißbier*, apple juice and Blue Curaçao.

Stammtisch Table for regular customers.

Central

Andechser am Dom, Weinstraße 7, t (089) 298481, *www.andechser-am-dom.de*. The only place in Munich where you can drink Bavaria's best beer freshly tapped. Brewed by monks

⭐ News Bar >

(see 'Kloster Andechs', below and p.120), the beer is the perfect prologue and companion to dishes made from the monastery's game, vegetables, mushrooms and cheese. Dinner will set you back €9–20.

Franziskaner-Fuchsenstubn, Perusastraße 5. A good place for a beer-and-sausage breakfast, right in the heart of town. There's been an inn on the site for 500 years, and Emperor Franz Joseph had a *Stammtisch* here. They serve the best *Weißwurst* in Munich. Meals cost €20 on average.

Hofbräuhaus, Platzl 9, *www. hofbraeuhaus.de*. Munich's most famous beer hall bursts at the seams with raucously singing Australians, Americans and Germans from the provinces. Everyone sways to the resonant oompah band, and many feel moved to dance. The Hofbräuhaus is the subject of a drinking song that is almost the Bavarian national anthem, but few locals go anywhere near the place.

Augustiner-Keller, Arnulfstraße 52, *www.augustinerkeller.de*. A leafy surprise off a tatty street behind the station, much favoured by staff from *Bayerischer Rundfunk* (the Bavarian TV station). If you sit at one of their *Stammtische* (regulars' tables) just near the entrance, the waiters will give you short shrift. The house-brewed beer is excellent, and the aroma of *Steckerlfisch* (chargrilled skewered fish) fills the neighbourhood.

Englischer Garten

Chinesischer Turm, southern end of the Englischer Garten, *www. chinesische-turm.de*, known to locals as the 'China-Turm'. On sunny days more students are here than at the university. Often has live music, and a kiosk sells *Steckerlfisch* for €9.

Aumeister, Sondermeierstraße 1, north end of the Englischer Garten, *www.aumeister.de*. The best place for a picnic, under the chestnut trees.

Seehaus, on the Kleinhesseloher See. Respectably quiet lakeside garden, full of dewy-eyed couples barely noticing the sunset. Mediterranean and Bavarian meals cost €20. (There's also a cheaper beer garden next door.)

Osterwald-Garten, Keferstraße 12, *www.osterwaldgarten.de*. Full of hairy academics and paunchy Schwabing die-hards drinking slowly and having grumbly conversations. The food is good – try the *Schweinsbraten* (roast pork) with giant dumplings.

Farther Afield

Kloster Andechs, just east of the Ammersee, *www.andechs.de*. A terrace where you can drink strong beer and eat scrumptious food (see p.120).

Schloßgaststätte Leutstetten, Altostraße 10, Leustetten (off the A95, or train in Starnberg direction). In a small village south of Munich, this is the real thing, with waitresses in traditional dress, FC Bayern football team at their *Stammtisch* and the best *Schweinsbraten* (roast pork) for miles.

Waldwirtschaft Großhesselohe, Georg-Kalb-Straße 3, Großhesselohe (S-Bahn Lines 7, 27), *www.wald wirtschaft.de*. A large beer garden on the Isar with a jazz band usually in full swing by mid-afternoon. This is the best place to sample *Ausgezogene* (doughnuts fried in lard and dipped in sugar). The *Steckerlfisch* (chargrilled fish) is superb.

Entertainment and Nightlife in Munich

Munich has possibly the best opera company in Germany, two top-class orchestras, over 40 theatres, a vibrant film industry, the country's leading theatre school, two excellent music academies and a lively jazz and modern music scene. The local listings magazines *Münchner Stadtmagazin* (available from newsagents), *In Munich* (free from cafés and theatres) and the English-language *Munich Found* (www.munichfound.com), published monthly, will guide you through the maze.

Classical Music and Opera

The **Münchner Philharmonie** and the **Bayrischer Rundfunk Sinfonie Orchester** are Munich's leading orchestras, but the **Münchner Kammerorchester** and ensembles from local academies also keep a high standard.

Munich's largest concert hall is the **Philharmonie Hall**, part of the **Gasteig Kulturzentrum**, Rosenheimerstraße 5, **t** (089) 5481 8181. A huge glass-and-brick arts centre just across the Isar from the city centre. It's the focal point of much of the city's best music and theatre, and also hosts the annual film festival. *General box office open Mon–Fri 10.30–2 and 3–6, Sat 10.30–2.* Classical concerts also take place in **churches** all over town, in the **Herkulessaal** (Residenz, **t** (089) 2906 7263) and in other parts of the Gasteig (above). Keep an eye out for concerts in the beautiful **Cuvilliés Theatre**, at Max-Josef-Platz.

Opera House, Max-Joseph-Platz, advance ticket sales office located at Maximilianstraße 11, **t** (089) 2185 1920. Operas often sell out well in advance, but you can get standing room and student tickets from the box office one hour before the performance. *Open Mon–Fri 10–6, Sat 10–1.*

Opera Festival (July–August). Ranking with those in Salzburg and Bayreuth.

Staatstheater am Gärtnerplatz, t (089) 202411. South of the Viktualienmarkt, this presents a frothier programme of operetta, ballet and musicals, with last-minute offers. *Open Mon–Fri 10–1 and 3.30–5.30, Sat 10–12.30pm.*

The best place to buy advance tickets is through **München-Ticket GmbH**, which has desks in the following tourist information centres:

Rathaus, t (089) 5481 8181; *open Mon–Fri 10–8, Sat 10–6.*

Hauptbahnhof, t (089) 5481 8181; *open Mon–Fri 10–6, Sat 10–2.*

Theatre and Cinema

Munich has eleven major theatres, as well as fringe and cabaret venues (amply supplied by out-of-work actors from the national drama academy). Performances are almost always in German; even if your German is good, the cabaret, which relies heavily on in-jokes and dialect, can be glumly incomprehensible. The outer reaches of the avant-garde, on the other hand, are equally confusing to all, no matter what your mother tongue is. Hardy perennial Alexeij Sagerer bewilders the establishment with performances involving live pigs, mud and noise.

The annual Munich Film Festival in June and July shows new cinema from around the world.

Deutsches Theater, west of the Hauptbahnhof, at Schwanthalerstraße 13, **t** (089) 5523 4444. Sometimes imports foreign musical and dance companies.

Nationaltheater, Max-Joseph-Platz, **t** (089) 2185 1940. Mainstream local theatre.

Werkraumtheater, Hildegardstraße 1, **t** (089) 237210, and **Theatre im Marstall**, Marstallplatz (tickets from the Residenztheater box office). Both stage more experimental work.

Münchner Lach- und Schiesgesellschaft, Ursulastraße 9, **t** (089) 391997, *www.lachund schiess.de*. Established cabaret venue.

Museum-Lichtspiele, Lilienstraße 2, **t** (089) 482403. A complex of three cinemas that shows films in the original language (usually English) – a rarity in Germany.

Live Music and Nightclubs

The *Münchner Jazz-Zeitung*, available from most music shops and jazz clubs, will tell you what's on and where. Avant-garde jazz and improvised music are particularly strong. Many nightclubs offer free or reduced admission early in the week; otherwise, you can expect to pay €5–20 to get in.

Atomic Café, Neuturmstraße 6, **t** (089) 548 18152, *www.atomic.de*. This small club, playing classic '60s and '70s rock and occasional bursts of indie and Britpop, makes a welcome change from the pretentiousness of so much of Munich's nightlife scene.

Backstage, Friedenheimer Brücke 7, *www.backstage089.de*. For up-and-coming bands, check the programme here. Good for rap, reggae and Afro.

Feierwerk, Hansastraße 39 (U- and S-Bahn Heimeranplatz), **t** (089) 72488, *www.feierwerk.de*. Good for new bands.

M-Park 4004, Landsbergerstraße 169, **t** 0171 154 8038, *www.m-park.tv*. Munich's newest big dance club, playing everything from house to salsa in more than 4000 square metres of space, with several stages.

P1, Prinzregentstraße 1, *www.p1-club.de*. Newly tarted up in 2009, P1 is a Munich legend. Originally a US officers' club, it is still the spot where Munich's smart set hang out. Dress up to get past the doormen.

Unterfahrt, Einsteinstraße 42, in Haidhausen, *www.unterfahrt.de*. Cellar venue, visited by many jazz greats.

Vogler, Rumfordstraße 9, *www. jazzbar-vogler.com*. Between the Viktualienmarkt and Gärtnerplatz, a groovy candlelit venue with a bohemian feel. Nightly jazz, latin, soul and rock gigs.

North of Munich

Dachau

Dachau
S-Bahn Line 2 to Dachau, then bus 722 to the Gedenkstätte (Memorial); Autobahn 8 exit Dachau/ Fürstenfeldbruck, then follow signs to KZ (Konzentrationslager); www.kz-gedenkstaette-dachau.de; open Tues–Sun 9–5; adm free; documentary film showings in English at 11.30 and 3.30

About 20km northwest of Munich is the **Dachau Concentration Camp Memorial**. Dachau was the Nazis' first concentration camp, set up in March 1933. It was used mainly for political prisoners, so, unlike Auschwitz and Belsen, it was not primarily a 'death camp'. Nevertheless, a visit is a sombre, disturbing and eye-opening experience.

The camp is now a bleak, windswept expanse of gravel and concrete: Allied soldiers razed the barrack huts to the ground in 1945. Next to the entrance gate, which like Auschwitz bears the infamous cynical motto *Arbeit macht Frei* (Work brings Freedom), is the old kitchen and laundry, now a **museum**. Here there is a display of photographs and documents relating to the camp, at once chilling and depressing, and a short but harrowing **documentary film**. Across from the museum are two reconstructed **barrack huts**. Each was built to accommodate 208 prisoners, with only two washrooms between them. By 1938 up to 1,600 people were crowded into each barrack. Inside you can see how the original prisoners' bunks were redesigned to become wooden three-tiered shelves on which the inmates slept, crammed against each other and stacked to the ceiling. The sites of the other 28 barracks are marked by neat gravel oblongs. At the end of the row is a Jewish temple, an International Memorial, and Catholic and Protestant churches. A path from the far corner of the camp takes you to the ovens and crematorium, and the **gas chamber**, camouflaged as a shower room. Lethal gas was to be channelled in through holes in the ceiling. You can still see the holes, though the chamber was never used. Dachau prisoners selected for gassing were transported to Hartheim Castle near Linz in Austria, where 3,166 were executed between 1942 and 1944 alone.

Schleißheim

Schleißheim
S-Bahn 1 towards Freising: Oberschleißheim

If your taste is for Baroque architecture, or looking at paintings and pottering around museums, you should take your cue from the

17th- and 18th-century dukes of Bavaria and break your journey at Schleißheim, 15km north of the centre of Munich, on the outskirts of the city. The **Altes Schloß** (Old Palace) began as a modest hermitage completed for the devout Duke Wilhelm V in 1597. In 1616 Duke Maximilian I acquired the estate from his father and the retreat grew into an Italianate Renaissance palace. Sadly, today's palatial complex is a pale image of what it used to be like before bombs destroyed it during the Second World War. A skilful reconstruction of the 17th-century original buildings, it now contains a permanent exhibition of domestic Christian *objets d'art*, such as nativity cribs, depictions of the Passion and Eastern European Easter eggs.

Altes Schloß
www.schloesser-bayern.de; open April–Sept Tues–Sun 9–6; Oct–Mar Tues–Sun 10–4; adm €2.50, or combined ticket to Old Palace, New Palace and Lustheim €6

The earlier residence is overshadowed by the grander **Neues Schloß** (New Palace). In 1693 Elector Maximilian II Emanuel decided to build an extension to the existing castle. The War of the Spanish Succession put a stop to building work until 1719, when Joseph Effner restarted the project, with new designs. The state rooms are paeans to Baroque opulence. Architectural big guns employed by Effner such as Cuvilliés, Johann Baptist Zimmermann and Cosmas Damian Asam (*see* p.34) became locked in a frantic competition to outdo each other, and it shows. The Augsburg woodcarver Ignatz Günther draped the eastern portal with mythological allegories. Amid all this splendour is the **Großer Saal** (Large Hall), its dazzling brightness outshone only by its stunning painted dome, with scenes from the Wittelsbachs' history. The Neues Schloß also houses the **Barockgalerie**, a spin-off from the Bavarian state collection of Baroque paintings in Munich's Alte Pinakothek (*see* p.81).

Neues Schloß
www.schloesser-bayern.de; open April–Sept Tues–Sun 9–6; Oct–Mar Tues–Sun 10–4; adm €4 or combined ticket €6

A stroll through the landscaped gardens offers little respite. Arabesques of blossoms and coloured pebbles, geometric hedges and a canal with cascades adorn the French-style formal gardens for over 330m. The **Gartenschloß Lustheim** (garden palace) to the east predates the completion of the Neues Schloß by some 30 years; it was built as a wedding present to the elector's wife, Maria Antonia, and designed by Enrico Zuccalli, who was cheated of seeing the project through because the War of the Spanish Succession so depleted the elector's coffers.

Gartenschloß Lustheim
open April–Sept Tues–Sun 9–6; Oct–Mar Tues–Sun 10–4; adm €3 or combined ticket €6

Freising

In the shadow of Munich's sparkling new airport lies Freising, one of Bavaria's oldest towns. There has been an episcopal diocese in Freising since the 8th century and, under Otto von Freising (*c.* 1115–58), uncle of Emperor Frederick Barbarossa, the see began an early spiritual and cultural boom. The town grew up around the bishopric, whose local dignitaries became powerful secular princes, remaining so until the beginning of the 19th century.

Getting to Freising

By **road**, Freising is 35km northeast of Munich on the B11.
Freising is connected to Munich's **S-Bahn** network. Take Line 1 for a 25-minute jaunt to the terminus at Freising. All the main sights are within easy walking distance of the station.

The Domberg

Perched casually on top of the low hill called the Domberg in the upper part of town is Freising's pre-eminent ecclesiastical monument, the **Mariendom**. From outside it's no beauty, stumpily fashioned out of blank masonry. The twin-towered basilica was originally built during the Romanesque period: on entering the Dom you see a sculpture of the Emperor Barbarossa, one of the church's early benefactors, on the left-hand side of an arched portal. The interior, however, is surprisingly opulent – a sumptuous feast of Baroque and rococo architecture. In 1724 Johann Franz Eckher von Kapfing set about countering severe Reformation aesthetics with new, sinuous forms that provided splendid backdrops for the pomp and ceremony of popular worship. The result is the sparkling white interior by Egid Quirin Asam, with energetic ceiling *trompe l'œil* by his brother, Cosmas Damian. In his depiction of the Second Coming, above the nave, little figures float up through the clouds. Contemporary with these frescoes is the rococo decoration of the church's late Gothic cloisters. The **crypt**, the oldest surviving part of the building, contains the empty tomb and the refashioned gold shrine (1863) of St Korbinian, the founder and patron saint of the church that preceded the Dom. Among the 24 columns is the mysterious **Bestiensäule** (Beast Column), one of the most distinguished pieces of early medieval sculpture in Bavaria; its eccentric yet highly skilled carvings consist of an entwined mass of men and beasts, symbolizing the struggle between the powers of darkness and light.

Abutting the Mariendom to the west is the 15th-century **Dombibliothek**. The library dates from the early days of the diocese in the 8th century, and this is where one of the oldest books in the German language, the *Abrogans*, was drafted by monastic scribes (see 'Literature', p.40). The library rooms were refurbished between 1732 and 1734, when the main hall acquired its vivacious, stuccoed ceiling fresco, designed by François de Cuvilliés.

Diözesanmuseum
www.dombergmuseum
-freising.de;
open Tues–Sun 10–5;
adm €2

The set of ecclesiastical buildings is completed by the Diözesanmuseum, the largest diocesan museum in Germany, displaying Christian religious art over nine centuries. The 17th-century seminary is an ideal setting for its collection of over 9,000 exhibits from Bavaria, Salzburg and Tyrol, including a stunning Byzantine icon, the *Lukasbild*.

Where to Stay and Eat in Freising

ⓘ Freising >
*Marienplatz 7, t (08161)
540, www.freising.de*

Freising

Dorint Hotel München Airport, Dr-von-Daller-Straße 3–5, **t** (08161) 5320, *www.dorint.de/muenchen-freising* (€€€). A touch less glamorous than the Marriott (below), though pricier, in an older building connected with a modern annexe.

Marriott München Airport Hotel, Alois-Steinecker-Straße 20, **t** (08161) 9660, *www.marriott.de* (€€€–€€). Brash modern conference hotel that offers service and trappings to the usual high standards.

Hotel Bayerischer Hof, Untere Hauptstraße 3, **t** (08161) 538300, *www.hotel-bayerischer-hof.eu* (€€). Warmly elegant and traditional, modernized and efficient. The restaurant serves regional specialities.

Around the Domberg

The **Altstadt**, below the Domberg, is a pleasant spot where you can stroll about and admire the fine Baroque façades of the beautifully restored canons' houses. Try to visit the **Asamsaal** in the former episcopal lycée at the Marienplatz. In 1707 Hans Georg Asam, father of the famous brothers, decorated it with allegorical representations of the triumphant progress of science and the divine virtues.

Asamsaal
*guided tours from
tourist office only*

Freising's other prime attraction sprawls over another gentle hill, southwest of the Altstadt. The former Benedictine monastery of **Weihenstephan** boasts the world's oldest brewery. In 1040 (locals put the date 150 years earlier) the local abbey was granted the privilege of brewing its own beer, which apparently appealed to the monks' temporal senses to the detriment of their spiritual devotion. Nowadays the students of the Faculty of Brewing at Munich's Technical College, present here since 1895, and the **Staatsbrauerei Weihenstephan** (State Brewery) make every effort to continue this tradition, possibly even surpassing the skills of their monastic forebears. You can also visit the adjoining *Bierstüberl* (beer tavern) to sample the various traditional brews, including the famed *Stephansquell* and *Weihenstephan*.

**Staatsbrauerei
Weihenstephan**
*www.brauerei-
weihenstephan.de;
Mon–Thurs guided
tours on the hour 9–2,
except 12 noon; adm €2
including beer-tasting*

Landshut

'*Landshut, du g'freist mi*' ('Landshut, you delight me') a Wittelsbach duke wrote at the foot of a letter to his Landshut subjects. Once-mighty Landshut, straddling the River Isar, still has much to delight the visitor. Landshut has been the capital of Lower Bavaria since the 13th century, when it ruled over a duchy stretching as far as Reichenhall and Kitzbühel (now in Austria).

History

Landshut began as a settlement at a bridge over the Isar, first mentioned in 1150. In 1204 Duke Ludwig I founded the town, the present Altstadt, below a new castle known as the Landshut. His

Getting to Landshut

Landshut is 70km northeast of Munich on the A11. This makes it a convenient stopping place if you're en route to the Bavarian Forest and Passau.

There are frequent **rail** connections to Munich (45–60mins) and Regensburg (1hr). The Hauptbahnhof is on the northwestern edge of town, a 15-minute ride to the centre by city bus.

---

son Otto II (the Illustrious) moved his ducal residence here from Kelheim in 1231. In the 14th century the Neustadt and Freyung quarters were laid out, spreading out to the east of the original settlement. The town soon burgeoned under the Landshut branch of the Wittelsbachs, who consistently outshone even their extravagant cousins in Munich. In 1475, at the height of its Golden Age, Landshut played host to the splendid wedding of Duke Georg to Jadwiga, daughter to the king of Poland. The feast became a medieval byword for lavishness (*see* 'Festivals in Landshut' p.102). When in the 16th century Ludwig X chose Landshut as his permanent base, he shifted his ducal residence from the incommodious castle to the Stadtresidenz, which he commissioned in 1537 as the first Renaissance-style *palazzo* north of the Alps. After the 16th century Landshut declined in importance – though from 1800 to 1825 the town nurtured Bavaria's Provincial University before it eventually settled in Munich.

Burg Trausnitz

Burg Trausnitz
*www.landshut.de; open
April–Sept daily 9–6;
Oct–Mar daily 10–4;
adm €4*

The massive **Burg Trausnitz**, which broods over the town, grew up over four centuries and is a haphazard mixture of Romanesque, Gothic and Renaissance styles. The Landshut, as the castle was known until the 16th century, was founded in 1204 along with the town that it was to guard and remained the residence of the Wittelsbach dukes until 1543.

Those with sufficient stamina can climb up the steep Burgberg, which connects the Altstadt to the castle complex, in 20 minutes, taking advantage of its panoramic vistas over the town. (Alternatively, take bus 7 from Altstadt). The Burgberg leads to the outer defences, which include well-preserved sentry walks. Passing through the late Gothic gatehouse you reach the central, arched courtyard, graced by a Renaissance loggia. The Fürstenbau to the west forms the visual centrepiece. Extended in the middle of the 15th century, the building is notable for its lavish Renaissance detail, the product of Prince Wilhelm's attempt to create a suitably elegant residence for his wife Renate of Lorraine. In 1573 he hired a band of Italian artisans to refurbish the interior with a balustraded staircase in an effusive Italianate style. Sadly, most of the grotesque characters that decorated the upper storey were destroyed in a fire in 1961, and the only survivors are the life-size paintings depicting animated groups of playful *commedia dell'arte* buffoons which pop out of the walls of the *Narrentreppe* (Fools' Staircase).

Before leaving, take a stroll through the Hofgarten, the castle's expansive gardens that stretch out below its eastern walls with fine views across the town.

The Altstadt

The busy shopping thoroughfare called the Altstadt runs almost the entire length of the town's original medieval core, beginning at the foot of **St Martin**, a bold Gothic hall church whose unusual brick steeple, shaped like a huge ballistic missile, tapers to a point 133m above the ground, making it the tallest masonry construction of its kind in the world. Unluckily for Master Hans von Burghausen, who started work on the church in 1389, he did not live to see his ambitious project through to completion. Inside the church, the lofty vaulted stonework forms a distant canopy to astonishingly narrow halls, lined by twin rows of slender columns. In the southern aisle is the *Rosenkranz-madonna*, a virtuoso piece of 16th-century woodcarving. This beautifully restored *Madonna and Child*, by the local sculptor Hans Leinberger, anticipates the Baroque style and plays tricks with perspective (try looking at the sculpture from different angles).

If you follow the Altstadt around to the northern edge of the old town centre, you'll become entangled in a lively jumble of brightly coloured façades, impeccably restored houses and romantic alleys of crumbling, very much lived-in old houses, often backing onto colourful, arcaded courtyards. Altstadt 81 is the 15th-century **Pappenbergerhaus**, with stepped gables, all castellated with little merlons and turrets. In Kirchgasse you'll find the **Pfarrhof St Martin**, which has a splendid wooden staircase leading up to various stuccoed rooms. Nearby, in Obere Ländgasse, is the eye-catching **Palais Etzdorf**, whose rococo façade was supposedly designed by Johann Baptist Zimmermann.

On the Altstadt, opposite the neo-Gothic **Rathaus**, is the 16th-century **Stadtresidenz**, which supplanted the Trausnitz as the seat of the Wittelsbachs until Bavaria was united under Munich in 1545. Behind a neoclassical façade (the result of an 18th-century facelift) is a palace constructed by Italian master builders and modelled on Mantua's *Palazzo del Tè*. A series of Renaissance arcades leads along an Italianate courtyard. A covered staircase from the vaulted western cloister climbs to the state rooms. These begin with the imposing Italienischer Saal (Italian Hall), lined with reliefs of the tasks of Hercules, capped by stunning coffer frescoes of ancient Greek philosophers, heroes and rulers. Then come a series of salons named for the subjects of their ceiling paintings: the Göttersaal (the gods), Sternenzimmer (celestial bodies), Apollozimmer,

Stadtresidenz
open April–Oct Tues–Sun 9–6; Nov–Mar Tues–Sun 10–4; adm inc. museums €3

(i) **Landshut >>**
in the Rathaus, Altstadt 315, t (0871) 922050, www.landshut.de

Festivals in Landshut

Landshut Wedding

Landshut is most famous as the scene of Germany's largest costume pageant, the Landshut Wedding, which is held every four years (next in June/July 2010; *www.landshuter-hochzeit.de*). For four weeks, mostly at weekends, more than 2,000 locals revel in period costume against the backdrop of the historic townscape, re-enacting the splendid marriage festivities of five centuries ago (*see* History, p.22). The celebrations include the wedding procession, tournaments and recitals of medieval music.

Other Festivals

The annual *Frühjahrsdult* and *Herbstdult* (Spring Festival and Autumn Festival) in late April and late August are of slightly more modest proportion.

Where to Stay and Eat in Landshut

Landshut

Romantik-Hotel Fürstenhof, Stethaimer Straße 3, t (0871) 92550, *www.fuerstenhof.la* (€€€). A stately *Jugendstil* hotel on the outskirts of town, with a genuinely welcoming atmosphere. Soft blue and pink pastel hues, designer curtains and an abundance of floral arrangements add a gentle touch. The *maître d'* comes from Britain and serves delightful new German cuisine in two stylish restaurants.

Hotel-Gasthof Zur Insel, Badstraße 16, t (0871) 9231 60, *www.insel-landshut.de* (€€–€). A clean and conveniently situated guesthouse, to the northeast of the Altstadt.

Venuszimmer and Dianazimmer. Also in the Stadtresidenz is the **Stadt-und-Kreismuseum**, which contains some fine locally produced ceramics and an interesting collection of medieval armour, produced by the town's renowned armourers.

The Hallertau

The Hallertau
www.hallertau.info

Fifteen per cent of the world's hops originate from the rich agricultural land of the Hallertau, lining the B13 north of Munich. Undulating fields of crops coat the rolling countryside, punctuated by rectangular patches of tall hops forming delicate pinnacles up and down the hillsides. As each crop comes into season, alternating patches of dark green, yellow-gold and bright green appear, dotted with the white and yellow of a few sleepy villages and scattered farmsteads. Here and there the rhythm is broken by stretches of deciduous and coniferous forest.

Once, swarms of pieceworkers came to help harvest the overflowing gardens; nowadays machines have replaced all but a few manual labourers. The region still maintains its traditional harvest-time festivity, each year choosing a *Hopfenkönigin* (hop queen) amidst much feasting and drinking. The heartiest bash is in **Abensberg** around the beginning of September.

The bulk of each year's hop harvest is sucked up by the breweries in and around Bavaria, which fervently observe the *Reinheitsgebot* (*see* p.51). Locally, hops have an additional market: in mid-March to mid-April succulent, asparagus-like *Hopfensprossen* (hop shoots) appear on the menu of various Hallertau restaurants – a culinary experience not to be missed.

Fans of good asparagus should put aside 24 June (St John's Day) to visit the little town of **Schrobenhausen**, in the west of the Hallertau, when the asparagus harvest comes to a festive close. The town also has the **Europäisches Spargelmuseum** (asparagus museum), where you can find out everything there is to know about it.

Europäisches Spargelmuseum
open May–June daily 10–5; July–Aug Wed, Sat and Sun 2–4; adm €3

Ingolstadt

Ingolstadt is perhaps best known for the Audi assembly plants that mass-produce '*Vorsprung durch Technik*'. The story goes that when the Horch motor company moved production from Zwickau in eastern Germany to Ingolstadt after the Second World War, the new management mulled over the need to improve their international image. The old family name of Horch (which in German means 'Listen!') was given a Latin translation, believed to be more appealing to non-German ears. Those wishing to learn more about the prestigious Audi road machines should visit the **Audi Museum**, which displays the most impressive cars Audi has produced over the past 100 years and explores the company's role in racing history, beginning with its pre-war Grand Prix racers.

Audi Museum
t 0800 2834 444, www.audi.com; open Mon–Sat 9–6; adm €4

History

Ingolstadt began as a seigneurial estate of the Franks around AD 800, but was ceded to the Wittelsbachs in the early 13th century. After 1253 Duke Ludwig the Severe fortified it and made it his ducal residence. The Danube was diverted in 1363 to link up with the fledgling town. In the 14th and 15th centuries the town became the ducal capital of the Ingolstadt branch of the Wittelsbachs and was made a military stronghold, guarding a vital causeway over the Danube. In 1472 Duke Ludwig the Rich founded the first provincial university in Ingolstadt (it lasted until 1828). The town remained an important military centre until 1945: at times during the 19th century, military personnel in Ingolstadt outnumbered its citizens.

The Altstadt

Friedhofstraße, approaching the Altstadt from the west, takes you through the **Kreuztor**, the emblem of the city. Built in 1363 as part of new fortifications for an expanding city, the gate stood guard over what once was the western thoroughfare into the old town. It is the only surviving gate out of four, a triumphant and defiant pile, with pixie-capped hanging turrets and weathered red-brick masonry.

Getting to Ingolstadt

Ingolstadt is on the A9, 60km north of Munich and 90km south of Nürnberg.
Most of the Altstadt is pedestrianized, but there is ample **parking** around the outskirts.
Ingolstadt is on the main Munich–Nürnberg and Ulm–Regensburg **rail** lines, and so is served frequently by fast trains (Munich 45mins; Nürnberg 60mins). The Hauptbahnhof is about 2km south of the Altstadt. Regular bus services connect both.

A little farther down Kreuzstraße, the two asymmetrical, square brick towers of the **Liebfrauenmünster** appear like equally formidable redoubts. Duke Ludwig the Bearded began this Gothic hall church in 1425 as a suitable place to put his tomb. Inside, most of the church is in the usual cathedral gloom, but rows of windows in the central section flood the nave with light, lending a preternatural glow to the side chapels. Of these, the most impressive are the six on the western side, where double-ribbed vaulting is entwined in a fragile network of branches, at points dangling like slender stalactites from the ceiling. The painting at the late Gothic high altar is the *Adoration of the Madonna*, one of the most celebrated works of the 16th-century Renaissance artist Hans Mielich.

To the north of the minster, Konviktstraße leads to Ingolstadt's other magnificent church. Hemmed in by town residences on Neubaustraße, the unprepossessing, spireless **Asamkirche Maria de Victoria** conceals outrageous Baroque embellishments.

Asamkirche Maria de Victoria
open Mar–Oct Tues–Sun 9–12 and 1–5; Nov–Feb Tues–Sun 1–4; organ recitals Sun 12pm; adm €2

Commissioned as an oratory by the eminent Jesuit seminary of Ingolstadt, the church (1732–36) is a virtuoso masterpiece by the celebrated Asam Brothers. Here Baroque fantasy reaches hallucinogenic proportions in a breathtaking **ceiling fresco** of the *Incarnation* by Cosmas Damian Asam, supposedly finished in six weeks. The sexton will point you to a circle on the ground near the door, where, as you look up, everything resolves into 3D. It is said that King Ludwig I spent hours flat on his back looking at the painting. Another focal point is the *Lepantomonstranz*, in the sacristy. Again, if you ask, someone will open the gates to reveal the sublime gold and silver monstrance, designed by the Augsburg goldsmith Johann Zeckl in 1708 in honour of the Battle of Lepanto (1571), a famous Christian victory over the Ottoman Turks.

Back south along Neubaustraße is the **Tillyhaus**, where Johann Tilly, the field marshal of the Catholic armies during the Thirty Years' War, died in 1632.

Farther down towards the core of the Altstadt, on Ludwigstraße, is the **Ickstatthaus**, a patrician mansion built in 1749 for a local professor and displaying one of the most opulent rococo façades in town. South of Ludwigstraße is the Rathausplatz and the **Altes Rathaus** with intriguing touches of refashioned neoclassical achitecture. A few yards to the east of Rathausplatz is the

13th-century **Herzogskasten** (duke's treasury or granary), or Altes Schloß, with 14th-century stepped gables at each end.

Just to the southwest of the Herzogskasten, on the banks of the Danube, an erstwhile barracks has been put to good use: since 1992 it has housed the **Museum für Konkrete Kunst** (Museum of Concrete Art). In a series of well-fitted-out halls you are given a perspective on avant-garde aspects of contemporary, tangible art forms covering media ranging from painting to poetry.

Museum für Konkrete Kunst
www.mkk-ingolstadt.de; open Tues–Sun 10–5; adm €3

The Ramparts and the Neues Schloß

Since the early 19th century, Ingolstadt has been surrounded by a ring of stone-parapeted fortifications. Between 1828 and 1848 King Ludwig I ordered some 20,000 men to transform Ingolstadt into Bavaria's most formidable fortress town, so that it would live up to its strategically important position on the Danube. The Schanz (bulwark), as the massive military fortifications were known, bore the unmistakable stamp of the architect Leo von Klenze (famed for his buildings in Munich), who was eager to demonstrate that military architecture needn't be purely functional, but could also be aesthetically appealing. The remains of the fortress (large sections were blown up by the Allies in 1945) surround the Altstadt in a polygon, one of the typical forms of 19th-century military architecture.

It's worth making your way to the **Glacis**, a broad green belt on a sloping bank around the **Knüttegraben** (town moat), just west of the Altstadt. The **Fronte**, one of the former bastions, now adrift among the fronds and lichen of the park, has been tastefully converted into workshops and a youth centre, while the **Kavalier Hepp**, designed to bolster the town's western entrance, houses Ingolstadt's **Stadtmuseum** (Town Museum), where you can trace the town's architectural development and visit the **Spielzeug-museum** (Toy Museum) with its superb collection of early sheet-metal playthings. The contrastingly curved ramparts along the southern bank of the Danube were also subject to a post-war pep up. Here the neoclassical **Reduit Tilly**, built as a last-ditch stronghold for the Wittelsbach dynasty in time of war, and the whimsical **Turm Triva** have been landscaped into the **Klenzepark**, a large, peaceful recreation area, laid out and arranged for Bavaria's Garden Show in 1992. The park is an unusual and agreeable contrast to the town and offers fine views of the Altstadt.

Stadtmuseum
Tues–Fri 9–5, Sat–Sun 10–5; adm €3

Spielzeugmuseum
open Tues–Fri 9–5, Sat–Sun 10–5; adm €2.50, under 15s free

Another blatant expression of military power is the **Neues Schloß** to the east of the Altstadt, not far from the Herzogskasten. The fortress-like palace dates from the early 15th century, when the massive structure of 3m-thick walls and defensive towers was built on the orders of Duke Ludwig the Bearded. Appropriately, it is now home to the extensive collection

ⓘ Ingolstadt >
Altes Rathaus:
Rathausplatz 2,
t (0841) 305 3030,
www.ingolstadt.de

Hauptbahnhof:
Elisabethstraße 3,
t (0841) 305 3005,
www.ingolstadt-
tourismus.de

Festivals in Ingolstadt

The first weekend in July sees the *Bürgerfest*, when the town celebrates its civic prowess. At two-year intervals, in August (next in 2010) Ingolstadt celebrates the *Reines Bierfest* (Real Beer Festival), commemorating the proclamation of the *Reinheitsgebot* here in 1516. Beer-drinkers go to great lengths to turn the event into a bacchanalian revel.

Where to Stay and Eat in Ingolstadt

Ingolstadt

Ambassador Hotel, Goethestraße 153, t (0841) 5030, *www.nh-hotels.com* (€€€). Swish, slickly run and central, with views across the Altstadt. Famed for the groaning buffet at breakfast.

Hotel Rappensberger, Harderstraße 3, t (0841) 3140, *www.rappensberger.de* (€€€–€€). Classy: combines a historic house, renovated in 2002, with a newly built annexe.

Donau Hotel, Münchener Straße 10, t (0841) 965150, *www.donauhotel.de* (€€). Well-run little hotel in the town centre with friendly service, and convenient for all the sights. Attached to a cheery, traditional inn.

Hotel Zum Anker, Tränktorstraße 1, t (0841) 30050, *www.hotel-restaurant-anker.de* (€€). Comfortable family-run hotel in the Altstadt, with a good restaurant.

Bayerisches Armeemuseum
www.bayerisches-armeemuseum.de; open Tues–Sun 8.45–4.30; adm €3

of the Bayerisches Armeemuseum (Bavarian Army Museum), which spans seven centuries of Bavarian military history. Most famous is the splendid booty of the 17th-century wars with the Turks, including ornate helmets, horse armour and banners.

Around Ingolstadt

Neuburg and Weltenburg

The small town of **Neuburg** on the River Danube, 26km southwest of Ingolstadt, could have popped up straight out of a Renaissance picture book. Although it dates back to Roman times, Neuburg's glory days started in 1505 when the town became detached from Wittelsbach rule and was governed as capital city of the tiny, newly founded principality of the Junge Pfalz (Young Palatinate) by the prince-electors of the Palatinate in Heidelberg. When Prince Ottheinrich converted to Protestantism in 1542, he set about the construction of sumptuous palaces. His new subjects, eager to echo their leader's every whim, followed suit and a building boom ensued.

Neuburg Schloß
open April–Sept Tues–Sun 9–6; adm €3

The focal point of Neuburg's Renaissance building is the Schloß, with its massive outer walls lining the tall hill at the town centre. This red sandstone mass appears to arrange itself into towers, domes and graceful arches. But what really catches your eye is the courtyard with arched loggias asymmetrically grouped around three flanks, its Mediterranean character heightened by the black and white *sgraffito* paintings of the *Fürstenspiegel* (representations of the princes, harking back to a book on princely conduct by that name) that adorn the inner walls. Tiers of images represent Old Testament heroes and hunky Greek deities.

Another example of Protestant fervour in Neuburg is the **Hofkirche St Maria**, on Karlsplatz. This early 17th-century church was to be a beacon of Protestantism in Catholic Bavaria, but its intended role was thwarted when Ottheinrich's successor reconverted to Catholicism in 1614, and instituted more stuccoed embellishments to the interior than had been originally planned. Today it is a colourful potpourri of architectural styles from Gothic to Baroque.

Another 19km upstream lies **Kloster Weltenburg**, where you're really spoilt for choice. It's hard to decide whether the abbey or its scenic setting is more spectacular. At Weltenburg the Danube makes a tight loop and shrinks to just 80m wide, cutting through a gorge of densely forested limestone rocks eroded into truly bizarre shapes. The aptly named **Donaudurchbruch** (Danube's Cleft) forms the perfect scenic backdrop for the monastic complex on the sandy banks. The best way to take in the whole panorama is to arrive by boat (*see* 'Cruises', p.113). The **Klosterkirche**, attached to a Benedictine abbey that's supposedly Bavaria's oldest monastic establishment (*c.* AD 620), is one of the finest examples of Baroque and rococo architecture along the Danube. A pale building of ochre stone, it maintains a stately serenity despite the hordes of tourists that invade it daily. Inside the church, which was begun by Cosmas Damian Asam in 1716, the *stuccatori* have let loose with rococo swirls and flourishes. In the hallway before you reach the nave, look out especially for the stuccoed allegories of 'the four last concerns': Death, Last Judgement, Hellfire and Heaven. In his *trompe l'œil* painting of the *Assumption of the Virgin Mary* over the domed nave, cherubs float up into the sky, past a pyramid of clerics, Old Testament heroes, saints and the Holy Trinity. There's also a finely painted *Last Judgement* by Franz Asam, Cosmas Damian's son, in the porch. Another highlight is the splendid four-columned tableau over the high altar, with a dazzling depiction of a mounted St George slaying the dragon.

Should you find these outbursts of rococo fantasy somewhat overwhelming, then the beer garden of the adjoining **Klosterschänke** (Abbey Inn) is a good place to stop and recover, with a glass of the abbey's own dark beer.

Klosterkirche
open daily 7–9pm; adm free

Klosterschänke
open daily 9–7

07 München | North of Munich: The Altmühl Valley

The Altmühl Valley

Like the Bavarian Forest, the Altmühl Valley (*Altmühltal*) has been consistently bypassed by foreign tourists, unaware of what they are missing. The River Altmühl gives its name to a Jurassic valley that winds its way from the heart of the Franconian highlands following a placid, gently rolling course to the resort of Treuchtlingen, then twists through dramatic loops and tight hairpin bends to meet the Danube at Kelheim. Until about 150

Getting around the Altmühl Valley

A **car** is the most convenient way to travel around the valley. The A9 traverses the central Altmühl Valley in its Munich–Nürnberg section, while the B2, B13 and the B299 crisscross the river and take you to dozens of small towns and villages. For a jaunt along the river itself you have to rely on smaller country roads.

Chief **rail** stations in the valley, on the main rail line from Munich to Würzburg, are at Eichstätt, Treuchtlingen and Gunzenhausen. There are regular **bus** services centering on Treuchtlingen and Kelheim that can take you to many of the smaller resorts. Ask at the local tourist offices for details.

million years ago, the valley was the shoreline of a gigantic primordial lake that did a lot to shape the local landscape, leaving large deposits of fossils. Nowadays the most scenic parts are the river's central reaches, where glistening forests and rows of fissured limestone crags drop down to the banks, and shallow rivulets branch out into valleys of lush meadowland and juniper-covered heath.

Geological faults that caused individual hills to become detached from the main mass provided the perfect natural defences for feudal overlords, and many are still crowned by castles. But the Altmühl Valley has few major towns and even less in the way of major man-made sights. Some 3,000 square kilometres of the valley have been declared Germany's largest **nature park**, with rare specimens of flora and fauna and trees up to 900 years old. The limestone is riddled with some 300 caves, many of them inhabited during the Stone Age.

The surrounding countryside is at its most beguiling in autumn, when the white limestone rocks of the valley are offset by the golden tones of the trees; but the landscape is remarkable at any time of year. It is a relatively deserted region, popular mainly with Germans on activity holidays.

From Gunzenhausen to Eichstätt

A few kilometres northwest of Gunzenhausen, the Altmühl and its tributaries have been dammed to create the **Altmühlsee**, a lake that, with four smaller man-made lakes, spreads over 25 square kilometres and forms a kind of Bavarian Riviera. There are numerous water sports facilities around the lakeside, and the **Vogelinsel** (Bird Island) to the north is famous for bird-watching (mostly rare storks and herons).

At **Treuchtlingen**, 20km upstream, where three tributaries join the Altmühl, you can relax in the **Altmühltherme**, an indoor leisure centre with pools, sauna, solariums and thermal springs. The town also boasts a 16th-century **Schloß** and the ruins of a 14th-century **Burg**. North of the resort lies the *Fossa Carolina*, a medieval canal project (*see* 'The Main-Donau-Kanal', p.110).

Beyond Treuchtlingen you can leave the Altmühl for a short detour to **Weißenburg**, a small town that offers a graphic demonstration of Rome's control over the frontier regions of its empire. Just north of

Altmühltherme
*www.altmueltherme.de;
open Sat–Mon 9–8,
Tues–Thurs 9–9,
Fri 9–10; €14.50 day,
€7.50 for 2½hrs*

the town a 550km line of old Roman **Limes** fortifications linked the Rhine and the Danube, preventing Germanic incursions into the province of *Raetia* after AD 89. Archaeological monuments of the time have been preserved and reconstructed following 20th-century excavations. The whole northern section of the Altmühl Valley is dotted with the remains of Roman occupation, notably military forts and farming *villae rusticae*. Two reconstructed Roman military camps, one in stone and an earlier one protected by palisades, plus the foundations of **Roman baths** can be seen around Weißenburg. A visit to the **Römermuseum** in town helps to show what life in the Roman marches must have been like through a collection of Roman treasure, ranging from silver votive offerings to bronze statues of deities.

Back on the main route, lying on a picturesque bend of the Altmühl 7km beyond Treuchtlingen, is **Pappenheim**. Its charming little cluster of stone and half-timbered buildings rises up towards a skilfully restored 11th-century **Burg** with an interesting museum containing an assortment of arms and instruments of torture. Next stop, just a few kilometres out of Pappenheim, is **Solnhofen**, which likes to advertise itself as a 'world in stone'. This little resort is a mecca for fossil-hunters and hobby geologists who descend each year on the nearby chalk quarries in search of the petrified remains of prehistoric animals. (The local tourist office will even lend you a hammer and chisel.) Solnhofen also prides itself on being the birthplace of lithography, the art of stone-block printing, and its residents have honoured its 19th-century inventor, Alois Senefelder, with a statue in the middle of town. The impressive **Bürgermeister-Müller-Museum** in Solnhofen's town hall is packed with exhibits illustrating both the history of lithographic printing and the much older imprints of many Ice Age fossilized creatures, including one of the rare fossils of the archaeopteryx.

After Solnhofen the Altmühl passes through a series of loops to the **Zwölf Apostel** (Twelve Apostles), a wooded range of eerie, fissured boulders, best seen from a canoe or kayak. The postcard-pretty hamlet of **Dollnstein** marks the end of the primeval Uraltmühl Valley, in which the river follows the former course of the Danube. After Dollnstein the twisting valley opens out between rugged slopes.

At one of the tight hairpin bends straddling the river, about 11km upstream from Dollnstein, lies the town of **Eichstätt**, capital of the Altmühl Valley. This wonky old town has a special link with the English-born missionary St Willibald, who arrived here in AD 745 and became its first bishop. On the east side houses pass through the Baroque spectrum of white to yellow to cream, propping each other up around the town's two main squares, the Marktplatz and the Domplatz. Standing in their midst is the pale Baroque **Dom**,

Roman baths
open Mar–Dec Tues–Sun 10–12.30 and 2–5; adm €2

Römermuseum
open Mar daily 10–12.30 and 2–5; April–Oct daily 10–5; closed Nov–Feb; adm €2, or €4 for combined ticket with baths

Burg
www.grafschaft-pappenheim.de; open Mar–Nov Tues–Sun 10–5; adm €3

Bürgermeister-Müller-Museum
www.solnhofen.de; open April–Oct daily 9–5; Nov–Mar, Sun 1–4; adm €3

07 München | North of Munich: The Altmühl Valley

The Main-Donau-Kanal

The idea of a navigable continental waterway to link the Black Sea with the North Sea has existed since the 8th century. In AD 793 Charlemagne ordered some 6,000 workmen to drive a ditch between the Rivers Rezat and Altmühl, tributaries of the Main and Danube, at a point where they were just 2km apart. But the attempt was thwarted by incessant flooding. Nowadays the remnants of this, the *Fossa Carolina* (Latin for Carolingian ditch), form a leafy pond to the north of Treuchtlingen that is celebrated among fishermen.

Only in the 19th century did Ludwig I's engineers restart this ambitious canal project. Between Dietfurt and Kelheim the Altmühl was deepened and cleared by dredgers, straightened and canalized to a width of 12m. Eleven locks were built to cope with the changing water levels. After ten years of construction the 'Ludwig-Donau-Main-Kanal' was opened to shipping in 1846, but the venture failed with the advent of steam railways. Today this old canal is like an outdoor museum of industrial archaeology, full of musty bridges, romantic lock-gates, rusty sluices, mossy wharves and diminutive, forlorn lock-houses, many of them designed by the famed Leo von Klenze. An easy way to spot the route of the erstwhile canal is by the fruit trees that line the crumbling towpaths. It is said that the income generated by the trees soon outstripped that of the canal.

In 1992 Charlemagne's vision again became a reality when the Danube was linked by canal to the Rhine, after 32 years of construction and at a cost of DM5.6 billion (€2.9 billion), creating a 3,500km waterway. In the process, the Altmühl's lower reaches were transformed beyond recognition by the disproportionate widening of the river and by four huge concrete sluice gates – ugly and out of place in the enchanting river landscape. At the time, some 850,000 protesters aired their vexation at the wanton destruction of the ecologically sensitive environment, describing the canal as 'the silliest project since the building of the tower of Babel'.

But the Bavarian state government has more plans up its sleeve. Now they want to straighten out the Danube for some 70km between Straubing and Vilshofen, so that the watercourse will be navigable throughout the year. Conservationists have warned that the new project will precipitate another ecological disaster, and claim that its commercial viability is questionable. It seems that the Danube and the Altmühl Valley may face another period of change and controversy.

which shelters the famous **Pappenheimer Altar** (*c.*1490) with its striking Crucifixion group. Across the river high above the town is the splendid 17th-century **Willibaldsburg**, built as a residence for Eichstätt's prince bishops. Nowadays the complex houses two museums, the **Historisches Museum** and the **Jura-Museum**, focusing on local history and the palaeontological and geological aspects of the town's environs.

Willibaldsburg
www.schloesser-bayern.de; open April–Sept daily 9–6; Oct–Mar Tues–Sun 10–4; adm €4 inc. museums

From Eichstätt to Kelheim

First stop after Eichstätt is **Pfünz**, which greets visitors with life-size bronze statues of two Roman legionaries at the entrance to the town. Pfünz's reconstructed Roman fort, **Vetoniana**, complements the Roman encampments of Weißenburg.

From Pfünz the river follows some tight turns to **Kipfenberg**, a pretty little village on the southern bank that marks the geographical centre of Bavaria. Surrounded by wooded hills on all sides, Kipfenberg is dominated by its 12th-century **Burg**, set high on a bluff above the village. On the diminutive Marktplatz you can visit the inspiring **Fasenickl-Museum**, a colourful and cleverly presented display of costumes and masks pertaining to the village's long carnival tradition.

Vetoniana
open daily; adm free

Burg
outbuildings only open to the public

Fasenickl-Museum
www.fasenickl.de; open first Sun of every month or by arrangement, t (08421) 905761

After Kipfenberg the river meanders gently on to **Beilngries**, 14km downstream on the northern side. Here, at the junction with the River Sulz, the walled medieval town nestles in the tranquil surroundings of a little bowl-shaped valley covered largely with a coniferous forest. Out of this rise the two soaring stone towers of

Schloß Hirschberg
www.bisturmshaus-hirschberg.de

Schloß Hirschberg. This Baroque residence was built by the prince-bishops of Eichstätt to keep the locals under the thumb, and today houses a Catholic seminary.

The high point of the Sulz Valley is **Berching**, 8km north of Beilngries, which has benefited greatly from the recent completion of the Main-Donau-Kanal, since boats from Kelheim now moor alongside the 1,100-year-old Altstadt (*see* 'Cruises', p.113). With its creaky half-timbered houses, cobbled squares and medieval town walls (complete with nine towers and covered sentry walk), the beautifully preserved town seems stuck somewhere in the 1300s.

Back on the Altmühl, past **Dietfurt** with its medieval patrician houses, you reach the hamlet of **Altmühlmünster** on the opposite bank. Until the 14th century the local monastery was an important stronghold of the Templars. The town is the starting point for a 14km-long circular footpath through the thickly wooded Brunn

Schloß Eggersberg
www.schloss-eggersberg.eu

Valley to **Schloß Eggersberg**. This 15th-century manor house in the rural obscurity of the quiet hamlet of Obereggersberg was built as the hunting lodge of a local aristocratic dynasty and recently converted into a hotel and restaurant, with sweeping views over the Altmühl (*see* p.113). A small part of the complex houses the

Hofmarkmuseum
open daily 12–6; closed 23 Dec–9 Jan; adm €3

Hofmarkmuseum, presenting local history and archaeology. The Schloß can also be reached by car from Riedenburg.

The buzzing town of **Riedenburg** seems a world away in spirit, destined to prosper as one of the regional tourist magnets. For this it can thank the Main-Donau-Kanal and the day-trippers converging on the town by boat. Completely dominating the townscape are Riedenburg's three **castles** of the 12th and 13th centuries, perched high on the encircling craggy hills. As you

Kristallmuseum
www.kristallmuseum-riedenberg.de; open Mar–Oct daily 9–6; adm €3

explore, look out for the **Kristallmuseum**, where the prize exhibit is the world's largest clump of rock crystals, from Arkansas.

Around the next twist of the now canalized river, on the southern bank, you'll find the 11th-century **Burg Prunn**, whose strong stone

Burg Prunn
guided tours only, April–Oct daily 9–6; Nov–Mar Tues–Sun 10–3.30; adm €3

walls tower precariously over a 70m-high chalky promontory above the treetops. Once the most formidable fortress in the Altmühl Valley, Schloß Prunn is now the well-preserved showcase of a fully appointed medieval castle complex. (It's a long and daunting walk from Nußhausen, below, to the castle, so try to come by car.)

Following the northern bank of the Altmühl east from Riedenburg brings you to the tiny village of **Essing**. This was founded by the Celts in 500 BC, but there's nothing exceptional to see apart from the **wooden footbridges** that span the river's old basin, and the new Main-Donau-Kanal. The romantic old *Brücke* (bridge) and its *Brückturm* (gate tower), against a backdrop of village houses rising up the steep limestone crags, are in stark contrast to the swaying, 193m-long, state-of-the-art timbered bridge over the canal (the longest of its kind in Europe). Across the latter are the **Schulerloch stalactite caves**, about 2km to the east. The caves, with a total length of 400m, were inhabited in the Stone Age. From the Schulerloch caves, you can walk back across the river front of the Schellnecker Wand to the vestiges of the 19th-century Ludwig-Main-Donau-Kanal (*see* p.110).

Schulerloch stalactite caves
www.schulerloch.de; guided tours only, Easter–Oct daily 10–4; adm €3.50

Four kilometres upstream, **Kelheim**, at the confluence of the Altmühl and the Danube, is the most touristy town on the river, its moored pleasure boats lending a Mediterranean seaside atmosphere. In summer it is a bustling place, thronging with coach parties and day-trippers, but somehow preserving its romantic charm. Hemmed in between the river, the Main-Donau-Kanal and the sloping flank of the Donaudurchbruch to the west (*see* p.107), it has the reckless mood of a holiday island. The Wittelsbach dukes resided here until 1231 when, by a tragic quirk of fate, the assassination of Duke Ludwig I on the town's bridge caused his successors to steer clear of the place and move to Landshut. There's an **Altstadt** full of evocative nooks and crannies, a **Schloß** dating back to the 12th century, a famous 17th-century **Weißbier brewery** and the three original town gates.

Befreiungshalle
www.schloesser-bayern.de; open mid-Mar–Oct daily 9–6; Nov–mid-Mar daily 9–4; adm €3

From one of these, Mittertor, you start the slow ascent to the imposing **Befreiungshalle** on its hill just outside town. The massive, drum-like monument commemorating the Bavarian dead in the wars against Napoleon (surprisingly numerous given that Bavarian troops had been an ally of Napoleon for most of the time) was started by King Ludwig I in 1842 and completed by his architect Leo von Klenze five years later. Inspired by ancient Greek architecture, the mostly brick-built domed rotunda is supported by eighteen marble columns, each topped with an oversized limestone statue representing one of the peoples that rose against Napoleon.

ⓘ **Altmühl Valley Nature Park >**
Information Centre, Notre Dame 1, Eichstätt, t (08421) 98760, www.naturpark-altmuehltal.de; open April–Oct Mon–Sat 9–5, Sun 10–5, until 6 in summer; Nov–Mar Mon–Thurs 9–12 and 2–4, Fri 9–12

Tourist Information in the Altmühl Valley

The **Nature Park Information Centre** (*see* left) is a real treasure trove to anyone wanting to explore this wilder sector of the Altmühl Valley. Friendly, efficient staff help with the region's topography, museums, castles, hotels and farming holidays as well as sports and outdoor activities. An educational display on the first floor explains the ecology of the valley's habitats.

Festivals in the Altmühl Valley

The main regional bashes around the Altmühl Valley are essentially local affairs, though this doesn't mean strangers aren't welcome.

Around *Fasching* (carnival) in February–March the inhabitants of Kipfenberg dress outlandishly and parade through the streets, while during their *Limesfest* the menfolk

(i) **Weißenburg**
*Römermuseum,
Martin-Luther-Platz 3,*
t *(09141) 907124, www.
weissenburg.de*

(i) **Beilngries**
Hauptstraße 14,
t *(08461) 8435,
www.beilngries.de*

(i) **Kelheim**
*Rathaus, Ludwigplatz
14,* **t** *(09441) 701234,
www.cms.kelheim.de*

confront each other as Roman legionaries and Germanic warriors.

The *Weltumsegler Niederlandt* (derisory German for the Dutch circumnavigators) festival, at the end of May, is the point of revelry in Pappenheim when a group of gallants whirl about the town in costumes of various periods, making a mockery of the world's major historic events.

Sports and Activities in the Altmühl Valley

Tourist information offices (*see* left) can help with advice and information on all sports.

Cruises

This is a sublime way to see the region, if you have the time. A number of *Schiffstour* companies are based at Kelheim, offering round-trips and pleasure cruises on the Altmühl and Danube (see *www.schifffahrt-kelheim.de*).

Travelling the full length of the Altmühl involves a cruise on the **Main-Donau-Kanal** from Beilngries to Kelheim (*services mid-April to mid-October Mon, Wed, Thurs and Sat, 4½hrs; single €13, return €19*), or any of the stops in between. The **Danube** offers the most attractive stretch, however, between Kelheim and Weltenburg; between mid-March and October boats ply the river in and out of the scenic Donaudurchbruch (*30–45 mins; single €4, return €7.50*).

Cycling

One of the great attractions of the Altmühl Valley is the comprehensive network of **cycle routes**, often following the hiking trails. There's a 164km-long cycling route, the **Altmühltal-Radweg**, between Gunzenhausen and Kelheim, most of it quite easy going. There are plenty of places to hire bicycles, and you can get maps and information from any of the tourist offices along the way.

Hiking

By far the best way to see the valley is on foot. Marked trails give you the option of anything from an afternoon stroll to a fortnight's serious walking. Tourist offices give advice on walks

and sell maps of the trails. Some travel companies organize long-distance and circular group hikes, and will cart your luggage on ahead of you.

Rock-climbing

Rock-climbers (*Kletterer*) enjoy the challenge of the cliffs, especially around the Dohlenfelsen near Wellheim-Konstein and around Riedenburg.

Water Sports

With its 200km of gently flowing water, the Altmühl offers the perfect environment for pleasant and undemanding *Bootswandern* (travelling about by boat) and is particularly suited for novices in **canoeing** and **kayaking**. The Altmühlsee near Gunzenhausen and the Kleiner Brombachsee at Absberg are popular lakes for **windsurfers**.

Where to Stay and Eat in the Altmühl Valley

Hotel Adler, Marktplatz 22, Eichstätt, **t** (09421) 6767, *www.adler-eichstaett.de* (€€). Modernized, 17th-century Baroque mansion. Traditional touches, such as candelabras, remain, but the comfortable rooms are uniformly furnished.

Hotel zur Post, Bahnhofstraße 7, Gunzenhausen, **t** (09831) 67470, *www.hotelzurpost-gunzenhausen.de* (€€). In a former posthouse, this hotel's restaurant and wood-panelled day rooms are especially attractive.

Ringhotel Gams, Hauptstraße 16, Beilngries, **t** (08461) 6100, *www.hotel_gams.de* (€€). Situated in the town centre, clean and comfortable, despite the rustic touches. Amenities include three different saunas and bicycle loan.

Hotel Schloß Eggersberg, Obereggersberg, Riedenburg, **t** (09442) 91870, *www.schloss-eggersberg.com* (€€). In a historic hunting lodge with expansive park, this stately country hotel offers outdoor pursuits such as horse-riding, angling and cross-country skiing. Here you can live in pampered luxury, among Persian rugs and fine period furniture. The adjoining restaurant is renowned for its ever-so-refined cuisine and hefty bills.

Goldene Rose, Rosenstraße 6, Weißenburg, t (09141) 2096, *www.hotel-goldene-rose.de* (€). Long-established hotel across from the Rathaus, which justifiably prides itself on its antique-furnished rooms, friendly service and solid *gutbürgerliche* cuisine.

Hotel Aukofer, Alleestraße 27, Kelheim, t (09441) 2020, *www.hotel-brauerei-aukofer.de* (€). A good hotel with eager management, well-appointed rooms and two conservatories. Close to the Befreihungshalle. Serves its own beer and hearty fare.

East of Munich: Inn-Salzachgau

With some justification, the Inn-Salzachgau, southeast of Munich, styles itself as 'the other Upper Bavaria'. This triangular patch of land, bounded by the converging Rivers Inn and Salzach (marking the Austrian border to the east), is a secluded spot, comprising fertile upland farmland, here and there broken by patches of deciduous woodland. The highlights of the area are thinly spread, but through its scattering of sights it constitutes one of the best areas to observe the gradual unfolding of the architectural innovations that reached Bavaria via trade routes from beyond the Alps.

Wasserburg

This small town, lying just shy of where the River Inn snakes round a narrow tongue of land, is another medieval gem barely touched by foreign tourists. The town's prime location on a peninsula first recommended it to a local princely family who made Wasserburg their seat in 1137. From here, they kept tabs on the important salt route from Reichenhall to Munich and could control the waterway trade between the Adriatic Sea and the Danube.

Most of Wasserburg's prime attractions are grouped together on the spacious **Marienplatz**, which looks at its most impressive when approached over the Inn bridge and through the massive 15th-century **Brücktor**. To the east of the square is the **Kernhaus** with its rococo façade of 1740. Opposite lies the high-steepled, Gothic **Rathaus**. On the far side of the square is the 14th-century **Frauenkirche,** whose interior underwent a Baroque renewal in around 1750. Some of Wasserburg's most evocative streets lie just off the Marienplatz. Follow the narrow, colourful alley marked 'Schmiedzeile' (on the western side of the square), where ancient shops have fancy wrought-iron guild signs. This will lead you to the **Burg**, resting on a gentle elevation on the bank of the Inn. This 12th-century castle was extended in the 16th century and is now an old people's home; the only part accessible to the visitor is the late Gothic chapel in the inner courtyard.

Getting around East of Munich

Four major *Bundesstraßen* (federal **highways**) cross the region. Most of the important towns lie along the B12 from Munich (A94 up to Markt-Schwaben) to Altötting (90km) and on to Passau. The B299 runs from Landshut to Altötting (60km), while the B20 connects the latter with Burghausen (15km). The B304 links Munich with Wasserburg (55km).

There are two **car ferries** from Mühldorf on the River Inn, one providing a service to Annabrunn, the other to Starkheim.

The main **rail** lines serving the region run from Munich to Mühldorf with connections to Altötting (1hr 30mins) and Burghausen (2hrs), and from Munich to Wasserburg (1hr 20mins), where a branch line follows the Inn to Mühldorf.

Altötting

Altötting is Bavaria's answer to Lourdes in France or Czestochowa in Poland. By the 15th century a series of miraculous healings – such as a boy killed by a cart and a drowned child being brought back to life – had elevated this erstwhile Carolingian settlement to a thriving place of pilgrimage. Given the 700,000 or so wayworn devotees who still flock to Altötting each year, particularly around the months of May and October, the town is the one place where you cannot fail to appreciate that the Catholic Church is alive and kicking in Bavaria.

Altötting's adulation of the Virgin Mary centres on the **Gnadenkapelle**, a tiny Gothic brick chapel built around an even smaller octagonal cell, which you reach from the wide, central **Kapellplatz**, and a bevy of booths selling every conceivable kind of devotional souvenir. Its history goes back to a Carolingian baptistry, in which St Rupert is said to have christened a Bavarian duke as early as the 7th century. Before entering the outwardly unprepossessing chapel, have a look around the **cloisters**, covered with votive icons and girdled with bundles of the broad wooden crosses that penitents traditionally hump around the chapel. Inside, the gloomy candlelit nave is encased in black marble. A myriad colourful rosaries and other *ex votos*, dangling from the soot-blackened walls, usher you to the chapel's centre point, the luminous silver shrine of the **Black Madonna** (*c.* 1300). The Virgin and Child are carved in limewood, swathed in dazzling ceremonial robes and sport glittering coronets. Opposite, an eerie row of urns contain the hearts of 21 Wittelsbach rulers, including that of Ludwig II. Similarly preserved is the heart of Field Marshal Johann Tilly, Catholic hero of the Thirty Years' War and a devout pilgrim to Altötting. His other remains are displayed in a tomb in the vaults of the Stiftspfarrkirche.

Opposite the south face of the Kapellplatz and completely overshadowing the Gnadenkapelle is the twin-towered **Stiftspfarrkirche**, built in the so-called transitional style. It was completed around the same time as the late Gothic nave was

Stiftspfarrkirche treasury
open April–Oct Tues–Sun 10–12 and 2–4; adm €2

added to the Gnadenkapelle, but is more cautiously Romanesque than go-ahead Gothic. The calibre of the pilgrims that came to visit Altöttingen can be appreciated in the adjoining treasury. It wasn't just hoi polloi who begged for forgiveness over the centuries. From early on, the high and mighty Wittelsbachs and Hapsburgs abased themselves before the Black Madonna, repented their sins and showed their gratitude with a welter of votive offerings. Prize of the collection is the magnificent *Goldene Rössl*, a heavily decorated and gilded filigree masterpiece of French origin (*c.* 1400) that depicts the Adulation of the Virgin Mary by King Charles VI of France, with a manservant holding the reins of an enamelled white mare on the base.

Wallfahrts- und Heimatmuseum
open April–Oct Tues–Fri 2–4, Sat 10–3, Sun 10–12 and 1–3; adm €2

At the northern end of the Kapellplatz, facing the Gnadenkapelle, lies the **Wallfahrts- und Heimatmuseum** (Pilgrimage and Local History Museum), really only worth a visit if you feel a craving for total immersion in Altöttingen's history of Christian devotion.

Burghausen

'*Voilà la ville souterraine!*' ('Behold the subterranean town!') exclaimed Napoleon as he looked out over Burghausen. His remark seems a fitting reflection on the town's defensive posture as an important military stronghold on the Bavarian-Austrian border. Wedged between the Salzach to the east and a former arm of the river, the Wöhrsee, to the west, Burghausen sprang up under the protective watch of its massive fortress. Today, street after street has retained its bright, decorative houses that distinguish the architecture of the Inn-Salzach.

The steep but straight Burgsteig brings you to the **Burg**, Germany's longest castle complex, with a kilometre of bristling towers and baileys. Begun in the 13th century, for the next 300 years it was the guardian of Burghausen's lucrative salt trade, controlled by the Landshut branch of the Wittelsbachs. The castle fortifications were last extended between 1480 and 1490, in an attempt to ward off an imminent onslaught by the Turks. You enter the *Hauptburg* (main castle) through a medieval gateway. Here the main buildings around the inner courtyard date back to the oldest-surviving Gothic origins of the castle complex. Altogether five more baileyed quadrangles spread out to the north, all linked by massive gateways and bridges, progressively marking the tran-

Historisches Stadtmuseum
open May–Sept daily 9–6.30, Nov–Mar 10–4; adm €2

sition from Gothic to early Renaissance. There are two interesting museums within the castle precincts: the **Historisches Stadt-museum** (Historic Town Museum) in the Hauptburg and the **Foto-museum** (Photography Museum) at the northern entry to the Burg.

Fotomuseum
open April–Oct Wed–Sun 10–6; adm €2

Down below, the **Altstadt** hugs the bank of the River Salzach. Space is at a premium on the narrow strip of land, and the old town's generous layout comes as a surprise. Don't be put off by the dull row of riverfront houses: behind them a mesh of gracious burgher houses fans out, a lively jumble of brightly painted façades with many false frontages concealing the high gables. The focal point is the oblong **Stadtplatz**, the main thoroughfare and social hub of Burghausen. At the southern end of the square stands the 15th-century **St Jakobskirche** with its onion-shaped twin domes. Across the square is the 14th-century **Rathaus**, and a colourful potpourri of stately buildings, including the late Gothic **Wachszieherhaus** (Candle-maker's House). Ranged around the Stadtplatz are two more 17th- and 18th-century churches, the castellated former **Kurfürstliche Regierungsgebäude** (Administrative Building of the Prince-Elector), now housing the town library and conference rooms, and the splendid rococo **Taufkirchen Palais**. Not far from where Burghausen's only bridge crosses over the Salzach to Austria, you'll find the mooring from which converted salt barges leave for river jaunts in the summer (*see* 'Sports and Activities East of Munich' p.117).

Festivals East of München

The region's main cultural event, the *Musiksommer zwischen Inn und Salzach* (Musical Summer betwixt Inn and Salzach) is shared by several of the region's resorts (Altötting, Burghausen, Kloster Au and others) and attracts top-drawer artists from around Germany.

There are two other, contrasting music festivals: the **Week of Church Music** held in Altötting each year in October, and the **International Jazz Week** in March at Burghausen, which includes open-air performances.

Sports and Activities East of München

Boat Trips

If you have time to spare for leisurely journeys, converted **salt barges** (*Plätten*) can take you on a gentle dawdle from Burghausen along some fine stretches of the River Salzach (May–Oct).

Cycling

By far the most pleasurable way of seeing the countryside is by bicycle. Most of the land is fairly flat, and there is a comprehensive network of cycle routes. Maps and details are available from tourist offices.

You can hire bicycles very cheaply from the parcel counters at most German rail stations (*see* **Planning Your Trip**, p.60).

Hiking

Walking is also a good way to get around, but get a copy of the local *Wanderkarte* (walking map), as it's all too easy to get lost.

Where to Stay and Eat East of München

Wasserburg

Hotel Fletzinger, Fletzingergasse 1, t (08071) 90890, *www.fletzinger.de* (€€). Historic building in the centre, newly renovated and well-equipped.

Altötting

Hotel zur Post, Kapellplatz 2, t (08671) 5040, *www.zurpostaltoetting.de* (€€). The grandest hotel in town. Spacious rooms with a Roman bath and five in-house restaurants.

Burghausen

Hotel Glöcklhofer, Ludwigsberg 4, t (08677) 96170, *www.hotelgloeckhofer.de* (€€). Sits at the entrance to the castle, is comfortable and modern.

ⓘ **Wasserburg >>**
Rathaus,
t (08071) 10522,
www.wasserburg.de

ⓘ **Altötting >>**
Rathaus, Kapellplatz 2a,
t (08671) 8069,
www.altoetting.de

ⓘ **Burghausen >>**
Rathaus, Stadtplatz 112–114, t (08677) 2435,
www.burghausen.de

Hotel Lindacher Hof >

Hotel Lindacher Hof, Mehringerstr 47, t (08677) 9860 www.lindacherhof.de (€€). In the centre, just a short distance from the castle, this stylish traditional hotel has modern four-star facilities such as a gym and sauna.

Klostergasthof Raitenhaslach, Raitenhaslach 9, t (08677) 9730, www. klostergasthof.com (€€–€). Occupies a tastefully converted wing of a 16th-century monastery, 5km southwest of the town centre, with vaulted dining halls and monastic vestiges.

South of Munich

On fine days thousands of *Münchners* flock out to the southern **lakes** to swim, waterski, windsurf, sunbathe and enjoy all the commercial trappings of German *Freizeit* (leisure time). In just one hour you can be out of the city, breathing bracing Alpine air at the seethingly popular Ammersee or Starnberger See, or at the smaller Tegernsee or Schliersee. The more distant Chiemsee has the added attraction of King Ludwig II's grandest palace.

The Lakes

The **Ammersee** and the **Starnberger See**, just a few kilometres apart, are both large, pretty lakes lined with rich *Münchners'* holiday villas. In places it is hard to find a stretch of public beach, and when you do it is likely (in good weather) to be packed with fellow pleasure-seekers. Both lakes allow waterskiing (banned on most other Bavarian lakes), and the water is skimmed by powerboats, yachts and windsurfers.

The main resort on the Ammersee is **Herrsching**, which can get very crowded (you can find quieter public beaches by following the path around the lake). From Herrsching you can walk up through the woods (5km, not all easy going) or catch a bus (no.951 or 956) to **Andechs**, a beautiful 14th-century hill-top monastery. The Gothic church has a fussy rococo interior and the tomb of the composer Carl Orff, but the monks are more famous for their potent beer (*see* 'Where to Stay and Eat South of Munich', p.120).

Most of the eastern shore of the Starnberger See is private property (though there are public beaches at Berg, Leoni and Ammerland). **Starnberg**, right at the top of the lake, is the main resort. From here the cafés, ice-cream stands and windsurfer hire shops spread out down the western shore – a peculiar mixture of Alpine charm and seaside tat. The main beach is at **Possenhofen**, where King Ludwig II drowned (*see* p.175). Today a small wooden cross (occasionally stolen by devotees) marks the spot where he was found, and there is a chapel to his memory nearby.

Tegernsee, surrounded by forests and lush countryside, against a backdrop of the Alps, is a parade ground for Munich's *nouveaux riches* and wealthy industrialists from the north. The best thing to

Getting around South of Munich

Ammersee

40km southwest of Munich, off Autobahn 96; S-Bahn Line 5 to Herrsching (1hr). **Ferries**, run by Schifffahrt auf dem Ammersee (**t** (08143) 229, *www.bayerische-seenschifffahrt.de*) cross the lake to quieter spots (round-trip fares €9.90–15.90).

Starnberger See

30km southwest of Munich, off Autobahn 95; S-Bahn Line 6 to Starnberg (40min). Rent **bicycles** at S-Bahnhof. **Ferries** (*www.bayerische-seenschifffahrt.de*) cost €14.30 round trip or €2.50 per stop.

Tegernsee and Schliersee

Two lakes 8km apart and 50km south of Munich, off Autobahn 8. **Rail** connections from Munich Hauptbahnhof (just over 1hr).

Chiemsee

80km southeast of Munich, on Autobahn 8. Frequent **rail** connections from Munich Hauptbahnhof to Prien am Chiemsee (1hr); **ferries** cross to the islands, contact Chiemsee Schifffahrt, Seestraße 108, **t** (08051) 6090, *www.chiemsee-schifffahrt.de* (grand tour €10.70).

Wallberg
www.wallbergbahn.de;
Wallbergbahn cable car
goes from the southern
village of Rottach-
Egern; €14 return

do is to join the hang-gliders on the peak of the 1,722m-high Wallberg, from where you get a detached and spectacular view. The Benedictine **Kloster** dates from the early 16th century. Maximilian I turned it into a summer home, and nowadays it is a beer tavern. The tiny **Schliersee**, on the other hand, is far less crowded and uptight, and has a charming country atmosphere. People still wear traditional dress on feast days for their own sakes, and not for tourist photographs. You can mess about in little boats with no fear of being flattened by something fast, and the hang-glider air traffic is not quite so thick. It is also a pleasant place to swim, as the water in summer can reach 25°C, a good 5°C warmer than the larger lakes.

Schloß
Herrenchiemsee
www.herren-
chiemsee.de; open
April–Sept daily 9–6;
Oct daily 10–5;
Nov–Mar daily 10–4;
adm €7

Chiemsee, 40km further west, is a vast lake popular with water sports enthusiasts, but best known as the location of **Schloß Herrenchiemsee**, Ludwig II's final and most ambitious building project. Ludwig idolized the Sun King, Louis XIV of France, and was determined to build a replica of Versailles in Bavaria. With this in mind he bought **Herreninsel**, an island on the Chiemsee, in 1873. The cornerstone of the new palace was laid five years later. Ludwig's generous patronage of the composer Wagner, and earlier fantasy castles at Linderhof and Neuschwanstein, had all but bankrupted state coffers. This time the king's ministers tried to temper his ambitious plans, but in the end Ludwig got his own way. He sent back plan after plan drawn up by the architect George Dollmann, until finally his proposed palace reached the dimensions of the French original. The garden façade at Herrenchiemsee is an exact replica of the Versailles garden façade, but money ran out in 1885 after only the central part of the palace had been built.

The ferry (*see* above) drops you off at a wooden jetty on the northern end of the island. After running the gauntlet of souvenir kiosks, you follow leafy avenues across the meadows, to come somewhat abruptly upon the formal gardens and splendid façade of the castle. You can only see the **interior** on a guided tour, but this is well worth it for the sumptuous Parade Chamber (an audience hall even more ornate than the one in Versailles); the king's bedroom with its rich, blue, heavily gilded, boat-like bed; the Dining Room with a 'magic table' like the one at Linderhof (*see* p.125) and an exquisitely worked 18-arm Meissen porcelain chandelier; and the stunning Gallery of Mirrors (an exact replica of its Versailles counterpart, with nearly 2,000 candles in the chandeliers and candelabras).

Before Ludwig bought Herreninsel, there was a monastery on the island. **Fraueninsel**, a few hundred yards across the water, was (and still is) the site of a Benedictine nunnery. Most visitors head back to the mainland after seeing Herrenchiemsee, so Fraueninsel is left to the relative calm of the nuns, birds, fishermen and a scattering of holiday residents and tourists. The whitewashed church is a quaint mixture of Romanesque, Gothic and Baroque. Next to it is a distinctive 9th-century octagonal bell tower, topped with a 16th-century onion dome. The Torhalle (gatehouse) has a chapel in the upper storey containing splendid Carolingian frescoes.

Torhalle
open mid-May–end Sept daily 11–5

(i) **Schliersee >>**
Kurverwaltung, Schliersee, t (08026) 60650, www.schliersee.de

(i) **Ammersee >**
Rathausplatz 1, Schondorf, t (08192) 8899, www.ammersee.de

(i) **Chiemsee >>**
Rathausstraße 11, Prien am Chiemsee, t (08051) 69050, www.chiemsee.de

(i) **Tegernsee >**
Kuramt, Hauptstraße 2, Tegernsee, t (08022) 180140, www.tegernsee.de

(i) **Starnbergersee**
Kirchplatz 3, Starnberg, t (08151) 13008, www.sta5.de

Where to Stay and Eat South of München

Ammersee

Kloster Andechs, Ammersee, *www.andechs.de*. Brews potent beers, which you can drink overlooking the valley below the monastery. In deference to the surroundings, there are signs commanding *Singen und Lärmen nicht gestattet* (noise and singing not permitted). The *Bockbier* is so powerful it's only served during the week – it caused too many road accidents at weekends. They serve delicious fare (try the creamy beer soup).

Tegernsee

Bräustüberl, north wing of the Kloster, Tegernsee, *www.braustuberl.de* (€). Beer hall that's popular with thirsty local farmers. A spirited (if at times rowdy) alternative to the chic cafés elsewhere on the lake.

Fischerstüberl am See, Seestraße 51, t (08022) 919890, *www.hotel-fischer stueberl-tegernsee.de* (€). Cosy inn with a leafy terrace overlooking the lake. The restaurant serves superb fresh fish.

Schliersee

Haus Huber am See, Seestraße 10, t (08026) 6619, *www.landhotel-huber.de* (€). Simple, cheery boarding house a few mins' walk from the lake.

Chiemsee

See Hotel Wassermann, Ludwig-Thoma-Straße 1, Seebruck am Chiemsee, t (08667) 8710, *www.hotel-wassermann.de* (€€€). Large rooms with balconies smothered in geraniums, and inspirational views of Chiemsee and the Chiemgauer Alps; small pool and sauna downstairs. The owners rent bicycles and organize tours.

Herrenchiemsee Beer Terrace, Herreninsel, near the jetty (€€–€). Shady spot with a fine view over the lake. Despite being in such a tourist trap, the food (*Schnitzels*, sausages and other tourist standards) is well cooked and reasonable.

Klosterwirt Café, Fraueninsel, next to the Kloster, *www.kloster wirt-chiemsee.de* (€). Charming café overlooking the lake on the pretty and reposeful nuns' island. Try the fiery *Klostergeist* (a liqueur distilled by the nuns themselves).

Bavarian Alps

The craggy Bavarian Alps stand shoulder to shoulder, just an hour's drive from Munich. At times they plummet abruptly to the edges of icy, sparkling lakes, or stretch out into luscious meadows and rolling forest-land. The air is invigorating and clear: the mournful tune of cowbells carries for miles across the valleys. The hillsides are dotted with traditional chalets, with long balconies cascading with flowers.

In winter, skiers shoot about the slopes and crowd into warm Gaststätten *to drink* Glühwein *or hot chocolate. In summer you can see women in headscarves working in the fields, cowherds leading prized animals up to mountainside grazing lands, and village folk in traditional* Tracht (costume) *for a wedding or feast day.*

This part of Bavaria appeals particularly to nature-lovers and winter-sports enthusiasts, though here you will also find King Ludwig II's most charming and eccentric castle, and high culture in the form of the famous Oberammergau Passion Play.

08

Don't miss

🟊 *Lüftlmalerei* and the Passion Play
Oberammergau **p.122**

🟊 Ludwig II's retreat
Schloß Linderhof **p.124**

🟊 Autumn *Viehscheid*
Allgäu villages **p.131**

🟊 Alpine hiking trails
Around Oberjoch **p.132**

🟊 Heal yourself with water
The Kneipp spa belt **p.137**

See map overleaf

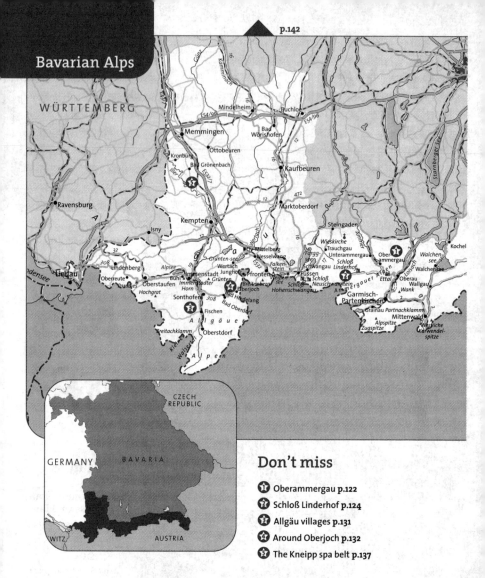

Bavarian Alps

Don't miss

🟊 Oberammergau **p.122**

🟊 Schloß Linderhof **p.124**

🟊 Allgäu villages **p.131**

🟊 Around Oberjoch **p.132**

🟊 The Kneipp spa belt **p.137**

Oberammergau and its Surroundings

🟊 Oberammergau

Oberammergau, about 90km southwest of Munich on the B23 (off Autobahn 95), is a small town crushed against a sheer granite mountain face and teeming with tourists nearly the whole year through. Most come simply because the town is famous, and are surprised by how pretty it is. Wander through the streets to look at the *Lüftlmalerei*, the bright frescoes that adorn many Alpine homes. These paintings (usually of biblical scenes) became the

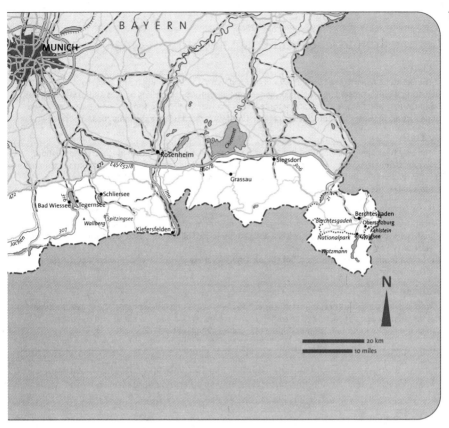

rage in the Counter-Reformation, when displays of religious zeal were encouraged. Fresco-painting was an expensive business, but this town prospered from Passion Play tourism and woodcarving even in the 18th century. Old *Lüftlmalerei* abound, and the tradition continues. Some of the best examples are by local artist Franz Seraph Zwinck (1749–92). His **Pilatushaus** (in Verlegergasse) is an exquisite work of controlled design and skilful *trompe l'œil* that far surpasses the other façades, some of which seem wilfully kitsch.

When they aren't donning robes and learning lines, a large proportion of Oberammergauers are chipping away at blocks of wood. The town is renowned for its **woodcarving**, and the streets are lined with shops selling crucifixes, cherubs, Nativity scenes and chunky toys. Some shops (such as Holzschnitzerei Josef Albl in Devrientweg, and the Pilatushaus, which is now a crafts centre) have workshops attached where you can watch the craftsfolk chiselling.

Four kilometres down the B23 is **Kloster Ettal**, a 14th-century Benedictine monastery that got a facelift during the Counter-

Getting around Oberammergau and Surroundings

By Car

The **Deutsche Alpenstraße** (German Mountain Road) is a signposted route from Lindau to Berchtesgaden. Completed in 2002, this engineering feat, with 105 tunnels, 15 bridges and 10 viaducts, was begun in 1933, and follows a spectacular route. Minor roads are well made, though some passes are steep and twisting. In winter, fit snow tyres or carry chains if you intend to leave the main road.

By Train

The only track along the length of the Alps is in Austria (linking Feldkirch with Innsbruck and Salzburg). However, there are numerous rail routes from Munich: Mittenwald and Oberammergau (both 1hr 40mins), Berchtesgaden (2½–3hrs), Garmisch-Partenkirchen (1hr 20mins). A *Sonderrück-fahrkarte*, round-trip ticket, almost halves the cost.

Bus Tours

Berchtesgaden Mini Bus Tours, at Berchtesgaden tourist information centre, t (08652) 64971, *www.eagles-nest-tours.com*. Eagles Nest Tours offers a detailed 4hr tour of all the sites associated with Hitler and the Nazi Party. Space is limited, so book.

Panorama Tours, Arnulfstrasse. 8, t (089) 591504. Offers a variety of trips: Berchtesgaden (€41), Linderhof/Neuschwanstein (€43).

Walking

A great way to explore. Local tourist offices can suggest routes and provide maps. The state government has declared six areas of pasture to be common land, where you roam as you please and come across cabins offering snacks and fresh milk. Tourist offices have details of these, too.

Reformation. Ettal pales by comparison with other Bavarian churches, but it does have a splendid cupola fresco by the Tyrolean artist Johann-Jakob Zeiller.

Schloß Linderhof

⭐ Schloß Linderhof
www.schloss linderhof.de; open daily April–mid-Oct 9–6; mid-Oct–Mar 9.30–4; adm €7 including Grotto and Kiosk, €6 in winter

Ten kilometres to the west of Kloster Ettal is the oddest and most bewitching of King Ludwig II's castles. Ludwig was an absolutist, deeply opposed to his father's namby-pamby ideas of constitutional monarchy. He hero-worshipped the French Bourbons, especially Louis XIV. He wanted to replace Maximilian II's modest hunting lodge at Linderhof with a copy of the palace of Versailles, which he planned to call Meicost Ettal (an anagram of Louis XIV's motto *L'état, c'est moi*). He eventually set his ersatz Versailles on Herreninsel (*see* p.119). Linderhof was a retreat where he built a modest 'Royal Villa' (in which the bedroom is by far the biggest room) and filled the park with quirky pavilions and stage sets for re-enacting scenes from Wagner's operas. Like an enchanted prince, Ludwig would descend on Schloß Linderhof in a golden rococo sleigh, with attendants in period livery.

fountain
every hour on the hour 9–5

The Schloß is a modest, dumpy Baroque imitation, crisply white and heavily ornamented. It is periodically upstaged by a 30m spurt of water from the gilded fountain set in the middle of a formal parterre garden. In one corner of the garden is the old linden tree that gave the castle its name. Inside, the palace is encrusted with gilded stucco and smothered in tapestries, rich fabrics and exotic carpets (one made of ostrich plumes). The high point is the huge **bedroom** with its 2.7-by-2.1m blue velvet bed, fenced off by a carved and gilded balustrade. In the garden outside, an artificial cascade (built to cool the room in summer) tumbles almost up to the window. In the dining room you can see Ludwig's famous **magic table**, which sank through the floor to be loaded up in the kitchens below, so that the reclusive king could eat alone, often dressed as Louis XIV or the Swan Prince.

Beyond the formal parterres, a wilder 'English Garden' extends for another 50 hectares, gradually blending into the countryside. One of Ludwig's favourite buildings is here, the **Venus Grotto** (1876). This is a 10m-high cavern with a small lake that reproduces the scene in the first act of *Tannhäuser*. Garlands of roses hang between sparkling stalagmites and stalactites made from canvas, cement and lustrous stones. Hidden lights, some underwater, throw streaks of bright, changing colour across the shadows – a spectacular feat of electrical engineering for the time. The gilded shell-shaped boat in which Ludwig loved to be rowed waits empty on the water.

The **Moorish Kiosk** was built for the 1867 Paris Exhibition, then bought by Ludwig. Its stylish minarets look out of place against a backdrop of the Alps. Inside, the enamelled feathers of the **Peacock Throne** stand out even against the kaleidoscopic walls and windows. At the eastern edge of the park is the simple wooden **Hunding's Hut**, based on Wagner's stage directions for the first act of the *Walküre*. It is a recent replica of the original hut (which burnt down in 1945), but isn't worth the walk unless you're an avid Ludwig- or Wagnerophile.

Garmisch-Partenkirchen and Mittenwald

Garmisch-Partenkirchen, Germany's leading ski resort, is on the B2 south of Oberammergau at the foot of the Wetterstein range. The two merged villages retain different atmospheres: Garmisch is glitzy, modern and pricy; Partenkirchen has more village charm and is a little cheaper. Ludwigstraße in Partenkirchen even has some traditional *Lüftlmalerei*.

Most people leave Garmisch-Partenkirchen quickly, either to ski, or for the magnificent views from the mountains. The **Zugspitze** (2,963m) is the highest peak in Germany. To get to the top by public transport, take the *Zugspitzbahn* (electric railway) from central Garmisch to Eibsee; then either a dizzy ride on the

Zugspitze
www.zugspitze.de; both routes from Garmisch €50 return

Eibseebahn cable car to the summit, or rack railway through a tunnel to Hotel Schneeferhaus (2,645m, good skiing in winter) and the *Gipfelbahn* cable car the rest of the way. A cheaper option, with nearly as good a view, is Wank (1,780m), via cable car from the outskirts of Garmisch, where souvenir kiosk proprietors are bemused by the number of postcards sold to British visitors. Hikers can tackle the challenging **Alpspitze** (2,628m), or strike out on a path hewn from the rock in the dramatic **Partnachklamm** gorge, to the southeast.

Wank
€18.50 return, €12 single

Mittenwald (20km farther southeast, just off the B2) is prettier, less touristy and has a far more authentic atmosphere. Chalets with bright frescoes and overhanging eaves snuggle in the shadow of jagged peaks; neighbours greet each other in the street; occasionally an ancient tractor chugs through town. The pews in the local church have family name-plates fixed on the end. In Obermarkt and around Im Gries are some of the richest *Lüftlmalerei* in the district. In 1683 Mathias Klotz, a local who had worked with the great violin-maker Nicolò Amati in Cremona, returned to teach his craft to local woodcarvers. Mittenwald violins, violas and cellos are now world-coveted. The Geigenbau-museum (Museum of Violin-making) at Ballenhausgasse 3, recently renovated, displays some of the finest instruments and documents the history of the craft. Mittenwald's pet mountain is Karwendl (2,385m). The views from the top, over the valley and the Wetterstein range, are even more breathtaking than those from the peaks around Garmisch.

Geigenbau-museum
Ballenhausgasse 3; open Jan–mid-Mar, mid-May–mid-Oct and mid-Dec–mid-Jan Tues–Sun 10–5; other months Tues–Sun 11–4; closed Mon and Nov–mid-Dec; adm €10

Karwendl
cable car €20 return, €11 single

Berchtesgadener Land

Berchtesgadener Land
www.nationalpark-berchtesgaden.de

In the southeast corner of Germany, on the Austrian border, is the Berchtesgadener Land, where (local legend goes) dawdling angels distributing wonders and beauty around the globe were so startled by a divine order to hurry up that they dropped the lot. Some of the mightiest mountains of the Alps crowd around a slender lake and a lush valley, now a National Park.

At the beginning of the 12th century, Augustinian monks built a priory at Berchtesgaden and established what was to become one of the smallest states in the Holy Roman Empire. In 1190 the discovery of huge deposits of salt ('white gold') made the prince-provosts of Berchtesgaden as wealthy as their neighbours in Salzburg (Salt City). The state was incorporated into Bavaria in the 19th century, and the Wittelsbachs converted the priory into a royal residence. But the name Berchtesgaden has a more sour historical connotation: it was here, in a village just above the town, that statesmen (including Neville Chamberlain) came to visit Hitler in his country retreat, in the vain hope of preventing an invasion of the Sudetenland (*see* **History**, p.26).

The hillside town of **Berchtesgaden** teems with tourists. The frantically busy road through the centre quenches any Alpine charm, but Berchtesgaden has more than pretty houses and winter sports. In the Renaissance rooms of the Wittelsbach **Schloß** is part of the sacred art collection of Crown Prince Ruprecht, son of the last King of Bavaria, who lived here from 1923 to 1955. The German woodcarving is especially good, and there is fine porcelain and Italian furniture. A charming Romanesque cloister and Gothic dormitory survive from the medieval priory.

Schloß
*www.haus-bayern.com;
open Pentecost–15 Oct
Sun–Fri 10–1 and 2–5,
closed Sat;
16 Oct–April Mon–Fri
11–2; adm €8*

In the simple **Franziskanerkirche** at the southern end of town you can see a graceful Baroque carving of Christ, and (in the adjoining graveyard) convincing testimony to the healthy mountain air – the tomb of one Anton Adner who lived from 1705 to 1822.

A tour of the disused shafts of a working salt mine, the **Salzbergwerk** may not sound enticing, but is not to be missed. Men don traditional thick leather kidney-warmers; women get baggy white trousers (skirts are not advisable). You huddle together astride a wagon that carries you down a tunnel deep into the mine, then slide down a 30m-long chute into an enormous vault, glittering with salt crystals. Here you're shown a film and a real miner explains how the equipment works. Then it's off down another long chute to an enormous underground lake where, a little like Ludwig II in his magic grotto at Linderhof (*see* p.125), you are borne across the black water on a wooden boat. Finally you're whisked back up to the surface by lift and train.

Salzbergwerk
*www.salzzeitreise.de;
open May–1 Nov daily
9–5; Nov–30 April
Mon–Sat 11.30–3; tour
1½hrs; adm €12.50*

The **Königssee** (5km south of Berchtesgaden, buses from Hauptbahnhof) is a thin, fjord-like lake hooked around the foot of the **Watzmann** (2,713m), Germany's second-highest mountain. Crowds flock here whatever the weather; escape them by taking the electric ferry which makes a round trip past dramatic mountain scenery.

Ferry
round trip €14

High in the mountains east of Berchtesgaden is **Obersalzberg**, the site of Hitler's **Berghof**, his mountain retreat. The house was badly bombed in the war, and destroyed by US troops in 1952. A better reason to visit is the 'Eagle's Nest', a restaurant at the summit of the 1,834m **Kehlstein**. The Eagle's Nest was built as a teahouse and given by Martin Bormann (Hitler's adviser) to his boss as a birthday present, but it was seldom used. Today it is very commercialized, but nothing can detract from the splendid view across the Alps – as far as Salzburg in clear weather.

Kehlstein
*May–Oct, special buses
take you from the
village up a magnificent
winding road, and you
travel the last 124m in
a lift inside the
mountain; €19 return
from Berchtesgaden*

08 Bavarian Alps | Obergammergau and its Surroundings: Berchtesgadener Land

Festivals around Oberammergau

Oberammergau Passion Play

The Passion Play began in 1634 after residents, worried by signs of plague in the village, vowed that if it developed no further their descendants would perform the Passion of Jesus every ten years, forever. No one in Oberammergau died of the disease, and for generations townsfolk have honoured the pledge, though in 1680 the performance date was moved to coincide with the beginning of the decade (the next one is in 2010).

The text has had a chequered history. A bawdy original was cleaned up in 1750 and put into high Baroque verse. The 19th century saw the first prose version; recent modernizations have expunged rampant anti-Semitism.

Nowadays the Passion takes place in a vast 1930s open-air theatre. The spectacle lasts the whole day (with a 2hr lunch break); nearly half a million people see the 100-odd performances between May and September. *Passion Oberammergau* is Village Hall Nativity Play writ enormous. Only locals (1,500 of them) take part, men cultivating their biblical beards for months beforehand. Even the props are made by local craftspeople alone, and tradition dictates that a local virgin plays Mary. There was outrage in 1990 when not only was the Mother of God portrayed by a mother of two, but (even worse in Bavaria) another of the lead actors was a *Protestant*.

Other Festivals

As a Roman Catholic stronghold, the Bavarian Alps have many religious festivals, often involving street processions, dressing up in *Tracht* and feasting. **Corpus Christi** has the richest local dress, especially around Oberammergau: men wear knee breeches and bright waistcoats; women have brocaded dresses and otter-fur bonnets. On **Palm Sunday** the rites have intriguing pagan undertones. Churches, streets and homes are decorated with *Palmbosch'n* (silvery willows) festooned with *Geschabertbandl* (dyed woodshavings). Cuts are made in the bark to let out witches and druids (not viewed as favourably in Bavaria as in Wales). Children carry the branches to church to be blessed, and then out into the fields where they are left to ensure protection for the year ahead.

The *Viehscheid*, the autumn cattle-drive, is the most colourful of all village events. Hardy cowherds decorate their animals with elaborate *Faikl* – headdresses made of ribbons, leaves, feathers and flowers, sometimes up to a metre high – and bring them down from the high Alpine pastures. This takes place around *Michaeli* (29 September), though much depends on the weather and it is better to enquire locally. In **May or June** the cowherds and their charges head back for the mountains (without quite so much display). The cattle drives take place in towns throughout the mountains and foothills; the earliest autumn drive is usually in Garmisch-Partenkirchen (early September), and the last in Königssee (as late as October), where the cows have to make the last part of their journey by boat. *See also p.133.*

Shopping around Oberammergau

Violins

If you have money to spend on a violin, head for **Mittenwald**, where Anton Maller (Stainergasse 14) sells instruments of world renown. Or you can settle for a chocolate or marzipan version, on sale all over town.

Woodcarvings

For centuries **Oberammergau** dealers have sold woodcarvings from local workshops. Most carving has a religious theme, and much is churned out for the souvenir market, but there are some fine artists at work. For a bit extra you can commission a piece.

Toni Baur, Dorfstraße 27. Vibrant secular pieces.

Josef Albl, Devrientweg 1. For more traditional religious work.

Pilatushaus, in Verlegergasse. Prices are slightly lower at this craft centre and co-op.

In **Berchtesgaden** the carvers concentrate more on dolls, toy horse-carriages and *Spanschachteln*, brightly painted wooden boxes. You can get all of these at Schloß Adelsheim (Schroffenbergallee 6).

Sports and Activities around Oberammergau

Hiking and Rock-climbing

Hikers are very well catered for. Alpine refuges all over the mountains offer shelter, refreshment and often overnight facilities at minimal cost. There are some excellent marked routes: local tourist offices have maps and details. **Mountaineering** schools, such as the **Bergsteigerschule Karwendl-Wetterstein**, Dekan-Karl-Platz 29, Mittenwald, **t** (08823) 93002, offer courses and guides.

Winter Sports

The best **skiing** is in the western part of this region. Garmisch-Partenkirchen is still a World Cup downhill, super-giant slalom and ski jump centre, and cheaper than most Swiss resorts. There are two classic black pistes on the Zugspitze and Kreuzeck Hausberg; beginners will be happier on the gentler slopes of Wank. Mittenwald and Oberammergau specialize in cross-country skiing. The season is generally Dec–April, though it can last longer.

Runs are not as exciting around Berchtesgaden, though they are pretty, but the town is a vibrant centre for other winter sports such as **tobogganing**, **skating**, **curling** and **ice-skittles**.

Other Sports

Hang-gliding, **ballooning**, **cycling** and **white-water rafting** are popular. You can hire equipment and get tuition in most of the resorts. Try **Outdoor Club Berchtesgaden**, Gmundberg 7, Berchtesgaden, **t** (08652) 97760, *www.outdoor-club.de*; or **Heinzelmann-Reisen**, Artenreitweg 13, Schönau am Königssee, **t** (08652) 2530, *www.mix-tours.de*.

Where to Stay and Eat around Oberammergau

Private rooms in local houses go for just €30–40 per person (including breakfast). Look out for signs saying *Fremdenzimmer*, or ask at the tourist office. You will have most luck in Oberammergau, or nearby Unterammergau, an authentic little farming village. In **youth hostels B&B** will cost you only €20–25.

Oberammergau

Hotel Böld, König-Ludwig-Straße 10, **t** (08822) 9120, *www.hotel-boeld.de* (€€). Smart hotel with a lick of Alpine charm and a herbal sauna, steam bath, solarium and Jacuzzi – in fact most of what you need for a hedonistic holiday.

Hotel Wolf, Dorfstraße 1, **t** (08822) 92330, *www.hotel-wolf.de* (€€). Modern Bavarian-style hotel just a few minutes' walk from the Passionstheater. Rooms in the top two storeys have wooden balconies, window boxes and mountain views. A hotel for dog lovers, with doggie showers and lots of four-legged activities.

Hotel Alte Post, Dorfstraße 19, **t** (08822) 9100, *www.altepost.com* (€). Rustic Bavarian hotel braving a busy junction in the middle of town.

Pension Almrose, Pürschlingweg 3a, **t** (08822) 4369 (€, without private bath). Clean and friendly, with an Alp at the bottom of its garden.

Jugendherberge, Malensteinweg 10, **t** (08822) 4114. Youth hostel.

Berggasthof Kolben-Alm, take Kolben-Alm cable car, **t** (08822) 6364, *www.kolbenalm.de* (€€–€). Small hillside guesthouse that serves great cold meat platters and steamy noodle-rich Bavarian food. You might catch a *Hüttenabend* if you're lucky, when locals and hikers get together for a festive sing song.

Café Hochenleitner, Faistemantel-gasse 7, **t** (08822) 1312 (€). The best place to head to sample Bavarian country baking: good coffee and a tempting array of *Torte*.

Zauberstuberl, Eugene-Papst-Straße 3a (€). Cosy spot for lunch, especially

---

(i) **Oberammergau >>**
Eugen-Papst-Straße 9a,
t *(08822) 92310,*
www.oberammergau.de

(★) **Hotel Böld >>**

(i) **Garmisch-Partenkirchen** >
Kurverwaltung, Richard-Strauss-Platz, t (08821) 180700, www.garmisch-partenkirchen.de

(i) **Berchtesgaden** >>
Königsseerstraße 2 (near Bahnhof), t (08652) 9670, www.berchtesgadener-land.com

(★) **Alpenhof** >

(i) **Mittenwald** >
Dammkarstraße 3, t (08823) 330

(★) **Die Alpenrose** >

in winter when the chef comes up with five or six hearty, warming soups.

Garmisch-Partenkirchen

Posthotel Partenkirchen, Ludwigstraße 49, t (08821) 93630 (€€). Atmospheric old coaching inn.

Ohlsenhof, Von-Brug-Straße 18, t (08821) 2168, www.ohlsenhof.de (€). Friendly, well-run and popular with young travellers.

Jugendherberge, Jochstraße 10, t (08821) 2980, www.hihostels.com. Youth hostel.

Alpenhof, Bahnhofstraße 74, t (08821) 59055 (€€€–€€). Wide variety of local cuisine, from snacks to finely cooked fish, served up in defeatingly generous portions.

Mittenwald

Die Alpenrose, Obermarkt 1, t (08823) 9270, www.hotel-alpenrose-mittenwald.de (€€–€). A 13th-century merchant's house with painted ceilings, panelled nooks and flourishes of carving in the bedrooms, right in the centre of one of the prettiest towns in the region.

Alpengasthof Groebl Alm, Mittenwald/Oberammergau, t (08823) 9110, www.groeblalm.de (€). Located above Mittenwald, a chalet-style hotel run by the Leuthner family, with spectacular Alpine views, nice rooms and a generous breakfast. Shepherds bring their goats down the hill right in front of your balcony.

Post Hotel, Obermarkt 9, t (08823) 9382 333, www.posthotel-mittenwald.de (€). Considers itself a dash above the Alpenrose up the road. More upmarket, but not as cosy.

Jugendherberge, Buckelwiesen 7, t (08823) 1701, www.hihostels.com. Youth hostel.

Berchtesgaden

Hotel Vierjahrszeiten, Maximilianstraße 20, t (08652) 5026, www.hotel-vierjahreszeiten-berchtesgaden.de (€€–€). Sleepy old hotel with a modern, angular extension. Ask for a room with a balcony and mountain view. The popular **restaurant** serves excellent fish and game dishes such as venison *tournedos* in a sauce of three kinds of mushrooms.

Hotel Krone, Am Rad 5, t (08652) 9460, www.hotel-krone-berchtesgaden.de (€). Quiet, family-run hotel with fine views, away from the bustle of town, and with a sunny breakfast terrace.

Hotel-Pension Floriani, Königsseer Straße 37, t (08652) 66011, f (08652) 63453 (€). Close to town; the affable owners, Wilfred and Ursula Conserti, speak English. Most rooms have balconies.

Pension Haus am Berg, Am Brandholz 9, t (08652) 94920 (€). On the hillside above the town, and good value. Most rooms have a balcony.

The Allgäu

Legend has it that it was in the Allgäu that the Devil tempted Christ. The offer must have been hard to refuse: it's an alluring mix of lush pastures and towering mountains. This archetypal Bavarian countryside in fact belonged to neighbouring Swabia, and locals still have a reputation for Swabian staidness. Closer to Augsburg, the countryside opens up a little and sightseeing gives way to outdoor fun. The health resorts and magnificent mountain churches are popular with the Germans, though foreigners tend to whizz by on their way to better-known Alpine resorts. This is also cheese country (*see* box, p.132): no visit is complete without sampling some of the local fare.

Getting around the Allgäu

By Train

There are regular connections between Augsburg, Bad Wörishofen and Füssen; and between Augsburg and Oberstdorf (change here for Lindau and Pfronten).

By Car

The best way to see the Allgäu Alps is using your own transport. The 120km stretch from Füssen to Lindau follows the breathtaking route of the Deutsche Alpenstraße (*see* 'Getting around Oberammergau: By Car', p.124). At Sonthofen the B308 meets the B19 to Oberstdorf.

By Bus

Regional bus services are run by German Rail, operating Füssen–Oberstdorf, Füssen–Pfronten, Sonthofen–Oberstdorf and Oberstaufen–Lindau. Local services run between Oberstdorf and the Kleinwalsertal.

Hiking

To appreciate both the scenery and the rural life you really need to get out and walk in the Allgäu Alps. There's a profusion of well-signposted hiking trails. These 4–6hr hikes wind among towering peaks, including the Heilbronner Weg near Oberstdorf and the less demanding Hörnertour near Fischen. Tourist offices can give you advice on guided walks, and sell trail maps.

Cable Cars

Several cable car services offer pain-free ascent to many peaks and panoramic viewpoints. The Untere Breitenberg (10mins), the Nebelhorn (20mins), the Fellhorn (15mins), the Kanzelwand (20mins), the Walmendiger Horn (15mins) and the Hochgrat (20mins) are accessible by gondola.

08

Bavarian Alps | The Allgäu: The Allgäu Alps from Füssen to Lindau

The Allgäu Alps from Füssen to Lindau

⭐ Allgäu villages

The Allgäu Alps, between the Upper Bavarian Alps to the east and the Austrian border to the south, peter out towards the west and the shores of the Bodensee. Romantic foothills build up to a more rugged landscape strung with highland **villages**. The peaks of this 150km mountain range don't rise as high as in the Upper Bavarian Alps (none is above 2,600m), but belvederes dotted about the area offer vast panoramas of picture-book scenery. **Füssen** is a popular starting point for visits to the royal castles of Neuschwanstein and Hohenschwangau (*see* pp.173–6), and is the southernmost town of the Romantic Road (*see* chapter 09). The health resort isn't an auspicious beginning to this well-trodden route since, despite its age and pretty river setting, there is not much to see except for an odd 17th-century Dance of Death fresco in the **St-Anna-Kapelle**, attached to the church of St Mang.

Skirting the Weißensee and a plateau area offering wonderful views of Füssen against the Säuling (2,041m), the road goes to **Pfronten**, a federation of 13 villages in the Pfrontener Tal dating back to a medieval 'farmers' republic' with its own constitution. The 'sun terraces' on the Breitenberg (1,838m) and the Falkenstein (1,277m), as well as the Hochalpe skiing area (1,500m), offer hiking and winter sports, while the villagers get on with cattle-farming.

The Allgäu Cheese Industry

The Allgäu is renowned for the quality of its cheese and is glibly referred to as Germany's *Käseküche* (cheese kitchen). Today, half a million Allgäu cows produce more than two billion litres of milk every year. Two-thirds of this output is made into cheese, accounting for 25 per cent of the German market.

The Allgäu has long been a dairy-farming area, but cheese is a relatively recent product. Carl Hirnbein, a farmer from Grünten, brought in Dutch and Swiss cheesemakers in the mid-19th century. Within 50 years, brands such as Allgäuer Limburger, Emmentaler and Bergkäse won nationwide recognition. Within a further 20 years the cheesemaker Josef Kramer from Wertach added the Weißlacker cheese to the list. Experts are still not sure whether the distinctive nature of Allgäu cheeses was developed intentionally or accidentally as a result of the failure to imitate other cheeses. But whether scientific discovery or happy accident, the cheeses are full of flavour and well worth sampling.

North of Pfronten, on the B309, lies Nesselwang. Just before you reach this health and winter sports resort, turn left and continue to the **Wallfahrtskirchlein Maria Trost** at the foothill of the Alpspitze (1,575m). This Baroque pilgrimage church, built between 1662 and 1725 and draped with rococo frescoes, is one of the finest small churches in the Bavarian Alps.

Down the B310 from Oy-Mittelberg, past the Grüntensee, is **Wertach**. Both towns are health resorts famed for their peaceful, recuperative atmospheres. It's then just a few kilometres to **Jungholz**, an Austrian enclave only accessible from the German side. For just under 700 years this resort has been Austrian and enjoys the same economic status as the Kleinwalsertal (*see* box, p.134).

A few kilometres from where the B310 runs into the B308, the Jochstraße winds up to the **Kanzel**, a vantage point overlooking the magnificent Ostrach valley (famous for its wild flowers), and farther on to the high mountain village of **Oberjoch**, before turning into the valley to **Bad Hindelang**. Together with neighbouring **Bad Oberdorf**, this town is one of the most important health resorts in the Allgäu Alps. Its most intriguing sight is the **St Jodok-Kirche**, an ordinary little church that contains the **Hindelanger Altar**, a beautiful 16th-century altarpiece by Jörg Lederer, one of the region's most celebrated artists. For keen hikers, this area offers numerous beautiful **trails** through uninhabited forests and along the jagged limestone heights of the surrounding mountains. It is possible to reach the summits of three peaks from here: the Daumen (2,280m), the Geißhorn (2,249m) and the Hochvogel (2,593m).

⭐ Alpine hiking trails

Beyond Hindelang, below the Grünten (1,738m), is **Sonthofen**, site of the **Ordensburg**, built in 1935 as a training centre for Hitler's military élite and still a military barracks. The old winter sports resort suffered severe war damage, though the most important monuments have been carefully restored. The Gothic **Pfarrkirche St Michael** is particularly interesting. Rebuilt in the Baroque style, the church contains wooden altar-figures carved by Anton Sturm in 1748 that resemble those he made for the better-known Wieskirche (*see* p.173).

From Sonthofen you can either head due west or take a much more rewarding detour that cuts deep through the most spectacular mountain valleys and peaks of the **Upper Allgäu**, eventually ducking into the Tyrolean Alps. Skiing in the area is second only to that in the Bavarian Alps, and there's an excellent network of marked hiking trails. The upland plateaux are covered with forests of pine and fir, while May to July sees the Alpine countryside awash with cyclamen, rhododendron, anemones, gentian and – still farther up – the edelweiss.

First stop along the B19 is the picturesque resort of **Fischen**. Just beyond it lies **Oberstdorf**, the southernmost village in Germany. The resort is now a popular winter sports centre, but its quaintness remains: it has never outgrown the characteristics of a mountain village. Oberstdorf forms the end of the Iller valley, and the slowly rising, rocky mountainsides that surround the place make hill-walking much the best way to explore the area. One of the most spectacular hikes takes you east along the peaks and gorges of ten 2,000m-high mountains to the lush Oy valley. The **Breitachklamm** is a deep, impressively curling riverine gorge, very narrow in places, with the gushing white water of the Breitach shooting over mossy rocks and lined by ancient forests. Until the turn of the 19th century this amazing gorge was known as the Zwing, and was allegedly haunted by gruesome spectres called *Zwinggeister*. As you near the Austrian border the road runs to the **Kleinwalsertal**, on the Austrian side (*see* box, p.134).

On the B308 past Immenstadt is the **Großer Alpsee**, a mountain lake around the foot of a set of craggy heights. For a great view of the lake and surrounding peaks ascend on foot to the hilly **Immenstädter Horn** (1,489m).

08 Bavarian Alps | The Allgäu: The Allgäu Alps from Füssen to Lindau

The *Viehscheid*

The clanking of cowbells could be the Allgäu's theme tune. Agricultural life makes itself felt splendidly in the pastoral tradition of the *Viehscheid*. The autumn events that take place in villages all around the Allgäu Alps (usually in the second or third week of September) are among the bucolic highlights of the Bavarian calendar.

At the end of summer grazing, herds of cattle are driven down from pastures high in the alps. Before reaching the villages, the herds are decked out in colourful finery: the lead cows (only one in every herd) wear large ornamental headdresses made by the farmers' wives, and often huge ceremonial cowbells. The rest of the cows are decorated with smaller bunches of brightly coloured flowers. The herds are then driven into the villages, where the inhabitants offer thanks for their safe return.

So many people, tourists and locals alike, come to see these events each year that the accompanying beer tents are often larger than the pastures that the cows have come from. Some villages don't even advertise their *Viehscheid* festivals any more in the hope that they won't get overwhelmed by outside visitors. The festivals can seem very touristy, but they are usually a serious matter for the villagers. The thanksgiving is a solemn tribute to the animals they depend on for their livelihood. If a cow is killed in an accident in the high pastures, there is usually no *Viehscheid* that autumn.

The Kleinwalsertal

The Kleinwalsertal, jutting into the Allgäu Alps from Austria, is an oddity. In the 13th century the *Walser* (emigrants from the Upper Valais, now in Switzerland) populated this valley, and soon found themselves subjects of the dukes of Tyrol.

Through the centuries, the *Walsers'* economic survival as highland farmers proved barely tenable. They felt cut off from Austria by the Allgäu Alps, especially in winter. In 1891 the situation was reversed when this isolated valley was granted the special status of a *Zollausschlußgebiet* (customs-free zone). The result is a mix of Austrian sovereignty and German economic administration. Today the hamlets of the Kleinwalsertal have Austrian police under Austrian law (passport not required), German customs and a German postal service but Austrian stamps. In the days before the euro, the only legal tender was the Deutschmark, and the Austrian phone boxes only took German coins. Look out for the unusual costume of the female Walser, consisting of loose-fitting black dresses and brown fur hats.

Oberstaufen
www.oberstaufen.de

Down the road, along the beautiful Konstanzer Tal, is **Oberstaufen**, at the foot of the Hochgrat massif (1,834m). Until 1947 this spa was a sleepy village known for its pure air. Then a refugee physician set up a clinic modelled on the unique Schroth dietetics, which claim to purge the body through special dietary rules, towel-packs and drinking cures. Oberstaufen, the only approved Schroth health resort in Germany, has over 80 clinics, sanatoriums and health hotels. Seek out the **Bauernhofmuseum** (Farming Museum), a little way back at **Knechtenhofen**. It has an original Alpine farmhouse on site and offers fascinating insights into the rural culture of the Allgäu as it was and, to some extent, still is.

Bauernhof-museum
open May–Oct Wed 2–5, Sun 10–12; adm €2

Westwards the B308 tops the **Paradies** (908m), in a high horseshoe bend that winds its way along a steep gradient down into the Weißach valley. Do take time to stop at the atmospheric **Café Paradies** on this road, as it affords stunning vistas over some fine forested hills of the Bregenzer mountains – as far as the distant Appenzell Alps in Switzerland on a clear day.

Lindenberg
www.lindenberg.de

Hutmuseum
Hirschstraße; open Wed 3–5.30, Fri–Sun 10–12; adm €1

Northwest of Oberreute is the small, well-preserved town of **Lindenberg**. It is now chiefly known for the quality of the Allgäu cheese from its dairies (*see* box, p.132). Before leaving, have a look at the **Hutmuseum** (Hat Museum). In the 18th century local horse dealers adopted the art of straw-weaving from Italy and developed a thriving hat factory. The museum contains specimens of hats from around 1850 to the present, and includes live demonstrations showing how straw hats are made. Towards Lindau the road weaves from the eastern foothills of the Pfänder (1,064m), running close to the Austrian border, with amazing views of the **Bodensee** (Lake Constance).

Lindau

Tourists flock across the causeway to the island resort of Lindau and its bustling, colourful, rather Mediterranean town. Lindau has little bits of everything, from 13th-century fortification towers to the spanking new *Inselhalle* recreation centre.

In town (on Reichsplatz, near the harbour) look out for the delightfully eccentric 15th-century **Altes Rathaus** with its curly gables, witty *trompe l'œil* and gaudy frescoes. On Marktplatz, to the north, is the **Haus zum Gavazzen**, a Baroque patrician palace with rather more muted murals, which houses the Stadtmuseum (Town Museum), an ideal museum for a rainy day. Downstairs are *Totentafeln*, wooden fold-out tables from the 17th century, used to depict a dead notable's life and achievements. The first floor has some fine period rooms; further up are old clocks, dolls' houses, traditional painted furniture and occasional glimpses out across the red roofs of Lindau. The collection of **mechanical musical instruments** is a good place to round off your visit.

On the other side of town, beneath the multi-turreted **Diebsturm** (Thief's Tower, built in 1350) is the earthy little 11th-century **St-Peter-Kirche**, which houses a superb *Passion Cycle* by Holbein the Elder – his only surviving frescoes.

Stadtmuseum
open April–Oct Tues–Fri and Sun 11–5, Sat 2–5; adm €2.50; for the mechanical musical instruments, guided tours only, at 3 and 4.45pm, 30mins

08 Bavarian Alps | The Allgäu

(i) **Lindau >>**
Ludwigstraße 68, t (08382) 260030, http://lindau-tourismus.de

(i) **Füssen**
Kaiser-Maximilian-Platz 1, t (08362) 93850, www.stadt-fuessen.de

(★) **Gasthof-Pension Grüner Baum >>**

(i) **Oberstdorf >**
Marktplatz 7, t (08322) 7000, www.oberstdorf.de

(★) **Pension Wiese >**

(★) **Restaurant Weinstube Frey >>**

Where to Stay and Eat in the Allgäu

Pfronten

Hotel Bavaria, Kienbergstraße 62, t (08363) 9020, *www.bavaria-pfronten.de* (€€). Modern, chalet-style, with traditional Alpine flair and cuisine, located in the village of Pfronten-Dorf. Rates include use of the 'wellness centre', with indoor and outdoor pools, sauna and whirlpool.

Oberstdorf

Pension Wiese, Stillachstraße 4a, t (08322) 3030, *www.hauswiese.de* (€). Although the Wiese family originate from Hamburg, they have managed to fill each room with an authentically local and charming ambience. It has no restaurant, however.

Oberstaufen

Kurhotel zum Löwen, Kirchplatz 8, t (08386) 4940, *www.loewen-oberstaufen.de* (€€). A centrally located spa hotel in one of the resort's most beautiful houses. The gourmet restaurant excels in salmon dishes and delicious salads.

Lindau

Hotel Bayerischer Hof, Reutemann und Seegarten, Seepromenade, t (08382) 9150, *www.bayerischerhof-lindau.de* (€€€–€€). Large, efficiently run hotel complex set slightly back from the throng, on the promenade.

Hotel Stift, Stiftsplatz 1, t (08382) 93570, *www.hotel-stift.de* (€€). Relaxed, friendly hotel in the Altstadt.

Gasthof-Pension Grüner Baum, Bodenseestraße 14, t (08382) 55 52, *www.gruenerbaum-oberreitnau.de* (€). Hotel with a cozy *Gäststube*, beer garden and sauna. A swimming pool is just down the road and it's a short bus ride to Lindau island.

Restaurant Weinstube Frey, Maximilianstraße 15, t (08382) 5278 (€€). Nondescript from the outside, this place only reveals its historic character in the dining room. The menu focuses on fish from the Bodensee and light, tart wines produced by local vintners.

Gasthaus zum Sünfzen, Maximilianstraße 1, t (08382) 5865 (€). This converted 14th-century house in the Altstadt serves good, plain meals.

North of the Allgäu Alps

This is a gentler, less spectacular journey than the one that leads through the Allgäu Alps, but its course through the Alpine foothills of central Allgäu is nonetheless full of seductive charm. Both Memmingen and Kempten, at the north and south points of the itinerary, are attractive and richly historic. Between them, and in the broad spread of countryside to the east of the road that connects them, lie several towns and villages that in the modern era have become famous as spa resorts.

Memmingen

You don't need to go on a guided walk to get to know Memmingen. The clear arrangement of the historic town with its tiny crisscrossing ducts suits this unhurried provincial market town southwest of Augsburg. Add to this highly original townscape a rich history and a tradition of agreeable festivals, and you have what deserves to be called one of the most enticing small towns in the Allgäu. It's at its most animated during its annual *Fischertag* (*see* p.139).

Memmingen, a Free Imperial City, guarded its municipal wealth behind the **Stadtmauer**, of which five impressive 15th-century gateways survive. The importance of commerce to the town (whose merchants were the first in Germany to establish trade posts in the New World) is shown by the mansions that overshadow the 16th-century **Rathaus**. The most impressive is the **Siebendächerhaus** on Gerberplatz.

Grouped around the Marktplatz, another ensemble of municipal buildings includes the cheerful late 15th-century **Steuerhaus**. This underwent a rococo transformation, tattooing the walls above its ground-level arcades with exuberant green and russet frescoes. Also marking the town's era of prosperity here is the Baroque **Großzunft**, the town's early 18th-century guildhall, its façade enlivened by a graceful balcony.

Buxheim Carthusian monastery
www.kartause-buxheim.de; open April–Oct daily 10–12 and 2–5; Nov–Mar guided tours by arrangement, t 08 33 161804, info@heimatdienst-buxheim.de; adm €2.50

Northwest of Memmingen, **Buxheim**'s former **Carthusian monastery** tells an extraordinary story. In 1691 sculptor Ignaz Waibel carved an elaborate set of 31 early Baroque choir stalls for the *Klosterkirche*. When the monastery was secularized in 1803, these magnificent pieces were sold overseas and eventually found their way to the Bank of England. They were given to an Anglican convent in 1891. When some 70 years later the convent moved from London to Kent, a new Mother Superior pleaded for the return of the stalls to Germany. Only in 1979, though, did the Bavarian authorities succeed in bringing back these lost pieces which, after

Getting around North of the Allgäu Alps

Memmingen is 35km from Kempten on the A7. The best way to visit the small towns and villages along the way, though, is to use the crisscrossing main **roads** in the region.

Rail connections run between Memmingen and Augsburg and Memmingen and Ulm. Kempten can be reached from Munich, Ulm and Augsburg via Kaufbeuren.

Regionalbus offers services from Kempten to Kaufbeuren, Kempten to Füssen, Memmingen to Ottobeuren and Memmingen to Buxheim.

painstaking repair work, were eventually restored to the Carthusian church in Buxheim in July 1994.

Around Memmingen: Kneipp Country

⭐ **The Kneipp spa belt**

The area between Memmingen to Kempten is known as Kneipp country, as each year thousands of *Kneippianer* throng to a belt of spa towns to seek health and rejuvenation (*see* box, p.138). Down the A7 is **Grönenbach**, a quaint resort and health spa. Just northwest lies the village of **Kronburg**, with its mighty Renaissance castle above the town. The most intriguing place to visit here is the Schwäbisches Bauernhofmuseum, laid out at the western end of the town, at Illerbeuren. The open-air museum brings together some 20 original buildings from the rural Allgäu foothills, including farmsteads and workshops of traditional crafts.

Schwäbisches Bauernhof- museum
www.bauernhof museum.de; open April–Sept Tues–Sun 9–6; Mar and Oct–Nov Tues–Sun 10–4; adm €4 inc. guided tours

Along serene country roads that weave back across the A7, you come to the **Benedictine abbey** at **Ottobeuren**. Its Baroque architecture (1737–1766) is mainly the work of Johann Michael Fischer. Leading sculptor Johann Joseph Christian and the Augsburg artist Johann Michael Feichtmeier were the driving force behind the interiors. A deliberately dim porch opens into a vast, bright hall with high pulpits, flocks of putti, and licks and curls of stucco and gold. Behind all this joyous abandon, however, is a controlling hand. Especially worth seeking out are the carved choir stalls and the reliquaries in the side altars. Human skeletons recline on two of the tombs, decked out in gauze, velvet and gold. The three organs, built by the master Karl Joseph Riepp, rank with the most beautiful church organs in the world. In the adjoining museum is more religious carving and painting, exquisite 18th-century inlaid furniture, a Baroque **theatre** and an elegant **library**.

Abbey museum
open Palm Sun–1 Nov daily 10–12 and 2–5; adm €2

Health-seekers can follow a number of Kneipp exercise trails along the Günz valley. The outlying village of **Stephansried** to the north is Kneipp's birthplace. Some 25km on the B18 to the northeast of Ottobeuren lies **Mindelheim**, which has a graceful Baroque **Liebfrauenkirche** and a 14th-century bastion, the **Mindelburg**. Tucked away in the Baroque **Silvesterkirche** is the Schwäbisches Turmuhrenmuseum (Swabian Tower Clock Museum), where you can delve into the history of the clocks that

Schwäbisches Turmuhren- museum
open Wed 2–5, plus last Sun in month 10–12 and 2–5; adm €2

The Kneipp Story

Kneipp treatment has a special place among Germany's spa cures. This health-care programme, devised by Catholic parson Sebastian Kneipp (1821–97), is based on natural healing powers. Kneipp drew on the area's bountiful natural resources – water, sunshine and pure mountain air – and combined them into a health regime. The Rothschilds, Pope Leo XIII and Theodore Roosevelt all consulted Kneipp. Today, water-treading in specially devised exercise pools has become synonymous with Kneipp's proven methods, but, with over 60 Kneipp spas in Germany, the cures encompass a wider synthesis of hydrotherapy, herbal therapy, nutritional therapy, physiotherapy and biorhythmic balance.

once graced the region. Mindelheim has a special relationship with Britain. In 1704 the town, with the Mindelburg, became the personal property of John Churchill, Duke of Marlborough, after the Battle of Blenheim, and for the next ten years it remained an outpost of Britain in the Allgäu.

The B18 takes you to **Bad Wörishofen**, the undisputed centre of natural cure therapies in the region, which rose to fame after Kneipp made it his base in 1855. The hub of the spa quarter is the **Sebastianeum**, founded by Kneipp, which now houses sanatoriums and overnight facilities for some 7,000 visitors. Look out for the **Dominikanerinnen-Kloster** with its Baroque **Marienkirche**, decorated by the fresco-painting brothers Dominikus and Johann Baptist Zimmermann. The abbey also houses the **Kneippmuseum**, with artefacts and printed material relating to the life and work of the Allgäu 'water healer'.

Kneippmuseum
www.kneipp-museum.de; open 15 Jan–15 Nov Tues–Sun 3–6; adm €2

Turning south at Buchloe, follow the B12 to **Kaufbeuren**. The town's medieval centre and 15th-century walls contain splendid Gothic and Renaissance buildings. The **Fünfknopfturm** (Five-button-Tower) is the town landmark and, with the **Blasiusturm** of the Gothic **Blasiuskapelle**, forms an impressive part of its military architecture.

Kempten

In the gently rolling countryside along the Iller valley, on the B12, lies the town of Kempten. This medium-sized town is a treat, with an impressive array of monuments. The site has been inhabited since Celtic times. Romans, Alemannic kings and Benedictine prince-abbots were rulers, and the town was made a Free Imperial City in 1361. Modern-day Kempten represents a merger between two separate towns. When in 1527 the more progressive free burghers adopted the Reformation, the people from around the abbey remained loyal to the Catholic prince-abbots. This caused a deep divide, and both towns alternately found themselves at the receiving end of the ravages of the Thirty Years' War. Architectually, the erstwhile religious division is still detectable and the

Freitreppe, a steep ascent built in the 19th century to disguise the visible signs of the split, marks the borderline between the two. On one side the domed **Stiftskirche St Lorenz** rises over the maze of Catholic Kempten. This abbey church, built between 1652 and 1666, is part of an extensive complex of ecclesiastical buildings and adjoins the **Residenz**, the former palace to the prince-abbots. The ensemble is one of the earliest examples of Baroque architecture in Bavaria. Imperiously boasting Protestant control of the burgher part of town, the more economical late Gothic **St-Mang-Kirche** on the other side honours the 8th-century patron saint of the Allgäu. The burgher church is fitting company for the nearby **Rathaus**, a step-gabled Renaissance construction with rococo exteriors, and the **Ponikauhaus**, a 16th-century merchant's house.

Archäologischer Park Cambodunum
www.apc-kempten.de;
open Tues–Sun 10–4.30;
adm €3

Should the idea of exploring ancient Roman Kempten (*Cambodunum*) appeal to you, go to the **Archäologischer Park Cambodunum**, east of the River Iller. In 1885 the town's Roman remains were discovered nearby and unearthed, revealing a forum, basilica, temple and thermal baths. To give a graphic idea of the excavation site, an archaeological park was designed and a full-size Gallo-Roman temple precinct was reconstructed on its original stone foundations. The result is conjectural and may upset archaeological purists, but to the uninitiated this glimpse of ancient culture may come as a revelation. Roman artefacts of the conventional kind are found in the **Zumstein-haus** on Residenz-platz; this houses the **Römisches Museum** (Roman Museum).

Römisches Museum
open Thurs–Sun 10–12 and 2–4; adm €2

Festivals North of the Allgäu Alps

ⓘ **Memmingen**
Marktplatz 3,
t (08331) 850172,
www.memmingen.de

Fischertag

Memmingen celebrates its famous annual *Fischertag* in July: a spectacular fish hunt in the Stadtbach, the town's largest canalized pond. More than 800 amateur fishermen from Memmingen, armed only with landing nets, vie with each other to catch the largest trout and thus become the *Fischerkönig* (Fisher King). The locals claim that the tradition has a practical background as, in the old days, each year the pond was drained, and the fishermen's competitiveness provided a convenient way of emptying it of fish – and most of the mud.

Tänzelfest

At the end of July the whole town holds a celebration centring on its schoolchildren. Emperor Maximilian I of Austria used to stay in his 'beloved' Kaufbeuren whenever he could and in 1497, it is said, he initiated the festivities. Nowadays some 1,600 local youngsters act scenes from the town's 1,000-year-old history in colourful processions, including scenes played by the emperor and his jester, Kunz von der Rosen.

Wallensteinfest

The *Wallensteinfest*, also at Memmingen, is held at four-year intervals (next in July 2012). This costumed festivity commemorates the town's occupation in 1630 during the Thirty Years' War, when the Imperial army's headquarters under the fearsome Albrecht von Wallenstein set up camp here.

Other Festivals

Elsewhere, rural festivals fill the calendar. Every five years (next in 2010) the *Wilder-Männdle-Tanz* takes place in the Oybele hall in Oberstdorf; 14 local men wearing lichen skirts and head-dresses made of forest leaves, pound a wild dance in 17 curious scenes, wielding clubs and large wooden tankards in an attempt to exorcise the evil spirits of the mountain forests. The *Fastnacht* (*Fasching*) comes in February or early March; this festival is an offshoot of the Swabian carnival season and features processions of colourfully dressed imps, fools and witches in wooden masks.

ⓘ **Kaufbeuren** >>
Kaiser-Max-Straße 1,
t (08341) 40405,
www.kaufbeuren.de

ⓘ **Kempten** >>
Rathausplatz 24,
t (0831) 2525 237,
www.kempten.de

⭐ **Hotel Fürstenhof** >>

Where to Stay and Eat North of the Allgäu Alps

Kaufbeuren

Hotel Goldener Hirsch, Kaiser-Max-Straße 39–41, **t** (08341) 43030, *www.goldener-hirsch-kaufbeuren.de* (€€–€). Central, smartly modernized, historic hotel.

Kempten

Bayerischer Hof, Füssener Straße 96, **t** (0831) 57180, *www.bayerischerhof-kempten.de* (€€). Converted from a stately mansion, an imaginatively decorated, friendly hotel in the town centre with a small Chinese restaurant.

Hotel Fürstenhof, Rathausplatz 8, **t** (0831) 25360, *www.fuerstenhof-kempten.de* (€€–€). Attractive conversion of a 17th-century patrician residence. Several Hohenstaufen and Hapsburg emperors and princes have stayed here.

The Romantic Road

You might expect Germany's oldest tourist route to be associated with the Romantic movement: Wagner's powerful operas or Caspar David Friedrich's dramatic paintings. In fact the Romantische Straße is romantic with a small 'r' – more *Love Story than* Wuthering Heights; *cosy firesides and soft focus grassy meadows, rather than surging passions and dramatic scenery.*

From the university town of Würzburg it meanders through vineyards and rolling countryside, past the medieval gem of Rothenburg and through the Fugger family stronghold of Augsburg. From here it follows the ancient Via Claudia Augusta connecting Augsburg and Rome, and ends in Füssen in the Alpine foothills, a total of 343km. Your progress is punctuated by stops in Baroque palaces, grand churches and Fachwerk villages, and as you near the mountains you find two of Ludwig II's whimsical castles.

09

Don't miss

⭐ **Intriguing alleys and the Residenz**
Würzburg **p.143**

⭐ **Wine-tasting**
Stein vineyards **p.150**

⭐ **Pretty *Fachwerk* buildings**
Rothenburg **p.157**

⭐ **Fine rococo architecture**
Wieskirche **p.173**

⭐ **Ludwig's castles**
Neuschwanstein and Hohenschwangau **pp.173/176**

See map overleaf

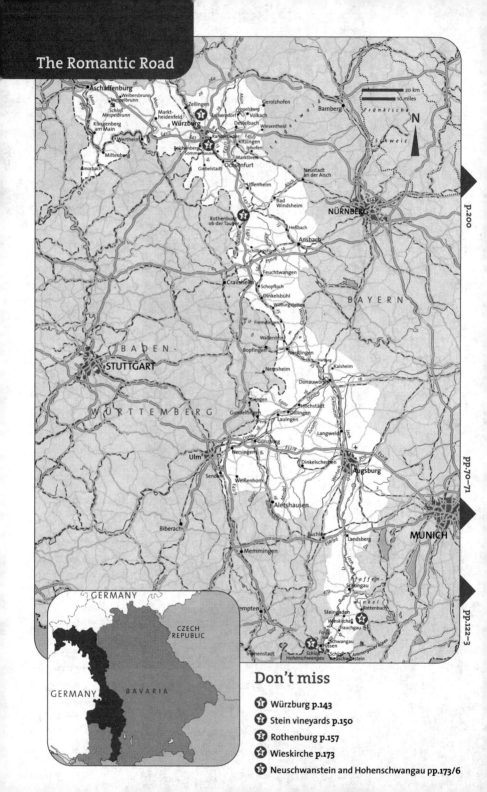

The Romantic Road

p.200

pp.70-71

pp.122-3

Don't miss

⭐ Würzburg **p.143**

⭐ Stein vineyards **p.150**

⭐ Rothenburg **p.157**

⭐ Wieskirche **p.173**

⭐ Neuschwanstein and Hohenschwangau **pp.173/6**

Getting around on the Romantic Road

By Car

The Romantic Road is motoring country. The route is well signposted in both directions, and for visiting some sights and doing your own exploring a car is essential. You could cover the full 343km in a day, but there would be little point.

Most of the delights of the Romantic Road are architectural, and it takes time to savour them. Simply trundling through the pretty but uneventful countryside would be monotonous. Allow five days to a week for a reasonably unhurried tour.

By Bus

It is possible, though time-consuming and tedious, to attempt the journey by a combination of rail and local buses. A far better idea, if you are relying on public transport, is to take the **Romantic Road Bus**, a festive coach, popular with backpackers and trippers. It runs daily from May to October, stopping at all the main sights. Often stops are only long enough for a quick look around, but you can stay overnight and catch the next bus through. You can of course also travel the Romantic Road from south to north (the bus runs both ways), but the route builds up in a more logical crescendo if you start in the vineyards of the north and end up in Ludwig's castles in the Alps.

Deutsche Touring GmbH, Am Römerhof 17, 60486 Frankfurt/Main, **t** (069) 790 3501, *www.touring.de*. For the Romantic Road Bus (Eurobus Line 190 A). A ticket for the full journey costs €70; the company gives a 60% discount if you have a German rail pass, Eurail pass or Eurail Selectpass.

Romans, rampaging emperors, crusaders and pilgrims to various churches trod the Romantic Road. Nowadays your fellow travellers are most likely to be busloads of tourists, devoutly following the route signs and alighting at the marked sights. But even the smallest deviation from the very well-beaten track can take you to forgotten corners, ignored by the throngs pounding by.

Würzburg

 Würzburg

Würzburg is wine, water and light. To the west the brawny Marienberg fortress swaggers above the town; to the east the Baroque Residenz rests gracefully in its gardens; through the middle flows the Main – 'like a child between father and mother', remarked the writer Heinrich von Kleist in 1800. Vineyards slope right into the centre of the town. On sunny days the sharp light reflects off the Main and throws everything into vivid relief.

Around AD 500 the Franks began to wipe out local tribes, and by AD 650 they had established a duchy at 'Virteburch'. A few decades later the Irish bishop Kilian came to preach Christianity. He was killed, thus ensuring his canonization, but he had done his work: by AD 742 Würzburg was a bishopric, and in the 12th century it got its own cathedral. In 1397 King Wenzel the Lazy promised to make Würzburg a Free Imperial City, but never got round to it. Only in the late 17th century, with the powerful Schönborn family as prince-bishops, did Würzburg really come into its own.

This dreamy town of Baroque palaces, *Fachwerk* houses and shady corners was flattened in 20 minutes by Allied bombers on

Getting around Würzburg

By Car

Würzburg is on the A3, 110km from Frankfurt, 130km from Nürnberg.
Car hire is available at: **Europcar**, at the Hauptbahnhof, t (0931) 12060; **Hertz**, Wörthstraße 10, t (0931) 413183; **Mitfahrzentrale**, Bahnhofsvorplatz-Ost, t (0931) 19440.
If you need a **taxi**, call t (0931) 19410.

By Train

Würzburg is on the main ICE rail route from Hamburg to Munich. Connections to other German cities are fast and frequent. There's an hourly train to Frankfurt Airport (1hr 20mins). For information, t 19419.

Public Transport

Once you arrive in central Würzburg, all the main tourist sights can be found within walking distance of each other. If you do find you need to use public transport, you could invest in a 24-hour **pass** (€4.10). A pass bought on Saturday is also valid on Sunday.
The main **bus station** is just outside the Hauptbahnhof.

16 March 1945. Of the 108,000 inhabitants, barely 5,000 survived, and Würzburg became known as the *Grab am Main* (the grave on the Main). Much of the city is new, but the monuments have been carefully restored, and you can find quiet old courtyards, madonnas on the streets, elaborate Baroque fountains and poky, gas-lit alleys.

The best time to visit Würzburg is in the autumn, when the grapes are harvested and you can huddle in *Weinstuben*, at the end of long 'golden days', sipping freshly fermented wine. The city is popular with Germans for short-break holidays. In season it becomes crowded over weekends, but it's much quieter during the week and outside August and October.

The Residenz

The Residenz
www.residenz-wuerzburg.de; open daily April–Oct 9–6; Nov–Mar 10–4.30; adm €7, concs €6

To the east of the city is its pearl, the prince-bishops' Residenz, a good place to start. In 1720 Johann Philipp von Schönborn wanted a grander, more modern palace than the draughty old fortress of his predecessors. The problem of how to finance it was solved when he confiscated the 600,000-florin fortune of a disloyal chamberlain. His uncle, the Elector of Mainz and Prince-Bishop of Bamberg, wryly suggested that a monument to the hapless official should be erected in front of the palace.

The Schönborns were an influential family (spawning at least a dozen bishops), infected with the *Bauwurm* ('building worm', the lust to build) and graced with good taste. Johann Philipp showed great foresight in choosing as his chief architect a young bell-founder and cannon-maker who had some flair as an amateur draughtsman (he had designed his own house and a city plan for Würzburg). Balthasar Neumann became one of the greatest German architects of the age, and through him the prince-bishop realized his dream of building a *Schloß über die Schlösse* (castle to beat all castles), a massive, U-shaped Baroque sandstone pile,

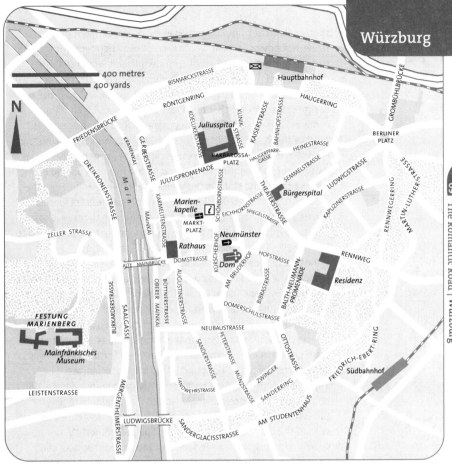

resplendent in its own square. After its completion, the Residenz was the talk of the civilized world. Fifty years later it impressed Napoleon, who said that it was 'the loveliest parsonage in Europe'.

The **Vestibule** (big enough for a coach-and-six to turn in) has a low ceiling with a half-hearted *trompe l'œil* dome and some restrained classical decoration. Neumann's original design was even plainer, intensifying by contrast the surprises to come. Guests stepped out of their carriages right on to the magnificent **staircase**. Here the low vaulting of the vestibule seems to break open to reveal the blue sky and wispy clouds of a ceiling **fresco** high above. The painting (by Giovanni Battista Tiepolo) depicts allegories of the four known continents paying tribute to the prince-bishop. Neumann sits astride a cannon on the cornice below his patron, proudly surveying his work. (Neumann, plus staircase, once appeared on the DM50 note). At 18m by 32m, the fresco is the biggest in the world, yet it arches over the staircase unsupported by a single pillar. Neumann carried off this spectacular feat by building the ceiling of feather-light pumice stone. Nobody believed it would work. A rival architect threatened to hang himself from the roof, confident that it would collapse under his weight before he died. Neumann suggested that the prince-bishop fire a battery of artillery in the stairwell to prove his design's strength. Neither test was carried out, but Neumann's confidence was vindicated in 1945, when Allied bombs destroyed most of the Residenz, but neither the stairway nor its vaulting. Each step is a few centimetres high, and they are perfectly spaced, inducing an exhilarating Hollywood glide as you sail up and down.

At the top of the stairs is the **Weißer Saal** (White Hall). Here the stucco artist Antonio Bossi, on the brink of madness, let loose a feverish blaze of stucco work before succumbing to his psychosis. The room is painted white to give prominence to the stucco, and to rest the eyes before the onslaught of the State Rooms.

The first of these, the oval **Kaisersaal** (Imperial Hall: the German Emperor used the Residenz whenever he was in the area) was also decorated by Tiepolo and Bossi. The frescoes, showing scenes from Franconian history, rank with Tiepolo's finest work. They bristle with life and play delightful tricks, at times even popping out into 3D. The classical deities get the same meticulous treatment as the main players. (One amorous couple has been featured in *Playboy*.) Seventy metres to the right and left of the Kaisersaal are the Imperial Apartments. This part of the Residenz suffered from Allied bombing, but has been lovingly rebuilt. From room to room you can sense the restorers' growing confidence as they refined their skills at the old crafts. Don't miss the **Spiegelkabinett** (Mirror Room), with its hand-painted mirrors and gilded stucco, or the **Grünes Zimmer** (Green Room) with exquisite rococo lacquer work.

Downstairs, off the eastern end of the vestibule is the **Gartensaal** (Garden Hall). Gardens offered an escape from formal 18th-century courtly behaviour. Beyond the palace walls you could let your hair down (courtiers often got into the spirit by dressing up as carefree peasants.) The Garden Hall was used to serve food and as a setting for musicians. In his stucco work Bossi hid mirrors that flicker with a magical light when the chandeliers are lit. The fresco (by Johann Zick) explores the contrast between courtly formality and happy abandon. Smaller pictures of putti send up the more serious treatment of a 'Banquet of the Gods' in the main painting.

There are more cheeky putti on the bastions in the garden behind the Residenz, carved by the court sculptor Peter Wagner. Things take a more disturbing turn south of the building, where rape is the theme, with two heavy statues, the *Rape of Proserpine* and the *Rape of Europa*. Before leaving, have a look at the **Court Chapel** (in the southern wing of the building), another Neumann triumph, with spiralling columns, curving balconies and graceful arches.

Around Town

The town centre, bounded by gardens following the line of the old city wall, is nicknamed the *Bischofsmütze* (Bishop's Mitre) because of its shape. Würzburg is not a museum piece, but among the everyday bustle you suddenly come across quiet pockets of another age, or turn a corner to a surprise view, past glass and concrete to the river, mountains and vineyards beyond.

The Dom

Walk from the Residenz down Hofstraße for the Dom. The 12th-century church seemed to survive the 1945 air raid intact (though the heat from surrounding fires melted the bells), but a year later the roof of the nave collapsed, and the cathedral had to be substantially rebuilt. It is worth a visit mainly for the vast array of Franconian sculpture, seven centuries' worth of bishops' effigies. Most impressive is the portrait of the 92-year-old Rudolf von Scherenberg (1499), carved with discomfiting realism by Germany's most eminent late Gothic sculptor, **Tilman Riemenschneider** (1460–1531). Riemenschneider came to Würzburg in 1483, and became *Bürgermeister* twice. He was imprisoned in 1525 for persuading the city council to join the Peasants' Revolt. Some say he was tortured and his hands were crippled; others say it was his spirit that was broken; but after his release he never carved anything of note again. Look out also for the intricately carved lectern (possibly also by Riemenschneider) and a 13th-century Epiphany group where the kings' robes are patterned with the heraldic eagle, rose and fleur-de-lys to represent Germany, Britain and France, then the world's leading nations.

The Neumünster

After the timeless hush of the Dom the city centre seems hectic. To the right, on Kürscherhof, is the Neumünster, built in the 11th century to house the remains of St Kilian and his fellow missionaries, but now largely dramatic, sweeping Baroque. Beyond the northern exit of the church is the peaceful **Lusam Garden**, where you can see one remaining wing of the original 12th-century cloisters – a dainty row of carved Romanesque pillars and arches. In one corner, the minstrel Walther von der Vogelweide (d. 1230), Germany's equivalent of Chaucer (*see* p.41) , lies buried. There are little shallow water bowls on each corner of the memorial, fulfilling the poet's last wish that birds should always have a reason to visit his grave. He was wildly popular in his time and, 750 years on, the locals still make sure that the grave is never without flowers.

The Marktplatz

West of the Neumünster, cut through some intriguing alleys of shops to the Marktplatz. On the north side of the square is the **Haus zum Falken**, a 14th-century priest's house given a rococo stucco façade when it became an inn in 1751. Next door is the Gothic **Marienkapelle**, most interesting for its exterior carvings. Above the north portal is a rather odd *Annunciation*. God talks to the Virgin through a speaking tube, down which the baby Jesus is surfing earthwards. Riemenschneider's lithe, erotic *Adam and Eve* on the south portal caused a scandal when they were first seen, mainly because a beardless Adam was thought disrespectful. The statues you see are 19th-century copies; the originals are in the Mainfränkisches Museum (*see* opposite). Balthasar Neumann (*see* pp.144–6) is buried in the church – called a 'chapel' because it was built by burghers, and the stuffy bishop refused to grant it the status of a parish church.

There was a constant battle between the townsfolk and clergy of Würzburg, where one in five of the population was a priest. The **Rathaus** on the west of the square was bought by burghers in 1316, and continually enlarged to cock a snook at the bishops – but it remains in the shadow of the church buildings. Inside is the Romanesque **Wenzel Hall**, where in 1397 the burghers tried to woo King Wenzel into granting the city Free Imperial status in a fruitless attempt to snatch power from the bishop.

Wenzel Hall
can be visited during office hours, when not in use

Along Juliuspromenade

Halfway along Theaterstraße is the **Bürgerspital**: 14th-century almshouses that derive their income from vineyards. A narrow arch leads to the quiet courtyard, where grannies sit happily on benches along the walls. A possible explanation for their smiles is that the Bürgerspital administration traditionally grants residents a glass of wine a day, and a bottle over weekends.

Around the corner on the Juliuspromenade is the **Juliusspital**, founded by the prince-bishop in 1576 and now a hospital. The Baroque **Fürstenbau** was once residence of the prince-bishop. At harvest-time the gardens at the back buzz with activity as grapes are carted in to the winery.

Farther down Juliuspromenade, you come to the River Main and a twin-armed 18th-century **crane** built by a son of Balthasar Neumann. It is a pleasant walk south along the river to the **Alte Mainbrücke**, a beautiful bridge dating from the 17th century, decorated with 12 enormous statues of saints.

Festung Marienberg

Across the bridge, on the hill, is Festung Marienberg, a hotchpotch of fortifications dating back to the 13th century that formed the prince-bishops' palace prior to the building of the Residenz. The buildings are carefully restored, but devastation during the Thirty Years' War, by the Prussians in the 19th century and during the Second World War, spared little of the original interior. The dinky 8th-century **Marienkirche** is one of Germany's oldest. The **Zeughaus** (arsenal) now houses the **Mainfränkisches Museum** with a superb Riemenschneider sculpture collection and wine museum.

Mainfränkisches Museum
www.mainfraenkisches-museum.de; open April–Oct Tues–Sun 9–6, Nov–Mar closes 4; adm €3

On top of the next hill is the **Käppele**, a compact pilgrimage church (the devout climb the hill on their knees) built by Neumann in the 1740s. However you've managed your passage to the top, you'll find the view back across town exhilarating.

Services in Würzburg

ⓘ **Würzburg** ›
Haus zum Falken, Marktplatz, t (0931) 372398, www.wuerz berg.de; open Jan–Mar Mon–Fri 10–4, Sat 10–1; April–Dec Mon–Fri 9–6, Sat 10–2, Sun (May–Oct only) 10–2

Post office: Bahnhofsplatz 2. Also runs a *bureau de change. Open daily until 8pm.*

Police, t 110

Doctor or **dentist, t** 19222.

Festivals in Würzburg

Würzburg holds a world-renowned **Mozart Festival** every June. Concerts are held in the Residenz, with the highlight being the *Kleine Nachtmusik* concert (first and last Saturdays) performed by lamplight in the gardens. On the first Saturday in July Würzburg erupts with the *Kiliani*, a procession followed by a fortnight of partying to celebrate St Kilian's Day.

At the end of September there's a huge **wine festival** beside the Friedensbrücke, where all the local producers present their wares; a more intimate alternative is the **Burgerspital Wine Festival**, held towards the end of June in the Burgerspital courtyard.

There is a **Bach Festival** towards the end of November.

Where to Stay in Würzburg

★ **Schloß Steinburg** ›

Würzburg

In the summer and early autumn, booking at least a fortnight ahead is advised.

Schloß Steinburg, Steinburg, **t** (0931) 97020, *www.steinburg.com* (€€€–€€).

From the balconies of this turn-of-the-century villa, your view sweeps from 'Stein', Franconia's famous vineyard north of the centre, across to the Würzburg fortress of Marienberg. The restaurant shows off the richness of Franconian cooking.

Hotel Würzburger Hof, Barbarossaplatz 2, **t** (0931) 53814, *http://hotel-wuerzburgerhof.de* (€€). This hotel has been run by the same family for nearly a century, and is getting grander all the time.

Hotel Zur Stadt Mainz, Semmelstraße 39, **t** (0931) 53155, *www.hotel-stadtmainz.de* (€€). Old inn, recently renovated and fitted with comfortable old furniture. All rooms have TV and double glazing.

Hotel Alter Kranen, Kärrnergasse 11 (behind Mainkai), **t** (0931) 35180, *www.hotel-alter-kranen.de* (€€–€). The best bargain: central and cosy, with friendly management. Front rooms overlook the Main.

Jugendherberge, Burkarderstraße 44 (behind Saalgasse), **t** (0931) 42590. Bed and breakfast from €17.50 (must be 26 or under).

Eating Out in Würzburg

The local Würzburger wines are among the best in Germany (see below). At harvest time, try *Federweißer* (also called *Bremser*): fermenting grape-must that tastes like fruit juice, looks like scrumpy, and has you under the table in minutes. With a slice of *Zwiebelkuchen* (a sort of onion quiche) it's a fine way to end the day.

Moszuppe, a rich wine and cream soup, is a tasty starter. Follow this up with hearty dishes such as *Schmeckerli* (stomach of veal), or nibble on a *Blooz* (plate-sized salty crackers) or *Blaue Zipfel* (sausages poached in spicy vinegar). These go an odd blue colour when cooked, but taste delicious. Carp comes baked or served '*Sud*' (poached in heavily spiced wine and vinegar). *Meefischli* is whitebait from the Main. Locals say the fish should never be longer than the little finger of St Kilian's statue on the bridge, and that they should swim three times – in water, fat and wine.

Haus des Frankenweins, Kranenhai 1, next to the old crane, **t** 390110 (€€€). As well as being a vortex for oenophiles, the restaurant lures gourmets to its fresh carp, exotic roulades and upmarket versions of an old Franconian *Brotzeit*.

Fischbäuerin, Katzengasse 7, **t** 42487 (€€). The best place to try *Meefischli* and other seasonal fish dishes.

Hotel zur Stadt Mainz Restaurant, Semmelstraße 39, **t** 53155 (€€). Run by the sort of cook who can turn the simplest ingredients, like oxtail and brown sauce, into a heavenly experience, but on some nights it seems that every visitor to Würzburg has heard about her.

Bürgerspital Weinsruben, Theaterstraße 19, **t** 352880, *www.buergerspital_weinsruben.de* (€€–€). Cellar restaurant of a famous local wine producer; offers the complete range of in-house wines (the dry Kerner is particularly good) and tasty Franconian dishes.

(★) **Zum Stachel >>**

Juliusspital-Weinstuben, Julius-promenade 19, **t** 54080, *www.julius spital.de* (€€–€). Atmospheric, if cavernous. Their wines are world-renowned and they serve a good harvest-time *Federweißer*. The Franconian cooking is good too.

Weinhaus Schnabel, through a plain door at Haugerpfarrgasse 10, **t** 53314, *www.weinhaus-schnabel.de* (€€–€). A good no-nonsense establishment with stolid waitresses, bright lights and inexpensive servings of many Franconian specialities.

Bars and Cafés in Würzburg

Locals call their cafés *Bäcken*. In the summer there is a jovial temporary beer garden on the east bank of the Main, in front of the Haus des Frankenweins. Look up across the old bridge to the Marienberg and sip your drink in one of the best spots in Würzburg.

Brückebäck, Alte Mainbrücke, across the bridge from the centre. Trendy bar where the youthful smart set line up against the plate-glass windows, and look out across the river.

Zum Stachel Gressengasse 1, *www.weinhaus-stachel.de*. Once the headquarters of the local farmers during the Peasants' Revolt. The tiny courtyard is a jigsaw of balconies, loggias and stairways, draped with creepers.

Sternbäck, Domstraße. Welcoming bar squeezed into an old house; in the summer people sit outside under the trees.

A Wine Tour around Würzburg

(★) **Stein vineyards**
(see box oppposite);
www.franken-weinland.de

Gastefuhrer
Weinerlebnis Franken,
Donat-Gromling
Strasse 10, Rimpar,
t *(09365) 2251*

South along the B13 is **Randersacker**, where the Pfülben vineyards produce good Rieslings. For guided tours contact **Gastefuhrer**.

Sommerhausen, a few kilometres on, is an enchanting cluster of grey stone houses, with vines and geraniums bursting out of cracks in the walls. There's a 16th-century **Rathaus** with pinnacled gables, and a **Renaissance castle** in the high street. In autumn the whole village bustles with the harvest, and you catch fragrant whiffs of ripe pears and crushed grapes. A colony of artists works here and sometimes contributes to the small **Christmas market** during Advent. There is also a minuscule theatre above the old tower gate, which attracts audiences from as far away as Würzburg. **Weingut Konrad Schwarz** uses grapes from the excellent Ölspiel vineyards to make velvety Spätburgunder reds.

Weingut Konrad Schwarz
Schleifweg 13, t (09333) 221 for appointment

Eastwards past Ochsenfurt and Marktbreit (both with typically Franconian red and grey half-timbered houses) is **Kitzingen**. In a yard behind the Landratsamt, past the Rathaus, are the cellars of the **Alte Kitzinger Klosterkeller**, part of an 8th-century Benedictine nunnery founded by Hadeloga, sister of the Frankish king Pepin the Short, to get over the shock of seeing her paramour dancing with another woman. Today you can visit their cellars (the oldest in Germany) and sit among the huge vats sampling wines. Try one of the more recent varieties, such as the fruity, rather flowery

Alte Kitzinger Klosterkeller
t (09321) 91690; shop open Thurs–Fri 9–6, Sat 10–8

Franconian Wine

Dagegen sende mir noch einige Würzburger; denn kein anderer Wein will mir schmecken, und ich bin verdrüßlich wenn mir mein gewohnter Lieblingstrank abgeht.

(Send me more Würzburger, for no other wine is so much to my taste, and I get grumpy without my favourite drink.)
Goethe, in a letter to Christiane Vulpius, 1806

Goethe put his money where his mouth was: he ordered 900 litres of Franconian wine in 1821 alone. The superb wines from around Würzburg are one of Germany's best kept secrets. Most of the vines are tucked away between stretches of forest and pasture to escape the crippling frosts, so you hardly notice them. Yields are small, so when the wines do make it to the outside world, they are expensive, and hence often ignored. A Franconian wine represented Germany at Queen Elizabeth II's coronation banquet, and Pope John Paul II drank it when he visited Germany in the 1980s.

The wines come in dumpy, flat, round-shouldered flasks called *Bocksbeutel*, supposedly invented by grape-growing monks who wanted to smuggle wine out into the fields. Almost exclusively white, the wines are mostly dry, pithy, flavoursome (often similar to burgundies) and heartily alcoholic. At one time most Franconian wines were made from the Silvaner grape – a bit of a non-starter in other regions, but here producing rich, honeyed wines. Sadly, Silvaner has been supplanted by the ubiquitous Müller-Thurgau, the wine-drinkers' equivalent of easy listening. Yet even this usually wimpish grape manages to pack a few beefier punches in Franconian wines. Heavy frosts and short summers mean that growers have a struggle getting Riesling grapes to ripen, but when they do (in hot years) the results are extraordinary.

In **Würzburg**, Riesling and Silvaner grapes bake away on the heat-retaining limestone slopes below the Marienberg fortress and in the famous Stein vineyard south of the city. These supply three of Germany's greatest wine producers: the **Bürgerspital** (*Theaterstraße/Semmelstraße; cellars open Mon–Thurs 7.30–12 and 1–4.45, Fri 7.30–12; shop open Mon–Fri 9–6, Sat 9–3*), the **Juliusspital** (*bulk purchases from Klinikstraße 5, Mon–Thurs 8–12 and 12.30–4.15, Fri 8–12; smaller quantities from Koellikerstraße 1–2, Mon–Fri 9–6, Sat 9–1*) and the **Hofkeller** (*Residenzplatz; open Mon–Fri 8.30–5.30, Sat 8.30–12*). Each offers wine-tasting, but for a more general introduction to local wines visit the **Haus des Frankenweins**, on the Main next to the old crane (*open Mon–Fri 10–6 and Sat 10–1*), which offers a wide selection from all over the region and can give helpful guidance. Try Rieslings and Silvaners from the Stein vineyards, and some of the newer wine varieties, which are just as exciting. Kerner in particular (a blend of red Trollinger and Riesling) can produce a strong, fruity, dry white wine.

Bacchus. Kitzingen also has the official German carnival museum, the **Deutsches Fastnachtsmuseum**, at Falterturm, with costumes, masks and other bits and bobs.

From Kitzingen, you can follow the B8 south to **Iphofen**, where the fertile red marly soils produce delicious, mouth-filling wines. Here even Müller-Thurgau grapes manage an aromatic bouquet. It's a good place to try some of the newer hybrids, such as Scheurebe or Perle. The town itself seems dreamily lost in time. The quaint 13th-century *Fachwerk* **Rödelseer Tor**, with a jumble of roofs, seems to lean in all directions. A sumptuous Baroque **Rathaus** is a surprise after narrow streets of half-timbered houses; in the late-Gothic **St Veit's** church are some fine Riemenschneider carvings.

The best place to begin your exploration of Iphofen's wines is the town's **Vinothek**, the showplace for 21 local vintners, located in a lovingly restored medieval warehouse. Rieslings and Sylvaners from the Julius-Echterberg and Kronsberg vineyards are superb (wines chosen for Queen Elizabeth II and the Pope, *see* box, p.151). **Johann Ruck** is a local institution, highly regarded for traditional wine-making techniques. **Weingut Hans Wirsching** has been in the same family for 15 generations, and is revered for dry Rieslings and crisp Sylvaners. **Weinbau Hans Dorsch** makes wines from the superior Kalb slopes.

North of Iphofen, off the B286, is **Volkach**, a busy little wine town. There's a 16th-century Rathaus and some romantically crumbly bits of old city wall. Down a side street off the Marktplatz is the **Schelfenhaus**, a Baroque house with some fine stucco work by a Bamberg artist named Vogel ('bird'), who used to sculpt a bird somewhere into his work as a trademark.

On a hill above the town, in the little church of **Maria im Weingarten**, is one of Riemenschneider's most exquisite works, the *Madonna im Rosenkranz* (Madonna in a Wreath of Roses; 1524). It shot to international fame when it was 'art-napped' and held for a ransom in 1962. The poor parish couldn't find the money, so the editor of *Stern* offered DM50,000 for its return. At **Weinbau Max Müller I** you can taste Rieslaner wines – a new hybrid fast becoming a local speciality.

Near Volkach, at the top of the **Vogelsburg**, admire the view while sipping spicy Traminer wines made by local nuns. The village of **Escherndorf**, down the hill, is famed for a vineyard called Lump that produces some of the region's best wines. **Weingut Egon Schäffer** creates sensuous wines from the Sylvaner grape and also makes *Birnenschnapps* (pear schnapps) and wine vinegar. **Weingut Fröhlich** excels at Sylvaner, too, as well as pale reds made from Schwarzriesling, a form of the Pinot grape.

Deutsches Fastnachtsmuseum
open April–Nov Sat and Sun 2–5; adm €1

Vinothek
Kirchplatz 7,
t (09323) 870317,
www.vinotekiphofen.de

Johann Ruck
Marktplatz 19,
t (09323) 800880,
www.ruckwein.de

Weingut Hans Wirsching
Ludwigstrasse 16,
t (09323) 87330,
www.wirsching.de

Weinbau Hans Dorsch
Rödelseerstr. 8, t (09323) 1375, www.weingut-dorsch.de; open Mon–Sat 8–6, Sun 9–12

Weinbau Max Müller I
Hauptstraße 46,
t (09381) 1218,
www.max-mueller.de;
open Mon–Fri 9–6, Sat 9–3, Sun 10–12

Weingut Egon Schäffer
Astheimer Straße 17,
t (09381) 9350,
www.weingut-schaeffer.de

Weingut Fröhlich
Bocksbeutelstraße 41,
t (09381) 2847,
www.weingut-michael-froelich.de

Festivals around Würzburg

Wine-growing towns have the best festivals of all – less raucous than beer festivals, but with more style and an infectious conviviality. The townsfolk will often elect a Wine Queen (as much for her knowledge of wine as good looks and personality) and there is much eating, dancing and drinking of local wines.

As well as the Würzburg wine events (*see* p.149), there are well over 100 smaller village festivals held between May and November. Rather like traditional British fêtes, many of these are organized by local associations, such as sports clubs or Voluntary Fire Brigades. Look out for wayside signs advertising a *Weinfest* in the early summer and autumn, especially in the villages around Volkach.

Where to Stay and Eat around Würzburg

You can base yourself in Würzburg and visit the wine villages on a day trip. The most idyllic of the villages for a longer stay are Sommerhausen, Iphofen, Volkach and Dettelbach.

Sommerhausen

If you wish to stay in a private room in Sommerhausen, expect to pay around €25 per person.

Gästehaus am Schloß, Hauptstraße 19, t (09333) 91710, *www.sommerhausen.com* (€€–€). Right at the heart of things; all rooms have television, and guests can hire bicycles for jaunts into the vineyards.

Mönchshof, Mönchshof 7, t (09333) 758, *www.moenchshof-brennerei.de* (€). Tucked away in its own historic courtyard, with contemporary comforts in upstairs rooms and a cosy medieval cellar below. The owners, the Oehler family, proudly serve local wines and schnapps they distill themselves.

Weinhaus Düll, Maingasse 5, t (09333) 220, *www.weinhaus-duell.de* (€). Half-timbered Franconian inn where travellers have dined and slept since the 16th century. Local ingredients appear in most dishes on the restaurant menu: game and farmer's produce, wild berries and Sommerhausen wines.

Iphofen

Romantic Hotel Zehntkeller, Bahnhofstraße 12, t (09323) 8440, *www.zehntkeller.de* (€€). Set in its own park just inside the ancient city wall. It is also a wine estate, producing wines from vineyards on the nearby slopes that pair well with the Franconian specialities in its restaurant.

Gästehaus Fröhlich, Geräthengasse 13, t (09323) 3030, *www.gaestehaus-froehlich.de* (€). Charming guesthouse run by German-Canadian Ruth Perry. All the rooms are warmly and individually decorated with old furniture, and there is a café downstairs that serves delicious home-made cakes.

Gasthof Goldener Stern, Maxstraße 22, t (09323) 3315 (€€€). Looks ordinary but has scrumptious food. Iphofen is renowned for asparagus, which gets on to the menu in a variety of guises.

Zur Iphöfer Kammer, Marktplatz 24, t (09323) 804326 (€€). Traditional meals based on local seasonal ingredients (sausages cooked in spiced vinegar, white asparagus salad, pan-fried Waller fish) and share the table with bottles of some of Iphofen's finest, from wine-maker Wirsching.

Volkach

Zur Schwane, Hauptstraße 10, t (09381) 80660, *www.schwane.de* (€€–€). Family-run hotel with its own vineyard and *Schnapps* distillery, and a breakfast buffet that even locals try to get in on.

Hotel Vier Jahreszeiten, Hauptstraße 31, t (09381) 84840, *www.vier-jahres zeiten-volkach.de* (€). Grand affair, built in 1605 as a residence for the prince-bishop. The rooms are sumptuously decked out with antiques and cabinets of Bohemian glass.

Hotel Zur Schwane Restaurant, Hauptstraße 10, t (09381) 80660, *www.romantikhotels.com/volkach*

ⓘ **Iphofen** >>
Kirchplatz 7,
t (09323) 870306,
www.iphofen.de

ⓘ **Randersacker**
Markt Randersacker,
Maingasse 9,
t (0931) 7053 17,
www.randersacker.de

ⓘ **Kitzingen**
Schrannenstraße 1,
t (09321) 920019,
www.kitzingen.info

ⓘ **Sommerhausen** >
Hauptstraße 15,
t (09333) 8256,
www.sommerhausen.de

ⓘ **Volkach** >>
Rathaus, t (09381) 40112,
www.volkach.de

★ **Zur Schwane** >>

★ **Mönchshof** >

(€€€). Restaurant of the hotel, which deserves its place in the list of the top 444 restaurants in Germany, serving adventurous concoctions such as venison in a red cabbage and walnut sauce.

Schloß Hallburg, between Volkach and Sommerach, t (09381) 2340 (€). Converted Schloß that's popular on Sunday mornings, when you can have a delicious brunch with some Franconian wine or Sekt to the accompaniment of a live jazz band, and then wander around the romantic gardens.

Weinstube Torbäck, Hauptstraße (€). Has a hearty board of sausages, breads and cheeses (or home-made Zwiebelkuchen) to go with your harvest-time Federweißer.

Dettelbach

Himmelstoß, Bamberger Straße 3, t (09324) 4776 (€€€). Offers heavenly Festtagesuppe (festival soup), rack of lamb and fish cooked by chef Herr Kuffer and served by his charming wife, with vintages from their small wine estate.

West of Würzburg: The Spessart and Odenwald

Between Würzburg and Frankfurt, stretching over more than 100km, is some of Germany's most extensive forest. Through it the River Main cuts a deep, winding valley into northwest Bavaria. North of the river, spreading across the border into Hesse, is the **Spessart**. South of the river is the **Odenwald**, which reaches into Hesse in the west and Baden-Württemberg to the south. The passion of the prince-bishops of Mainz for hunting saved the acres of beech and oak from the axe in past centuries, and strict legislation protects them now.

Both the Spessart and Odenwald are quiet regions of gently rolling hills, forests and small villages, long known to local trippers for their lonely walks, but relatively undiscovered by outsiders. The most popular long-distance hike on the Bavarian side is the 111km *Eselsweg* (Mule's Path), following the old salt route through acres of woodland and across expansive meadowlands from Bad Orb to Miltenberg.

Weibersbrunn, a small resort some 13km southeast of Aschaffenburg, is also a walkers' hot spot. The village itself is attractive, with an unassuming **parish church** whose *Crucifixion*, dated 1470, is a perfectly preserved example of a rustic depiction. Neighbouring **Rohrbrunn** was the site of the notorious **Wirtshaus im Spessart** (Spessart Inn), immortalized by the writer Wilhelm Hauff (1802–27) in his tale about highwaymen. (Sadly, the robbers' hide-out was flattened by a motorway.)

Several footpaths converge at Rohrbrunn, among these a walk that trails past the **Forsthaus Echterspfahl** (a converted forester's house that offers delicious meals), then meanders the fine hilltops to **Schloß Mespelbrunn**, a dreamy, moated Renaissance palace with exhibits of some fine suits of armour and weaponry.

Schloß Mespelbrunn
www.schloss-mespelbrunn.de; open daily 9–5; adm €3.50

Getting around West of Würzburg

By **road**, the A3 (one of Germany's main north-south arteries) runs from Frankfurt to Aschaffenburg (40km), through Aschaffenburg to Würzburg (97km), and on to Nürnberg. Most of the important towns of the Odenwald lie along the B469, which dips south from Aschaffenburg to Miltenberg (37km) and Amorbach (42km).

Aschaffenburg is the hub of **rail** lines to Frankfurt (30mins) and Würzburg (40mins). There are regular connections to Miltenberg (45mins) and to Amorbach (1hr 15mins via Miltenberg).

Aschaffenburg

Approaching from Würzburg on the A3, the first city of note you come to is Aschaffenburg, 'giving the Bavarian lion the wag in its tail', as one Bavarian poet described it. Since the Second World War much of this wagging has been done by American GIs: thousands of US troops are still stationed here.

In stark contrast to the surrounding countryside, Aschaffenburg raises a line of massive stone façades along the River Main. The largest and most imposing of these is square-built **Schloß Johannisburg**. This Renaissance palace was commissioned by archbishop Johann Schweickard von Kronberg and built between 1604 and 1614. The prince-bishop was fired with aspirations to the grandeur befitting his status as Elector of the Holy Roman Empire. The palace grew into a massive red-sandstone pile, costing the equivalent of €23 million. It was carefully restored after extensive damage during the Second World War. Inside is a branch of the **Bavarian State Gallery**, with fine paintings by Lucas Cranach and other Franconian artists. Each August hundreds of visitors come to hear virtuoso bell-ringing (*see* 'Festivals West of Würzburg', p.157).

If you want relief from the tourist throngs, and the dings and the dongs, head for the **Pompejanum**, King Ludwig I's Roman villa folly on a hill north of the castle. Or, to set quite another peal ringing, visit the **Schloßweinstube** (Palace Wine Tavern), where there is a tantalizing selection of Franconian wines.

The Altstadt, southeast of Schloß Johannisburg, centres on the Stiftsplatz, which is dominated by the late Romanesque basilica of the **Stiftskirche** (with an interesting medieval crucifix depicting the *Mourning of Christ*). Nearby, in Wermbachstraße, is the **Schönborner Hof**, a fine Baroque mansion now home to the **Naturwissenschaftliches Museum** (Science Museum), with displays on the zoology, mineralogy and geology of the Spessart. To the east of the Altstadt is the **Schöntal**, a landscaped garden with Mediterranean magnolia groves and a pheasantry that neatly complement the wild, romantic layout of **Schönbusch** on the western side of the River Main, one of the first English-style gardens in Germany. Set around a diminutive 18th-century Baroque palace, the **Pavillon**, are wild flowers, open meadows and a whimsical series of pint-size follies including man-made ponds, islets, canals and temples.

Schloß Johannisburg
www.schloesser-bayern.de; open April–Sept Tues–Sun 9–6; Oct–Mar Tues–Sun 10–4; adm €4

Bavarian State Gallery
open same times as Schloß

Naturwissenschaftliches Museum
open Thurs–Tues 9–12 and 1–4; adm €1

Pavillon
open April–Sept Tues–Sun 9–6; adm €3

09 The Romantic Road | West of Würzburg: Aschaffenburg

Miltenberg

Emerging absolutely unscathed from the Second World War, Miltenberg is by far the most romantic town in the region. Streets of decorated half-timbered houses – around 150 buildings in all, spanning four centuries – stretch out along the River Main below an old hill-top castle.

The best place to begin a walk around is the triangular **Schnatterloch**, the town's historic market square with its cascades of step-gabled façades that prickle with decorated portals and corner oriels. Most imposing is **Hauptstraße**, a pedestrianized shopping street running east from the Schnatterloch. The half-timbered houses are mostly built on ground-floor walls of red sandstone, using the square-framed *Ständerbau* technique. Today the wooden beams are painted ochre or grey, but originally they were daubed with ox blood, in striking contrast to the white walls. The street leads past the 15th-century **Altes Rathaus** down to the five-storeyed **Haus zum Riesen**, Miltenberg's best-known pile of *Fachwerk* architecture, a guesthouse since at least 1504 and the cosiest, most atmospheric of the town's hotels (*see* 'Where to Stay and Eat West of Würzburg', opposite).

Mildenburg
open Tues–Sun;
adm free

Back uphill from the market square is the **Mildenburg**, which rises up over the town. First mentioned in 1226, the castle was strengthened by the archbishops of Mainz as a check to their rivals at Würzburg, and to keep better watch over the trading stations on the River Main. Star attraction in the courtyard is the **Teutonen-stein**, a puzzling 5m-high monolith discovered nearby in the 19th century, with a cryptic set of initials ('CAHF'). The stone seems to date from Roman times but so far no one has explained the letters.

Amorbach

Amorbach gets its name from the Benedictine Abbot Amor of Aquitaine, who founded a monastery here in AD 734. Benedictine monks lived here until secularization in 1803. The abbot's relics, kept in the abbey, were held to be particularly useful to couples praying for fertility.

Nowadays the small town, which is brimming with handsome half-timbered buildings, stands in the shadow of the **Abteikirche**, once the abbey's church, built between 1742 and 1744. The plain Baroque interior is considered architect Maximilian von Welsch's masterpiece. White stucco predominates, with the ceiling frescoes and side altars adding discreet touches of colour. The best view of the interior is from just in front of the wrought-iron rood screen. From here you also have a fine view of the **organ**, the church's

Festivals West of Würzburg

In Amorbach each year, especially around Easter and Pentecost, there is a cycle of excellent **organ concerts** in the Abteikirche.

Aschaffenburg's favourite folk festival is the 10-day mid-June **Volksfest**, with feasting and fireworks in the Altstadt. For bell-ringers, travelling to Aschaffenburg is a pilgrimage. Every summer at the beginning of August, campanologists head for Schloß Johannisburg for the **Carillonfest**.

Hundreds of people pour into Miltenberg for its **Michaelis-Messe**, a nine-day funfair in the last week of August. In October and November Miltenberg hosts the **Kulturwochen im Herbst**, a weekly sequence of concerts and exhibitions. Details for all festivals are available from the tourist office.

Where to Stay and Eat West of Würzburg

Aschaffenburg

Aschaffenburger Hof, Frohsinnstraße 11, t (06021) 3868 10, www.aschaffenburger-hof.de (€€). Aschaffenburg's classiest address attracts conference-organizers with its modern-style appearance and spacious rooms, but scores badly when it comes to atmosphere. Good, inexpensive restaurant.

Ringhotel Wilder Mann, Löherstraße 51, t (06021) 3020, www.hotel-wilder-mann.de (€€). A modernized 16th-century building on the edge of the Altstadt. Quiet and folksy, but a touch stuffy.

Miltenberg

Haus zum Riesen, Hauptstraße 98, t (09371) 989948, www.riesen-miltenberg.de (€€–€). Reputedly Germany's oldest guesthouse, with upmarket, understated service. Rooms are named after former aristocratic guests. You can sleep surrounded by heavy antique furniture in the room where Emperor Frederick or Empress Maria once spent the night. There is a snug little restaurant on the ground floor where you can eat good, hearty dishes.

Amorbach

Relais et Châteaux Hotel Der Schafhof, Schafhof 1, t (09373) 97330, www.schafhof.de (€€€). Romantic building on the very edge of town, 3km west of the centre. Once an 18th-century Benedictine monastery, it's now a comfortable modern hotel with Baroque furnishings. The restaurant uses produce from its own garden.

Miltenberg >>
Rathaus, t (09371) 404119, www.stadt-miltenberg.de

Amorbach >>
Altes Rathaus, t (09373) 2090, www.amorbach.de

Aschaffenburg >
Schloßplatz 1, t (06021) 395800, www.aschaffenburg.de

09 The Romantic Road | Rothenburg ob der Tauber

greatest treasure. The 18th-century instrument is an astonishing piece of work with over 5,000 pipes, 30 bells and 63 stops. The Abteikirche is the venue for several prestigious annual organ recitals (see 'Festivals West of Würzburg', above).

On the south side of the church is the rambling 18th-century monastic **Residenz**. Inside, the original design is lost under layers of redecoration commissioned by the Princes of Leiningen when they acquired the building in the 19th century. The neoclassical **Grüner Saal** (Green Hall) is grand in white and green; the **library** has an energetic ceiling fresco, glorifying the Virtues, Wisdom and Science.

Residenz
guided tours; open Mon–Sat 9.30–5.45, Sun 11–5.45; adm €2

Rothenburg ob der Tauber

Rothenburg

Rothenburg lies 110km south of Würzburg, along the Romantic Road. A prosperous town until the 17th century, Rothenburg never quite recovered from a sequence of occupations during the Thirty

Years' War, and no new building took place for centuries. Although it was badly bombed in the Second World War, Rothenburg was painstakingly rebuilt exactly as it had been. It's all very pretty: the **sentry walk** around the top of the city wall has a splendid view of the *Fachwerk* (half-timbered) alleys, gables, turrets, spires and decorated façades that draw tourists all year. 'Gingerbread architecture', sniff some people contemptuously – and, like gingerbread, a little of Rothenburg goes a long way.

The best time to see the town is very early in the morning, before the hordes hit the streets. As the mist drains out of the alleys down to the River Tauber in the valley far below, you quite expect to see someone in tights and a floppy hat trundle past in a heavy wooden cart. Even when the streets fill up with tourists, Rothenburg doesn't entirely lose its medieval atmosphere.

In the **market square** farmers rub shoulders with trinket-sellers. In the autumn there are stalls selling *Federweißer* wine direct from the barrel, and during Advent a Christmas market clusters around the side of the Rathaus, up against St Jakobskirche. In the gable of the **Ratsherrntrinkstube** overlooking the square, little figures in the windows near the clocks act out Rothenburg's most historic moment. In 1631, during the Thirty Years' War, General Tilly captured the town but agreed to spare it if one of the councillors could down a *Meistertrunk* (a 3-litre tankard of wine) in one go. Georg Nusch, a former *Bürgermeister*, took up the challenge. He saved Rothenburg in ten minutes, but needed three days to sleep off the effects.

On the west side of the square is the **Rathaus**. The front part of the building is Renaissance, but behind it a Gothic hall pokes up a slender, 61m-high tower. Inside you can see the bare Imperial Hall, and descend to the gloomy dungeons. Just behind the Rathaus is Rothenburg's famous **Christkindlmarkt**, a shop that sells all the traditional trappings of a German Christmas the whole year round.

Impressive old mansions line the Herrngasse (which extends westwards past the Rathaus), though the grandest home is the **Baumeisterhaus** in Schmiedgasse. Statues of the Seven Virtues grace the first floor, while the Seven Deadly Sins frolic above. (It is now a restaurant – *see* opposite). North of the market looms the Gothic **St Jakobskirche**, where you can see the superb *Heiligblut-Altar* (1504), carved in limewood by Tilman Riemenschneider.

In miserable weather head for one of the small museums. The best are an originally furnished **Handwerkerhaus** (Craftsman's House) at Alter Stadtgraben 26, and the **Kriminalmuseum** at Burggasse 3, with its medieval punishment and torture instruments. The **Puppen-und-Spielzeugmuseum** (Doll and Toy Museum), at Hofbronngasse 13, has a vast selection of dolls from all over the world, and some exquisite dolls' houses; and the

Ratsherrntrink-stube show
on the hour, 11am–3pm, and at 8, 9 and 10pm

Rathaus
Imperial Hall
open daily 8–6; adm free; **tower** *€1 to ascend by stairs and ladder*

Handwerkerhaus
t (09861) 5810; open Easter–Oct Mon–Fri 11–5, Sat–Sun 10–5; Nov–Jan daily 2–4; adm €2.50

Kriminalmuseum
www.kriminalmuseum. rothenburg.de; open April–Oct daily 9.30–6; Nov–Feb daily 2–4; adm €3.80

Puppen-und-Spielzeugmuseum
www.spielzeugmuseum. rothenburg.de; open Jan–Feb daily 1–5; Mar–Dec daily 9.30–6; adm €4

Reichsstadtmuseum
open April–Oct daily 10–5; Nov–Mar daily 1–4; adm €3

Reichsstadtmuseum, Klosterhof, housed in a former Dominican convent, preserves many of the old fittings and equipment, as well as relics of Rothenburg's 13th-century Jewish community.

Feuchtwangen

Stiftskirche cloisters
guided tours only, t (09852) 90455

Fränkisches Museum
www.fraenkisches-museum.de; open May–Sept Wed–Sun 11–12 and 2–6; Mar, Nov and Dec Wed–Sun 2–5; adm €2

The **Stiftskirche** that dominates the colourful Marktplatz of this small town, 30km south of Rothenburg, was built in the 13th–14th centuries and has a high altar dating from 1484, featuring side panels painted by Dürer's teacher, Michael Wohlgemut. Abutting the church to the south are the Romanesque **cloisters**, a popular venue for open-air concerts between June and August. Craft workshops crowd the cloisters' half-timbered upper storey. The **Fränkisches Museum**, at Museumsstraße 19, focuses on the furnishings of local homes over the centuries.

Festivals in Rothenburg

On **Whit Monday** locals in costume act out Bürgermeister Nusch's drinking feat (*see* left), though no one really attempts to match it.

One Sunday each month in spring and summer you can see the jolly *Schäfertanz* (Shepherd's Dance) in front of the Rathaus. (The dance supposedly began as a celebration of Rothenburg's deliverance from the Plague.) Vast crowds turn out to watch both events.

The **Advent Christmas Market** has a long-established reputation as one of the best in Germany.

Where to Stay and Eat around Rothenburg

(i) Rothenburg ob der Tauber >
Marktplatz, t (09861) 404800, www.rothenburg.de; open Mon–Fri 9–12 and 1–6, Sat–Sun 10–3; Nov–Mar open fewer hours and closed Sun

Rothenburg ob der Tauber

Most of Rothenburg's visitors are day-trippers. An overnight stay is not as expensive as you might expect in such a tourist trap, and it does mean that you can see the town at its quietest. **Private rooms** in the Altstadt work out at around €45 for a double. Try **Herr Hess** (Spitalgasse 18, t (09861) 6130, www.das-laedle.de), or enquire at the tourist office.

Hotel Reichs-Küchenmeister, Kirchplatz 8, t (09861) 9700, *www.reichskuechenmeister.de* (€€).

Attractive modern conversion of a 16th-century patrician house, with its own sauna, steam room and Jacuzzi.

Hotel Roter Hahn, Obere Schmiedgasse 21, t (09861) 9740, *www.roterhahn.com* (€€). Cosy family-run hotel in a 14th-century building.

Hotel Hornburg, Hornburgweg 28, t (09861) 8480, *www.hotel-hornburg.de* (€€–€). Old Franconian villa just outside the town wall. The friendly staff lend books and bicycles to guests. No restaurant.

Baumeisterhaus, Obere Schmiedgasse 3, t (09861) 3404 (€€). Has heavy-beamed dining rooms, and a medieval courtyard draped with creepers. Munch *Apfelgebäck* in the café, or try the restaurant serving fine Franconian food (carp dipped in egg and breadcrumbs, then fried).

Glöcke, Am Plönlein 1, t (09861) 95899, *www.glocke-rothenburg.de* (€€). Tasty, simple cuisine; popular with locals.

Feuchtwangen

Romantik Hotel Greifen-Post, Marktplatz 8, t (09852) 6800, *www.greifen.de* (€€€–€€). Situated in the town centre, perfectly clean and comfortable, with classy antique furniture and a swimming pool in the former Renaissance courtyard. The restaurant serves good, hearty Franconian food.

Dinkelsbühl

Dinkelsbühl, 40km south of Rothenburg, vies with it for the position of most romantic town in Germany, but is more compact and less touristy. Dinkelsbühl claims to be older, dating back to the 7th century AD. By the end of the 13th century the town was an influential member of the Swabian League, with a ring of impressive protective defences. Nowadays Dinkelsbühl invites aimless wandering. Side streets lure you into inviting alleys of overhanging houses in *Fachwerk*, Gothic and Renaissance styles. Even the tourist strips seem jolly rather than tacky.

Dinkelsbühl's medieval core is protected by the **Stadtmauer**, which is guarded by 17 towers and pierced by four massive gateways. To enter the **Altstadt** use the east gate, the 13th-century **Wörnitz Tor**. This offers a picturesque view of the River Wörnitz and the moat against a backdrop of the ancient wall, dotted with towers of all shapes and sizes. Sadly the walls have lost most of their parapets: the **Alte** and **Neue Promenade** outside the western defences may give you an idea of the appearance of Dinkelsbühl's walls in the Middle Ages. The Altrathausplatz leads past the old Rathaus building to a larger square, the **Marktplatz**, fenced off at its eastern end by the **Münster St Georg**, the town's symbol (1448–99), a fine late Gothic *Hallenkirche* (hall church). From the outside the Münster looks fairly ordinary, but the interior is startling, surrounded by soaring spear-shaped windows. The delicate stonework rises between the windows, then fans out into the vaults in slender, graceful lines. The **high altar** seems enormously distant; on it a late Gothic *Crucifixion* panel glows mysteriously.

A few metres northwest across the Weinmarkt towards the **Rothenburger Tor** is the 16th-century **Deutsches Haus**. Its richly decorated façade makes it one of the finest examples of Renaissance half-timbering in Germany. Look out for the beautifully carved corbels of miniature figurines sprouting from the vertical beams. Separated from it by a small alleyway is the

---

Where the Night Watchman Still Calls

Dinkelsbühl preserves an age-old tradition, once a feature of towns across Europe: the night watchman. He begins his round from the Marktplatz every night at 9pm (9.30pm in summer) from April till October and at Christmas. In buckskin breeches, grey cloak and black felt hat and equipped with a halberd, horn and lantern, he sets off through the streets and narrow alleys, blows his horn and sings out loudly at more than 20 fixed stops along the way: *'Hört Ihr Leut und laßt Euch sagen...!'* ('Listen well, you burghers, to what I've to tell you...!').

Until 1889 the town had four night watchmen who served as sergeants-at-arms, imposed the night's curfew, kept watch for fires and checked the gates and sentries. Today the watchmen are more of a tourist attraction and many visitors follow in their footsteps through Dinkelsbühl.

Festivals in Dinkelsbühl

① Dinkelsbühl >>
*Altrathausplatz 14,
t (09851) 90240,
www.dinkelsbuehl.de;
has an outstanding
collection of maps and
information, including
details of walks with
the town's night
watchman*

For 10 days in the mid-July, Dinkelsbühl celebrates the **Kinderzeche**, a series of plays, parades, dances and fireworks commemorating an incident of the Thirty Years' War. In 1632, the story goes, the weeping of a contingent of local children mollified the Swedish commander, who had besieged the town and threatened its destruction. The main event of the festival, the re-enactment of the crucial meeting, takes place in the *Schranne*, an old 17th-century grain market in the town's historic Marktplatz. Open-air concerts by the renowned *Knabenkapelle* (boys' choir), dressed in 18th-century uniforms, are a celebrated feature of the festival.

The second Sunday of September usually sees the **Stadtfest** in Dinkelsbühl, and with it more pageants and bacchanalian revels.

Where to Stay and Eat in Dinkelsbühl

Dinkelsbühl

Hotel Deutsches Haus, Weinmarkt 3, t (09851) 6058/59, *www.deutscheshaus-dkb.de* (€€). Original period furniture graces the entrance hall and the décor of most rooms harmonizes with the historic exterior. Its elegant restaurant serves sumptuous meals.

Goldene Kanne, Segringer Straße 8, t (09851) 572910, *www.hotel-goldenekanne.com* (€€–€). This dainty hotel in the Altstadt has won a Bavarian state government award. If you can afford it, try to stay in one of the two suites overlooking the town centre.

Hotel Eisenkrug, Dr.-Martin-Luther-Straße 1, t (09851) 57700, *www.hoteleisenkrug.de* (€). Has a pink façade and lots of individual touches. Good restaurant; wine bar in the cellar.

Gasthof Restaurant Zum Goldenen Anker, Untere Schmiedegasse 22, t (09851) 57800, *www.hotel-zumgoldenen-anker.de* (€). Small, family-run, traditional guesthouse; timber-panelled rooms on the ground floor.

17th-century **Schranne**. This brick structure with dainty Renaissance gables, formerly a granary, now serves as a festival hall, where the annual *Kinderzeche* is performed (*see* above).

Nördlinger Straße, with its closely packed half-timbered façades, leads to the **Nördlinger Tor**. Just outside the wall and gate stands the 15th-century **Stadtmühle**, one of the most unusual buildings in Dinkelsbühl. Although a mill, it was fortified with barbicans, gun loopholes and a protective strip of water. Inside, the **Museum of the 3rd Dimension** has state-of-the-art displays of optical imagery.

Museum of the 3rd Dimension
open April–Oct daily 10–6; Nov–Mar Sat and Sun 11–4; adm €7

Nördlingen im Ries

The area south of Dinkelsbühl is known as the **Ries**, a fertile basin about 25km across surrounded by a range of hills that are about 100m high. For a long time scientists believed that the odd landscape was the result of some prehistoric volcanic activity. However, deep-earth rock samples extracted between 1961 and 1974 prompted geologists to come up with a new explanation. They established that, some 15 million years ago, a giant asteroid of around 1,200m in diameter, travelling at a speed of 30 to 50km

Nördlingen's *Türmer*

Twice during the Thirty Years' War, in 1634 and in 1645, Nördlingen was besieged by rival armies, culminating in fierce battles just outside the town. The burghers set great store by their walled defences, the guards who manned all five gates, and the Daniel, which served admirably as the town's tallest watchtower. According to local lore, though, it was an alert woman who saved the town from a raid in 1440. She apparently noticed a pig rubbing against one of the town's wooden gates, which was unlocked and opened. Uttering the words '*So G'sell so!*', she drove the animal off and was able to bolt the gate just in time. After that the woman's words became the password for Nördlingen's sentries. Nowadays the *Türmer* stand in for their erstwhile colleagues as night watchmen, taking it in turns to occupy the lookout post near the top of the Daniel. Every night, at half-hour intervals between 10pm and midnight, the traditional 'All's well!' rings out across the roofs of the slumbering town.

per second, must have hit the earth's surface here, making a crater 1,500m deep. Nowadays the lush loess soil in the Ries gives the region the fitting name of 'Bavaria's Breadbasket', yet it was thought close enough to a lunar terrain for NASA to send their Apollo 14 and 17 astronauts here as part of their field training. In the middle of the basin lies Nördlingen, with its old town walls oddly echoing the almost perfect circle of the surrounding crater hills.

There has been an Alemannic settlement here since the 6th century AD. The town's golden age came between the 14th and 16th centuries when its busy *Pfingstmesse* (Whitsun fair) attracted traders from all over Germany. By 1327 the town had outgrown its old circular defensive moat, prompting the building of the present **Stadtmauer** with eleven towers, five gateways and two bastions; 3km of the wall is still intact. You can walk around the entire parapet in an hour (the **Reimlinger Tor**, the town's oldest gateway, provides an access point).

After the ramparts, head straight for the **Georgskirche**, the mighty parish church, the best starting point from which to explore the Altstadt. This 15th-century late Gothic hall church is Nördlingen's pride and joy. The highlight of the interior is the soaring Baroque **high altar**, with an ornate Crucifixion group believed to be by the celebrated sculptor Nikolaus Gerhaert van Leyden. The building's focal point, however, is the 89.5m-high **Daniel**, a steeple named after the Old Testament leader. You can climb up the 365 steps for a fine view of the town and the outlying villages of the Ries.

Daniel
open daily 9–dusk;
adm €2

On the north side of the Georgskirche is the **Marktplatz**, where several municipal buildings compete with each other in gaudy brilliance. The 14th-century **Rathaus** wins by a long chalk, thanks to its magnificent exterior stone stairway with its four fluted columns of Gothic and Renaissance origin. Diagonally opposite is the 16th-century **Leihaus** and local tourist office. To the west is the timber-framed **Brot- und Tanzhaus**, a former trading hall. On

Baldinger Straße, which runs northwards from the Marktplatz past the Gerberviertel (Tanners' Quarter), is the former **Spital zum Heiligen Geist**. Established in the 13th century as a hospital and almshouse, with its own church, the complex now houses the **Stadtmuseum** with an astonishingly fresh set of reredos panels and an interesting diorama of the Battle of Nördlingen of 1634 (*see* box, left). From here you can amble down along the semicircular **Herrengasse**, atop part of the razed town defences, to reach the Weinmarkt and the adjoining **Hallgebäude**, an old salt and wine storehouse of the 16th century. On its southeast edge the Weinmarkt blends into the Neubaugasse where you'll find one of the most attractive houses in town. The mellow reddish tones in the restored timber-framed façade of the 17th-century **Wintersche Haus** look magnificent when seen from a distance. Come closer, and you will marvel at the beautifully carved front door with Baroque arabesque embellishments.

Rieskrater-Museum
open Tues–Sat 10–12 and 1.30–4.30; adm €3

The **Rieskrater-Museum** gives fascinating insights into the geological history of the region. The museum occupies a 16th-century barn, in sharp contrast to its innovative displays. The staff can arrange geological tours of the Ries for groups.

Festivals in Nördlingen

Stabenfest

Stabenfest takes place in mid-May, when locals mark spring with a 16th-century festival for children. The central feature is the procession of sumptuously dressed boys and girls from the Weinmarkt to the Kaiserwiese outside the town walls, where in good Bavarian fashion the event erupts into general merry-making. At this point the proceedings are punctuated with *Stabenlieder*, witty bardic lyrics, often with caustic references to the town's history.

Nördlinger Pfingstmesse

Mid-June brings the 14-day *Nördlinger Pfingstmesse* to the *Kaiserwiese*, a folk festival with funfair and lots of beer in the unbroken tradition of Nördlingen's formidable medieval Whitsun fairs.

Other Festivals

The *Historisches Stadtmauerfest*, a medieval pageant, is performed every three years (next in September 2011). The townsfolk dress up in period costumes. There are also displays of traditional crafts.

The *Scharlachrennen*, held at two-year intervals (next in 2011), sees a celebrated horse race, first held in 1438, when the winning jockey received a bale of handsome scarlet cloth – hence its name. Since then, the event has expanded to include not only the traditional flat racing, but foot races for the youngsters of Nördlingen.

Where to Stay and Eat in Nördlingen

Nördlingen

Hotel Klösterle, Beim Klösterle 1, t (09081) 87080, *www.nh-hotels.com* (€€). This stylish hotel, an intriguing example of medieval architecture blended with top-class hospitality, combines the former abbey building (1243) and the half-timbered Pflug (1420). The restaurant, in the former abbey church, serves regional specialities.

Gasthof Zum Engel, Wemdinger Straße 4, t (09081) 3167, *www. gasthofzumengel.de* (€). Pleasant converted brewery near the town walls, with a restaurant.

ⓘ Nördlingen >>
Leihaus, Marktplatz, t (09081) 841165, www.noerdlingen.de

Around Nördlingen

Neresheim and Kaisheim

At **Neresheim**, 19km to the southwest of Nördlingen, the **Abteikirche St Ulrich und Afra** was the last work of the Baroque architect Balthasar Neumann, who started rebuilding the abbey church of the Benedictine monastery in 1747. Master masons from Donauwörth concluded it. The airy and spacious interior, with domed ceilings and energetic ceiling frescoes by Martin Steinach, is its main attraction.

Six kilometres from Donauwörth lies the former Cistercian abbey church of **Kaisheim**. Smarting under their austere monastic restrictions, the Cistercian monks put their all into a small number of furnishings. There's a graceful Baroque high altar (1673) and some fine choir stalls. The wistful decoration that covers the organ parapet with cherubs, putti and drapery makes a rare spot of near-opulence in the church.

Harburg

Harburg, 15km southeast of Nördlingen, is a pretty town with half-timbered houses on the River Wörnitz. What really draws the crowds, however, is the imposing **Schloß**, above the town. First mentioned in 1093, the Staufian castle was given to the loyal Counts of Oettingen in 1295, a privilege that became hereditary in 1407 (it is still owned by their descendants). The rambling castle is one of the best preserved complexes of its kind in southern Germany – an architectural potpourri spanning seven centuries. The main courtyard is reached via a series of medieval defensive structures and is surrounded by some interesting buildings, such as **Burgvogtei**, the 16th-century castle manor, now an inn and small hotel. The 12th-century western keep, known as the **Diebsturm** (Thieves' Tower), adjoins the courtyard and is the castle's oldest surviving structure.

Harburg Schloß
guided tours Tues–Sun 10–5; adm €4.50

For many people, the castle's highlight is the treasures held in the **Fürstenbau**. This 16th-century building contains the lavish art collection of past and present burgraves, including spectacularly carved masterpieces by Tilman Riemenschneider.

Fürstenbau
adm €4.50

Höchstädt and the Battle of Blenheim

Leaving the main route of the Romantic Road at **Donauwörth**, the B16 takes you 30km southwest to **Höchstädt**, on the northern bank of the Danube, indelibly associated with the Churchills. On 13 August 1704, in a decisive battle of the War of the Spanish Succession, an Allied army under John Churchill, Duke of? Marlborough, combined with Habsburg troops under Prince

Eugene of Savoy to defeat a Franco-Bavarian army. The actual site of the **Battle of Blenheim**, as it became known in the English-speaking world (hence Blenheim Palace in Oxfordshire), lies close to the village of **Blindheim** and is easily accessible. Nowadays a sombre **sword-shaped monument** not far from where the B16 leaves Höch-städt towards Blindheim, as well as a small memorial in the village and a plaque on its cemetery wall, commemorate those who died in the battle. The **Heimatmuseum** in the former Rathaus of Höch-städt makes an essential supplement to a visit, as it includes two interesting dioramas and artefacts that were collected from the battlefield.

Heimatmuseum
*open first Sun in month
2–5; adm free*

Dillingen

The restful town of Dillingen, 10km further southwest along the B16, stretches gracefully along the Danube. The town dates from the 13th century, but soon developed as the ancestral residence of the prince-bishops of Augsburg. In 1564 the town's university was handed over to the Jesuit order, and soon became a centre of the Counter-Reformation in southern Germany.

Dillingen is dominated by Baroque Jesuit architecture, although there are earlier structures of other monastic orders as well. The main buildings are concentrated in the **Altstadt**, between Konviktstraße, Kardinal-von-Waldburg-Straße and Königstraße.

Start in front of the early Baroque basilica of the **Stadtpfarrkirche St Peter**. Immediately your eye is caught by the 18th-century blue-gold column of the **Immaculata-Säule**, backed by the mellow russet portal of the early 18th-century **Franziskanerinnenkirche Mariä Himmelfahrt**.

Past the **Rathaus**, an amalgam of the 15th-century town hall and a 17th-century patrician house, and the one-time **Dominikanerinnenkloster St Ulrich** (which now houses a girls' school), is the extensive complex of the **Jesuitenkolleg** and the 17th-century **Universität**. Following the suppression of the Jesuit order in 1773 and the secularization of all church property in 1803, the buildings now serve as a seminary for the Catholic church and a modern teacher-training college. Especially impressive is the **Goldener Saal** (Golden Hall), the erstwhile auditorium with resplendent rococo interior and vivacious ceiling frescoes by the 18th-century artist Johann Anwander, visual hymns of praise to the Virgin Mary.

Goldener Saal
*open April–Oct Sat–Sun
10–5; adm €1*

Towards the end of the central faculty buildings is the **Studienkirche**, whose converted rococo furnishings are said to have inspired many churches in southern Germany simply because cohorts of Catholic priests passed through the stringent seminary here at Dillingen.

09 The Romantic Road | Nördlingen im Ries: Around Nördlingen

Getting around Augsburg

Augsburg is on the A8, 60km northwest of Munich and 160km southeast of Stuttgart.

For **car hire**: **Avis**, Klinkerberg 31, **t** (0821) 3 82 41. **Taxis**: **t** (0821) 35025.

Augsburg is a busy **rail** junction. Over 90 trains a day will bring you here from all over Germany (Munich 30mins ICE; Würzburg 2hrs ICE; Frankfurt 3hrs). The Hauptbahnhof is west of the centre amidst modern buildings; it's a 15min walk to the Altstadt past the tourist office and local bus station.

A **day ticket** for the trams and buses costs €5.50, though you are unlikely to need it unless you are staying in the suburbs.

Augsburg

Augsburg has been hoarding treasure for over 2,000 years. Its Romanesque cathedral is outshone by the Gothic St Ulrich's, and both are eclipsed by the Renaissance Rathaus. Garlands of Baroque gables hang between rococo palaces, and the streets are so wide that some look more like squares.

Luminaries connected with the city include the Emperor Augustus (after whom it was named), Hans Holbein the Elder and Younger, Martin Luther, Mozart (whose father was born here, and who often returned to give recitals) and the 20th-century engineers Rudolf Diesel and Willi Messerschmitt. Augsburg doesn't commemorate Messerschmitt because of his Nazi sympathies; and for a long time they also ignored another famous son, the left-wing playwright Bertolt Brecht, who dismissed his home town as a bourgeois *Scheißstadt*.

History

Augsburg was founded by Tiberius (stepson of Augustus) in 15 BC, and soon became a prosperous trading city. By the 13th century it was a Free Imperial City, and reached its zenith in the 15th century with the rise to power of local merchant families the Fuggers and the Welsers. Despite constant battles of one-upmanship, they amassed fabulous amounts of money, and wielded extraordinary international influence. Between them they came to own entire countries in South America, propped up the royal houses of Europe and made Augsburg the financial centre of the world. Their wealth put the Medicis' fortunes in the shade.

Yet as well as this grand heritage, Augsburg also has the world's first social housing complex (built by the Fuggers in 1514), charming alleys and crumbly stone houses. It is a university town with a warm café life that takes the hard gloss off its stately façade.

The Rathausplatz

The city's elegant **Rathaus** is a good place to start. Augsburg's 17th-century Master Builder, Elias Holl (1573–1646), was one of the most important architects of the German Renaissance. In 1614

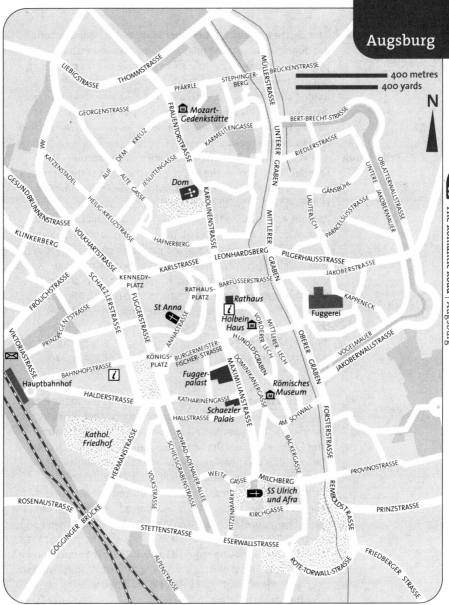

Holl returned from a trip to Italy brimming with new ideas. His rhetoric was as skilful as his draughtsmanship. Within weeks he had persuaded the city council to rip down the old Gothic Rathaus and commission him to build a more majestic expression of their might. Holl's monumental building, with its simple, clean proportions and twin onion-domed towers, is a gem of civic architecture.

Goldener Saal
open Mon–Fri 9–5

Inside, the magnificent **Goldener Saal** (Golden Hall) was burnt out during an air raid and finally restored (to a somewhat over-pristine state) only in the 1980s. Every crinkle, twirl or protruding finial of the carved wooden ceiling has been lavishly gilded. Set among all this nutwood, limewood and gold, 14m above your head, are panels of richly coloured paintings depicting personal and civic virtues. Grisaille frescoes and a gentle pastel-coloured marble floor help to subdue the riot.

Perlachturm
carillon at 11am, 12 noon, 5 and 6pm

Next door to the Rathaus is the 70m-high **Perlachturm**. The foundations date from the 11th century, but most of the rest was built 200 years later to serve as a watchtower. Then in 1615 Elias Holl rounded it off with a dome to complement those on his Rathaus, and to house the bells from the old city hall. The word 'Perlach' comes from the Old German for 'bear dancing', and was probably the name of a Roman amphitheatre on the site. Today the bruins could jig to merry Mozart tunes played on a carillon installed in 1985. In the middle of Rathausplatz is the ornate **Augustusbrunnen** (1594), a fountain built to honour Augustus Caesar. In the summer, this vast square is packed with tables, benches and umbrellas, and becomes one enormous *Bierstube*, while on the far side of the square, in hushed, carpeted cafés, spruce pensioners keep each other company over *Kaffee und Kuchen*.

The Dom

A short walk northwards up Hoher Weg brings you to the Dom (begun 1060), a hotchpotch of different architectural styles. Shadows of the original Romanesque arches can be seen above later Gothic windows; the twin spires date back to the 11th century; the high altar was installed in 1962; and there is a sugary rococo chapel (a favourite for weddings) off the north aisle. The cathedral's art treasures should not be missed. The series of **Prophet Windows** (1140) is the oldest stained-glass cycle in the world. Five prophets are depicted in bold colours and simple designs. All (except David, who is crowned) wear the pointed hats that medieval Jews were required to wear. There is an outstanding **bronze portal** – most of it dating back to the 12th century – and an eloquent cycle of paintings by **Holbein the Elder**, showing scenes from the life of the Virgin. In the courtyard are foundations of the ancient church of St John the Baptist (c. 960), including a full-immersion font that was probably part of a secret Christian baptistry in the cellars of a 6th-century Roman house.

Mozart-Gedenkstätte
Frauentorstraße 30; open Tues–Sun 10–4; adm €1.50

Just beyond the Dom is the **Mozart-Gedenkstätte** (Mozart House), mainly on the life of Mozart Senior, who was born in Augsburg but soon left for Salzburg and Vienna. Young Wolfgang frequently gave concerts in his father's home town, his recitals on one occasion coinciding with a heady romance with his cousin Bäsle.

St Anna

A wander back down Annastraße brings you to St Anna, built as a Carmelite monastery in 1321. You could easily think that this church was the wrong way round: a memorial chapel built in 1509 by Jakob Fugger and his brothers fills the *whole* of the west chancel and completely upstages the rest of the simple basilica. This **Fuggerkapelle**, with superb marble carving by Hans Daucher, became the touchstone for Renaissance design in Germany. In the east cloister, simple wooden stairs (the **Lutherstiege**) lead to an exhibition on the life of Martin Luther. Unfortunately, most of the exhibits are textual, and commentary is only in German.

From here make your way across to **Maximilianstraße**, south from Rathausplatz. Until 1957 Maximilianstraße was named after King Maximilian I Joseph of Bavaria. Then it was renamed after Emperor Maximilian I, a great lover of Augsburg, a gesture that in effect changed nothing. Two stylish 16th-century fountains grace the street, the first topped with a statue of Mercury, the second with a robust Hercules, designed by Dutch sculptor Adriaen de Vries to symbolize Augsburg's merchants and master craftsmen respectively. Just before the Hercules fountain, at Maximilianstraße 36–38, is the conglomeration of three houses that formed the 16th-century **Fuggerpalast**. The building is still home to Fugger descendants, but you can nip around the back for a look at the **Damenhof**, a pretty Italianate courtyard with arcades of Etruscan pillars, a musicians' balcony and traces of the original frescoes.

Schaezler Palais
open Tues–Sun 10–5;
adm €3

Farther down Maximilianstraße (opposite the Hercules Fountain) is the **Schaezler Palais**, built in 1770 for a wealthy silversmith. Inside is a compact rococo ballroom, almost in its original resplendent shape, with deep mirrors, glittering crystal chandeliers and a ceiling painting showing Europe as the centre of the world. Marie-Antoinette, on her bridal procession from Austria to France, popped in for three minuets during the grand opening ball, and the room at once became the social hub of Augsburg. At the back it connects up with a 16th-century convent, now the **Staatsgalerie**, with a

Staatsgalerie
same opening times as
Schaezler Palais

Luther and the Fuggers

In 1518 Luther was summoned to a court of the Inquisition in Rome. His patron, Johann Friedrich of Saxony, fearing for the priest's life, persuaded the Pope to hold the hearing in Augsburg. The pretext was that an ailing Luther couldn't make the journey to Rome (though he did manage to walk the full 500km from Wittenberg to Augsburg, where he stayed at St Anna). He was interrogated by Cardinal Cajetan at the home of Jakob Fugger between 12 and 14 October, but they couldn't reach an agreement. On 20 October, under threat of arrest, Luther slipped out of town.

At the next Diet, in 1530, the Augsburg Confession set out the basic tenets of the Lutheran faith, but it wasn't until 1555, with the signing of the Peace of Augsburg (*see* **History**, p.22), that the struggle between the two churches was resolved. Later, St Anna became a Lutheran church. Jakob Fugger, a fervent Catholic who imported bands of Jesuits to try to tip the balance in Augsburg, must be turning in his monumental grave.

striking portrait of Jakob Fugger in his favourite Venetian brocade cap by Albrecht Dürer (1518), and a series of paintings of Roman basilicas (1499–1504) by Holbein the Elder and local artist Hans Burgkmair (1473–1531).

Maximilianstraße runs up to the church of **St Ulrich und Afra** – a lofty Gothic structure with a Bavarian onion spire added in the 16th century. Shrines to Ulrich and Afra are inside, and three golden altars (1607) packed with saints and cherubim tower up above the choir. The adjacent **Ulrich Lutheran Church** used to be a sort of clerical souvenir shop, selling trinkets and indulgences, but after the 1555 Peace of Augsburg it was given to the Lutherans.

The Jakobviertel and Fuggerei

Duck east off Maximilianstraße for the **Jakobviertel**, once the poorer part of town. Among the clutter of medieval houses and narrow streets you'll find galleries and craft shops. The **Römisches Museum** (Roman Museum) is housed in an old Gothic hall church. The **Holbein Haus** commemorates its famous resident with a few documents, but is mainly used for contemporary art exhibitions.

Smarting from the insults Brecht heaped upon it, Augsburg only recently swallowed its pride and opened the **Brecht Haus**. The playwright was born here in 1898. The exhibition centres mainly on Brecht's life in Augsburg – not the most enthralling part of his career.

Jakob Fugger wanted to be sure that he would go to heaven. Reliable sources had it that this was difficult for a rich man – but a good stock of prayers could ease the passage. So in 1523, Fugger

Römisches Museum
Dominikanergasse 15; open May–Sept Tues–Sun 10–5, Oct–April Tues–Sun 10–4; adm free

Holbein Haus
Vorderer Lech 20; open Tues–Sun 10–5

Brecht Haus
Auf dem Rain 7; open Tues–Sun 10–4; adm free

The Richest Men in the World

The Fugger fortune was largely established by Jakob Fugger the Rich (1459–1525). The youngest son of a merchant family, he wanted to become a priest but at 19, following the deaths of his father and older brothers, he was hauled back out of the monastery to run the family firm. He went off to Venice for business training and was so fired by the Italian way of life that on his return he almost single-handedly introduced the Renaissance to Germany. The buildings he commissioned became models for the movement throughout the country. He brought in double-entry book-keeping, took risks in buying up some flooded mines and ended up with monopolies over Hungarian copper, Austrian silver and Spanish quicksilver. Soon he had amassed a fortune that historians estimate was the equivalent of the combined assets of today's top ten multinational companies. The rulers of Europe came to him to borrow money to pay their armies, and for the bribes needed to put a new emperor on the throne. (The election of Emperor Charles V in 1519 was financially secured through 543,585 florins from the Fuggers and 143,333 florins from their arch-rivals the Welsers.) In return Jakob Fugger extracted concessions and favours that increased his wealth and power even more. In his late forties he married a woman half his age. For 20 years he showered her with gifts and they entertained lavishly, but had no children. Jakob died in 1525, leaving his fortune to his nephew Anton. His wife remarried three weeks later – to some scandal, but very little surprise.

Anton ran the firm well, but lost his nerve over the dangerous trade with the Americas and the West Indies. (Charles V gave the Welsers control over Venezuela; the Fuggers were offered Chile and Peru, but declined as Anton felt that pirates and conquistadors made the venture too risky.) The family fortune gradually crumbled. Today's Fuggers own a bank and some property, but are not nearly as well off as their predecessors.

built a housing estate for Catholics who had been made poor 'through no fault of their own', setting the rent at one Rhenish guilder per annum – and one 'Our Father', one 'Hail Mary' and one 'Creed' daily, in his favour. Today the **Fuggerei** in Jakoberstraße is still financed and run by the Fugger family. Residents pay 88 cents in rent per year (the equivalent to a Rhenish guilder) and still offer up prayers for their benefactors. The estate, designed by Thomas Krebs, is a model of social housing way ahead of its time. Houses are separated by wide lanes; there are trees, fountains and individual gardens. You can visit **No.13**, in its original state, to marvel at the ingenuity of the design. The bright front room (used as a workroom) has windows onto the street, and backs into the kitchen. A special handle allows you to open the door to customers without leaving the work bench. The stove that heats the room is loaded from behind the wall in the kitchen (to reduce the fire risk). In the bedrooms there are niches for candles (also to prevent fires). The cottages are cosy and compact, and modern residents look blissfully content – even if they have to put up with tourists and pay a fine to the night watchman if they come home after 10pm. Mozart's great-grandfather lived at **No.14**. He was ostracized and reduced to poverty after burying the corpse of an executioner.

No.13, Fuggerei
open Mar–Oct 9–6; adm €1

09 | The Romantic Road | Augsburg

Services in Augsburg

Post office: Viktoriastraße 3 (near the station).

Festivals in Augsburg

There are two big **folk festivals**, at Easter and at the beginning of September. Both have accompanying street markets in the Jakobviertel. The *Christkindlmarkt* during Advent is one of the best Christmas markets in Germany, and is especially renowned for the quality of its live music, and for its 'alternative' Christmas stalls selling environmentally sound and politically correct products.

Where to Stay in Augsburg

(i) **Augsburg >**
Bahnhofstraße 7, t (0821) 502070, www. augsburg-tourismus.de; open Mon–Fri 9–5

Rathausplatz: open Mon–Fri 9–6, Sat 10–4

Augsburg

Steigenberger Drei Mohren Hotel, Maximilianstraße 40, t (0821) 50360, *www.augsburg.steigenberger.de* (€€€). Mozart, Goethe and any number of archdukes and princes have stayed here before you. This is the poshest address in town, though

modernization has all but destroyed the old atmosphere.

Hotel Ost am Kö, Fuggerstraße 4–6, t (0821) 502040, *www.ostamkoe.de* (€€). Quiet, central hotel with friendly management. It's 5mins' walk from the Bahnhof, and there's a parking garage nearby. No restaurant.

Pension Georgsrast, Georgenstraße 31, t (0821) 502610 (€). Very good value: central, quietly situated, with special deals on Chinese massage and health cures. No restaurant.

Bayerischer Löwe, Linke Brandstraße 2, t (0821) 702870 (€). Among the cheapest and most cheerful of the pensions in the northeastern suburb of Lechhausen.

Youth hostel, Beim Pfaffenkeller 3, t (0821) 33909. Bed and breakfast costs around €14.

Eating Out in Augsburg

Though it is technically in Bavaria, Augsburg is really the easternmost outpost of Swabia, and the cooking is appropriately refined. You'll find *Spätzle* (shredded noodles) with nearly everything. They are delicious covered with brown butter and breadcrumbs or cheese and fried onions. *Zwetschgendatschi* is a local speciality that earned Augsburgers their nickname (*Datschiburgers*): a yeasty lump of pastry smothered with plums and cinnamon sugar that you'll find in cafés all over town.

Welser Küche, Maximilianstraße 83, t (0821) 96110 (€€€). Hosts a nightly banquet where meals from Philippine Welser's 16th-century cookbook are served.

Fuggerei-Stube, Jakoberstraße 26 (€€). At the Fuggerei, and one of the best places in town for Swabian food. Try *Krautspatzen* (noodles with bacon and sauerkraut – surprisingly delicate, and far tastier than it sounds).

Vierunddreissig, Hunoldsgraben 34, t (0821) 39294 (€€). Crammed with junk-shop furniture and draped with pearls and feather boas, it serves whatever inspires the Italian, Greek and Swabian chefs (the fillets of pork in Armagnac are delicious).

Bars and Cafés in Augsburg

Kreßlesmühle, Barfüßerstraße 4, t (0821) 37170. An arts centre in an old mill. The place to be if you're a student, school truant or jazz fan. There's a café with a popular beer garden, live music (anything from blues singers to wandering Sephardic balladeers), and good theatre and film.

Perlach Stübe, t (0821) 510960. Tucked into the wall of the church at the Perlachturm and overlooked by nearly everyone, a cupboard-sized-bar where you can sip a *Schnapps* on a freezing winter's afternoon.

Café Eber, Rathausplatz, t (0821) 36847. The best place to join the *Datschiburgers* at their favourite culinary pastime.

Zeughaus, Zeugplatz 4, t (0821) 511685. Has a beer garden that's popular with thirtysomethings reluctant to shake off their student years. The restaurant serves good, inexpensive meals.

Landsberg

The town of Landsberg dates from Henry the Lion's 12th-century castle, built here to control the lucrative salt trade on the old road from Salzburg to Memmingen. The castle has long gone, and a small town is left (40km from Augsburg), rising steeply from the River Lech. It's another beautifully preserved medieval site that seems stuck in the days of yore, with timber-framed houses. Hitler spent nine months in the local prison following his unsuccessful *Putsch* of 1923 – time that he put to use in writing *Mein Kampf*.

The **Rathaus** on the central Hauptplatz makes a good starting point for a walk around the town. The floridly stuccoed rococo façade of the town hall (home to the local tourist office) was designed and realized by Dominikus Zimmermann, architect of the Wieskirche (*see* below). Zimmermann settled in Landsberg from 1716 and was *Bürgermeister* between 1749 and 1754. He also built the **Johanneskirche** (1750–52), south of the Hauptplatz, modelled on his more famous pilgrimage church.

The signposted ***Stadtrundgang***, a walk through the city, takes in the best sights, weaving through crooked alleys and arches, and climbing up to the fortified wall, of which around 300m, with a series of barbicans, survives intact. From here you see a huddle of red-tiled roofs. Brightly coloured roughcast shops and houses pop out of it, and it has grown a few eccentric gateways – odd

(i) Landsberg >
in the Rathaus,
Hauptplatz 152, t (08191)
128246, www.lands
berg.de; the free town
map outlines the
Stadtrundgang

Where to Stay in Landsberg

Landsberg

Hotel Goggl, Herkomer Straße
19–20, **t** (08191) 3240, *www.*

hotelgoggl.de (€€). Built on the base walls of an older hotel from 1670, the Goggl successfully captures the rich tradition of its predecessor.

Bayertor
*open May–Oct 10–12
and 2–5; adm €1*

patchworks of different period styles. The most striking of these is the 15th-century Gothic **Bayertor**, the town's heraldic emblem.

Ludwig's Castles and the Wieskirche

Soon after Augsburg, the faint smudge on the horizon begins to resolve itself into the peaks and shadows of the Alps. As you travel nearer, the atmosphere seems to sharpen, there's a growing chill and the countryside erupts in rocky outcrops.

In the middle of the rolling fields that lead up to the foothills, you'll find the **Wieskirche**, a pilgrimage church that tourist brochures refer to as 'The Church of our Flagellated Lord in the Meadow'. The object of veneration is a wooden statue of Christ, which was rejected as too ugly for the local Good Friday procession. Later it was found that, if you prayed hard enough, the figure shed real tears. Pilgrims flocked from afar, and in 1746 Abbot Marianus II built a grand church to accommodate them. The result was one of the finest examples of rococo architecture in Germany. The architect Dominikus Zimmerman (*see* p.34) was so pleased with it that he came to live in nearby Landsberg for the rest of his life. Light streams in, reflects off the brilliant white walls and pillars and picks out the curls and licks of gilded stucco. Cherubs and angels peek out from behind garlands of foliage, and in the middle of an effervescent ceiling fresco (by J.B. Zimmerman) the resurrected Christ sits resplendent on a rainbow.

Despite its isolated setting, the Wieskirche swarms with tourists. Coaches and souvenir kiosks cluster all the way up to the door; there's even piped music. When the church was finished, the abbot used his diamond ring to scratch on the window of the prelates' chamber the words: 'At this place abides happiness, here the heart finds peace'. He must be turning in his grave.

Just as you get to the Alpine foothills you come to Neuschwanstein and Hohenschwangau, two castles that once belonged to the dreamy, eccentric King Ludwig II of Bavaria (1845–86). Ludwig drew up plans for **Neuschwanstein** with the help of a stage designer rather than an architect. Work began in 1869 and went on right up to Ludwig's deposition in 1886. The sparkling white *Schloß*, with its sprinkling of spires and turrets, became a prototype for Walt Disney fairy-tale castles.

⭐ Wieskirche

⭐ Neuschwanstein

09

The Romantic Road | Ludwig's Castles and the Wieskirche

King Ludwig II of Bavaria

In Bavaria King Ludwig II has cult status. Perhaps his hopeless, self-destructive romanticism appeals to the national psyche. To foreigners he is known mainly as the builder of Neuschwanstein, the white castle featured in countless German tourist leaflets. But his real contribution is far more significant. Without Ludwig's support, the composer Wagner would never have the opportunity to produce the work he did.

Ludwig was born on 25 August 1845. Three years later his grandfather, King Ludwig I, abdicated after a scandalous affair with the 'Spanish' dancer Lola Montez (alias Mrs Eliza Gilbert, a British housewife). Ludwig's father, Maximilian II, became king but reigned for just 16 years, so the young prince assumed the throne at 19. He was fastidious about his appearance ('If I didn't have my hair curled every day, I couldn't enjoy my food,' he said) and enjoyed the costumes of his new role. Affairs of state held little appeal for him though, and he soon antagonized his cabinet.

Even as a toddler Ludwig revealed the proclivities that were later to seal his fate. His mother, Queen Marie, noted in her diary that the infant Ludwig loved art, would build churches with his toy bricks, enjoyed dressing up and was always giving away his toys and money. Another cause for complaint was the king's infatuation with Wagner. Ludwig heard his first Wagner opera (*Lohengrin*) in 1861. In the words of an attendant the music had 'an almost demoniacal' effect on the young prince, who became convulsed with excitement. At that time many considered Wagner's music to be cranky, ugly, even dangerous. In 1871 Mark Twain wrote: 'The banging and slamming and booming and crashing were something beyond belief. The racking and pitiless pain of it remains stored up in my memory alongside the memory of the time I had my teeth fixed...' Certainly in the 1860s Ludwig's conviction that no one could 'possibly remain unmoved by this magical fairy-tale, by this heavenly music' was not a common one – though it also hints that the monarch was captivated less by Wagner's music than by the world of fantasy the operas evoked.

As soon as he became king, Ludwig set about tracking down his hero. Wagner had gone into hiding; *Der Ring der Nibelungen* and *Die Meistersinger* were unfinished, all the leading opera houses had declared *Tristan* impossible to stage, and the extravagant composer had run up enormous debts. Ludwig's cabinet secretary spent three weeks in pursuit of the elusive Wagner, who thought powerful creditors were on his tail, but finally unearthed him in Stuttgart and whisked him back to Munich.

An intense and passionate friendship developed between the two, amounting to far more than straightforward royal patronage. Ludwig worshipped the composer. Wagner wrote of Ludwig that 'he knows and understands everything about me – understands me like my own soul'. He wrote of the tremendous inspiration he derived from Ludwig, and the two kept up a relentless correspondence. The king paid off Wagner's debts, set him up in a villa in Munich, granted him a stipend that exceeded that of a senior minister and promised him an enormous sum on completion of the *Ring*. The cabinet, however, became increasingly alarmed at the influence Wagner wielded, and Cabinet Secretary Pfistermeister and Minister-President von Pfordten (nicknamed Pfi and Pfo) connived to get rid of him. By December 1865 Ludwig was convinced that he was alienating his subjects, and asked Wagner to leave Munich. But the friendship and patronage continued.

His relationship with Wagner was almost certainly platonic. Ludwig was homosexual but, when he wasn't agonizing over this 'mortal sin' and swearing himself to celibacy, he was in love with a succession of grooms, handsome cousins and attentive aides-de-camp. He loathed his mother and referred to her alternately as 'that old goose', 'the widow of my predecessor', or 'the Colonel of the Third Artillery Regiment'. The only woman he had any real time for was his cousin, the Empress Elisabeth of Austria (*see* p.77). They had been friends from childhood, and they remained deeply attached until his death. Apart from Elisabeth, Wagner and a few long-lasting loves, Ludwig had few close friends. He was a shy, solitary figure who slept most of the day and went for long, lonely rides in the dead of night. At Linderhof there was even a device that lowered his entire dining table into the kitchens, where it could be replenished with food so he could eat alone.

Ludwig lived more and more in his dream world, neglecting affairs of state. The splendours of Versailles and the rich romance of German legends such as that of Lohengrin inspired him later to build three dream castles: Neuschwanstein (1869), a shrine to Lohengrin, Tannhäuser and other medieval German heroes; Herrenchiemsee (1878), a mock Versailles; and Linderhof (1879) with its magical grotto.

These three castles cost around 31 million Marks – about the amount of the indemnity paid to Prussia after the Seven Weeks' War. Ludwig ran up huge debts, and by 1884 there seemed a real possibility that Linderhof and Herrenchiemsee would be repossessed, but nothing could dissuade him.

Finally, the cabinet decided that Ludwig had to go. As Ludwig's brother, Otto, was insane, his mild-mannered uncle Prince Luitpold had to be persuaded to act as regent. The easiest way to do this was to have Ludwig declared insane too – since it ran in the family. Apart from Otto (who had suffered from convulsions since childhood) there was a string of odd, bewildered souls on his mother's side, and also the Princess Alexandra, a highly strung aunt who was convinced that she had swallowed a glass piano. Ludwig's own bizarre behaviour was a rich source of evidence against him. Early in 1886 the Minister-President Freiherr von Lutz and some cabinet colleagues gathered a thick wad of 'evidence' – much of it gossip from servants who had been dismissed and bore grudges. The prominent Dr Bernhard von Gudden certified Ludwig on the basis of this report, without having once examined him.

Certainly Ludwig was subject to violent outbursts of frenzied temper and was obsessively shy of the public; at banquets he would hide behind banks of flowers and have the band play so loudly that conversation was impossible. He occasionally demanded to be dressed in full regalia (which had to be fetched from a strongroom in Munich) for his midnight rides; after reading a book on the Chinese court he went through a phase of demanding that servants prostrate themselves before him; he meted out extraordinary medieval punishments ('Pluck out his eyes!') – though courtiers only pretended to carry them out. He was very odd, but there is little evidence of true madness. Ludwig was a dreamy eccentric with the power to make his fantasy world real. As much as he loathed his administrative role, he had an astute understanding of international affairs and was capable of rational, intelligent political argument. He could also be disarmingly down-to-earth, and was adored by local peasants as the tall, handsome king who would suddenly appear from nowhere, sit himself down next to some woodcutters and share their lunch.

The night Dr Gudden and a deputation from the cabinet came to apprehend Ludwig was cold and rainy. The party arrived at Hohenschwangau around midnight, planning to cross the valley to Neuschwanstein, where the king was staying, the next morning. However, a loyal coachman cottoned on to what was happening and warned the king. When the officials noticed the coachman was missing at 3am, they suspected the secret was out and immediately set off. They found their paths blocked by the police, the fire brigade and crowds of loyal locals.

The commissioners were arrested, but the machinery of Ludwig's downfall was in motion. Ludwig neither fled to the Tyrol, nor appeared in public to show that he was not mad. On 12 June 1886 a second commission arrived to take him to the castle at Berg, on the Starnberger See. Ludwig was devastated, drinking heavily and threatening suicide. But the next evening he seemed calm enough to go for an unaccompanied walk in the grounds with Dr Gudden. The two never returned. Later that night both of their bodies were fished out of shallow water at the lake's edge.

What happened remains a mystery. Perhaps Ludwig attempted suicide, and Gudden drowned while trying to save him; or maybe Ludwig murdered Gudden, but suffered a heart attack while doing so. Whatever the explanation, Ludwig's death was tragic and pointless. The Empress Elisabeth, who perhaps understood him better than anyone, burst out when she heard the news: 'The king was not mad; he was just an eccentric living in a dream world. They might have treated him more gently...'

Neuschwanstein opened as a museum three weeks after Ludwig's apparent suicide, and has been a tourist trap ever since. Notices command you to obey all members of staff and keep with your tour group and warn that you are not guaranteed a tour in the language of your choice. You are churned through the castle in groups of 60, as guides mechanically reel off their spiel in 35 minutes flat (probably half as long as you waited for a ticket). Then it's off down the hill and up the other side to Hohenschwangau to start all over again.

For all that, Neuschwanstein is worth the battle. The castle is ingeniously situated. From one side you look out across flat grassland to the shimmering Alpsee; other windows open straight onto an Alpine gorge with bounding cascades. You slip from stagy Byzantine halls into heavily carved wooden dens. (Fourteen woodcarvers toiled for nearly five years just to finish the king's bedroom.) Corners, windows and doorways are draped in rich brocades (usually in Ludwig's favourite blue); the walls are painted with scenes from legends that inspired Wagner's operas.

★ **Hohenschwangau**
same times and prices

Hohenschwangau is less impressive but has more historical interest. Maximilian II (Ludwig's father) rebuilt it from the ruins of a 12th-century castle in the 1830s. Ludwig grew up and spent much of his reign here. (He only stayed in Neuschwanstein for six months.) Lohengrin, the Swan-King, is supposed to have lived in the original *Schloß*. Ludwig was obsessed with swans and the legend; he loved to dress up as Lohengrin, and often got Prince Paul von Thurn und Taxis (a young favourite) to act out the story in a swan-shaped boat on the Alpsee, while a band played appropriate snippets from Wagner's opera.

The rooms in Hohenschwangau are mostly tame neo-Gothic. When Ludwig became king he changed the ceiling fresco in the Royal Bedroom from a day to a night sky, with an artificial moon and twinkling stars lit by lanterns from behind. This bedroom was the scene of a fracas between a young Ludwig and seasoned actress Lila von Bulyowsky. Afterwards, *she* claimed that she had been shocked by the nude women in the murals and, besides, would never dream of seducing a mere boy. *He* claimed that she had chased him around the room. Both said that they spent most of the evening sitting on the bed reciting *Egmont* – up to the scene of the kiss.

ⓘ **Schwangau**
Münchnerstraße 2,
t *(08362) 81980,*
www.schwangau.de

Where to Stay and Eat around Ludwig's Castles and the Wieskirche

Of the three *Gaststätten* that have been built next to the Wieskirche, the Moser is the best value. Like the others, it serves up Bavarian tourist favourites, with lots of cheese and beef from the ubiquitous Allgäu cows.

Schloßhotel Lisl, Neuschwansteiner-straße 1–3, **t** (08362) 81006 (€€€–€€). In the valley between Ludwig's castles, with good views of both. Despite being in such a popular location, standards are high and staff are attentive and courteous. Beer garden and two restaurants.

Hotel Weinbauer, Füssener Straße 3, **t** (08362) 9860, *www.hotel-weinbauer.de* (€€). Right on the road to Ludwig's castles; has solid comforts and *gutbürgerliche* cooking.

Hotel-Restaurant Rübezahl, Am Ehberg 31, **t** (08362) 8327 (€€–€). Has many rooms with postcard views of the castle. The restaurant serves *edelbayrische Küche* – refined regional specialties using ingredients from its own garden. The owner organizes mountain treks and after-dinner, torch-lit processions.

Hotel Neuschwanstein, Geblerweg 2, **t** (08362) 8209, *www.hotelneuschwanstein.de* (€). Perfect views across to Neuschwanstein and the Alps. In the style of a traditional Alpine chalet, so all rooms have a small wooden balcony (though not all have a view). The café downstairs serves tasty home-made cakes. *Closed 28 Oct–10 Nov.*

Eastern Bavaria

From a natural fountain in a palace garden near the Black Forest, the River Danube flows eastwards across Germany to the Black Sea. One of the most captivating stretches is in eastern Bavaria, just before the river crosses the Austrian border. It runs through fertile meadows, under medieval bridges, past castles and monasteries and through the merchants' city of Regensburg. Then it flows past the Bavarian Forest – the largest natural wilderness in Europe – before slipping by Italianate Passau and out of Germany.

During the Cold War this corner of Bavaria, wedged between the Alps and Czechoslovakia, was all but ignored by the Germans, let alone foreign visitors. It is still removed from mainstream tourism and offers intriguingly different architecture, unrivalled natural beauty and glimpses of a way of life that has barely changed since the end of the 19th century.

10

Don't miss

⭐ A huge *Dom* and sturdy *Steinerne Brücke*
Regensburg p.179

⭐ The 'Bavarian Venice'
Passau p.190

⭐ Wildflowers and wilderness
Bavarian Forest p.194

See map overleaf

CZECH

REPUBLIC

Bayreuth

Marktredwitz
Waldsassen

Erschenreuth

Windischeschenbach

Weiden i.d. Opf.

Vohenstrauß

Pfreimd

Hirschau

14

Ober-
Viechtach

Amberg

Altendorf

Waldmünchen

Schwarzenfeld

Rötz

Fuhrn

Neunburg
vorm Wald

Furth im Wald

Eschlkam

Neumarkt
i.d. Opf.

Schwandorf

Pemfling

Cham

Chamerau

Englshütt

Teublitz

Stamsried

85

Burglengenfeld

Nittenau

Roding

Kötzting

Schwarzenfeld

Regen

16

Großer Arbersee

Großer Arber

Regensburg

Walhalla

Bayer

Konzell

Viechtach

Bodenmais

Zwiesel

Stallwang

Frauenau

Nationalpark
Bayerischer
Wald

Böbrach

Klingenbrunn

Bogen

Donau

Bernried-Bishofsmais

Grafling

Grafenau

Spiegelau

533

Hohenau

12

Straubing

Deggendorf

Zenting

Mallersdorf-
Pfaffenberg

Schöllnach

Tittling

Landau
an der Isar

Vilshofen

Eichendorf

Vils

Dingolfing

Vils

BAYERN

Arnstorf

Passau

Griesbach
im Rottal

Rott

Pfarrkirchen

Eggenfelden

Bad Füssing

20 km

10 miles

Simbach am Inn

N

AUSTRIA

GERMANY

CZECH
REPUBLIC

GERMANY

BAVARIA

Don't miss

⭐ Regensburg p.179

⭐ Passau p.190

⭐ Bavarian Forest p.194

Regensburg

🟡 **Regensburg**

Regensburg is a mosaic of romantically crumbly plasterwork in ochre, pale green, faded pink and terracotta, with the odd bump of Roman wall and flounce of medieval stonework. Despite an august history as an important trading and administrative centre, it is an intimate, lived-in town – its fabric patched, darned and lovingly restored, but never charmlessly pristine.

Regensburgers prefer to inhabit old buildings, not just revere them. In many of its shops you may have to manoeuvre around Romanesque pillars; a changing room might be wedged under a Gothic arch; the deli over the road was probably once a chapel. In the evenings, as lights come on in apartments, you glimpse vaulted ceilings, Gothic carving and dark panelled walls. A university town with first-rate breweries, Regensburg brims with good cheer. Visitors from Charlemagne to Mozart and Goethe have admired its felicitous position on the Danube. Choice museums and the angelic *Domspatzen* ('cathedral sparrows', a boys' choir) add to the attraction.

History

The French call Regensburg *Ratisbonne*, from the old 'Radasbona', which suggests early Celtic origins. But the first known settlement was *Castra Regina*, a Roman fortress from AD 179. Despite hostility between the Romans and natives, there must have been fraternizing, for soon a mixed-race tribe, the *Baiuvarii*, outnumbered everyone else.

By the 6th century the last Romans had disappeared, and the new Duchy of Bavaria was ruled by the Agilolfing dynasty: Frankish rulers installed by the Merovingian kings. The Agilolfingers made Regensburg their seat, and under the Carolingian king Charlemagne (who resided here from 791 to 793) it remained a city of administrative and ecclesiastical importance, playing host to the occasional Imperial Diets. When the Diets became permanent in 1663 – in effect the first German parliament – the Regensburg Rathaus was chosen as their venue, and remained so until 1803.

Because of its position on the Danube (an important east–west European thoroughfare) and near the Brenner Pass over the Alps to Italy, Regensburg flourished. Medieval Regensburger coins have been found from Venice to the Scandinavian coast, and as far away as Kiev. Arbeo of Freising, an 8th-century monk, marvelled at the 'gold and silver, purple cloths, iron, wine, honey and salt' that filled the city's warehouses and weighed down the boats on the Danube.

Getting to and around Regensburg

Regensburg is about 120km from Munich (on Autobahns 9 and 93) and 100km from Nürnberg (on Autobahn 3). For **car rental**, try the following companies: **Sixt Budget**, at the Hauptbahnhof, **t** (01805) 252575, *www.sixt.co.uk*; **Mitfahrzentrale**: Prüfeningerstraße 13, **t** (0941) 22022, *www.regensburg.mifaz.de*. For a **taxi**, call **t** (0941) 57000.

Trains run frequently to Munich (1½hrs) and Nürnberg (1hr), and seven times daily to Cologne (5¾hrs) and to Vienna (4¼hrs). The Hauptbahnhof (information **t** (0941) 19419) is about 15mins' walk from the centre of town, straight down Maximilianstraße.

Regensburg is compact, so everything you're likely to want to see is within easy **walking** distance. If you do find that you need **buses** you can pick up a route plan from the bus information office at Ernst-Reuter-Platz 2, near the Hauptbahnhof.

A brisk trade in slaves and weapons further swelled the city's coffers to make 13th-century Regensburg the largest and richest city in southern Germany. By the time it became a Free Imperial City in 1245 it was also a centre of culture and learning. Two of the first epic poems in German, the *Kaiserchronik* and the *Rolandslied*, originated here. Generations of merchants built showpiece town houses. Fortified mansions with high towers, inspired by Italian city villas, rose up all over town. At the peak of Regensburg's prosperity there were over 60 of them; around 20 still survive. (Apart from a battering by Napoleon, the city has been left relatively unscathed by war.)

The Wittelsbachs succeeded to the duchy in 1180 and moved the capital first to Kelheim and then to Landshut and Munich. New trade routes bypassed Regensburg and by the end of the 14th century the town had been overtaken as a trading centre by Nürnburg and Augsburg. Regensburg has never forgiven the Wittelsbachs. The bitterness intensified in the 19th century when the rulers plundered Regensburg's monasteries and churches for art treasures to add to their private collections and top up state funds. Locals speak of 'the largest art robbery of the 19th century', saying: 'They would have taken the cathedral if they could have moved it.'

In 1853 the town scraped together funds to build a Royal Villa, hoping to lure the Wittelsbach monarchs for an occasional visit. Ludwig III treated this gesture with contempt, dismissing the little palace as 'an aviary' and carting off its furniture too. Even today Regensburgers bristle at the fact that the Royal Villa is neglected, used as government offices and has not been restored as a museum (unlike other Wittelsbach residences). On the other hand, centuries of neglect meant that Regensburg became a sleeping beauty, unable to replace its historic buildings with new ones and ignored by rampaging armies. Today the town remains pretty much in its medieval shape, although the establishment of the university in 1967, new BMW, Toshiba and Siemens factories and a blossoming tourist industry have provided an awakening kiss. In 2006 Regensburg joined UNESCO's list of World Heritage sites.

The Cathedral and Around

Regensburg's giant **Dom**, the finest Gothic church in south Germany, looms over the town's low red rooftops, looking as if it had been dropped there by accident. Construction began after 1260 on the site of an earlier Romanesque building but, as with so many German Gothic churches, it was only finished when the twin towers went up in the 19th century. In the back courtyard is the **Eselsturm** (Donkey Tower), part of the Romanesque original, called after the donkeys who carried building material. The architect of this church made a bet with the builder of the Steinerne Brücke that he would finish first (see below). He lost dismally: the bridge was finished in 11 years, long before the cathedral. On the roof of the Eselsturm is a statue of the hapless architect, who threw himself off the tower when he lost the bet.

Work on the present cathedral came to a complete halt for 100 years during the Reformation, when the Protestant city fathers refused to grant the bishops any money. When work resumed in the 17th century, the interior was decorated according to the new Baroque fashion – which meant that all the medieval stained-glass windows were replaced with clear glass. Recent restoration work has tried to recapture the old Gothic mood, and all that remains from the Baroque period is a splendid gold and silver altar. One set of 14th-century windows was left (in the south transept), containing parts of windows (exquisitely made with fingernail-sized pieces of glass) from the original Romanesque church. In the north transept is a modern window in a bold, rather ethnic design. This caused a rumpus when it went up – people said it looked like a totem pole. Other highlights include 13th-century statues of the Annunciation, with a beaming Gabriel and stunned Mary, both in swathes of perfectly carved cloth; and two niches at the western nave entrance containing grotesque figures of the Devil and his grandmother.

Cloisters
guided tours May–Oct Mon–Fri 10am, 11am and 2pm, Sat–Sun 1 and 2pm; Nov–April Mon–Fri 11am, Sat–Sun 1pm; adm €2.50

To see the **cloisters** you must go on a guided tour. This is worth it for a look at the **Allerheiligenkapelle**, a graceful Romanesque chapel with traces of original 12th-century frescoes; and the 11th-century **Stephanskapelle**, which still has its original altar, with openings at the base for the faithful to pop in notes with requests to the saint, whose relics lay inside.

Domschatzmuseum
open Tues–Sat 10–5, Sun 12–5; adm €2

On the north side of the cathedral the **Domschatzmuseum** (Cathedral Treasures Museum), housed in a former bishop's palace, has richly embroidered vestments dating back to the 11th century and rooms of sacramental treasures, including some fine *Jugendstil* pieces. The **Diözesanmuseum St Ulrich**, at the back of the cathedral, is worth a visit for the building itself, a 12th-century court chapel. The elegant arches inside are covered in ornamental frescoes from the 16th to 17th centuries. Most notable of the collection of paintings and sculptures to be seen here is the aptly named *Beautiful Madonna* by the great Regensburg painter Albrecht Altdorfer (1480–1538). Altdorfer's *Madonna* once hung in the tiny Gothic church of **St Johannes**, at the entrance to the cathedral and formerly its baptistry. In 1992 the priest in charge of St Johannes decided that its tower needed a clock and, much to the consternation of the purists, he put one up, a rather elegant timepiece complete with musical bells.

Diözesanmuseum St Ulrich
open Tues–Sun 10–5

Across the square, directly opposite the cathedral, is a former patrician palace, the **Haus Heuport**. In the porch are the 14th-century carvings of a wicked seducer (with a snake crawling out of his back) luring a virgin with an apple. The maid has just spilt her cup of oil. The exact history of the statues isn't known.

A few strides south is Neupfarrplatz. On a concrete island in the middle of this expanse of tarmac and paving is the **Neupfarrkirche**, a church built on the site of a synagogue which had been destroyed in 1519. Just before the church was finished the city council adopted the Reformation, so this became Regensburg's first Protestant church. Nearby, on Pfauengasse (off the south side of Domplatz), through an unassuming door, is Regensburg's smallest chapel, the **Mariae Laeng Kapelle**. In the 17th century the notion arose that if you wrote your prayer on a piece of paper as long as Mary, your request would be granted. The Church didn't approve, but the belief was tenacious and the chapel is still cluttered with notes and messages of thanks.

A walk back eastwards across the Domplatz brings you to the Alter Kornmarkt, where you'll find the **Herzoghof** (Ducal Court), a 13th-century mansion with a stone tower, probably the site of the first Agilolfinger residence (it belongs to the Post Office nowadays). On the south side of the Alter Kornmarkt is the **Alte Kapelle**, a sober church from the outside, but a rococo riot within. Off the northern end of the square is the **Niedermünster**, a Romanesque basilica, now the cathedral parish church. Recent excavations have uncovered Merovingian, Carolingian and even Roman predecessors. Down towards the river, on Unter den Schwibbögen, are the heavy stone blocks of **Porta Praetoria**, once the northern gate of the Roman fort. Part of the tower and one of the arches survive.

Niedermünster
viewing by appointment only,
t 865500

Along the River

After the cathedral, Regensburg's most prominent landmark is the **Steinerne Brücke**, a stone bridge of 16 graceful arches that spans the Danube. It was built between 1135 and 1146 in preparation for a crusade. The builder supposedly made a pact with the Devil: if Satan helped him to win his bet with the cathedral's architect by finishing the bridge first, then the first soul that crossed it would be despatched to Hell. The wily builder won his bet and foxed Satan too: first to cross the bridge was a donkey. As the only strong, defendable river crossing along the Danube at the time, the Steinerne Brücke contributed greatly to Regensburg's success as a trading town. Two of the three **gates** on the bridge were blown up by Napoleon, but he left the third intact for his triumphal entry into the city. The bridge rests on its original foundations, sturdy piles of stone that have never had to be repaired and that confuse the powerful Danube into a series of whirlpools. Legend had it that only a virgin could sail across these rapids and survive. Undaunted, local companies offer boat trips across them.

Beside the gate is the **Salzstadel** (City Salt Store, now a restaurant), built 1616–20. Boats carried the 'white gold' along a canal that went right into the building. Inside you can see the lift shaft up which the salt was hauled to safe storage. If you look carefully at the old wooden beams in the ceiling, you'll see that they are still encrusted with white crystals. Next door is the **Historische Wurstküche** (*see* 'Eating Out in Regensburg', p.189), a sausage kitchen probably built as the bridge-workers' canteen. Mozart munched the delicious Regensburger *Wurst* here, and lodged across the way in the **Zum Weißen Lamm**, as did Goethe some years later.

A short walk west along the river brings you to **Keplerstraße**, named after Johannes Kepler (1571–1630) whose work on planetary motion ranks him as a founder of modern astronomy. He lived here for much of his life, and died in No.5, now the Kepler-Gedächtnishaus, which has a so-so collection of period furniture and instruments, and displays on Kepler.

Kepler-Gedächtnishaus
open Sat–Sun 10–4.30;
adm €2.20

Also on Keplerstraße is the **Runtinger Haus**, a Regensburg patrician palace built for the Runtinger family around 1400. Matteus Runtinger joined two older houses with a grand banqueting hall seating nearly 120 and copied features of Italian villas. Unfortunately, you can't visit the house, which is now the offices of the Bavarian Monuments Bureau. Rich merchants such as Runtinger, bringing back these new ideas from Italy, sparked off a fashion for fortified mansions with solid castle-like towers. The towers were merely a status symbol: most were empty save for a chapel at ground level. The houses were built around courtyards, entered through an arch large enough to drive a coach through and closed off by a heavy wooden door. All around town you can see these courtyards, often with Italianate first-floor loggias.

The Merchant Quarter

Altes Rathaus
guided tours May–Sept,
tours in English
Mon–Sat at 3.15pm;
tours in German
Mon–Sat 9.30, 10 and
11.30am, 2, 3 and 4pm,
Sun 10am, 11am and
12pm; adm €2.80,
tickets from the tourist
office – ask for
Reichstagmuseum
Führung

The **Altes Rathaus**, on Rathausplatz just west of the cathedral, was the centre of medieval Regensburg. The oldest section was built in the mid-13th century. A banqueting hall was incorporated in around 1360, and a Baroque eastern wing was added in the early 18th century. From the outside the Rathaus is an unassuming building with just one flourish – a decorative Gothic balcony from which the Holy Roman Emperor would wave to a respectful populace. The square itself was the scene of much imperial pomp. When Ferdinand III was crowned in the 16th century, the streets as far as the cathedral were covered in red, white and yellow cloth, coins were thrown to the crowd and a fountain gushed red and white wine.

To see the magnificent **interior** you need to go on a guided tour. The highlight is a visit to the **Imperial Hall** (once the banqueting chamber) where the Perpetual Imperial Diet of the Holy Roman Empire sat from 1663 to 1806. It is a small, sumptuously decorated room with a free suspended wooden ceiling, and is laid out as it was when nobles from around the empire came to wrangle about imperial policy. There is a simple canopied chair for the emperor, and punishingly hard, colour-coded benches (green for princes, red for electors) for the rest. The tour also includes a well-equipped **Torture Chamber**; torture was only abolished in 1806.

The streets around the Rathaus still follow Roman and medieval lines. **Wahlenstraße**, south of Rathausplatz, and the surrounding alleys, such as Obere-Bachgasse, Untere-Bachgasse and Kramgasse, are the best spots for looking at historic architecture. Wahlenstraße is the oldest street, with the **Goldener Turm**, the highest remaining patrician tower (it now has a wine bar at the top). Obere-Bachgasse 7 was the painter **Albrecht Altdorfer's house**, and at No.15 are the remains of one of the **private chapels** that used to grace the merchants' towers. Obere-Bachgasse, at its northern end, becomes Untere-Bachgasse.

If you duck down the quaint little medieval alley of Hinter der Grieb, then along Rote-Hahnen-Gasse, you come to **Haidplatz**. This vast square was once a jousting arena and the scene of a bloody battle in the 10th century, between one Krako the Hun and local hero Dollinger. Dollinger won, and earned himself (as well as the usual purse of gold) immortality in the form of the Dollinger Ballad, still recited today. These days Haidplatz is the stamping ground of scruffs with loud stereos. On the northern end of the square is the former inn **Zum Golden Kreuz** which, from the 16th to the 19th century, was the lodging place of princes visiting the town to attend the Diet. The 46-year-old Emperor Charles V caused tongues to wag when he used the hotel as a trysting place during his affair with the local teenage beauty Barbara Blomberg. One of the results of the liaison was a son, Juan de Austria, born here in 1547. He banished his mother to a nunnery (she continued her errant ways long after Charles V died) and went on to become a heroic soldier and governor of the Netherlands. Farther along the square is the big neoclassical **Thon-Dittmer Palace**, which unites several earlier Gothic houses and is now an arts centre with an elegant wood-panelled concert hall. The large courtyard is surrounded by graceful Renaissance galleries and is used in the summer for outdoor performances.

A few minutes west of Haidplatz (along Ludwigstraße, down Drei-Mohren-Straße and across Bismarckplatz) is the mysterious **St Jakobskirche**, called the *Schottenkirche* (Scots' Church) after the

Irish monks who founded it in 1090. (In those times the Irish were referred to as *Schotte*; ironically the monastery became a Scottish one in the 16th century, and remained so until its dissolution 300 years later.) The Romanesque portal is covered in puzzling pagan-like designs: whores, hangmen, mermaids, monsters and more conventional Christian iconography. The two most feasible interpretations are that the carvings depict a scene from the Last Judgement, or tell the story of the Irish monks' voyage across the seas in answer to Charlemagne's call. The dim interior, with its low arches and oddly carved pillars, evokes an early Christianity, rich with ancient rites and rituals. In the Byzantine apse is a carved 12th-century crucifixion group with a dramatically miserable Virgin and Mary Magdalene.

Ostdeutsche Galerie
*open Tues–Sun 10–5;
adm €4; bus 6 or 11*

At Doktor-Johann-Maier-Straße 5 is the **Ostdeutsche Galerie** (East Germany Gallery), a collection of 19th- and 20th-century works by artists who lived or worked in the former East Germany. As well as pieces by Otto Dix, Lovis Corinth and the expressionist Karl Schmidt-Rottluff, there is some odd, rather kitschy surrealist work from the 1960s and 70s. There is also a good collection of 20th-century sculpture, including Käthe Kollwitz's poignant *Soldatenfrauen* (1937).

South of the Centre

Obere-Bachgasse leads south to Emmeramsplatz, dominated by the church of **St Emmeram**'s monastery, founded in the 8th century and for centuries a main centre of learning in Europe. In the 19th century the monastery was secularized. Its new owners, the Princes von Thurn und Taxis (*see* below), kitted it out with new inventions like flushing toilets, running water and electric lights. The church itself, however, remains in use. Part of the interior was splendidly reworked in 1730 by those famous Baroque designers the Asam brothers, though the older parts of the church (notably the 12th-century vestibule) have more charm and mystique. Around the right-hand side of the main altar you can see fragments of a wall that dates back to Carolingian times, and in the crypt there are remnants of 8th-century wall paintings.

Schloß Thurn und Taxis
*www.thurnundtaxis.de;
guided tours only, daily
1pm, weekends only in
winter; adm palace
and cloisters €11.50,
treasure chamber
€4.50; information
t (0941) 5048 133*

The **Schloß Thurn und Taxis** is immediately behind the church. The fortune from pioneering a European mail service in the 16th century (and cornering the monopoly well into the 19th) has made the 'T und Ts' probably the richest family in Germany. They own 17 per cent of Regensburg, vast tracts of forest in Germany and Canada, and the largest private Bavarian brewery (locals nickname the beer *Tod und Teufel* – Death and the Devil). The present *Fürst* (prince) is still a boy, but his mother Gloria (who was some 30 years her late husband's junior) cuts a dash on the Munich social scene. In Regensburg she is known as 'the punk princess', and at the Café

Princess in town you can buy succulent chocolates called *Kese Gloria* ('saucy Gloria'). Her Regensburg home boasts more rooms than Buckingham Palace and some of the finest furniture in the land. The family sold up castles in the west of Germany just before the Second World War and removed the contents to Regensburg, which escaped bombing. If the family is not at home, you are allowed in for a glimpse of the breathtaking **interiors**. The tour includes the beautiful former **cloisters** which exhibit the range of Gothic style from the 12th to the 14th centuries. There is also a Marstallmuseum (Museum of the Palace Mews), a glittering collection of carriages, sleds and sedan chairs.

Marstallmuseum
guided tours, Mon–Fri 10–5, Sat–Sun 11–5; adm €4.50

East of the Centre

Another museum is a short walk east of the Alter Kornmarkt. The Historisches Museum, in an old Minorite monastery, gives an overview of 2,000 years of Regensburg's history. Its 100 rooms of exhibits make viewing quite a task, but displays are well laid out. There is a cutaway model of a Roman house, and another of the Steinerne Brücke with all three gates intact. Regensburg's most famous artist, Albrecht Altdorfer (1480–1538), has a room to himself. He was a painter of the Danube School, who were known for the elaborate landscapes they used as back-grounds to their work – lush Austrian and Bavarian scenery that often completely overwhelmed the main subject of the painting. Altdorfer's art made him rich, and he became a town councillor and official city architect.

Historisches Museum
Dachauplatz 2–4, www.museen-regensburg.de; open Tues–Sun 10–4, Thurs 10–8; adm €2.20

Around Regensburg

Shining white on a hill above the Danube, 11km east of Regensburg, stands **Walhalla**, a pompous monument modelled on the Parthenon, put up by King Ludwig I in 1842 to honour Germany's heroes, though some have slipped in with dubious qualifications. Among the 200 or so plaques and busts of soldiers, artists, philosophers and other notables, you'll find the Dutch humanist Erasmus, Copernicus (a Pole) and scatterings of Austrians and Swiss. It is not a very enthralling site to visit, but the views over the Danube are pretty, and the surrounding park is good picnic territory. You can get to Walhalla by car (take the road along the north bank of the Danube, through Donaustauf), though it is more interesting to go by boat (*see* 'Activities in Regensburg', p.188).

Walhalla
www.walhalla-regensburg.de; open April–Sept daily 9–5.45; Oct daily 9–4.45; Nov–Mar daily 10–11.45 and 1–3.45; adm €3

An even lovelier boat trip follows the Danube to the Donaudurch-bruch and Klosterweltenburg, for which you board at Kelheim, 20km southwest of Regensburg (*see* pp.112 and 113).

Services in Regensburg

Post office: Main post offices are on Domplatz and next to the Hauptbahnhof.

Markets: Fruit and vegetable market, Alter Kornmarkt and Neupfarrplatz, *open Mon–Fri 6am–12 noon*. Flower market, Altdorferplatz, *Mon–Sat 6am–12 noon*.

Festivals in Regensburg

The biggest bash is the summer **Altstadt Festival** with jugglers, street theatre, a morality play about Emperor Charles V and Barbara Blomberg (*see* p.185), folk music and loads of food and drink. There are also two big beer festivals, the *Frühjahrsdult* (two weeks in May) and *Herbstdult* (two weeks in Aug/Sept).

Of the many annual music festivals the *Bach-Woche* (Bach week, June or July) is the most renowned, and the *Bayerisches Jazz-Weekend* (July) is the jolliest, with up to 50 amateur jazz bands blasting away in bars, squares and normally secluded courtyards.

As well as the usual **Christmas Market** (on Neupfarrplatz), there is a special **Crafts Christmas Market** on Haidplatz, where you can buy local carving, weaving and all types of hand-made gifts. The *Domspatzen* (cathedral choir) perform right through the year, with special concerts at the Christian festivals.

Activities in Regensburg

Boat Trips

Gebrüder Klinger, Steinerne Brücke, **t** (0941) 52104, *www.schifffahrt klinger.de*. Offers excursions and round-trips on the Danube (a trip to Walhalla and back takes about 2hrs, a one-way cruise to Passau takes most of the day).

You can also go on short city cruises to see Regensburg's skyline and brave the whirlpools under the Steinerne Brücke (€8). City trips leave from near the Historische Wurstküche and most Danube cruises leave from

Werftstraße on the island of Untere Wöhrd.

Short trips through the Donaudurch-bruch gorge leave from Kelheim (20km southwest of Regensburg off the B16, or rail to Saal then DB bus). Boats run daily from mid-May to early October (€10.50 return).

Where to Stay in Regensburg

Regensburg

Altstadthotel Arch, Haidplatz 4, **t** (0941) 58660, *www.altstadthotel arch.de* (€€). The connoisseur's address: a grand old patrician palace, stylishly converted. Its nickname ('Ark') comes from its odd, bulging boat shape. Most rooms are spacious and all are tastefully decorated.

Bischofshof am Dom, Krauterermarkt 3, **t** (0941) 58460, *www.hotel-bischofshof.de* (€€). Richly fitted-out inn that was once the bishop's palace, with elegant, comfortable rooms and impeccable service. Restaurant, *see* opposite.

Hotel Roter Hahn, Rote Hahnengasse 10, **t** (0941) 595090, *www.roter-hahn.com* (€€). Simple but atmospheric hotel in a 16th-century building in the Merchant Quarter. Some of the rooms are small, but still good value; staff are friendly and attentive.

Kaiserhof am Dom, Kramgasse 10–12, **t** (0941) 585350, *www.kaiserhof-am-dom.de* (€€–€). Old, family-run hotel in the shadow of the cathedral. Convenient but a bit spartan.

Münchner Hof, Tändlergasse 9, **t** (0941) 584440, *www.muenchner-hof.de* (€€–€). A smart hotel. The rooms are small, but often have quaint features such as a Gothic wall-niche or old wooden beams. Service is brisk and friendly.

Hôtel d'Orphée, Wahlenstraße 1, **t** (0941) 596020, *www.hotel-orphee.de* (€). In the medieval heart of Regensburg; every one of its 15 rooms is individually decorated. No.2 has an iron four-poster bed, crystal chandelier and terrace with a view.

Spitalgarten, St Katharinenplatz 1, **t** (0941) 84774, *www.spitalgarten.de* (€,

(i) Regensburg >>
Altes Rathaus,
t (0941) 5074 410,
www.regensburg.de;
open Mon–Fri 9–6,
Sat 9–4, Sun 9.30–4

★ Bischofshof
am Dom >>

without private bath). Romantic old building with the Danube and a beer garden right outside.

Eating Out in Regensburg

Historische Wurstküche >>

On a fine evening you can have great fun wandering about the medieval alleys and nosing out a restaurant, an old courtyard café or a beer garden hidden behind high stone walls. First just the clinking of glasses gives them away, then a shaft of light leads you through an arch or up a passage to a drink and good cheer. Here are a few tips to start you off.

Bischofshof am Dom, Krauterermarkt 3, **t** (0941) 58460 (€€€). The chef here worked for the *T und Ts* for over a decade. Now he runs this smart hotel and the restaurant is one of the best in town. Delicious variations on traditional German dishes.

David im Goliath-Haus, Watmarkt 5, **t** (0941) 58460 (€€€). Attractive, with a roof garden serving such perennials as prawn cocktail and duckling with orange.

Historiches Eck, Watmarkt 6, **t** (0941) 465 4734, *www.historisches-eck.de* (€€€–€€). Coolly decorated, with suave service and a well-prepared, imaginative menu: simple, succulent venison steaks, or delicate fare such as perch with an asparagus sauce, served with onion confit and wild mushrooms.

Vitus Café-Restaurant, Hinter der Grieb 8, off Untere Bachgasse, **t** (0941) 52646 (€€€–€€). Gothic chapel and courtyard reincarnated as a popular French restaurant with *chansons* on some evenings. Mussels are the house speciality.

Dicker Mann, Krebsgasse 6, **t** (0941) 57370, *www.dicker-mann.de* (€€). Upmarket restaurant in a medieval house with tasty Franco-German cuisine.

Bräuerei Kneitinger >

Bräuerei Kneitinger, Kreutzgasse 7, **t** (0941) 59302, *www.kneitinger.de* (€). Provides good, inexpensive Bavarian food in an old tavern atmosphere. Try the pancake soup or the baked carp.

Dampfnudel-Uli >

Dampfnudel-Uli, Watmarkt 4, **t** (0941) 53297, *www.dampfnudel-uli.de* (€).

Cluttered and eccentric little restaurant that occupies what was once a private chapel in the medieval Bamburger tower. Uli and Vroni Deutzer serve sweet Bavarian dumplings smothered in a variety of sauces, ranging from simple vanilla to concoctions of fruit, beer and wine.

Historische Wurstküche, Thundorfer straße 3, **t** (0941) 46621, *www.wurst kuchlade.de* (€). The medieval McDonald's: for 850 years the little hut on the Danube has dished out *Regensburger* pork sausages, grilled over beechwood fires and served with sweet mustard and *Sauerkraut*. The same family has owned the Wurstküche for the past 200 years. In summer you sit at long tables beside the river. In winter you crowd into the tiny, smoke-filled restaurant-cum-kitchen.

Bars and Cafés in Regensburg

Hemingway's American Bar, Obere Bachgasse 3–5, **t** (0941) 561506, *www.hemingway.de*. Fashion victims, dynamic young things with designer spectacles, and the occasional Bogart *manqué* eye each other up as they drink cocktails or eat salads out of huge glass bowls. Homesick Americans will find comfort in the menu.

Café Kaminski, Hinter der Grieb 6, **t** (0941) 599 9033. Another place to see and be seen as you sip your *Feierabend* drink.

Café Orphée, Untere Bachgasse 8, **t** (0941) 52977. Wood-panelled French-style café and crêperie. Around the back there is a pretty little garden with a fountain.

Türmchen, Wahlenstraße 14. Cosy wine bar at the top of a high fortified tower.

Café Prinzess, Rathausplatz 2, **t** (0941) 57671, *www.cafe-prinzess.de*. The oldest *Konditorei* (confectioner) in Germany. It opened in 1686 to serve pralines to the French delegates at the Imperial Diet, and still produces mouthwatering chocolates and cakes.

Beer Gardens in Regensburg

Bischofshof am Dom, t (0941) 7594 1010. Beautifully situated, right at the foot of the cathedral in what used to be the bishop's palace garden. The beer garden is still owned by the Bishop of Regensburg, and everyone drinks here – from tourists to the mayor. You can get a delicious *Brotzeit* (meat and cheese snack, €4–6) to go with your beer.

Kneitinger Keller, Galgenbergstraße 18, *www.kneitingerkeller.de*. Rip-roaring, 1,200-seater beer garden, within staggering distance of the University.

Spitalgarten, St Katharinenplatz 1, **t** (0941) 84774, *www.spitalgarten.de*. Right on the Danube, this is tucked in between the Steinerne Brücke and an old hospital, and is popular with laid-back locals.

Zum Gravenreuther, Hinter der Grieb 10, **t** (0941) 55050, *www.gravenreuther. de*. Old inn with a charming little courtyard garden. Work up an appetite for the hearty Bavarian fare, such as liver dumplings or roast pork with caraway seeds (€5–13).

Entertainment and Nightlife in Regensburg

There is a thriving classical music scene in Regensburg, with concerts taking place in atmospheric old halls and churches. The tourist office publishes a *Monatsprogramm* (monthly programme) of what's on, and offers a ticket reservation service.

Figurentheater, Dr.-Johann-Maier-Straße 3, **t** (0941) 28328, *www.regens burgerfigurentheater.de*. Children enjoy the marionettes here. *Performances Sept–May, Sat and Sun 3pm.*

Theater am Bismarckplatz, Bismarckplatz 7, **t** (0941) 5072 424, *www.theaterregensburg.de*. The city's main theatre, which reopened in 2001 after renovation. It now boasts state-of-the-art backstage technology.

Thon-Dittmer-Palais, Haidplatz 8, **t** (0941) 5072 432. The most vibrant venue in town, offering jazz, classical music and theatre. In summer, performances are often held outdoors in its graceful Renaissance courtyard.

Turmtheater im Goliathhaus, Watmarkt 5, **t** (0941) 562233. Sparkles with cabaret and small-scale musicals.

Nightlife in Regensburg centres on cafés and beer gardens, but there are a few clubs.

Scala, in the Pustet Passage, off Gesandtenstraße near Haidplatz, *www.scalaclub.de*. Noisy local youths frequent clubs such as this one.

Südhaus, Untere Bachgasse. If you feel like dancing, head for this place.

Passau

 Passau

All over Europe, towns with a few canals or more than one river are flattered with Venetian epithets. Passau, the 'Bavarian Venice', is one of the few that comes anywhere near deserving the hype. Napoleon felt it was the most beautiful town he had overrun in all Germany. The 18th- to 19th-century traveller and naturalist, Alexander von Humboldt, ranked Passau among the seven most beautifully situated cities in the world. If you stand on the high battlements of the Veste Oberhaus fortress and look out over the Altstadt, you might be inclined to agree.

Passau is set mainly on a peninsula at the confluence of the Danube, Ilz and Inn. Light off the water blanches the square

Getting to and around Passau

Passau is just off the A3: 90km from Linz, 170km from Munich, 100km from Regensburg and 225km from Nürnberg. If you are coming by **car** from Nürnberg or Regensburg, the regional road B8, which follows the Danube, is more scenic. Most parking garages are to be found along the southern bank of the Danube. For car hire, try **Europcar**, Hauptbahnhof, t (0851) 54235.

For a **taxi** in Passau, call t 57373.

The **Hauptbahnhof** (information t (0851) 55001) is 10mins' walk west of the Altstadt. There are frequent **rail** connections to Linz (1hr 10mins), Vienna (3hrs), Munich (2hrs), and Regensburg (1hr 10mins).

10
Eastern Bavaria | Passau

Italianate buildings, giving Passau the air of a sunny Mediterranean town. Only when you look closer, and notice how the outdoor tables with their bright umbrellas have been ranged in strict orderly rows, are you reminded that the piazza is a *Platz*.

Few foreigners know about this little town, yet in the 14th century Passau was a flourishing trading centre, with turnover on the three rivers more than double that on the Rhine. For centuries the burghers battled with the prince-bishops who owned the town. The merchants wanted independence, like their neighbours in Regensburg. But the bishops, ensconced in one of the most impenetrable fortresses in the land, always won. Passau craftsmen did succeed in developing the finest sword blades in Europe, and a 13th-century Bishop of Passau spent his quieter moments writing down the *Nibelungenlied*, Germany's most popular epic poem.

In 1662 a fire reduced the medieval town to rubble, and the present Baroque town was built by Italian architects. But, as with Regensburg, Passau's fortunes were on the wane, and the city's only recent claims to fame are that Wagner almost chose it over Bayreuth as the site for his music temple, and that a local invented the picture postcard. Today Passau is a university town with a small student population and a reputation for unpleasant right-wing politics.

The Altstadt

Even close up, the Altstadt's arcades, alleys, archways, covered stairways and wrought-iron gates seem more Italian than German. That said, once you've soaked in the atmosphere, there is not much to see. **St Stephan's Cathedral** is the best place to begin. The church is at the highest point in the Altstadt, built on the ruins of its predecessors and the original Roman fort. The Baroque church was built in the 17th century to replace a Gothic one all but destroyed by fire. The interior is laden with white stucco, with a gilded canopied pulpit crawling with cherubs and angels. The **organ** is the largest in the world, with 231 stops and 17,388 pipes; roughly twice the size of that in London's Royal Albert Hall.

St Stephan's Cathedral
organ recitals at 12 noon on weekdays in summer, or on Thursdays at 7.30pm; adm €3 lunchtimes, €5 evenings

Residenzplatz, behind the cathedral, is a small cobbled square lined with patrician mansions. From here you get the best view of the late Gothic east end of St Stephan's. Alongside it is the grand 18th-century **episcopal palace**. A walk down Schrottgasse brings you to the Gothic **Rathaus**, which defies the bishops' fortress across the river. It was the home of the wealthy Haller family, who for generations led citizens' rebellions, and as early as 1298 gave up some rooms for use as a town hall. Lovers of rich décor can pop inside for a look at the Großer Saal (Great Hall), a weighty affair of Baroque marble, 15th-century stained glass and enormous 19th-century wall paintings.

On the other side of the Rathausplatz in the Hotel Wilder Mann is the **Passauer Glasmuseum**, an excellent collection of glassware, well worth a visit even if you're not a connoisseur. Exhibits range from the exquisite to the wacky: painted glass, clear glass, garish colours and curious shapes. The *Jugendstil* and Art Deco pieces are particularly good, and there is some finely painted 19th-century work. East of the Rathaus, on Bräugasse, you'll find the **Stiftung Wörlen** (Wörlen Foundation), a museum of modern art. There is no permanent collection, but visiting exhibitions are of a high standard and the building, with its pretty arcaded courtyard, makes an attractive setting.

Großer Saal
*open Easter–Oct
Mon–Fri 10–12 and
1.30–4, Sat and Sun
10–4; adm €1.50*

Passauer Glasmuseum
*www.glasmuseum.de;
open daily 1–5;
adm €5*

Stiftung Wörlen
*open Tues–Sun 10–6;
adm €5*

Veste Oberhaus

Veste Oberhaus
*www.oberhaus
museum.de; open mid-
Mar–mid-Nov Mon–Fri
9–5, Sat–Sun 10–6; mid-
Nov–mid-Mar daily
10–6; general adm €5;
bus from Rathausplatz
April–Oct half-hourly
11.30–5*

The medieval fortress of Veste Oberhaus looms over the town from a rocky outcrop across the Danube. Reach it by crossing the Luitpoldbrücke, then walking up a precipitous flight of stairs cut into the rock; or catch a bus from the Rathausplatz. It is easy to see how the building became the focus of the citizens' anger, and why it proved unassailable over the centuries. It has been converted into a warren of museums. Once there, wander through the old rooms and courtyards for early Passau picture postcards and maps of Bavaria in the **Lithograph Museum**; nondescript contemporary art in the **20th-Century Gallery**; Gothic painting and sculpture in the **Diocesan Museum**; a collection of craftsmen's tools, and sculpture by the city's most famous artist, Hans Wimmer, in the **City Museum**; and some rickety old wagons in the **Fire Brigade Museum**. But by far the best reason for visiting the fortress is for the magnificent views over Passau and the three rivers. The pale Danube, the muddy Inn and the Ilz, turned a deep green-black by the marshy soil of the Bavarian Forest, swirl together in marble colours, before continuing eastwards. Interestingly, although the Inn is deeper, broader and has travelled further to get here than the Danube, it is still regarded as a tributary.

Services in Passau

Post office: Next to the Hauptbahnhof; *open Mon–Fri 8.30–12.30 and 2–5.30, Sat 8–12.*

Markets: Fruit and vegetable market, Tues and Fri mornings on Domplatz.

Festivals in Passau

During the *Maidult* in May, the whole town seems to become one large, bright market, and its citizens give themselves over to almost continuous beer-drinking. For the *Burgerfest* at the end of June the formula is enriched by dance, music and sports such as bungee-jumping. At the other end of the scale, the long-established **European Weeks** (EW) from June to August attract some astonishing European names from the worlds of opera, ballet and classical music.

Sports and Activities in Passau

Boat Trips

Passau is worth viewing from the water. Most boats leave from the Luitpold-Hängebrücke.

Wurm & Köck, Höllgasse 26, **t** (0851) 929 292, *www.wurm-koeck.de*. The leading shipping company on this stretch of the Danube; they offer a 45min *Dreiflüsse Rundfahrt* (Three Rivers Cruise, €6.50) as well as longer trips as far as Linz (€24).

Donau-Dampfschifffahrts-Gesellschaft (DDSG), Im Ort 14a, Dreiflußeck, **t** (0851) 33035, *www.ddsg-blue-danube.at*. This company can take you to Vienna.

Where to Stay in Passau

Passau

Hotel Wilder Mann, Am Rathausplatz, **t** (0851) 35071, *www.wilder-mann.com* (€€). This converted 11th-century palace on the Danube is one of the best hotels in the region. The rooms are sumptuously decorated (the best

ones are at the back, with balconies overlooking a quiet garden). The service is relaxed and friendly, there's a gourmet restaurant, a swimming pool in the Gothic vault, and even an in-house museum (*see* p.192).

Altstadt Hotel, Bräugasse 23–29, **t** (0851) 3370, *www.altstadt-hotel.de* (€€). Smart, modernized hotel with a terrace-restaurant overlooking the point where the three rivers meet. The hotel has its own underground garage.

Hotel König, Untere Donaulände 1, **t** (0851) 3850, *www.hotel-koenig.de* (€€). Modern, with comfortable rooms looking across the river to the Veste Oberhaus plus a sauna and solarium.

Pension Rößner, Bräugasse 19, **t** (0851) 2035, (€€–€). Family-run *pension* on the Danube. Rooms are small but cosy.

Wirtshaus Goldenes Schiff, Unterer Sandstraße 8, **t** (0851) 34407, *www.goldenes-schiff.de* (€). A traditional, friendly *Gasthof*, just 5mins' walk from the cathedral and the heart of the Altstadt. Aside from comfy rooms, there is a leafy beer garden and weekend pork roasts (with organically-fed, free range pigs).

Rotel Inn, Am Hauptbahnhof/Donauufer, **t** (0851) 95160, *www.rotel-inn.de* (€). One of Germany's quirkiest hotels, Rotel is built in the shape of a sleeping man on the shore of the Danube, a hundred metres from the train station. The rooms are only as wide as the bed. It lies right on a bike path and is popular with cyclists. *Open May–Oct.*

Eating Out in Passau

Heilig-Geist-Stiftschenke, Heiliggeistgasse 4, **t** (0851) 2607 (€€–€). *Weinstube* that dates back to 1358. Heavy wooden tables under low arches, bread in baskets and good wine in ceramic jugs. The food is mouthwatering, with fish from their private waters and a lengthy pancake menu (the wild mushroom fillings are delicious).

⭐ Wirtshaus Goldenes Schiff >>

ⓘ Passau >
*Neues Rathaus, Rathausplatz,
t (0851) 955980,
www.passau.de; open
April–Oct Mon–Fri
8.30–6, Sat and Sun
10–4; Nov–Mar
Mon–Fri 8.30–5*

*Infostelle, alongside
the Hauptbahnhof;
this can also give you
information on the
region – including
Austria and the
Bavarian Forest; open
Mon–Fri 9–5*

⭐ Heilig-Geist-Stiftschenke >>

⭐ Hotel Wilder Mann >

 Café Kowalski >>

Zum Jodlerwirt, Schrottgasse 12, **t** (0851) 2422 (€€–€). The venue for *Weißbier* aficionados, with yodelling and folk music on Saturdays and hearty Bavarian cuisine, such as venison ragout and potato dumplings.

Ristorante Zi'Teresa, Theresienstraße 26, **t** (0851) 30533, *www.zi-teresa.de* (€). Home-made pizzas and pasta in a popular restaurant with a small garden.

Bars and Cafés in Passau

Theresiencafé, Theresienstraße 14. Tranquil daytime café with a small courtyard garden, ideal for late breakfasts and lunches.

Café Kowalski, Oberer Sand 1, *www.kowalski-passau-live.de*. Away from the tourist crush, crammed with local trendies and students. The tiny balcony overlooking the Inn is popular at sundown.

Café Duft, Theresienstraße 22, *www.cafeduft.de*. Central café with a neighbourhood atmosphere, the honeypot of local gossip. You can also get a bite to eat.

TheaterCafé Aquarium, Unterer Sandstraße 2, *www.cafe-aquarium.eu*. Aptly named chrome and glass box, where people go to be seen.

The Bavarian Forest and the Upper Palatinate

⭐ Bavarian Forest

   The **Bavarian Forest** (Bayerische Wald), which gives its name to the easternmost strip of Bavaria, is one of the last wild areas in Europe. It spreads across the Czech border and merges in the north with the **Upper Palatinate** (Oberpfalz). This echo of the Rhineland region arises from the area's rule by the Electors Palatine of the Rhine, a senior branch of the Wittelsbachs. It's an idyllic land of meadows and wildflowers, forests in unimagined shades of green, hidden lakes and fast, chuckling streams. When the mists come down, the woods seem secret and isolated, but more often than not the sun is shining and the honey-scented air is filled with the warbles of birdsong. This is one of the few places where the road sign showing a leaping deer can be taken literally.

   City Germans scoffingly refer to this part of the country as the 'Bavarian Congo', yet this gives you the clue to its charm. Here you will find that life goes on in much the same way as it has done for centuries. There are storybook farmyards, colourful local festivals and hardly any foreign tourists at all. The food is excellent, and accommodation encouragingly cheap.

   Despite the lush appearance, the soil is rocky and hard to farm, but it does contain large silica deposits. This, and abundant firewood for furnaces, led medieval woodsmen to imitate their Bohemian neighbours and blow glass. (Town names that end in '-*hütt*' or '-*reuth*' derive from the old German word for a glassworks.) **Glass-blowing** is still more an individual craft than an industrial affair. Most factories use traditional methods, and

Getting to and around the Bavarian Forest and the Upper Palatinate

A **car** is essential to get about easily and explore remote corners. Roads are well made. The most scenic routes are along and around the B85 and B22.

If travelling by **train**, head for Grafenau or Furth im Wald, both handy bases for exploring the countryside. Trains leave from Regensburg and Passau, but you will have to change two or three times, and the journey will take up to 3hrs.

There are marked **hiking** routes around the forests and you can sleep in mountain huts. Tourist offices and bookshops have detailed maps. The determined could try the 180km *Nördliche Hauptwanderlinie* (Furth im Wald to Dreisesselberg, 7–10 days). The *Südliche Hauptwanderlinie* (105km, Rattenberg–Kalteneck, 5–7 days) near the Danube valley is easier, as is the route through the forest from Kötzting near Cham to Bayerisch Eisenstein on the Czech border (50km, 2 days).

Perhaps the ideal way to see the area is by **bicycle**: get about at a civilized speed, stop where you like, and really appreciate the countryside. You'll need a bike with gears, though, as some parts of the forest can be quite hilly. There are all sorts of marked routes ranging from those you can knock off in a few hours to some that take days. The **Bavarian Tourist Office** (Leopoldstraße 146, D-80804 München, t +49 89 2123 970, *www.bayern.by*) brings out a detailed brochure that grades cycle routes according to difficulty and also suggests those that are suitable for children (available from tourist offices throughout the area).

dotted around the forest towns are workshops where you can see craftspeople puffing and sweating beside glowing furnaces.

From Passau to Zwiesel

Museumsdorf Bayerischer Wald
open April–Nov daily 9–5; adm €3.50

After Passau, 20km up the B85 is **Tittling**, where you'll find the **Museumsdorf Bayerischer Wald**, an outdoor museum of reconstructed farmhouses from the 15th–19th centuries. Further along the B85 a side road goes to Grafenau, Spiegelau and Frauenau, three towns that border the National Park. The towns are not particularly attractive but are full of *pensions* and rooms to let, and make good bases for ventures into the forest. **Grafenau** is the most touristy, with a railway station and intermittent invasions of coach parties.

Freiherr von Poschinger Kristallfabrik
Moosauhütte, t (09926) 94010; guided tours Mon–Fri 9.30–2.30

Glashütte Valentin Eisch
t (09926) 1890, www.eisch.de

Glasmuseum
www.glasmuseum-frauenau.de; open Mon–Fri 9–5, Sat–Sun 10–4

At **Frauenau** you can visit the **Freiherr von Poschinger Kristallfabrik**, a glassworks that has been in the same family for 14 generations and that won worldwide fame for its *Jugendstil* pieces. Although the company now employs over 200 workers, they still use traditional glass-blowing methods. **Glashütte Valentin Eisch** also admits visitors and has a reputation for zanier, more avant-garde work. The **Glasmuseum**, at Museumpark, has a collection of glass from ancient Egyptian to modern times (though it isn't as impressive as the one in Passau) and gives you a thorough technical introduction to local glass-making. The nearby village of **Zwiesel** is a centre for many of the individual glass-blowers and smaller firms – most of whom welcome casual visitors. The **Bayerwald-Bärwurzerei**, 2km out of Zwiesel on Frauenauer Straße

80–82, distills over 20 types of *Schnapps* with names like Heartbreak, Forest Prophet and Merry Grandma.

Bavarian Forest National Park
Visitor Centre, Hans-Eisenmann Haus, Böhmstraße 35, Neuschönau (near Grafenau), t (08558) 96150, www.national park-bayerischer-wald.de; has slide shows about the Park and the Waldsterben, as well as tours, maps, and hiking suggestions; open Mon–Sat 9–5

The National Park itself is 13,000 hectares of rolling moorland, lush forest and mountains. It is dotted with inns and private guesthouses, and in some places there are reserves for animals (such as bears, lynx and bison) that used to roam freely. The air here is as unpolluted as in the centre of an ocean, but sadly the forests are succumbing to *Waldsterben*, the fatal disease that has affected nearly 80 per cent of Germany's trees. Many blame acid rain caused by pollution from British factories, but recent research points the finger at exhaust fumes from the millions of cars that shoot about the German *Autobahns*. Despite the alarming statistics, the forests appear healthy enough.

From Zwiesel to Waldsassen

Country roads winding north of Zwiesel bring you to **Bodenmais**, a bustling resort that seems made up entirely of glassware shops and *pensions*. It is, however, a good base for visiting the **Arbersee**, a dark lake squeezed between forested slopes at the foot of the region's highest mountain, **Großer Arber** (1,456m). The summit of the mountain, and a panoramic view, can be reached by chairlift. You can also hike along the River Arber, which drops in a series of falls and cascades through the **Risslochschlucht** gorge.

A few kilometres farther on, you come to the towns of **Kötzting** and **Furth im Wald**. The fearsome *Drachenstich* dragon can be seen all year round in a lair near the Furth im Wald tourist office; there is also a display on the history of the pageant (*see* 'Festivals in the Bavarian Forest', opposite).

Nearby is the small walled town of **Cham**, a hub of local transport and famous for its beers. The local Hofmark brewery produces the malty *Würzig-Mild* and tasty, somewhat bitter *Würzig-Herb*. Here the countryside opens out, and the B22 road takes you north through a lonely landscape dotted with copses, isolated farms and the odd ruined castle.

Waldsassen Stift and Stiftsbibliothek
www.abtei-waldsassen.de; open Mon 2–5, Tues–Sun 10–12 and 2–5; adm €3

The town of **Waldsassen**, 130km up the road from Cham, is, however, very much worth the journey for its impressive Baroque Stift (collegiate church) and Stiftsbibliothek (library). The library is a rich mixture of old volumes and elaborate woodcarving. Its upper gallery is supported by a series of figures carved to represent everyone connected with books. At times the connections become a little strained (such as the figure of the shepherd: the skins of his flock were used as bookbinding). From Waldsassen it is only a short journey west to Bayreuth or Nürnberg.

Festivals in the Bavarian Forest and teh Upper Palatinate

Roman Catholic farmers celebrate a lot, and the towns around the forest are alive with religious parades, seasonal festivals with pagan roots, and busy fairs. Festivities take many forms, from costume parades requiring months of preparation, to a village bash in a beer tent, accompanied by a man on an accordion. In early spring and summer, **Easter** and **Corpus Christi** are the most rewarding times of the year to catch the local revels.

The most famous festival in the region, and one of Germany's largest, is the Furth im Wald *Drachenstich* on the second and third Sundays in August. There's a fair, lots of food and beer and an opening procession with 200 horses and hundreds of people in *Tracht* (costume). The highlight is St George's battle with the dragon (a spectacle going back over 900 years: the oldest piece of folk theatre in Germany). A local lad in armour slays an 18m luminous green monster, which dies spurting blood all over the delighted onlookers. The performance lasts 75 minutes and is repeated at intervals throughout the festival. Tickets cost from €4.50 (standing) to €16 and can be booked through the **Drachenstichfestspiele**, Stadtplatz 4, t (09973) 50985.

The *Pfingstritt* is a Whit Monday procession of decorated horses and men in *Tracht* from Kötzting (near Cham) to the pilgrimage church at Steinbühl (starts 8am). A couple are symbolically married, and the show returns home for a party in the town square.

Where to Stay in the Bavarian Forest and the Upper Palatinate

Accommodation in the Bavarian Forest is plentiful and cheap. You can get **private rooms** for €15 or less per person. Many of these are in farmhouses or in cottages in the woods, and are often a much better bet than hotels. Look out for the '*Fremdenzimmer*' or '*Zimmer zu vermieten*' ('rooms to rent') signs. Small villages such as the romantic Klingenbrunn (5km from Spiegelau, on the edge of the National Park) are better than the towns, and will almost always have empty rooms.

Grafenau

Mercure Hotel Sonnenhof, Sonnenstraße 12, t (08552) 4480, *www.hotel-mercure-sonnenhof.de* (€€). Smart modern hotel designed to pamper your every whim. All the rooms have balconies, and in-house facilities include tennis courts, a steam bath, sauna, swimming pool, Jacuzzi and hunky ski instructors.

Säumerhof, Steinberg 32, t (08552) 408990, *www.saeumerhof.de* (€€). Comfortable, tastefully decorated rooms, and personal attention from the owner – who also cooks superb meals.

Hohenau

Die Bierhütte, Bierhütte 10, t (08558) 96120, *www.bierhuette.de* (€€). Cosy hotel between Grafenau and Freyung, set beside a small lake. The romantic old building was once a glassworks and brewery, and is these days run with tender loving care by the Störzer family.

Bodenmais

Hotel Hofbräuhaus, t (09924) 7770, *www.hotel-hofbraeuhaus.de* (€€€–€€). Traditional Bavarian hotel, owned by the same family for over 100 years. It is friendly, *gemütlich* and also offers a fitness centre and indoor pool.

Furth im Wald

Hotel Gasthof Himmelreich, Himmelreich 7, t (09973) 1840 (€). Quiet *pension*, set a little back from the busy High Street.

Hohenbogen, Bahnhofstraße 25, t (09973) 1509, *www.hotel-hohenbogen.de* (€). Cheery, down-to-earth *pension* with spotless rooms, and which also serves good meals.

ⓘ **Grafenau >>**
Rathausgasse 1, t (08552) 962 331, www.grafenau.de

ⓘ **Cham**
Cordonhaus, Propsteistraße 46, t (09971) 803 493. www.cham.de

ⓘ **Kötzing**
Herrenstraße 10, t (09941) 602 150

ⓘ **Waldsassen**
Verkehtsamt/Tourist-Info, Johannisplatz 11, t (09632) 88160, www.waldsassen.de

ⓘ **Furth im Wald >>**
Schloßplatz 1, t (09973) 50980, www.furth.de

Eating Out in the Bavarian Forest and the Upper Palatinate

Dotted all over the forest are inns and small villages with guesthouses where you can have a good meal for under €10 a head. The following suggestions might start you on your way:

Säumerhof, Steinberg 32, t (08552) 408990, Grafenau (€€€–€€). Superb, imaginative cuisine using local produce and game, and a relaxed friendly atmosphere. They offer a five-course gourmet menu.

Brauereigasthof Kamm, Bräugasse 1, Zenting, t (09907) 89220 (€€). House brewery serving some fairly hearty Bavarian dishes such as venison ragout and wild mushroom pancakes.

Brauerei-Gasthof Eck, Eck 1, Böbrach, 20km west of Zwiesel, t (09923) 685, *www.brauerei-eck.de* (€€–€). A picture-book hillside inn with a brewery. Excellent cuisine and good beer.

Franconia

Franconia was a patchwork of secular and ecclesiastically ruled states until the 18th century, when it was drawn into union with Bavaria (see 'The Kingdom of Bavaria', p.23). But even after this, Franconians retained their own dialect and cultural identity. They felt the Cold War division of Germany strongly: many communities were cut off from the ancient cultural and trade links with Thuringia and Saxony.

Now once again in the geographical centre of Germany, the region is becoming a popular tourist destination, with great stretches of nature reserves. Almost as enticing are the numerous towns, which are virtually period pieces of differing epochs. (See also The Romantic Road, *pp.141–76.)*

11

Don't miss

⭐ **Art treasures galore**
Germanisches Nationalmuseum, Nürnberg **p.207**

⭐ **Wagner festival**
Bayreuth **p.215**

⭐ **The Beer-and-Castle Road**
Kulmbach **p.218**

⭐ **Woodland walks**
Frankenwald **p.219**

⭐ **A vibrant, beautiful town**
Bamberg and its Domstadt **p.221**

See map overleaf

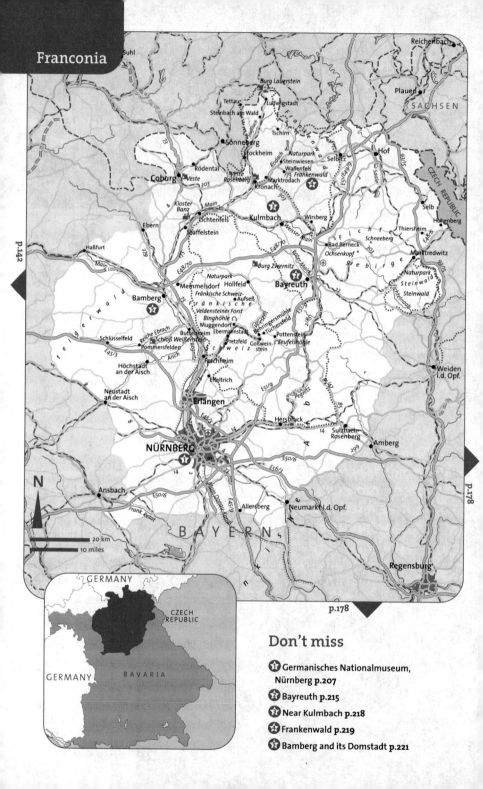

Don't miss

1 Germanisches Nationalmuseum, Nürnberg **p.207**

2 Bayreuth **p.215**

3 Near Kulmbach **p.218**

4 Frankenwald **p.219**

5 Bamberg and its Domstadt **p.221**

Nürnberg (Nuremberg)

Nürnberg is Bavaria's second largest city and the capital of Franconia. It is most recently remembered as the scene of vast Nazi rallies and the 1945–9 war crimes' trials. Before Allied bombers flattened most of the Altstadt in an air raid, however, Nürnberg was one of the most beautiful towns in Germany. It was a centre of art, science, trade and craft; home to Albrecht Dürer, Germany's most famous painter, to Hans Sachs, the original *Meistersinger* of Nürnberg, and to the inventors of the first world globe, the pocket watch and the lead pencil. Luther wrote that 'Nürnberg shines throughout Germany, like a sun among the moon and stars'. Pope Pius II praised the town's dazzling splendour and wryly remarked that 'the Kings of Scotland would be glad to be housed so luxuriously as the ordinary citizens of Nürnberg'. Adalbert Stifter, a 19th-century poet, enthused that the city was a work of art whose 'gracefulness, serenity and purity' of line filled him with irrepressibly gratifying feelings.

These days, Nürnberg is an odd mixture of dull modern ?architecture and painstakingly restored old buildings. No longer a vortex for art and industry, it is, however, an attractive and lively town, justifiably famous for its Christmas Market, scrumptious sausages and chewy gingerbread. There is some first-rate art to be seen, and the German National Museum, based here since 1852, has one of the most varied and impressive collections in the country.

History

Nürnberg's peak was in the Middle Ages. It was declared a Free Imperial City by Frederick II in 1219 and was at a nexus of main trade routes: the Balkans to Antwerp, Hamburg to Venice and Paris to Prague.

The city was famed for its bell-founders, candlestick-makers, woodcarvers, glass-painters and, above all, precision scientific instruments. By the 16th century Nürnberg had become equally celebrated for its painting and sculpture, and was beginning to achieve an almost mythic status in the eyes of many Germans. That is why, even after new trade routes to the Americas had robbed the city of its wealth by diverting trade with the east from land to sea, Nürnberg was the focus for the Pan-German movement in the 19th century. Later, the Nazis were to warp this symbolism even further. Hitler commissioned huge monuments to his Thousand Year Reich, to be built at the edge of the city, and Nürnberg became the scene of rousing Nazi rallies. The Allies, too, seemed to recognize this symbolic importance when they chose Nürnberg as the venue for bringing the surviving Nazi leaders to trial after the war.

Getting to and around Nürnberg

Nürnberg **airport** (t (0911) 93700, *www.airport-nuernberg.de*) is just 7km north of the centre. There are frequent flights to local German airports, and also connections to London, Amsterdam, Paris, Milan and Brussels. A bus shuttle service will run you to the Hauptbahnhof in 20 minutes (every 30mins, 5am–11.30pm).

The **Hauptbahnhof** is south of the Altstadt, just outside the old city wall. Intercity trains run hourly, with connections to Hamburg (4hrs), Frankfurt (2¾hrs) and Munich (1½hrs).

Autobahns connect you to every major city in Germany. The A9 to Berlin is very busy, and traffic is heavy and sometimes jams fast. If you're looking to **hire a car**, the following companies have local branches: **Avis**, Nürnberg airport, t (0911) 5298 966; **Europcar**, Essenweinstraße 3–7, t (0911) 214 930; **Mitfahrzentrale**, Allersberger Straße 31a, t (0911) 19444, *www.mfz.nuernberg.de*. If you need a **taxi** in Nürnberg, call t 19410.

The Altstadt is quite small enough to get about **on foot**, but there is a comprehensive network of **buses**, **trams** and **U-Bahn** lines, which all use the same tickets. Prices depend on how many zones you cross; tickets can be bought at most stops.

Today, Nürnberg still manufactures pencils and scientific instruments and is a leading manufacturer of children's toys. But, though a mecca for street entertainers in summer, Nürnberg has lost any claim to being the cultural centre of Germany.

The Kaiserburg

Kaiserburg
open April–Sept daily 10–6; Oct–Mar daily 10–4; adm €5, entry only with German-language guided tours

The Kaiserburg, on a rock over the northern edge of the Altstadt, gives Nürnberg its unmistakable skyline of odd stone blocks and quirky towers. The view over the jumble of red-peaked roofs takes you to medieval times, and shows the layout of the town.

The cluster of buildings that forms the Kaiserburg grew up over centuries: it is in fact two castles merged into one. On the eastern spur of the rock is the **Burgrave's Castle**. From the 11th–12th century this was a fortress belonging to the Salian kings (an ancient Frankish line) and then to the Burgraves (counts) of Nürnberg. When the last of the burgraves died in 1190, he was succeeded by his son-in-law, Frederic I of Zollern, founder of the Hohenzollern dynasty. During the 13th–14th centuries the castle was the Hohenzollerns' chief seat in Western Franconia, but the burghers of Nürnberg didn't take kindly to their rule. After some hostile clashes the Hohenzollerns were finally defeated. They sold the castle to the city in 1414.

The **Imperial Castle** on the western spur was a seat of the powerful Hohenstaufen line in the 12th century. The Hohenstaufens provided Holy Roman Emperors from 1138 to 1254. Even after the family's decline the castle continued to play an important role. In 1356, in the 'Golden Bull' decree, Emperor Charles IV commanded that the first Diet summoned by any newly elected German king had to be held at the castle. This held true for two centuries (until the Diet moved permanently to Regensburg), making Nürnberg one of the political centres of the empire. In 1427 the western spur too was taken over by the town and incorporated

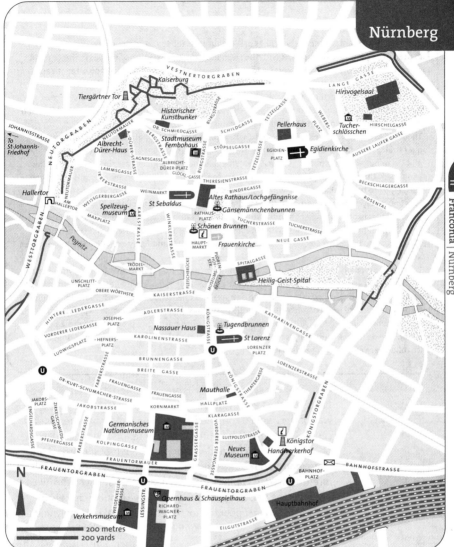

into the city defences, but it remained the property of the Holy Roman Empire.

The oldest part of the Kaiserburg is the gloomy **Fünfeckturm** (Pentagonal Tower, *c.* 1040), the only part of the original Salian building to survive. It shares the eastern spur with the solid **Luginslandturm**, a tower put up in the 14th century by burghers keen to keep a watchful eye on the Burgrave's castle. Once they had ousted the Hohenzollerns, the citizens joined the two towers with a Gothic **Kaiserstallung** (Imperial Stables, built 1494, now a youth hostel).

Franconia's Cuisine

Back in the 14th century, monastic scribes in Würzburg started to record their views on a healthy, balanced diet. They have provided us with the the the oldest known collection of recipes in the German language. Franconian cooking has come a long way since; to the visitor it may all too often mean sausages and *Sauerkraut*, but Franconia has a great deal more to offer, and views its gastronomy almost as an art form. Fertile land and a temperate climate fill the kitchen with an abundance of natural produce: Franconia is famous for potatoes, tomatoes, spinach, onions and asparagus. The land north of Nürnberg is known as *Knoblauchsland* (garlic country).

There are as many sausages as there are towns. Supreme is the original *Nürnberger Bratwurst*, no longer than a little finger, eaten in multiples of six. In Coburg, sausages are prepared over a charcoal fire of fir- or pine-cones, while the *Blaue Zipfel* (Blue Tail-Ends) of Bamberg are simmered in vinegar (giving them their bluish tinge) together with tarragon, onions, carrots, parsley, mustard and pepper. *Blaue Zipfel* are traditionally served with Sauerkraut and a horseradish sauce, or with potato salad.

Potatoes rarely appear *au naturel*, but come dressed up as *Knödel* (dumplings). The classic potato dumpling in Franconia is made of about two-thirds raw potatoes and one-third boiled ones, sometimes blended with flour, maize meal or toasted breadcrumbs. There are many variations on this theme, such as liver, bacon and bread dumplings. The latter must be soft and fluffy enough to be broken open with a fork.

Thrift is traditionally an important feature of Franconian cuisine. A meal must be satisfying, but not cost too much; a good example is the tasty cheese dish *Gerupfter*, made with Camembert and butter seasoned with paprika, rolled into a ball with egg yolk and finely chopped onions. Sometimes a little beer or wine is added for good measure. This rule of simplicity has inspired people to produce desserts from inexpensive ingredients. *Ausgezogene*, tiny slabs of filled pastry, are probably the most popular creation. The dish's name (literally 'something drawn out') describes how the sweetened dough was once rolled between the housewife's knees.

The main body of the castle is on the western spur. The Gothic **Palas** was the Hohenstaufen family living quarters. Only the east wall of the original Romanesque building remains; the rest is 15th century. The outside is impressive, but interiors tend to be devoid of atmosphere as the guided tour takes you through rather bare state rooms and suites. Most of the Kaiserburg had to be rebuilt after the Second World War. One building that survived the Allied bombs is the **Kaiserkapelle**, a *Doppelkapelle* (double chapel, *see* p.28) with an airy upper tier for the emperor and his family, and a squat, dim lower storey for humbler beings. A crucifix in the Upper Chapel is said to be by Veit Stoss. The Nürnberg Kaiserkapelle is the only *Doppelkapelle* known to have an additional west gallery and choir tower: the solid **Heidenturm** (Heathens' Tower). Out in the forecourt you can see the **Tiefer Brunnen**, a well probably as old as the castle itself and so deep that it takes six seconds for a stone dropped from the top to hit the water.

The Northern Altstadt

Just below the Kaiserburg is the **Tiergärtner Tor**, one of four gates in the wall that surrounds the medieval Altstadt. The area around here is one of the most attractive parts of the Altstadt. Lanes of half-timbered houses open onto a cobbled *Platz*, a hive of buskers, backpackers and merry youth, especially in the summer. Just

Johannisfriedhof
*open April–Sept daily
7–7, Oct–Mar daily 8–5*

outside the city wall (west along Johannisstraße) is the **Johannisfriedhof**, one of Germany's oldest and best-known cemeteries, with elaborate 16th- and 17th-century tombstones. Among locals buried here are the *Meistersinger* Hans Sachs (*see* p.42), sculptor Veit Stoss (*see* p.30), and Albrecht Dürer.

**Albrecht-Dürer-
Haus**
*open Mar–Oct, and
during Christkindels-
markt, Tues–Wed and
Fri–Sun 10–5, Thurs
10–8; adm €5*

The **Albrecht-Dürer-Haus**, where Germany's Renaissance Man lived from 1509–28, is just across the square from the Tiergärtner Tor. The house is worth a visit for its cosy atmosphere and authentic medieval interiors, though it has no original Dürer paintings. There are, however, a few engravings and first editions of his treatises. Modern artists have also contributed some odd homages to the great man.

Hausbrauerei
*hourly guided tours
Mon–Fri 2–7, Sat and
Sun 11–7; adm €3.50*

Down Bergstraße (also just across from the Tor), in the **Alt-stadthof** (a 16th-century courtyard), you'll find the **Hausbrauerei**, a working antique brewery, with cellars deep under the Kaiserburg. After your visit you can taste the murky beer in an adjoining pub.

Farther south, down Albrecht-Dürer-Straße and across Weinmarkt, you come to **Weißgerbergasse**, the most attractive lane of half-timbered houses in the city, now mainly given over to restaurants and cafés. Down Karlstraße, which also leads off

Spielzeugmuseum
*open Tues–Fri 10–5,
Sat and Sun 10–6; adm
adults €5, children €2.50*

Weinmarkt, is the **Spielzeugmuseum** (Toy Museum), worth a visit for its vast collection of mainly 18th–20th-century toys. Back eastwards along Schustergasse you come to the twin-towered **St Sebalduskirche** (1225–1379), Nürnberg's oldest parish church. Inside, resting on 12 bronze snails, is the richly decorated brass **Shrine of St Sebald**. Cast by Peter Vischer in 1491–7, it is generally considered to be the high point of German Renaissance metalwork. There is a moving crucifixion scene by Veit Stoss on the pillar behind the Shrine. On a pillar in the nave is a delicately coloured, early 15th-century carving of Mary with a halo.

**Stadtmuseum
Fembohaus**
*open Tues–Wed and
Fri–Sun 10–5, Thurs
10–8; adm €4*

Around the corner on Burgstraße is the **Stadtmuseum Fembohaus**, with heavy stucco ceilings and wood-panelled rooms. A more rewarding museum is the intimate **Tucherschlößchen**, a few minutes' walk east towards the university in the northeastern corner of the Altstadt. This was the Renaissance mansion of the Tucher family, who manufactured astronomical instruments, and later imported textiles and brewed beer. The house was destroyed during the war, but completely restored by the family themselves. There is a loving, personal touch to the displays of fine furniture and painting. The highlight of the tour is the *Tucherbuch* (1590–6), a family chronicle with stunningly beautiful illustrations. Tours are in German only, but you can ask for a printed English translation.

Tucherschlößchen
*Hirschelgasse 9; open
Mon 10–3, Thurs 1–5,
Sun 10–5; adm €5*

Around the Hauptmarkt

The **Hauptmarkt** is the centre of town, and scene of a bustling, countrified daily market for fruit, fresh herbs and home-made cakes and breads. Across the northern end of the square is an exuberant Renaissance **Altes Rathaus**, built in the style of a Venetian *palazzo*. Here you can visit the **Lochgefängnisse**, medieval prison cells with a fully equipped torture chamber. Outside, on the western side of the square, is a replica of the completely over-the-top **Schöner Brunnen** ('Beautiful Fountain'), a filigreed Gothic spire, gaudily painted and crowded with figures of electors, prophets and other church heroes.

Lochgefängnisse
*open April–Oct
Tues–Sun 10–4.30;
adm €3*

The pretty step-gabled **Frauenkirche**, erected by Emperor Charles IV in 1355, is just across the square. Although the church was badly bombed, the intricately carved tympanum above the entrance porch survived intact. In the 16th century a pretty oriel and clock were added to the façade. Above is a gold and blue ball that shows the current phase of the moon. Below is a glockenspiel (nicknamed the **Männleinlaufen**) that commemorates Charles IV's 'Golden Bull' (*see* p.202). At noon the carillon rings out merrily and figures of the seven electors circle three times around a statue of the emperor. Above the main altar in the church is the painting called the *Tucher Altar* (1445), a lively composition by the best artist working in Nürnberg prior to Dürer, an unknown painter now named the 'Master of the *Tucher Altar*'.

West of the Hauptmarkt (along Augustinerstraße and down to the river) is the half-timbered **Weinstadel** (medieval wine store) and the covered wooden **Henkersteg** (Hangman's Bridge). South of the Hauptmarkt you can cross the river over the **Museumsbrücke**. From here you can see the sprawling stone buildings of the **Heilig-Geist-Spital** (a medieval hospital) on the left, and the neat **Fleischbrücke** (modelled on Venice's Rialto Bridge) on the right.

The Southern Altstadt

Cross the Museumsbrücke and follow Königstraße (a brash, modern shopping precinct) to reach the **St-Lorenz-Kirche** (1250–1477). From the outside St Lorenz looks almost identical to St Sebald, begun some 25 years earlier: the communities on either side of the river were in fierce competition at the time. The parishioners of St Lorenz did eventually show a little more imagination by turning to models in France. The interior of the church is spectacular High Gothic, with a glittering rose window and a prickly 20m-high tabernacle, by the local mason Adam Kraft. Above the high altar you can also see Veit Stoss' polychrome *Annunciation*.

Outside the church is an eye-catching fountain, the **Tugendbrunnen**. The Seven Virtues look a little nonplussed as water squirts from their breasts, and from the raised trumpets of supporting cherubs. Across the square is the oldest house in the city, the 13th-century **Nassauer Haus**, which has a turreted upper storey and a prettily carved oriel window.

Around the **Königstor** (at the end of Königstraße, in the southeastern corner of the Altstadt) is the **Handwerkerhof** (Artisans' Courtyard). Here candle-makers, tinworkers, doll-makers and others ply their crafts in a twee medieval atmosphere.

Handwerkerhof
open Mon–Fri 10–6.30, Sat 10–4

The Germanisches Nationalmuseum

The imposing National Museum of German Art and Culture is on the Kornmarkt (just off Königstraße, across Hallplatz). Its enormous collection of German art and artefacts is housed in the **Karthaus**, a 14th-century Carthusian monastery. Modern buildings are integrated into the old Gothic fabric: plate glass and sharp angles contrast startlingly with gentler lines and worn stone. There are floor plans, but it's fun to explore at random. You can wander through cloisters resplendent with fine carvings, duck through low doors into dim little rooms stuffed with old furniture, climb up narrow stairs to see cabinets of seemingly forgotten cultural ephemera. You can be diverted for hours, and can get quite enjoyably lost.

★ **Germanisches Nationalmuseum**
www.gnm.de; open Tues and Thurs–Sun 10–6, Wed 10–9; adm €6

The **ground floor** is devoted to medieval art, prehistoric artefacts and collections of musical instruments and hunting equipment. The pick of the painting and sculpture is in **Rooms 8–14**. There is work by famous Würzburg woodcarver Tilman Riemenschneider (*see* p.30), as well as notable pieces by the local artist and villain Veit Stoss: in the latter's exquisite *Raphael and Tobias* (1516) the swirls and billows of the angel's cloak seem to float in the wind. He finished the carving soon after he had been convicted of forging promissory notes, branded on both cheeks, imprisoned and stripped of his status as a Master Craftsman. The gentle, touchingly intimate *Madonna of the Sweet Pea* (1410) by the Master of St Veronica is one of the finest examples of the 'soft style' of the Cologne School (*see* p.31), in contrast to the powerful, naturalistic 'hard style' of painters such as Konrad Witz. His *Annunciation* (1444) shows an attempt to portray perspective and a treatment of light that was revolutionary for the time. In the **southwest wing** is the Golden Cone of Ezelsdorf-Buch (1100 BC). The cone, stamped with intricate patterns, is over 88cm high and made from a single piece of paper-thin gold. The **southeast wing** contains a superbly displayed collection of musical instruments. A 12-minute slide show introduces the collection; headphones dotted around the hall allow you to hear the instruments.

The **upper floor** has a variety of traditional costumes; toys and domestic objects; sculpture and painting from the Renaissance onwards; arts and crafts of the 20th century; and the first ever world globe (designed by Martin Behaim in 1491) in pride of place

11 Franconia | Nürnberg

in Room 35. Nicknamed the *Erdapfel* (Earth Apple), it is, apart from the absence of Australia and the Americas (both then unknown to the Western world) and the odd bit of distorted coastline, remarkably accurate. Behaim based his globe on the latest charts supplied by Portuguese navigators, as well as Ptolemy's map of the 2nd century AD – information which led Columbus to believe that he had reached the Far East when he came across the Americas (and so called its people Indians).

Renaissance and Baroque paintings are hung in **Rooms 33–64**. Here you can see an extensive collection of works by Dürer, such as the eloquent portrait of his bright-eyed octogenarian teacher, *The Painter Michael Wolgemut* (1516). There is also fine work by Lucas Cranach the Elder. Look out for the wryly detailed *Venus with Cupid Stealing Honey* (1530). Hans Baldung (nicknamed 'Grien' because of his preference for green clothes) is also well represented. In his *Sebastian Altar* (1507), the artist himself (in a dashing red hat and the inevitable green cloak) stands next to the martyred saint, and confidently eyes the viewer. Most impressive are the objects from Nürnberg's Renaissance heyday as a centre of crafts (**Rooms 65–74**). The artistry of the *Schlüsselfelder Ship*, a gilded silver tablepiece (*c.* 1503) is breathtaking. A mermaid supports a three-masted ship which is finished in meticulous detail. The rudder can move and the deck and rigging swarm with 74 minute, individually cast sailors.

The 20th-century art in the museum is less exciting. However, in **Room G** (in the **northernmost wing**) you can see Ernst Kirchner's rather wretched *Self-portrait as a Drunkard* (1915), one of this Expressionist's best works.

South of the City Wall

The grey, looming, half-finished piles built by Hitler as monuments to his Third Reich are found in **Luitpoldhain** (tram 12), a park in the southeastern suburbs. From a podium draped with swastikas Hitler made his ranting speeches to the vast stadium, filled with a roaring sea of spectators all raising their hands in the *Sieg Heil* salute. Up to half a million Germans flocked to the week-long Nazi rallies, recorded by Leni Riefenstahl in the famous propaganda film, *Triumph of the Will*. At the northern entrance to the park is the Luitpoldarena, scene of SS parades.

Documentations-zentrum Nazi
open Mon–Fri 9–6, Sat and Sun 10–6, last entry 5pm; adm €5

The **Documentationszentrum Nazi** is located in the north wing of the **Kongresshalle** (modelled on the Colosseum in Rome but never completed). This €8 million museum is a bold attempt to confront Nürnberg's Nazi past and to answer the question that inevitably haunts the visitor: how could this happen? The permanent exhibition, entitled '*Faszination und Gewalt*' (Fascination and

Terror), combines educational exhibits with clips from Riefenstahl's film, and photographs and documents from the rallies. It also explores the 1935 Nürnberg anti-Semitic 'Race Laws', which paved the way for the Holocaust.

Across an artificial lake is the **Zeppelin Tribüne**, designed by star Nazi architect Albert Speer for the massive September rallies. The torches and colonnades have been stripped off the podium, but the huge stadium (holding 70,000) remains.

Services in Nürnberg

Post office: next to the Hauptbahnhof, at Bahnhofplatz 1. It has a *bureau de change*.

Police: t 110.

Medical emergencies: t 19292.

Markets: There is a good weekday fruit and vegetable market on the Marktplatz. At the beginning of the asparagus season in May, the market is devoted to the vegetable.

Festivals in Nürnberg

Christkindelsmarkt

Nürnberg has the largest, most famous *Christkindelsmarkt* ('Christ-child's market'; *see www.christkindels markt.de*) in Germany. In the 17th century it became the fashion to give presents at Christmas, not New Year, as previously. The market that grew up in Nürnberg to supply carved toys and tasty goodies became the prototype for similar fairs now held in nearly every town in the country.

From the Friday before Advent until Christmas Eve the Hauptmarkt is transformed into an enchanted land of wooden stalls and bright bunting, smothered in pine leaves and lit by lanterns. Despite the market's enormous popularity, you'll find little kitsch or tatty commercialism. Vendors pile their stalls with hand-carved wooden toys, traditional decorations and craftwork. Aromas of *Glühwein*, grilling sausages and freshly baked ginger *Lebkuchen* soften the sharp winter air. You can buy *Rauschgoldengel* (gold foil angels), *Zwetschgenmännle* (odd figures made from crêpe paper and prunes) and the straw wreaths that have decorated

Nürnberg homes at yuletide for centuries. At dusk on the first day a 'Christ-child' recites a prologue from the balcony above the entrance to the Frauenkirche, and little terrestrial angels peal out carols down below. A few days later, with strings of school chums bearing home-made lanterns, they wind in procession up the hill from the Market Square to the castle.

Other Festivals

The *Altstadtfest* (late Sept) is ostensibly a celebration of Franconian folk culture, but really a rollicking knees-up with food and beer flowing freely. The **Toy Fair** (the largest in the world) held every February is peopled mainly by parents and business folk walking between stacks of teddies and playing the latest computer games. Big boys' toys whizz about during the **Norisring car races** in late June. Roads southeast of the city are closed to make a long racetrack, traffic piles up, and you are deafened by car and helicopter engines for days on end.

Cultural events tend to cluster around the summer months. At the end of May you can catch *Musica Franconia*, a week of concerts of ancient music played on period instruments. The *Kulturzirkus*, an international theatre festival of increasing renown, is held in June – as is Europe's oldest sacred music festival, the *Orgelwoche* (organ week). Buskers and street entertainers descend on the city for two weeks in July/August for the *Bardentreffen* (Bards' Meet). They're joined by more established names who also give open-air concerts. In October the *Ost-West Jazzfestival* hosts bands playing anything from Dixie to free jazz.

Shopping in Nürnberg

For hand-made pewter, stained glass, pottery and jewellery, try the **Craftsmen's Courtyard** (*see* p.207).

The centre has the usual pedestrianized shopping zone. Königstraße, Karolinenstraße and Kaiserstraße have major department stores and a few swish boutiques. **Schmidt's bakery** on the Hauptmarkt sells *Lebkuchen* cooked to a recipe that has been a family secret for centuries.

Where to Stay in Nürnberg

Nürnberg

Expensive (€€€)

Ramada Nürnberg Parkhotel, Münchener Straße 25, **t** (0911) 47480, *www.ramada-nuernberg.de*. Classy, glassy modern hotel in the Luitpoldhain Park, with its own pool, sauna, gym and sun terrace.

Romantik Hotel Gasthaus Rottner, Winterstraße 17, Großreuth district, **t** (0911) 658480, *www.rottner-hotel.de*. Feels like a country house, although it's only 15mins from the Altstadt by public transport. The dining room is quaint and rustic, and the hotel's 36 rooms are rigorously modern and comfortable. After a day of sight-seeing, you can relax in the hotel bar, terrace café or beer garden.

Moderate (€€)

Burghotel, Lammsgasse 3, **t** (0911) 238890, *www.altstadthotels.com*. Folksy hotel at the foot of the Burg, with smart modern facilities and a swimming pool.

Hotel Elch, Irrerstraße 9, **t** (0911) 2492 980, *www.hotel-elch.com*. Lovely medieval inn in the Altstadt; small rooms, but the atmosphere and friendly service make up for it.

Hotel Marienbad, Eilgutstraße 5, **t** (0911) 226912, *www.hotel-marienbad.de*. One of the best of a bunch of nondescript hotels near the Hauptbahnhof. It is clean, efficiently run and there to fall back on if everywhere else is full.

Merian-Hotel, Unschlittplatz 7, **t** (0911) 2146 690, *www.merian-hotel.de*. Stylish, well-run hotel in a pretty area of the Altstadt, with comfortable, tastefully decorated rooms (some look out over a shady square with a fountain) and impeccable service.

Romantik Hotel am Josephsplatz, Josephsplatz 30–32, **t** (0911) 214470. Ideally situated in the Altstadt, this 300-year-old hotel surprises with mod cons, like a sauna and fitness room. *Closed 24 Dec–6 Jan.*

Inexpensive (€)

Vater Jahn, Jahnstraße 13, **t** (0911) 444507, *www.hotel-vaterjahn-parma.de*. Good-value relaxed *pension*, situated south of the Hauptbahnhof.

Eating Out in Nürnberg

Nürnberg's culinary claims to fame are *Nürnberger Bratwurst*, sausages the size of a little finger, and *Lebkuchen*, spicy gingerbread with honey and nuts. Traditionally, *Lebkuchen* are sold only at Christmas, but nowadays you can eat them all year round.

Bratwurst should be made entirely of pork. The sausages are served with *Sauerkraut*, potato salad or hot white radish. Six is the minimum order, 'real men' knock back a dozen at a time, and if you order more than ten you get them on a heart-shaped plate. Snack stalls sell them '*Zwaa in an Weckla*' (two in a roll). Usually *Bratwurst* are grilled over wood fires, but you can also get them *nackerte* ('naked' – raw, peeled, mixed with onions, pepper and paprika and spread on black bread), or as *Blaue Zipfel* – reputedly a hangover cure). *Bauernseufzer* are long, smoked *Bratwurst* which can be eaten raw or boiled. *See also* box, p.204.

Expensive (€€€)

Gasthaus Rottner, Winterstraße 15, Großreuth district, **t** (0911) 612032, *www.rottner-hotel.de*. Chef Stefan Rottner is one of a young generation of chefs going back to good old Bavarian cooking: one who can do justice to a local *Zander* fish, braised *Kalbsbackerl* (veal cheek) or wild boar and cabbage.

(i) Nürnberg >
opposite the Hauptbahnhof, t (0911) 2336 131, www.nuernberg.de; open Mon–Sat 9–7

Altstadt: Hauptmarkt 18; open Sept–April Mon–Sat 9–6; May–Oct and during Advent 9–7

(★) Gasthaus Rottner >>

Goldenes Posthorn, Glockleinsgasse 2, near St Sebaldus, **t** (0911) 225153. Romantic inn (once Dürer's local), serving Franconian meals. Delicious potato soup and asparagus dishes.

⭐ **Böhms Herrenkeller** >

Expensive–Moderate (€€€–€€)
Böhms Herrenkeller, Theatergasse 19, **t** (0911) 224465. Traditional tavern with a good wine list and hearty Franconian dishes. Try the *Schweinebraten* (roast pork with potato dumplings) or the *Krautwickala* (stuffed cabbage leaves).

Der Nassauer Keller, Karolinenstraße 2–4, **t** (0911) 225967, *www.nassauer-keller.de*. Low ceilings, low lights and suits of armour in the cellar of Nürnberg's oldest house. Renowned for their saddle of lamb and old Franconian cookery.

Moderate (€€)
Heilig Geist Spital, Spitalgasse 16, **t** (0911) 221761, *www.heilig-geist-spital.de*. This old hospital's 15th-century eating hall extends right out over the Pegnitz. Excellent, wide-ranging menu, with game and veal.

Irrer Elch, Irrerstraße 9, **t** (0911) 209544. Cosy medieval tavern with good home cooking. Game and carp dishes are a speciality.

⭐ **Bratwurst-Häusle** >

Inexpensive (€)
Bratwurst-Häusle, Rathausplatz 1, **t** (0911) 227695, *www.die-nuernberger-bratwurst.de*. The huge chimney puffs out grilled-sausage aroma right across the square. Locals and tourists flock for the best *Bratwurst* in town.

Bratwurst-Glöcklein, Handwerkerhof, at end of Königstraße, **t** (0911) 227625. In the Craftsmen's Courtyard, serves up good *Bratwurst*.

Prison St Michel, Irrerstraße 2. Popular French restaurant that serves everything from scrumptious *galettes* (wholemeal pancakes) to standards such as duckling with orange.

Bars and Cafés in Nürnberg

Café Kröll, Hauptmarkt 6–8, **t** (0911) 91122. Traditional café serving good coffee and mouthwatering cakes.

Café Sebald, Weinmarkt 14, **t** (0911) 381303. Lively, trendy café in the midst of a cluster of half-timbered houses. Also serves good salads and light meals.

Ruhestörung, Tetzelgasse 31, **t** (0911) 221921. Bar in the northern Altstadt, popular with students.

Entertainment and Nightlife in Nürnberg

The local listings magazine is called *Plärrer*; also, the tourist office publishes a monthly *Monatsmagazin*, and *Sommer in Nürnberg* is their free guide to summer events.

Cinema
Roxy, Julius Lossmannstraße 116 (tram 8), **t** (0911) 48840. Wide-ranging, changing programme; films in original languages.

Music, Theatre and Opera
The best music, theatre and opera in Nürnberg is during the summer arts festivals (*see* p.209). You can pre-book tickets at a booth on the second floor of the Karstadt department store, opposite the Lorenzkirche.

Opernhaus and **Schauspielhaus** on Richard-Wagnerplatz, south of the Altstadt just outside the city wall; box office **t** (0911) 2313 808. Both are of a fairly high standard.

Meistersingerhalle, Luitpoldhain (tram 12), box office **t** (0911) 492011. The Nürnberg Symphony Orchestra plays here.

Serenadenhof, Bayernstraße 100, **t** (0911) 55554. Pop stars often perform at this music venue.

Schmelztiegel, Bergstraße 21. Small cellar near the Tiergärtenertor; Dixieland is the sole fare.

Nightclubs in Nürnberg

Mach 1, Kaiserstraße 1–9. The trendiest club in town, often with live music.

Kilian, Kilianstraße 108–110, north of the city centre near Freudenpark. Also trendy; mostly house music.

Steps, Johannisstraße 83 (bus 34). A less hearty atmosphere, but better music.

Bayreuth

Before the border with the old DDR came down, Bayreuth was a sleepy little town, forgotten in an isolated pocket of West Germany and brought out into the light just once a year for the famous Wagner Festival. The inhabitants were prosperous and conservative, and seemed to begrudge the appearance of the Bayreuth University in the late 1970s, belittling it with the diminutive *Universitäla*. The hordes that poured in a decade later – five to a Trabant, peering out at the wealthy West through steamed-up windscreens – were almost too much to bear. Bayreuth is still reeling from the shock.

It is now a bustling town on the Berlin–Munich axis of Germany. The students are asserting their presence and give the town a little life and flair. This, and some fine 18th-century architecture, makes Bayreuth worth a visit in its own right.

The Baroque and rococo buildings are mostly the legacy of the Margravine Wilhelmina, sister of Frederick the Great. In 1731 the cultured, intelligent and passionate Wilhelmina was married to the Margrave of Bayreuth. Had it not been for her father's inept matchmaking, she could have been Queen of England. Instead she was lumped with a provincial lord known as a crushing bore. Undefeated, Wilhelmina set about transforming Bayreuth into a glittering centre of the arts and employed some of Europe's top architects to give the town a face-lift.

A century later the composer Richard Wagner chose Bayreuth as the centre for staging his operas. He came to live here with his wife Cosima and her father Franz Liszt, built a theatre, and laid the foundations for the annual festival. However, Wagner's nationalism and anti-Semitism appealed to the Nazis and the Bayreuth Festival, as Germany's cultural mecca, became tainted with a fanaticism that it is only just beginning to shake off. Many blame Wagner's English daughter-in-law, Winifred, for cultivating Hitler's patronage, and having him to stay as a house guest when he came to Bayreuth for festivals during the 1930s.

The City Centre

Margravine Wilhelmina's most impressive contribution to Bayreuth is the **Markgräfliches Opernhaus**: she commissioned the great Bolognese theatre builder Giuseppe Galli Bibiena and his son Carlo to design the Opera House. The exterior is insignificant, a simple grey foyer with wooden balustrades – but beyond the auditorium doors is one of the most beautiful and atmospheric theatres in the land, with all the magic of a stage set. The rococo interior is made of wood: carved, gilded, marbled and painted in deep greens. There's a scattering of garlands and putti, and rich

Markgräfliches Opernhaus
*Opernstraße;
guided tours April–Sept
Tues–Sun 9–6, Oct–Mar
Tues–Sun 10–4; adm €6*

Getting to and around Bayreuth

Bayreuth lies 85km north of Nürnberg on the A9, the main route between Berlin and Munich. Much of the centre of town is pedestrianized. The main **car parks** are located northeast of the centre off the Wittelsbachring.

For **car hire**, firms with local offices are as follows: **Avis**, Markgrafenallee 6, **t** (0921) 7857710; **Hertz**, Erlanger Straße 43, **t** (0921) 51155.

The **Hauptbahnhof** is 10 minutes' walk north of the city centre. There are hourly **trains** to Nürnberg (1hr).

ceiling paintings. The wood gives the theatre intimacy, warmth, excellent acoustics and also a sense of artifice. The bell-shaped stage is 27m deep, the largest in Germany until 1871. (Its size and acoustics helped lure Wagner to Bayreuth, but he later decided that even the Opernhaus couldn't cope with his productions, and built the even bigger Festspielhaus.) Margravine Wilhelmina was an accomplished painter, writer, actress and composer: on the tour you get a chance to soak up the atmosphere and listen to a recording of one of her works.

Running west from Opernstraße is the main shopping street, **Maximilianstraße**. At No.57 is the 400-year-old sandstone pharmacy, the **Mohren Apotheke**. The northern side of the street is dominated by one of Bayreuth's landmarks, the Baroque **Altes Schloß**, now a tax office. The *Schloß* has twice had to be completely rebuilt: once in recent history, after Allied bombing in 1945, and once in 1753 after it had burnt down. (Some say the margrave started the fire deliberately, as he wanted a new palace and his wife's extravagance had drained and alienated the treasury.) An elegant 16th-century octagonal stone tower juts up behind the *Schloß*. A ramp inside allowed the margraves to ride their horses right to the top, but today you can climb up for a splendid view of Bayreuth only if you go on the official City Tour.

Historisches Stadtmuseum
open July–Aug daily 10–5; Sept–June Tues–Sun 10–5, closed Mon; adm €2

In Kirchplatz (south off Maximilianstraße) is the **Historisches Stadtmuseum**, a run-of-the-mill museum enlivened by the model ships and miniature cannons used by the 18th-century Margrave Georg Wilhelm, for the spectacular naval battles he used to stage on the artificial lake behind his palace.

Farther on is the **Stadtkirche**, with a quaint stone bridge connecting the tops of its delicate towers. The church is the only building in town that predates the Renaissance. At the back of the church is the diminutive **Schwindsuchtshäuschen**, the town's smallest house, which is barely as wide as a car. Kanzleistraße leads into **Friedrichstraße**. Here Margrave Friedrich gave away land cheaply and donated building materials to anyone who would build according to plans approved by his architects (who were firmly under the control of Wilhelmina). The result is a sustained and grandiose stretch of Baroque architecture.

Some way off the northern end of Maximilianstraße is the **Brauerei- und Büttnerei-Museum** (Brewery and Cooper's Museum). The half-hour tour takes you through the fully functional 19th-century steam brewery, and ends up with free samples in a 1920s-style beer bar.

Brauerei- und Büttnerei-Museum
Kulmbacherstraße 40, www.maisel.com; guided tours Mon–Sat 10am; adm €4

The Neues Schloß and Villa Wahnfried

If you follow Ludwigstraße, south of Opernstraße, you come to the sumptuous **Neues Schloß**, built when the Altes Schloß burned down. Wilhelmina herself had a hand in the interior design. The showpiece is the **Zedernsaal** (Cedar Chamber), a warm, wood-panelled dining hall. In the **Spiegelzimmer** (Mirror Room), Wilhelmina intended the irregular fragments of mirror that line the walls to be a comment on the vanity of an age that was overly concerned with appearances.

Neues Schloß
guided tours April–Sept Tues–Sun 9–6; Oct–Mar Tues–Sun 10–4; adm €4

At the east end of a shady Hofgarten behind the Schloß is **Villa Wahnfried**, once Wagner's home, now the **Richard-Wagner-Museum**. Wagner designed the house and lived here (1874–83) with his second wife Cosima. The house is built around a large central hall, where the best musicians of the day gave recitals, and the Wagners held soirees with royals, intellectuals, musicians and artists in attendance. The museum houses an interesting collection of Wagner memorabilia, and costumes and photographs of past productions. In the cellar is an intriguing collection of set-designers' models. Wagner and Cosima lie buried in a simple grave behind the house.

Richard-Wagner-Museum
www.wagner museum.de; open April–Oct Mon, Wed and Fri–Sun 9–5, Tues and Thurs 9–8; Nov–Mar daily 10–5; adm €4, July–Aug €4.50

The Eremitage

Amidst wheatfields and woodland east of town is the **Eremitage**. Built by Margrave Georg Wilhelm as an ascetic retreat from his voluptuous court, the Eremitage and its park were later given to Margravine Wilhelmina, who gave vent to the tedium of her marriage by turning the retreat into a glamorous country seat. She escaped here with her talented friends and poured her heart out in memoirs that caused a scandal when they were published decades after her death.

Eremitage
along Königsallee, bus 2 from Marktplatz; guided tours 15 April–Sept Tues–Sat 9–6, Sun 9–8; Oct Tues–Sun 10–4; adm €4

The palace itself is a mildly interesting rococo building: the real attraction lies in the gardens, with extravagant **fountains**, a **water grotto**, an **artificial ruin** used as an open-air theatre where Wilhelmina herself played Racine's *Bajazet* with Voltaire, and the **Sonnentempel** (Sun Temple). This dumpy dome, to one side of the main palace, is covered with a sort of pebbledash of blue and green stones that sparkle in the sunlight. On top is a gilded statue of Apollo driving a chariot pulled by three horses.

Services in Bayreuth

Police: t 110.
Medical emergencies: t 19222.

Festivals in Bayreuth

🏆 Bayreuth's
Wagner Festival

ⓘ Bayreuth >>
*Luitpoldplatz 9,
t (0921) 88588,
www.bayreuth-
tourismus.de; staff can
help with booking
accommodation, and
offer good walking
tours around the town*

⭐ Hotel Goldener
Anker >>

Wagner Festival

Every year, for the five weeks from July to the end of August, around 60,000 people cram into Bayreuth for the Wagner Festival, the biggest and most important celebration of the composer's work in the world. The festival was founded by Wagner himself. After much bitter wrangling with the Bavarian finance ministry, but with the ardent patronage of King Ludwig II, the Maestro set about designing a theatre and creating a temple to his own art. The first festival opened with the *Nibelungen* in 1876 and was a complete flop. Wagner even had to sell the costumes to try and recoup costs.

It was his second wife, Cosima, who really established the event. She reigned over the festival until 1908, and administration remains a family affair: the show was run for 41 years until 2008 by Wagner's grandson Wolfgang. Performances take place in the original red-brick **Festspielhaus** (*guided tours Tues–Sun 10–10.45, 2.15–3; closed Nov; adm €2.50*) on a hill north of the centre (past the Bahnhof, along Bürgerreutherstraße). An imposing but not very beautiful building, it has punishingly hard seats and brilliant acoustics. Official **ticket prices** range from €12 to €195; tickets go on sale from mid-November. How they are meted out is a mystery (even to the Bayreuth tourist office, who will not be able to help you at all). Agencies around the world get batches seemingly at random. Individuals have to apply in writing the year before they hope to attend (to Kartenbüro, Festspielleitung, Postfach 100626, D-95402 Bayreuth, *www.bayreuther-festspiele.de*). The pattern here seems to be that you will strike lucky every fifth or seventh year.

Other Festivals

The townspeople's reply to the Wagner Festival is the *Frankische Festwoche* (Franconian Festival), which usually runs concurrently with the ***Bayreuther Volkfest*** (Bayreuth Folk Festival) for a week in May/June. Here, as well as top-rate cultural fare from the likes of the Bavarian State Opera, you'll find beer tents, a funfair and much merrymaking.

Where to Stay in Bayreuth

Bayreuth

Standard prices are given below. Expect an increase of *at least* 20% during the Wagner Festival. Rooms over this period are booked out months in advance.

Hotel Goldener Anker, Opernstraße 6, **t** (0921) 65051, *www.anker-bayreuth.de* (€€€). Old-style, with smallish but comfortable rooms, near the old Opernhaus and convenient for all the city sights.

Bayerischer Hof, Bahnhofstraße 14, **t** (0921) 78600, *www.bayerischer-hof.de* (€€). A plush modern hotel close to the station. The rooms are well-appointed, the staff unobtrusively attentive and the hotel has its own swimming pool and loads of parking space.

Fränkischer Hof, Rathenaustraße 28, **t** (0921) 64214, *www.fraenkischerhof-bayreuth.de* (€). Small, central hotel with friendly management.

Gasthof Goldener Löwe, Kulmbacher Straße 30, **t** (0921) 746060, *www.goldener-loewe-bayreuth.de* (€). Charming, countrified brewery-cum-guesthouse in a quiet spot conveniently still quite close to the centre of town.

Gasthof zum Edlen Hirschen, Richard-Wagner-Straße 75, **t** (0921) 512583 (€). Well-run family guesthouse with simple, comfy rooms.

Gasthof Zum Herzog, Kulmbacher Straße, **t** (0921) 41334, *www.gasthofherzog.de* (€). Clean, comfortable and good value, although unfortunately some of the rooms do not have their own private bathroom.

Youth hostel, Universitätsstraße 28, **t** 251262 (bus 4).

Eating Out in Bayreuth

Goldener Anker, Opernstraße 6,
t (0921) 65051, *www.anker-bayreuth.de*
(€€€). The old sandstone inn with the
Grand Duke's arms is utterly quaint
inside and out. The French-orientated,
classical cooking is deliciously
superior. *Closed Mon and Tues.*

Annecy, Gabelsbergerstraße 11,
t (0921) 26279 (€€€–€€). Relaxed
atmosphere and good, unpretentious
French cuisine – scrumptious
casseroles and poultry dishes.

Wölfel, Kirchgasse 12, **t** (0921) 68499
(€€). Cosy tavern, ideal for a meal after
a drink at the Eule (*see* right), that
serves excellent Franconian cuisine.
You can get delicious baked carp, or
ham cooked in a doughy pastry.

Brauereischänke am Markt,
Maximilianstraße 56, **t** (0921) 64919
(€€–€). A little touristy, but with a jolly
atmosphere and hearty Franconian
fare: good sausages and pork with
raw dumplings.

(⭐) Eule >>

Bars and Cafés in Bayreuth

Rosenau, Badstraße 29, **t** (0921) 65136.
Good beer hall with beer garden and
a friendly atmosphere.

Herzogkeller, Hindenburgstraße,
t (0921) 43419. Vast beer garden,
popular with students.

Eule, Kirchgasse 8, **t** (0921) 57554.
Bayreuth's Künstlerkneipe (artists'
pub). Musicians and singers used
to gather here after festival
performances. The walls are
covered with photos that span
decades of Wagnerian stars – it's
the nearest the town comes to a
festival museum, and worth a visit.

Café Florian, Dammallee 12a,
t (0921) 56757. The watering hole for
Bayreuth's 'in' crowd.

Operncafé, Opernstraße 16, **t** (0921)
65720. Elegant café next to the old
Opernhaus, good for coffee and
gooey cakes.

North of Bayreuth

The B2/B303 from Bayreuth leads about 35km to the heart of the
Fichtelgebirge (Spruce Mountains), passing through Bad Berneck, a
health resort in a picturesque setting, with a 15th-century fortified
chapel and the ruins of a 12th-century castle on a hill above the
town. East of **Bad Berneck**, conifers shroud the granite hills of the
Fichtelgebirge. The horseshoe-shaped range opens onto the
foothills of the Bohemian Forest in the Czech Republic. Although
the 'mountains' are no more than chunky hills, they do include the
Schneeberg (1,051m) and the **Ochsenkopf** (1,024m), two of
Franconia's highest peaks. The landscape is less dramatic than
farther southwest in Franconian Switzerland, so the area has
escaped the full impact of tourism and remains a sleepy backwater
of farms, villages and the odd dilapidated castle.

Tin, lead, silver and gold in the Fichtelgebirge made medieval
Franconia rich. As the minerals ran out, the locals turned to
textiles, glass-blowing and porcelain; the latter still plays a
significant role in the economy. Fichtelgebirge ceramics can be
found in classy shops throughout Europe, and the tourist office
has designated a 'porcelain road' along the B15, linking the towns
of Marktredwitz, Thierstein and **Selb**. In Selb, near the Czech border,
the whole town revolves around china, with the Rosenthal and

Hutschenreuther porcelain factories. A porcelain fountain stands imperiously in Selb's swish pedestrian precinct, and you even walk on porcelain cobblestones. The **Museum der Deutschen Porzellanindustrie** (Museum of the German Porcelain Industry) in **Hohenberg** gives a comprehensive account of the history of porcelain production, with examples of period styles.

Museum der Deutschen Porzellanindustrie
open Tues–Sun 10–5; adm €3.50

Another route northwest of Bad Berneck on the B303 goes to the Franconian Forest (about 50km). First stop is **Wirsberg**, a cluster of houses surrounded by forest. The village styles itself the 'Verdant Wedding Village' – a kind of Bavarian Gretna Green. As long as you have the correct paperwork (this is Germany), the *Bürgermeister* will marry you at any time of day. Beyond Wirsberg, the B289 leads to Kulmbach, a mecca for all serious beer-drinking folk in Bavaria.

Kulmbach

If Bayreuth caters to loftier cultural aspirations, Kulmbach takes care of the more mundane things in life. In a *Land* that boasts some 800 breweries (about half of all those in Germany) Kulmbach has the distinction of not only brewing more beer than anywhere else in Bavaria, but also drinking the largest share per capita. Beer-brewing has a long tradition in Kulmbach: up to the beginning of the 15th century each citizen was entitled to brew his own beer.

Today the four big breweries in town pride themselves on their attention to detail: in choosing their strain of barley, specifying how it should be kilned in the maltings, selecting hop varieties, finding the spring water of the requisite softness and breeding yeasts that confer subtle and complex background flavours. You can sample local brews on a pub-crawl of brewery-owned *Gaststätten*, or go on one of the rewarding guided tours (*see* p.219). The extremely powerful Eisbock is Reichelbräu's star product, but still considered small beer next to EKU's ominously named Kulminator 28: at 22 per cent proof, it's said to be the world's strongest brew.

Kulmbach is not all beer and skittles. In the **Unterstadt**, fine old burgher houses are grouped round a spacious **Marktplatz**. From here, walk up through the older **Oberstadt** to Kulmbach's other attraction, the **Plassenburg**, for panoramic views over the town and surrounding countryside. The castle dates from the 12th century, but most of what you see today was built 400 years later. Inside the walls a number of residential buildings are crammed round an impressively ornate Renaissance courtyard. The castle itself houses the **Deutsches Zinnfigurenmuseum** (National Museum of Tin Figurines), where a series of over 200 dioramas, with around

Deutsches Zinnfiguren-museum
open April–Oct Wed–Tues 9–6, Thurs 9–8; Nov–Mar daily 10–4; adm €3.25

Staatliche Sammlungen
same times; adm €2.50

300,000 figurines, takes you from the Middle Ages to modern times. Also on the Plassenburg is the **Staatliche Sammlungen** (Bavarian State Collection), displaying a good stock of hunting weapons and an Iron Age amphora containing sediments of beer brewed more than 2,500 years ago.

The Beer-and-Castle Road

✪ **Beer-and-Castle Road**
www.bierundburgen strasse.de

The B85 past Kulmbach is another theme road, the Beer-and-Castle Road (Bier- und Burgenstraße), stretching far into Thuringia past fortresses and towns with traditional breweries. Working your way up, you come to Kronach, another medieval gem of the Franconian heights.

Kronach

'*In Kronach schmeckt der Dreck wie Honig*' ('In Kronach even the dirt tastes like honey') goes a local saying. This charmed town has preserved many of its half-timbered buildings. The home town of Lucas Cranach the Elder, the quirky Renaissance painter (*see* p.32), has a bold Renaissance **Rathaus** and a **hall church** that is a high point in Franconian Gothic. The town lies in the shadow of the **Veste Rosenberg**, a fortress complex, dating back to the Staufian epoch, but much altered in the 16th and 17th centuries. Nowadays the impressive ring of pentagonal bastions has lost its menace, and the keep and the buildings round the inner courtyard houses the **Fränkische Gallerie** (Franconian Gallery), which has some fine works of Lucas Cranach the Elder and Younger.

Fränkische Gallerie
open April–Oct daily 9.30–5.30, Nov–Mar daily 10–4; adm €2.50

The Frankenwald (Franconian Forest)

Burg Lauenstein
open April–Sept Tues–Sun 9–12 and 1–5; Oct–Mar Tues–Sun 10–12 and 1–3.30; adm €3

Log raft
leaves from Wallenfels, northeast of Kronach, during May–Sept, usually on Sat and Sun

Flößermuseum
open Tues–Sat 9–11 and 2–4, Sun 2–4; adm €2

Back on the B85, which now closely follows the path of the River Haßlach, the road winds through the Franconian Forest, past Ludwigsstadt to **Burg Lauenstein**, high on a promontory overlooking the woods. Stretching south from the Thuringian Forest, the Franconian plateaux rise to a height of 600m. A sparsely populated stretch of woodland (most of it is a nature park), the Franconian Forest is dotted with half-forgotten villages whose residents once lived by processing timber. The rivers that cut through the attractive hillsides proved ideal for timber-rafting as well as being the source of power for numerous water mills. The Franconian Forest is popular with walkers, though a novel way of seeing some of the more unspoilt parts is on a reconstructed **log raft** down the River Wilde Rodach. In nearby **Marktrodach**, the **Flößermuseum** (Rafters' Museum) vividly depicts the harsh lives that the rafting folk once led.

Activities
North of Bayreuth

Brewery Visits

Generally, breweries can only be toured by groups. The following breweries and their museums are worth a visit:

Bayerisches Brauereimuseum Kulmbach, Hofer Straße 20, Kulmbach, t (09221) 80510, *www.bayerisches-brauereimuseum.de*. A hands-on museum detailing the complete beer-making process. Among the numerous relics, the star attraction is the oldest archaeological proof of wheat-beer brewing in Germany – a 2,500-year-old earthenware amphora discovered not far from Kulmbach, whose residues inside are from Bronze Age dark wheat beer. *Open Tues–Fri 10–5, Sat and Sun 9–5; from 10am in winter; adm €4, price includes beer tasting and souvenir tasting glass.*

Mönchshof-Bräu GmbH, Kulmbach, t (09221) 80519. Individuals can join a guided tour of the Mönchshof brewery; *Tues–Thurs at 1pm and Fri at 11am; adm €6, including beer-tasting and a snack.*

Festivals
North of Bayreuth

The main festival is the bacchanalian nine-day-long **Beer Week**, which takes place in a huge tent in Kulmbach in July and August. Less strenuous is the **Zinnfigurenbörse** (Tin Figurines Exchange), a collectors' fair in Kulmbach, held in early August in alternate years (next in 2011).

Where to Stay and Eat
North of Bayreuth

Kulmbach

NH Hotel, Luitpoldstraße 2, t (09221) 6030, *www.nhhotels.com* (€€–€). The town's most upmarket hotel. Attentive care and comfort, but little flair; situated on a busy traffic junction.

Hotel Kronprinz, Fischergasse 4–6, t (09221) 92180, *www.kronprinz-kulmbach.de* (€). Right in the historic Unterstadt, beneath the Plassenburg. Traditional décor, though some rooms are a little small.

Bad Berneck

Hotel Hartl's Lindenmühle, Kolonnadenweg 1, t (09273) 500650, *www.linden muehle.de* (€€–€). A quiet, well-equipped spa hotel with pool and views over the Kurpark.

ⓘ **Kulmbach >>**
Stadthalle, Suite 2,
t (09221) 95880

ⓘ **Kronach**
Marktplatz 5, near the
Rathaus, t (09261)
97236, www.kronach.de

ⓘ **Frankenwald**
Tourist Centre
Adolf-Kolping-Straße 1,
Kronach, t (01805)
366398, www.
frankenwald-
tourismus.de

🌲 **Frankenwald**
woodland walks

The best **walks** are in the glades around the Rivers Rodach and Tettau. Follow the **Rodach gorge**, passing timbered **sawmills**, then cross the river at Steinwiesen before heading north through the **Leitsch Valley** to the village of Tschirn. The **Rennsteig**, one of the region's oldest and finest long-distance wilderness footpaths, cuts through the northern Franconian Forest, from Tettau all the way to Steinbach am Wald.

Bamberg

Bamberg is a vibrant university town just west of Bayreuth, built on seven hills along the River Regnitz. It is a hot contender for the title of the most beautiful town in Germany, yet is inexplicably ignored by most foreign tourists. The Thirty Years' War and the Second World War, which caused the ruin of so many German cities, left Bamberg relatively unscathed: it has kept at least one

Getting to and around Bamberg

Bamberg is off the A70 to Würzburg (100km) and Bayreuth (70km), and the A73 to Nürnberg (60km). The biggest and most convenient undercover **parking garage** in the city is beneath Maximilianplatz, near the Rathaus. For a **taxi** in Bamberg, call **t** 19410.

The **Bahnhof** (**t** (0951) 19419) is 15mins' walk from the centre. (To get to the Rathaus walk down Luitpoldstraße, turn right into Obere Königstraße and then cross the Kettenbrücke.) There are hourly connections to Würzburg (1hr) and frequent **trains** to Nürnberg (45mins) and Munich (2½hrs).

Das ist eine Stadt, die steckt voller Raritäten, wie die Kommode einer alten Groß- mama, die viel zusammen- scharrte.

(This is a city stuffed with more curiosities than are in an old grandmother's hoard in a chest of drawers.)

Karl Immerman
(19th-century traveller)

good example of every European architectural style from Romanesque onwards. Without losing its medieval structure or charm, the town enjoyed a Baroque building boom when some of the era's greatest architects slipped decorous mansions in between the wonky half-timbered houses that prop each other up along its steep, winding alleys. Bamberg has a splendid cathedral, boisterous student life, a world-renowned orchestra and ten local breweries – the sort of mixed bag that makes a small German town a delight.

The Lower City

This is the scene of Bamberg's commercial life. The hub of the activity is **Maxplatz**, with a busy weekday fruit and vegetable market. On the north side of the square is the ponderous **Rathaus** (originally a seminary) designed by the great Baroque architect Balthasar Neumann. **Grüner Markt**, a wide boulevard, leads south off Maxplatz. The most impressive façade belongs to **St Martin's**, a Jesuit church built in 1686–93 by the Dientzenhofer brothers (who designed many of Bamberg's Baroque buildings). Inside there is a rather clever *trompe l'œil* dome. Grüner Markt leads to the Obere Brücke, a bridge over the Regnitz. Linking this and the Untere Brücke, a few yards downstream, is the **Altes Rathaus**, the oddest town hall in Germany. Covering an island in the middle of the river, it looks like a gaudy boat tethered to the bridges. The basic Gothic structure was given a rococo boost in the 18th century. A stone gateway arches over Obere Brücke. On one side stretches a wing emblazoned with bright murals, on the other a little half-timbered addendum hangs over the water.

From the Untere Brücke you can see **Klein-Venedig**, a cluster of half-timbered fishermen's houses. Over the river the hills bristle with church spires. To the east, in streets lined with ochre Italianate buildings, you'll find two of the most ostentatious mansions in the city. The **Böttingerhaus**, at Judenstraße 14, has an opulent portal and courtyard, bulging with stucco work by local artist Vogel. The Franconian *chargé d'affaires* built it in 1707–13, with a river palace almost next door. The **Concordia** (end of Concordiastraße) is, however, best viewed from across the water; go down an alley at the bottom of Concordiastraße and over the bridge onto the Geyersworth island.

E.T.A. Hoffmann-Haus
*open May–Oct
Tues–Fri 4–6, Sat and
Sun 10–12; adm €2*

The Nonnenbrücke takes you to Schillerplatz and the **E.T.A. Hoffmann-Haus**. Hoffmann (1776–1822) was a Romantic painter, composer and writer, most remembered for his bizarre short stories. Two of his tales inspired Romantic ballets – Delibes' *Coppelia* and Tchaikovsky's *Nutcracker*. Hoffmann's eccentric, even schizophrenic personality is the subject of Offenbach's opera *The Tales of Hoffmann*. The museum's large collection of memorabilia is really only worth a visit if you are a Hoffmann fan.

The Domstadt

 Bamberg and its Domstadt

In the 11th century Emperor Henry II established the Bishopric of Bamberg, hoping to make it the capital of the Holy Roman Empire, as important as Rome. His dreams weren't realized, but Bamberg became a medieval centre of learning, and the prince-bishopric lasted until Napoleon's secularization.

The cathedral and ecclesiastical palaces that crown Bamberg's main hill are called the Domstadt (Cathedral City), in contrast to the commercial town below. From the Altes Rathaus, wind through narrow alleys and up stairways to the large, sloping **Domplatz**. This square presents a magnificent spectrum of European architecture from Romanesque beginnings in the cathedral to Gothic, Renaissance and Baroque in the surrounding buildings.

The Cathedral

The first cathedral burnt down twice, and the present one was built as Gothic architecture bloomed (*c.* 1215–37). The cathedral's east chancel is earthy, rounded Romanesque; the west chancel flighty, pointed Gothic. Between them the nave is a perfect illustration of the transitional style. The four towers mirror each other, with just a slight distortion that reflects the changes those two important decades produced: the spires on the western end are a touch lighter, sharper and more delicate than their solid Romanesque counterparts. The **Fürstenportal** (Prince's Portal, 1228), on the north side of the nave, is a supreme feat of Romanesque carving. Apostles and prophets line arches that recede towards a heavy wooden door. On the tympanum, Christ presides over the Last Judgement. Inside, around the east choir, are more fine early **13th-century sculptures**. A youthful, pregnant Virgin is flanked by an aged Elizabeth (known as 'The Bamberg Sibyl'). Two simpler female figures, Synagogue and Ecclesia, represent the Old and New Testaments. Synagogue is blindfolded, skinny and wears a thin, seemingly transparent shift. Ecclesia has a crown, fuller garments and a smug smile. Most famous of all is the statue of the **Bamberger Reiter** (*Bamberg Rider, c.* 1235). No one knows who the horseman is – possibly Constantine the Great or one of the Magi. He sits proud on his steed, staring far into the distance. The whole statue quivers with energy, but holds unfortunate memories: Hitler saw it as a pinnacle of German artistic perfection, and during the Third Reich reproductions adorned public buildings everywhere. The **Imperial Tomb** in the centre of the nave contains the remains of the saintly 11th-century ruler Henry II and his consort Kunigunde; the top and sides are covered in carvings depicting events from their lives by the famous medieval sculptor Tilman Riemenschneider. To the left of the west chancel you can see the deeply burnished, though sadly unfinished, **Weihnachtsaltar** (Nativity Altar, 1520–3), one of the last works of the Nürnberg sculptor Veit Stoss.

The Alte Hofhaltung

Alongside the cathedral is the Alte Hofhaltung, a motley complex which comprises the former imperial and episcopal palace and old imperial Diet Hall. The **Ratstube**, a graceful Renaissance building on the corner nearest the cathedral, now houses the **Historisches Museum**, a missable collection of bits and bobs relating to the city's history.

Historisches Museum
open May–Oct Tues–Sun 9–5; adm €2.10

Next to this is a grand Renaissance stone gateway, the **Reiche Tor** (Imperial Gate). It is flanked by allegorical figures of the Pegnitz and Main rivers and shows Henry and Kunigunde carrying a remarkably accurate model of the cathedral. Through the arch you come to the big, uneven cobbled **inner court**. All around the edges are striking, four-storey, 15th-century half-timbered buildings with wooden galleries and heavy, drooping eaves.

The Neue Residenz

Neue Residenz
www.schloesser-bayern.de; open April–Sept daily 9–6; Oct–Mar daily 10–4; adm €4

The rest of the Domplatz is taken up by the huge **Neue Residenz**, another product of the powerful Schönborn family (*see p.144*) whose one-upmanship resulted in grand buildings across Germany. The Baroque Residenz was commissioned by Prince-Bishop Lothar Franz von Schönborn (also archbishop and elector of Mainz), and built by Leonhard Dientzenhofer in 1697–1703. The **interior** is worth a visit for a look at the bright frescoes in **Kaisersaal**, and a finely painted **Chinesische Kabinett**. The building houses the small **Staatsgalerie**, with works by Cranach the Elder and Hans Baldung (Grien). At the back of the palace is a **rose garden**, a fragrant retreat with serene statues, a rococo summer-house (now a café) and a magnificent view.

Michaelsberg and Altenburg

A footpath leads up from Aufseßstraße (behind the Residenz), through orchards to the top of Michaelsberg, another of Bamberg's seven hills. The **abbey of St Michael** on top of the hill is an old people's home, but you can visit its Baroque church with over 600 medicinal herbs painted on the ceiling. The cellars house the **Fränkisches Brauereimuseum**, a small museum of beer and brewing history. Outside, a spacious terrace looks out over Bamberg and the countryside, and there is a small café under the trees.

Fränkisches Brauereimuseum
open April–Oct Tues–Sun 1–5; adm €2.50

Retracing your steps down Michaelsberg and continuing along Maternstraße, you reach the **Karmelitenkloster**. The church is another Dientzenhofer Baroque showpiece, but the **cloisters** are serenely Romanesque. Nearby, on Unterer Kaulberg, is Bamberg's finest Gothic church, the **Obere Pfarrkirche**, while uphill (along Altenburger Straße) is the **Altenburg** (1109), a ruined castle complete with moat and bear pit.

Karmelitenkloster cloisters
open daily 9–11.30 and 2.30–5.30

Services in Bamberg

Post office: Ludwigstraße 25, near Bahnhof. *Open Mon–Fri 7.30–6, Sat 8–12.30.*

Banks: Branches of most German banks are on Hauptwachstraße/Grüner Markt.

Police: t 110.

Medical emergencies: t 19222.

Festivals in Bamberg

Roman Catholic Bamberg's main festival is **Corpus Christi** (May/June) when there is a church procession with many people dressed in *Tracht*. There is more traditional dress and dancing, as well as water-jousting during the *Sandfest* in August.

Activities in Bamberg

River Cruises

You get superb views of Bamberg from the river, especially in the early morning. Tickets are available from **Bamberger Veranstaltungstdienst**, at Langestraße 24.

Where to Stay in Bamberg

Bamberg

Romantik Hotel Weinhaus Messerschmitt, Langestraße 41, t (0951) 297800, *www.hotel-messerschmitt.de* (€€€). Bamberg's most traditional

hotel has been in the same family since 1832. In the corridor you'll come across photos of Messerschmitt, the engineer of Germany's first jet fighter and uncle of proprietor Herr Pschorn.

Barock-Hotel am Dom, Vorderer Bach 4, t (0951) 54031 (€€). Beautiful Baroque building in a quiet street behind the cathedral. The rooms aren't very imaginatively furnished, but they're comfortable enough and the management is helpful and friendly.

St Nepomunk, Obere Mühlbrücke 9, t (0951) 98420 (€€). Stylish hotel that teeters over the Regnitz on stilts. The rooms are sumptuously decorated and the service is impeccable.

Hotel Alt Ringlein, Dominikanerstraße 9, t (0951) 95320, *www.altringlein.com* (€€–€). Spruce and newly modernized hotel, part of which has been an inn since 1545. It nestles in the shadow of the cathedral and is run by a capable and attentive family.

Weierich, Lugbank 5, t (0951) 955660, *www.hotel-weierich.de* (€€–€). Rustic, cosy inn, centrally situated.

Spezial, Obere Königstraße 10, t (0951) 24304, *www.brauerei-spezial.de* (€). Comfortable tavern run by a local brewery, a few minutes' walk from the lower city.

Fässla, Obere Königstraße 19, t (0951) 26516/22998, *www.faessla.de* (€). This place is also owned by a brewery, but a little more upmarket, with televisions in the rooms. Offers a hearty breakfast buffet.

ⓘ **Bamberg >**
Geyerswörthstraße 3 (on an island in the Regnitz), t (0951) 2976 200, www.bamberg. info; open Mon–Fri 9.30–6, Sat 9.30–2.30

(★) Café
Domherrenhof >>

Youth hostel, Wolfsschlucht, Oberer Leinritt 70, t (0951) 56002. Bed and breakfast is €14.

Eating Out and Bars in Bamberg

Bamberg is most famous for its beer. There are ten local breweries, which together produce around 30 different kinds. Locals rate highly the *Rauchbier* (smoky beer) made from smoked malt following a 16th-century recipe. The taverns owned by the breweries are also often recommendable places for tasty, good-value meals.

Dom-Terrassen, Unterer Kaulberg 36 (€€). Unassuming *Gaststätte* near the Karmelitenkloster with a splendid terrace, with views over the Domplatz. There's a small café for *Kaffee und Kuchen*, as well as a larger *Gaststätte* on the Michaelsburg. Both have terraces overlooking the town.

Zum Schlenkerla, Dominikanerstraße 6, t (0951) 56060, *www.schlenkerla.de* (€€). Lively 17th-century tavern that serves good beer and light meals.

Spezial, Sternwartstraße (€€). Popular beer cellar with garden, serving well-prepared food.

Klosterbräu, Obere Mühlbrücke 3 (€). 16th-century tax collector's office turned brewery and pub.

Café Domherrenhof, Karolinenstraße 24 (€). Big basket chairs, high Baroque ceilings and a terrace with a view up to the Neue Residenz. A good place for breakfast or a snack.

Entertainment and Nightlife in Bamberg

The **Bamberger Symphoniker**, once the Deutsches Orchester of Prague, skipped the border just as the Iron Curtain was falling. They perform all over town, but the most enchanting way to hear them is at the regular candlelit performances in the Kaisersaal of the Neue Residenz. Members of the Symphoniker also form the **Bamberg Baroque Ensemble**, which plays chamber music, and various other groups of high quality perform around town. Tickets for all concerts can be obtained from **Bamberger Veranstaltungsdienst**, Langestraße 22, t (0951) 9808 220.

Downstairs, Langestraße 16. The nightclub most popular with Bamberg's trendies.

North of Bamberg

Just northeast, at Memmelsdorf, is **Schloß Seehof**, one of two palatial residences commissioned by the prince-bishops of Bamberg in the 17th and 18th centuries. (The other is Schloß Weißenstein at Pommersfelden.) Built at the turn of the 17th century, it had the full early Baroque treatment, with the addition of four octagonal towers. The *Schloß* now houses Franconia's office for the preservation of historic monuments. The adjoining landscaped gardens have been restored.

Städtisches
Museum
*open April–Oct Tues–Fri
10–12 and 2–5, Sat–
Sun 2–5; Nov and Mar
Sat 2–4; 26 Dec–9 Jan
Sat–Sun 2–4 by appt.
only; adm €1.50*

A few miles further on the B173 you come to **Staffelstein**, a charming string of Franconian half-timbered buildings, between a dolomite bluff and the River Main. On the little Marktplatz is the picture-postcard Baroque **Rathaus** (1687). At the **Städtisches Museum** (Town Museum), you can find out about **Adam Riese**, the mathematical wizard born locally in 1492 whose name has long been the byword for arithmetical accuracy to every German schoolchild.

Beyond Staffelstein, in an area of rugged little hills, two cheerful Baroque buildings appear on either side of the B173. High above the woods to the west is **Kloster Banz**. Founded in 1069 by the Benedictine order, the monastery received a Baroque facelift after 1695. The princely dimensions of the estate enticed the Wittelsbachs to buy it in 1814, with a view to turning it into a palace. Today it is home to a training and conference centre. The **church** at the far southwest corner is the most eye-catching building in the complex, and its interior is considered one of architect Johann Dientzenhofer's masterpieces: crimson, grey and golden tones suffuse the oval-shaped nave, with the delicate carving of the choir stalls adding a touch of class.

Crowning a slope on the opposite side of the main road, the **Vierzehnheiligen** counterbalances Kloster Banz. This church was built on the spot where, in 1519, a shepherd saw three successive apparitions of 14 of Franconia's patron saints. A chapel was built here as early as 1525, but the present Baroque church is based on designs by Balthasar Neumann. The church is a brilliant example of the spatial illusionism that was to become a Neumann speciality: the interior, based on a series of ovals, appears to be much larger than it is. The marble and the gold-leaf stucco combine to produce some dazzling effects, but even finer are the masterly, highly theatrical *trompe l'œil* ceiling frescoes by Giuseppe Appiani, with a foreshortened *Annunciation* above the choir and a central cycle illustrating the 14 saints who gave the church its name. The same saints adorn the **Gnadenaltar**, a free-standing altar with an ostentatiously ornamented *baldacchino*. This central altar is on a par with the outrageously tinselly rococo **high altar** at the east end, creating an equally inviting, joyful atmosphere.

From Vierzehnheiligen it is just 25km on the B289 and B4 past the town of **Lichtenfels**, famed for its wickerwork, to Coburg.

Coburg

Standing magisterially on a leafy hill above the town is one of the most outstanding sights of northern Franconia, the awesome **Veste Coburg**. From far away the castle's towers and gables poke up like the points of a crown from behind a mighty ring wall.

The Veste can look back on more than 750 years of history. From 1353 it was linked with the Wettin rulers of Saxony and Thuringia, becoming one of their chief residences in the 16th century. The descendants of the Wettins, the **Saxe-Coburg-Gotha** family, provided spouses for royal families all over Europe, including Queen Victoria's consort, Prince Albert. The complex was almost completely rebuilt in the 16th and 17th centuries, and is now a

Museum,
Veste Coburg
open April–Oct daily
10–5; Nov–Mar
Tues–Sun 1–4; adm €3

museum with a vast and important collection of engravings and other work by Rembrandt, Cranach, Dürer et al., and a captivating cross-section of over four centuries of period interiors in the timber-framed Fürstenbau.

Coburg's **Altstadt** is laid out in a series of twisting streets between the castle hill and the River Itz. In the middle is the **Stadtplatz**, dominated by the late 16th-century **Rathaus** and the Stadthaus (*c.* 1600), the former ducal chancellery. In both, the dying flickers of the Renaissance are fused with the new spirit of early Baroque. Close to the central square are two prime examples of half-timbered architecture: the **Münzmeisterhaus** (1348), generally regarded as one of the most beautiful examples of Franconian *Fachwerk*, and the **Hofapotheke** (*c.* 1400), a former apothecary's house with a late Gothic oriel projection.

Schloß Ehrenburg
guided tours Tues–Sun
at 10 and 11am, 1, 2, 3, 4
and 5pm; to 3.30 in
winter; adm €5

Proof that the new dynastic ties with (among others) the courts at St Petersburg, London, Lisbon and Stockholm did, in fact, pay off for the Saxe-Coburg-Gothas is the 16th-century **Schloß Ehrenburg**. This sumptuous Renaissance palace in the middle of town was given a neo-Gothic going-over in the 19th century. One of the curiosities on display is Germany's first operating water closet, installed for none other than Queen Victoria, who didn't want to do without the amenity that had grown so dear to her.

For those who like to people their rooms with porcelain figurines, the **Hummel porcelain works** in the small town of **Rödental**, just northeast of Coburg, give insight into the painstaking manufacturing techniques that go into the perky characters designed on paper by the Franciscan nun Maria Innocentia (1909–46) in the 1930s, which have since been successfully marketed the world over. The town of **Neustadt bei Coburg**, also to the northeast, is the centre of the German doll industry and holds an annual **International Doll Festival**.

International
Doll Festival
early May; www.
spielzeugmuseum-
neustadt.de

Where to Stay and Eat North of Bamberg

ⓘ **Coburg >**
Herrengasse 4,
t *(09561) 74180,*
www.stadt.coburg.de

Coburg

Hotel Goldener Anker, Rosengasse 14, **t** (09561) 55700, *www.goldener-anker.de* (€€€). Central, with good management and a respected restaurant.

Romantik Hotel Goldene Traube, Am Viktoriabrunnen 2, **t** (09561) 8760, *www.goldenetraube.de* (€€). Family-run 18th-century hotel, with lots of modern amenities. The gourmet restaurant and traditional *Weinstube* serves earthy Franconian specialities.

Hotel Festungshof, Festungshof 1, **t** (09561) 80290, *www.hotel-festunghof.de* (€€). Newly renovated, well-equipped small hotel on the foot of the hill that leads up to the Veste.

Staffelstein

Kurhotel, Am Kurpark 7, **t** (09573) 3330, *www.kurhotel-staffelstein.de* (€). Hotel on the outskirts of the town with its own sauna and solarium, and massage on offer. There's also easy access to the Obermain-Therme, Bavaria's latest and hottest thermal spring. It's generally full of elderly Germans taking the *Kur*.

Getting around Franconian Switzerland

Local **buses** are erratic and train routes tend to skirt the edges of the region, so a **car** is the best way to get around. Bamberg, Bayreuth and Nürnberg are equally good starting points. The B2, B470 and B22 cut across the area, but in order to see the more remote scenery it's best to resort to local roads.

Main **rail** lines run Forchheim–Ebermannstadt (connection to Behringersmühle); Nürnberg–Gräfenberg and Nürnberg–Neunkirchen, with a connection to Simmelsdorf-Hüttenbach.

Franconian Switzerland is very much an area to explore on **foot** or by **bicycle**. On 4,000km of signposted walking trails, you can follow in the footsteps of the Romantic literati who first trod this unspoilt beauty spot. The region is also well laid out with cycle paths (you can hire bicycles from the train stations at Bamberg and Forchheim).

Franconian Switzerland

Franconian Switzerland (Fränkische Schweiz) is the name given by the 19th-century German Romantics to the area between Bamberg, Bayreuth and Nürnberg. The landscape is far from Alpine, though it does have surprisingly deep valleys, lush meadows, cherry and apple groves, and sudden outcrops of dolomite rock, some with stalactite caves, topped by gaunt castle ruins. It has long been a popular holiday destination and is a good spot for hiking.

From Bamberg to Pottenstein

Schloß Weißenstein
guided tours April–Oct 10–5; adm €4

Pommersfelden, 20km south of Bamberg along the B505, is the site of **Schloß Weißenstein**. Set in the **Steigerwald**, the splendid Baroque palace was built by Prince-Bishop Lothar von Schönborn at the turn of the 18th century, about the same time as the Würzburg Residenz and the Neue Residenz in Bamberg. Much of the original architecture is there, including the grand three-storeyed flight of steps in the main building, and an eye-catching frivolity of marble and stucco at the entrance to the **Marmorsaal** (Marble Hall). Avid denim-wearers might head for **Buttenheim**, 17km northeast of Pommersfelden, the birthplace of Levi Strauss, a Jewish pedlar's son who emigrated to the United States in 1847 to become one of the most prolific producers of blue jeans.

A few kilometres southeast is **Forchheim**, a half-timbered town in forest along the Pegnitz, halfway between Bamberg and Nürnberg. Lovers of regional costumes should stop at the pretty village of **Effeltrich**, 8km south of Forchheim. Here, most weekends, villagers step out in a swish of frilly *Tracht* (traditional dress).

From Forchheim, you can either potter about Franconian Switzerland, or follow the B470, which hugs the River Wiesent. The road takes you to the cherry-growing village of **Pretzfeld** and its 16th-century castle. To the south, the gently undulating **Truppach Valley** stretches along the course of this tributary of the Wiesent.

At one time, the valley was crammed with over 200 **water mills**, used to process rich local deposits of iron ore. Today just eight remain, preserved under a protection order.

Zwernitz Castle
open mid-April–mid-Oct daily 9–6; adm €3.50

Yet farther north, at **Zwernitz Castle** near **Hollfeld**, you will find **Sanspareil**, a rugged, romantic garden laid out around the crag-top ruin of the castle, with fanciful grotto landscapes. Wilhelmina von Bayreuth modelled the garden on the one created at her brother's palace of Sanssouci in Potsdam in the late 18th century.

Sanspareil
same times and prices as Zwernitz Castle

Back on the B470, the countryside opens up a little as you get closer to **Muggendorf**, a town of richly coloured houses, idling beneath a ruined castle. This is the oldest resort in Franconian Switzerland. A remarkable group of stalactite caves can be found around the town; the largest of these, extending over a length of 400m, is the **Binghöhle**. From Muggendorf the road rambles on past **Gößweinstein** and **Behringersmühle**, around knobbly hills, to **Pottenstein**, a pretty village with a Gothic church and a 10th-century castle. The nearby **Teufelshöhle** is a 1,500m cave with stalactites even finer than those of the Binghöhle. In the nearby hamlet of Tüchersfeld is the **Judenhof**, an old Jewish stronghold now housing the **Fränkische Schweiz Museum**, where you can see local history exhibits, including the belongings of the former Jewish occupants.

Binghöhle
guided tours only, 13 Mar–10 Nov daily 9–5.30; adm €3

Teufelshöhle
guided tours only, Easter–Oct daily 9–5, Nov–Easter Tues and Sat 10–12; adm €3.50

Fränkische Schweiz Museum
open April–Oct Tues–Sun 10–5; adm €3

Festivals in Franconian Switzerland

Nearly every village in Franconian Switzerland has festivals to mark religious holidays or the arrival of spring and autumn. Many locals dress up in *Tracht*, and the bigger festivals often include folk-dancing contests.

One of the most spectacular events is in Forchheim at the end of July, when the *Annafest* is celebrated with a ten-day funfair. Muggendorf holds an annual *Kürbisfest* (Pumpkin Festival) in late September, and nearby Pottenstein observes Epiphany (6 Jan) with a *Lichterfest* (Festival of Lights), an evening candle- and torchlit parade.

(i) Ebermann-stadt
Tourismus-Zentrale Fränkische Schweiz, Oberes Tor 1, t (09194) 797779, www.ebermannstadt.de

(i) Forchheim
Rathaus, Hauptbahnstraße 24, t (09191) 714338, www.forchheim.de

(i) Pottenstein
Gästezentrum am Rathaus, t (09243) 70841, www.pottenstein.de

Where to Stay and Eat in Franconian Switzerland

Prices are relatively low, and even in summer finding accommodation is never a problem. If you want to take in the sights and scenery, or help out at some local cherry-picking between June and August, try the various **farming holidays** on offer in the region. In many ways the best bargains of all, a number of farmhouses provide full-board rates from as little as €35 per day. A list is available from **Verein Urlaub auf dem Bauernhof**, Löschwöhrdstraße 5, D-91301 Forchheim, t (09191) 65070.

Hotel Feiler, Oberer Markt 4, Muggendorf, t (09196) 92950, *www.hotel-feiler.de* (€€). An elegant, quiet, family-run hotel with some romantic timber-framed bedrooms. The restaurant offers excellent sole and fillet of lamb.

Hotel-Gasthof Resengörg, Hauptstraße 36, Ebermannstadt, t (09194) 73930, *www.resengoerg.de* (€). Rustic half-timbered house (including two outlying guesthouses) with commodious rooms, good cheer and hearty wine and beer tavern.

Scheffel-Gasthof, Balthasar-Neumann-Straße 6, Gößweinstein, t (09242) 201, *www.scheffel-gasthof.de* (€). An atmospheric Baroque mansion, now a jolly, traditional inn.

Language

German has never enjoyed a particularly good press. Holy Roman Emperor Charles V considered it fit only for speaking to his horse. Mark Twain sent it up wickedly in his essay *On the Awful German Language*, and the narrator of Anthony Burgess's novel *Earthly Powers* calls it 'a glottal fishbone-clearing, soulful, sobbing, sausage machine of a language'.

It is a language of devilish complexity. There are three, rather than two, genders; nouns and adjectives decline; it is full of irregular verbs and deceptive conjugations; and the syntax is ornate, and often littered with parentheses that lead the inexperienced astray. The verb often comes only at the end of one of these arduous syntactical journeys. *Punch* once carried a cartoon of 'The Man who Died of Boredom while Waiting for a German Verb to Arrive'. More recently, simultaneous interpreters at an international conference were struck dumb during one long, impassioned outburst by a German delegate, as they too awaited the elusive particle. (All a section of the audience heard through their headphones was 'I missed the bloody verb').

But there are some advantages. Nouns are capitalized and easy to spot. This helps you to make some sense of written passages, even if your knowledge of German is scanty. Spelling is phonetic, so once you have grasped the basics of pronunciation there are few surprises. And German is a precise language. Numbers of words can be combined into a single new one that hits the nail right on the head; sometimes, though, this gets out of hand. 'These things are not words,' lamented Twain, 'they are alphabetical processions.'

For a restaurant vocabulary list, *see* **Food and Drink**, pp.50–2.

Pronunciation

Most consonants are the same as in English. There are no silent letters.

g is hard, as in English 'good'
ch is a guttural sound, as in the Scottish 'loch' – though **sch** is said as *sh*
s is also often pronounced *sh*, when it appears before a consonant (especially at the beginning of a word), as in **stein**, pronounced *shtine*. Otherwise the sound is closer to 'z': **sie** (she) = *zee*
z is pronounced *ts*
d at the end of the word becomes 't'
r is rolled at the back of the throat, as in French
v is pronounced softly, somewhere between the English 'f' and 'v'
w is said as the English 'v'
a can be long (as in 'father') or short (as in 'hat').
u can be short, as in 'put' (*Hut*: hat), or long, as in 'boot'
e is pronounced at the end of words, and is slightly longer than in English.
Say: eh as in 'hay';
ai and ei as in 'pie';
au as in 'house';
ee and ie as in 'glee';
eu and oi as in 'oil'.
An **umlaut** (¨) changes the pronunciation of a word. Say ä like the 'e' in 'bet', or like the 'a' in 'label'. Say ö like the vowel sound in 'fur'. ü is a very short version of the vowel sound in 'true'. Sometimes an umlaut is replaced by an 'e' after the vowel.
ß The printed symbol *ß* is sometimes written ss, and is pronounced as a double '*ess*'.

Practice Sentences

Verstehen Sie Deutsch?
(*fairshtayen zee doitch?*)
Do you understand German?

Nein, ich verstehe kein Wort.
(nine, ich fairshtay kine vort)
No, I don't understand a word.

Haben Sie Zimmer frei?
(haben zee tsimmer fry?)
Do you have any rooms free?

Useful Words and Phrases

The standard of English in Bavaria is pretty good – though restaurants off the tourist track seldom have an English menu. In rural districts, however, you are advised to go armed with essential German phrases.

yes/no/maybe *ja/nein/vielleicht*
excuse me *Entschuldigung, bitte*
it doesn't matter *es macht nichts*
I am sorry *es tut mir leid*
please *bitte*
thank you (very much) *danke (schön);*
vergelt's Gott (in rural Bavaria)
it's a pleasure *bitte (schön)*
hello *guten Tag; hallo*
hello (in Bavaria) *grüß Gott*
goodbye/bye *auf Wiedersehen;*
tschüss/tschü; pfüat di (in rural Bavaria)
good morning/evening *guten Morgen/Abend*
good night *gute Nacht*
how are you? (formal) *wie geht es Ihnen?*
(informal) *wie geht es Dir?* or *wie geht's?*
I'm very well *mir geht's gut*
I don't speak German *ich spreche kein*
Deutsch
do you speak English? *sprechen Sie Englisch?*
do you understand me? *verstehen Sie mich?;*
host mi? (in rural Bavaria)
I don't know *ich weiß nicht*
I don't understand *ich verstehe nicht*
how do you say... *wie sagt man...*
my name is... *mein Name ist... ; ich heiße...*
I am a/an...
Englishman (-woman) *ich bin Engländer(in)*
American *Amerikaner(in)*
Australian *Australier(in)*
Canadian *Kanadier(in)*
New Zealander *Neuseeländer(in)*
I come from...
England *ich komme aus England*
Scotland *Schottland*
Ireland *Irland*
Wales *Wales*
the United States *den Vereinigten Staaten*
Canada *Kanada*

Australia *Australien*
New Zealand *Neuseeland*
leave me alone *lass mich in Ruhe*
and/but *und/aber*
is this table free? *ist der Tisch frei?*
the menu, please *die Speisekarte bitte*
the bill, please *die Rechnung bitte*
I would like... *ich möchte...*
with/without *mit/ohne*
how much does this cost? *wieviel kostet dies?*
cheap/expensive *billig/teuer*
where is/are...? *wo ist/sind...?*
who *wer*
what *was*
why *warum*
when *wann*
how do I get to...
(town) *wie komme ich am besten nach...*
(building or place) *wie komme ich am*
besten zur/zum...
how far is it to... *wie weit ist es nach...*
how long does it take? *wie lange dauert es?*
near/far *nah/weit*
left/right/straight on *links/rechts/geradeaus*
help! *hilfe!*
could you help me? *könnten Sie mir bitte*
helfen?
I am ill *ich bin krank*
I am lost *ich weiß nicht wo ich bin*
I am hungry/thirsty *ich habe Hunger/Durst*
I am hot/cold *mir ist warm/kalt*

Notices and Signs

open/closed *geöffnet/geschlossen*
closed (literally: rest day) *Ruhetag*
in this year *heuer*
entrance *Eingang*
exit (emergency exit) *Ausgang (Notausgang)*
no entry *Eingang verboten*
toilet *Toilette*
Ladies/Gents *Damen/Herren*
bathroom *Badezimmer*
push/pull *drücken/ziehen*
bank *Bank*
bureau de change *Wechselstube*
police *Polizei*
hospital *Krankenhaus*
pharmacy *Apotheke*
post office *Post*
airport *Flughafen*
customs *Zoll*
railway station *Bahnhof*
train *Zug*

platform *Gleis*
reserved *besetzt*
rooms to let *Fremdenzimmer*
pedestrian zone *Fußgängerzone*
picnic area *Rastplatz*
way round/circuit *Rundgang*

Days and Months

Monday *Montag*
Tuesday *Dienstag*
Wednesday *Mittwoch*
Thursday *Donnerstag*
Friday *Freitag*
Saturday *Samstag*
Sunday *Sonntag*
January *Januar; Jännar*
February *Februar*
March *März*
April *April*
May *Mai*
June *Juni*
July *Juli*
August *August*
September *September*
October *Oktober*
November *November*
December *Dezember*

Numbers

one *eins*
two *zwei*
three *drei*
four *vier*
five *fünf*
six *sechs*
seven *sieben*
eight *acht*
nine *neun*
ten *zehn*
eleven *elf*
twelve *zwölf*
thirteen *dreizehn*
fourteen *vierzehn*
seventeen *siebzehn*
twenty *zwanzig*
twenty-one *einundzwanzig*
thirty *dreißig*
forty *vierzig*
fifty *fünfzig*
sixty *sechszig*
seventy *siebzig*
eighty *achtzig*

ninety *neunzig*
hundred *hundert*
hundred and forty-two *hundertzweiund-vierzig*
two hundred *zweihundert*
thousand *tausend*
million *eine Million*
billion (thousand million) *eine Milliarde*
billion (million million) *eine Billion*

Time

watch/clock/hour *Uhr*
alarm clock *Wecker*
what is the time? *wie spät ist es?*
one/two o'clock *eine/zwei Uhr*
quarter past two *Viertel nach zwei*
half past two *halbdrei*
half past three *halbvier*
quarter to three *Viertel vor drei*
morning *Morgen; Vormittag*
afternoon *Nachmittag*
evening/night *Abend/Nacht*
week *Woche*
month *Monat*
year *Jahr*
season *Jahreszeit*
spring/summer *Frühling/Sommer*
autumn/winter *Herbst/Winter*
century *Jahrhundert*
today/yesterday/tomorrow
 heute/gestern/morgen
this/last/next week *diese/letzte/nächste Woche*

Driving

car hire *Autovermietung*
filling station *Tankstelle*
petrol/diesel *Benzin/Diesel*
leaded/unleaded *verbleit/bleifrei*
my car has broken down *mein Auto hat Panne*
I've had a car accident
 Ich habe einen Autounfall gehabt
garage (for repairs) *Autowerkstatt*
parking place *Parkplatz*
no parking *Parken verboten*
driver's licence *Führerschein*
insurance *Versicherung*
one-way street *Einbahnstraße*
except (on No-Entry signs) *außer*
get in correct lane *einordnen*
junction *Kreuzung*

Glossary

Altstadt old town
Bad spa town (precedes the town name)
Bahnhof railway station
Berg mountain
BRD Federal Republic of Germany
Brücke bridge
Brunnen fountain, spring, well
Bundes federal, hence **Bundestag** (Federal
  Parliament)
Burg castle
Bürgermeister mayor
Dom cathedral
Dorf village
Fachwerk half-timbered
Feierabend home time, used by shopkeepers
  to refuse service 10 minutes before closing.
Feiertag holiday
Festung fortress
Flughafen airport
Fluß river
Funk radio – hence **Funktaxi** and **Funktelefon**
  are not what might be expected.
Fürst prince
Gasse alley
Gasthaus/hof inn, guest house
Graf count
Hafen harbour
Hauptbahnhof main railway station
Hauptstraße main street
Heimat homeland, hometown
Herzog duke
Hof court (royal); also courtyard or mansion
Insel island
Jugendherberge youth hostel
Jugendstil German version of Art Nouveau
Kaiser Emperor
Kammer room, chamber
Kapelle chapel
Kaufhaus department store
Kino cinema
Kirche church
Kloster monastery, convent
König king

Kunst art
Kurhaus clinic of a spa town or health resort
Kurort health resort
Kurverwaltung tourist office in a spa town
Land state in the Federal Republic (pl. **Länder**)
Landgraf landgrave (in charge of a territory)
Lüftlmalerei frescoes
Margraf margrave (governor of a frontier
  province)
Markt market, market square
Meer sea
Münster minster, often any large church
Palast residential part of a castle
Platz square
Prinz prince, but since 1918 used as a general
  aristocratic title
Rathaus town/city hall
Ratskeller Rathaus cellar restaurant
Reich empire
Reisebüro travel agency
Residenz palace
Ritter knight
Saal hall
Sammlung collection
Schatzkammer treasury (e.g. of a cathedral)
Schickimiki yuppie (shortened to **Schicki**)
Schloß palace, castle
See lake
Stadt town, city
Strand beach
Straßenbahn tram
Tal valley
Tankstelle filling station
Tor gate (usually once part of a medieval
  wall)
Tracht traditional costume
Turm tower (often part of a medieval wall)
Verkehrsamt tourist office; also
  Verkehrsverein or **Fremdenverkehrsamt**
Viertel quarter, district
Volk people (folk)
Wald forest
Zimmer room

Chronology

BC

800 BC–400 BC Celtic tribes settle in the area that comprises modern Bavaria.

From 15 BC Roman invasion of the land between the Alps, Dolomites and the Danube. Provinces of Raetia and Noricum are protected by forts at Augsburg, Kempten, Regensburg and Passau.

AD

AD 488 Roman control of lands north of the Alps collapses under the onslaught of the Germanic *Baiuvarii*.

555–788 Frankish dukes of the Agilolfing family rule lands south of the Danube. Capital established at Regensburg.

7th–8th century Irish and Scottish missionaries convert central Bavaria to Christianity.

8th century A Merovingian dynasty establishes crown lands north of the Danube (modern Franconia).

788 Tassilo III, the last of the Agilolfing dukes, is deposed by Charlemagne, and the Bavarian duchy is absorbed by the Carolingian Empire.

843 Bavaria comes under the control of Louis the German, king of the eastern Franks.

907 Margrave Luitpold, founding father of the Babenburg dynasty, is killed by a Magyar army at the Battle of Pressburg. His son Arnulf takes over and defeats the Slavs.

937 Arnulf is demoted to his ancestral margravate by Emperor Otto I. The duchy becomes a bone of contention between the Welf and Staufian families.

1156 Emperor Frederick Barbarossa gives his cousin Henry the Lion, the powerful Saxon duke, the Bavarian duchy.

1158 Munich is founded by Henry the Lion as a salt-trading centre on the River Isar.

1180 Henry the Lion loses his Bavarian lands. Frederick I Barbarossa invests the Count Palatine Otto of Wittelsbach, descendant of the margraves of Schyren, with the duchy.

1183–1231 The adept Duke Ludwig triples his lands by inheritance, by purchase, by feudal acquisitions and by force.

1214 The Palatinate of the Rhine is secured for Bavaria.

1231 Duke Ludwig is murdered by a cloaked assassin at Kelheim.

1231–53 Otto II (the Illustrious) chooses to relocate his residence to the newly founded Landshut and expands his holdings by purchasing individual patches of land.

1247 The Wittelsbachs adopt the armorial bearings of the white and blue rhombuses (formerly held by the Counts of Bogen) as their family coat of arms.

1255 Territorial division into the separate duchies of Upper Bavaria and Straubing.

1392 Renewed fragmentation into four autonomous duchies (Landshut, Straubing, Ingolstadt, Munich).

1475 The Landshut Wedding between Prince Georg and Jadwiga, daughter of the king of Poland, marks the wealth of the Landshut branch of the Wittelsbachs.

1506 Duke Albrecht IV (the Wise) paves the way for territorial union and brings in primogeniture. He establishes Munich as main ducal capital for the Wittelsbachs.

1508–50 Duke William IV reunifies Bavaria. He champions the Counter-Reformation.

1550–79 Under Duke Albrecht V, the Protestants are persecuted. The Jesuit order gains the upper hand.

1555 The Peace of Augsburg establishes religious equality for Protestant and Roman Catholic faith – but subjects have to assume the faith of their rulers.

1609 Duke Maximilian I sets up the Catholic League in response to the Protestant Union.

1623 Maximilian becomes Elector of the Holy Roman Empire of the German Nation and seizes the Upper Palatinate for the Wittelsbachs.

1631–48 The Thirty Years' War (1618–48) devastates Bavaria. Following the defeat of Johann Tilly, the military champion of the Catholic armies, Augsburg and Munich are briefly occupied by the Swedes.

1679–1726 Elector Maximilian II Emanuel embarks on a building plan under the ?guidance of the Baroque masters, the Asam and Zimmermann brothers.

1701 Emperor Leopold I of Austria turns against Bavaria and unleashes the War of the Spanish Succession.

1704 Battle of Blenheim. A Franco-Bavarian army is defeated by the Habsburgs and British under Prince Eugene of Savoy and the Duke of Marlborough. Bavaria is ?occupied by the Austrians for 10 years.

1743 After the Austrian Succession, an Austrian Army of occupation arrives in Bavaria.

1745 The young Maximilian III Joseph is forced to retire from the war and concentrates instead on domestic reforms. The Academy for the Arts and Sciences is founded in Munich and the Jesuits banned from Bavaria.

1778–9 In the War of the Bavarian Succession between Austria and Prussia, Frederick the Great of Prussia ensures territorial integrity for the Wittelsbachs.

1805 Following the French occupation of Bavaria, Elector Maximilian IV becomes Napoleon's ally and his title is augmented to King of Bavaria. Bavaria is doubled in size, receiving Franconia and large parts of Swabia.

1813 Maximilian switches loyalties again and becomes a member of the Germanic Confederation.

1815 At the Congress of Vienna, Bavaria rises to become the third largest power in Germany, after Austria and Prussia.

1825–48 King Ludwig I promotes Bavaria's political and commercial standing and embarks on a neoclassical rebuilding of Munich under the aegis of court architect Leo von Klenze.

1837 Ludwig I creates the provinces of Upper, Middle and Lower Franconia.

1848 Ludwig I is forced to abdicate because of an affair with one of his mistresses. Political unrest in Munich.

1848–64 King Maximilian II brings Bavaria into an alliance with Saxony, Hanover and Württemberg to establish a strong third force in Germany.

1864–86 King Ludwig II supports Austria against Prussian Prince Otto von Bismarck. He sets out on an ambitious and costly building programme in Bavaria.

1866–7 The Seven Weeks War. Prussia defeats Austria and Bavaria. Ludwig II is coerced into paying financial reparations and into a defensive alliance with Prussia.

1870–1 The Franco-Prussian War. Bavaria is absorbed into a greater German Reich under Prussian domination. Bavaria keeps own army, postal service, railways and embassies abroad.

1918 Germany is defeated in the First World War. King Ludwig III is deposed and Bavaria is proclaimed a breakaway Soviet-style republic.

1919 After revolutionary councils spearhead a 'Red Terror' in Munich, the Bavarian Republic is quelled by the Freikorps. Bavaria becomes a constitutional state in the Weimar Republic.

1923 Failure of Hitler's Munich Putsch. He is imprisoned at Landsberg Prison.

1927 First all-German Nazi rally in Nürnberg.

1933 Hitler appointed Chancellor. Bavaria loses state privileges. Dachau concentration camp opened.

1935 Nazi Racial Purity Laws enacted in Nürnberg.

1938 Berchtesgaden and Munich provide the backdrop for the Munich Agreement, paving the way for the German occupation of the Sudentenland in Czechoslovakia.

1939–45 Bavaria's industry fuels Hitler's war effort from deep inside the Third Reich.

1942–3 The White Rose Society circulates a number of resistance leaflets at Munich University. Most members are tried and executed by the Nazis.

1944–5 Bavarian towns and cities suffer from incessant Allied carpet bombing.

1945 Bavaria becomes part of the US zone of occupation. Nürnberg is the location of the Allies' main war crime trials.

1946 Bavaria is re-established as a constitutional Land of the Federal Republic of Germany, but does not ratify its constitution. Thousands of eastern refugees are absorbed by Bavarian communities.

1947–1994 The right-wing Christian Social Union (CSU) emerges as pre-eminent ?political party in Bavaria.

1978 Franz-Josef Strauss heads the Bavarian state.

1980 Strauss states his candidature as all-German Chancellor at general elections.

1988 Strauss dies without a successor. Many party members switch their allegiance to the extreme-right Republikaner party.

1990 Reunification puts Franconia back in the heart of Germany.

1991 During the parliamentary debate about the return of the seat of government to Berlin, members of the CDU speak out against such a move, arguing that it would upset the political balance between the Federal government and its *Länder*.

2002 Federal Chancellor Gerhard Schröder and the Social Democrats (with their coalition partner, the Greens) win a second term by a painfully narrow margin against Conservative Bavarian challenger Stoiber. Schröder gains votes by opposing US policy on Iraq.

2005 Joseph Ratzinger, born in Bavaria in 1927, succeeds John Paul II to become pope, taking the name of Pope Benedict XVI.

2007 Gunther Beckstein becomes prime minister of Bavaria.

2008 Horst Seehofer replaces Beckstein as prime minister of Bavaria.

2010 Christian Democrat leader Angela Merkel re-elected as Chancellor of Germany in federal elections, and forms a centre-right coalition government with the Free Democrats.

Further Reading

History/General

Applegate, Celia, *A Nation of Provincials – the German Idea of Heimat* (UCL Press). A ?scholarly and absorbing study of one of the dynamos of the German psyche.

Ardagh, John, *Germany and the Germans* (Penguin). Far-reaching insights into a multifarious people, based on personal experience.

Blunt, Wilfred, *The Dream King* (Hamish Hamilton 1970). Thorough, intriguing biography of Ludwig II, builder of fairy-tale castles and patron of Richard Wagner.

Fulbrook, Mary, *A Concise History of Germany* (CUP 1990). The most compact, accessible account of German history – from murky beginnings to the 1989 revolution.

Huber, Heinz, with illustrations by Ronald Searle, *Haven't We Met Somewhere Before?* (Heinemann). Knowing, often funny, though at times dated view of the nation from the 1960s. Searle's cartoons are timeless.

Mann, Golo, *The History of Germany since 1789* (Penguin). Hefty tome, but a good read. Insider's account of the paradoxes of the nation – in history, philosophy and art – ending just after the Second World War.

Mikes, George, *Über Alles* (Allan Wingate). An opinionated, amusing personal account of the humorist's journey through a Germany recovering from the Second World War.

Schneider, Peter, *The German Comedy – Scenes of Life after the Wall* (Farrar Straus Giroux. First published in German as *Extreme Mittelage*). Essays and anecdotes that get under the skin of the new Germany.

Schulte, Michael, *Karl Valentin* (Hoffmann und Campe). A picture-a-page biography of Munich's odd comedian.

Tacitus, *The Germania* and *The Annals of Imperial Rome* (Penguin). Amusing, perceptive and at times delightfully personal account of the Germanic tribes knocking about in Roman times.

Art and Architecture

Anzelewsky, Fedja, *Albrecht Dürer – Malerische Werk* (Deutsche Verlag für Kunstwissenschaft). One volume of sumptuous illustrations and another of careful analysis of Dürer's paintings. Two further volumes – *The Complete Woodcuts* and *The Complete Etchings, Engravings and Drypoints* (both published by Dover) – make up an excellent record of the Master's work.

Greindl, Gabriele, *Barock in Ostbayern* (HB Bildatlas special series, no.21). A splendid survey of the work of the Asam brothers in eastern Bavaria.

Ranke, Winifred, et al, *Franz von Lenbach* (Prestel). A good biography and a well-illustrated survey of paintings by Munich's prince of the portrait (in German).

Prinz zu Sayn-Wittgenstein, Franz, *Schlösser in Bayern*. An insider's view of the castles and grand houses of Bavaria.

Simplicissimus (Haus der Kunst). The pick of cartoons and articles (1896–1944) from Munich's famous satirical magazine.

Toman, Rolf, *The High Middle Ages in Germany* (Benedikt Taschen). Lavishly ?illustrated series of essays on different aspects of medieval art and culture.

Watkin, David, *German Architecture and the Classical Ideal* (Thames & Hudson). Sets German neoclassicism in a European context. Good chapter on Leo von Klenze.

German Literary Landmarks

Böll, Heinrich, *The Lost Honour of Katharina Blum* (Penguin). Familiar to most non-Germans as a film. The best-known work of one of Germany's fêted modern novelists.

Brecht, Bertolt, *Poems and Plays* (Methuen). The influential 20th-century dramatist also wrote fine poetry, which has been sensitively translated.

Büchner, Georg, *Plays* (Methuen). *Woyzeck* and *Danton's Death* are perhaps the most extraordinary and powerful plays to come out of Germany – certainly the ones most frequently performed in other countries.

Goethe, Johann Wolfgang von, *The Sorrows of Young Werther; Faust; Selected Verse* (all published by Penguin). With these you have the core of the work of Germany's most prominent literary figure.

Grass, Günther, *The Tin Drum* (Picador). Gripping and fantastical novel about the curious Oskar, whose scream can shatter glass. Grass digs about in the German psyche to unearth the causes and effects of the success of the Nazis.

Grimmelhausen, Johann Jacob Christoffel von, *Simplicius Simplicissimus* (Dedalus). Epic novel written and set in the early 17th century, and one of the most important German works of its time.

Hesse, Hermann, *Narziss and Goldmund* (Penguin). The adventures of a beautiful medieval monk – suffused, some say, with repressed homo-eroticism.

Hoffmann, E.T.A., Heinrich von Kleist, Ludwig Tieck, *Six German Romantic Tales* (Angel). A handy anthology of tales by masters of the art.

Mann, Thomas, *Buddenbrooks* (Penguin). A semi-autobiographical novel that charts the decline of a wealthy German merchant family.

Remarque, Erich Maria, *All Quiet on the Western Front* (Picador). The book that has become the classic tale of the First World War, for German and English readers alike.

Schiller, Friedrich, *The Robbers, Wallenstein* and *William Tell* (Penguin). Main works by Germany's most respected dramatist after Goethe.

Index

Main page references are in **bold**. Page references to maps are in *italics*.

4th edition published 2010

Cadogan Guides is an imprint of
New Holland Publishers (UK) Ltd
London • Cape Town • Sydney • Auckland

New Holland Publishers (UK) Ltd	80 McKenzie Street	Unit 1, 66 Gibbes Street	218 Lake Road
Garfield House	Cape Town 8001	Chatswood, NSW 2067	Northcote
86–88 Edgware Road	South Africa	Australia	Auckland
London W2 2EA			New Zealand

Cadogan@nhpub.co.uk
www.cadoganguides.com
t 44 (0)20 7724 7773

Text Copyright © Rodney Bolt 1995, 1999, 2005, 2010
Copyright © 2010 New Holland Publishers (UK) Ltd

Cover photographs: © Jon Arnold Images Ltd/Alamy (front), © FB Fischer/Photolibrary (back)
Photo essay photographs: All photographers © *www.istockphoto.com* unless otherwise credited: p.10
(top) © Manfred Ball/Photolibrary, p.10 (bottom) © Norbert Probst/Photolibrary, p.11 (top) ©
Corbis/Photolibrary, © p.14 Superstock/Photolibrary
Maps © Cadogan Guides, drawn by Maidenhead Cartographic Services Ltd
Cover design: Jason Hopper
Photo essay design: Sarah Gardner
Updater: Robin Gauldie
Managing Editor: Guy Hobbs
Editor: Dominique Shead
Proofreading: Linda McQueen
Indexing: Isobel McLean

Printed in Italy by Legoprint
A catalogue record for this book is available from the British Library

ISBN: 978-1-86011-428-1

The author and publishers have made every effort to ensure the accuracy of the information in this
book at the time of going to press. However, they cannot accept any responsibility for any loss, injury or
inconvenience resulting from the use of information contained in this guide.

Please help us to keep this guide up to date. Although we have done our best to ensure that the information in this guide is correct at the time of going to press, laws and regulations are constantly changing and standards and prices fluctuate. We would be delighted to receive any comments concerning
existing entries or omissions.

All rights reserved. No part of this publication may be reproduced, stored in a retrieval system, or
transmitted, in any form or by any means, electronic or mechanical, including photocopying and
recording, or by any information storage and retrieval system except as may be expressly permitted by
the UK 1988 Copyright Design & Patents Act and the USA 1976 Copyright Act or in writing from the
publisher. Requests for permission should be addressed to Cadogan Guides/New Holland Publishers,
Garfield House, 86–88 Edgware Road, London, W2 2EA, United Kingdom.

Bavaria touring atlas

BONN

Aachen

Koblenz

Wiesbaden

Mainz

FRANKFURT
Offenbach

Fulda

Aschaffenburg

Würzburg

Ludwigshafen

Kaiserslautern

Heidelberg

Saarbrücken

Trier

Karlsruhe

BADEN
BADEN

Pforzheim

Ansbach

Heilbronn

STUTTGART

Böblingen

Balingen

Tübingen

Freiburg

Strasbourg

Konstanz

Singen

FRANCE

SWITZERLAND

CZECH
REPUBLIC

Aue

Zwickau

Reichenbach

Plauen

Sonneberg

Coburg

Kulmbach

Bayreuth

Bamberg

Erlangen

Fürth

NÜRNBERG

Schwabach

Amberg

Weiden i. d. Opf.

Schweinfurt

Regensburg

Straubing

Deggendorf

Passau

Ingolstadt

Eichstätt

Augsburg

Freising

Dachau

MUNICH

Fürstenfeldbruck

Kaufbeuren

Kempten

Biberach

Ulm

Ravensburg

Rosenheim

Salzburg

AUSTRIA

40 km
20 miles

N

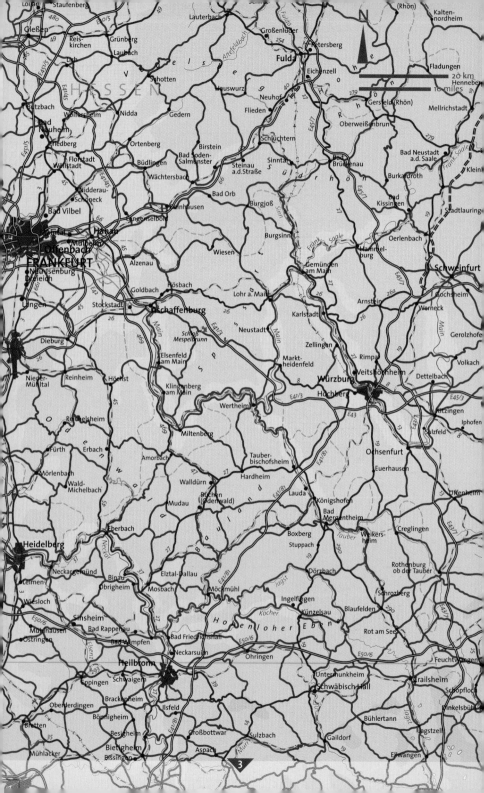

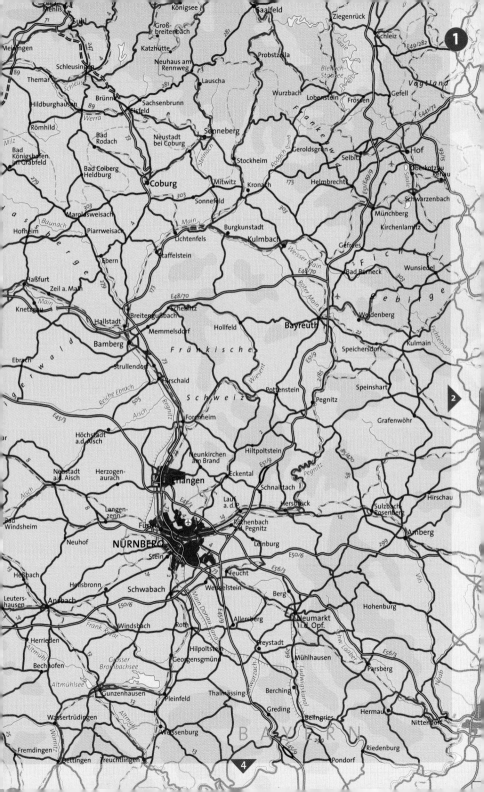

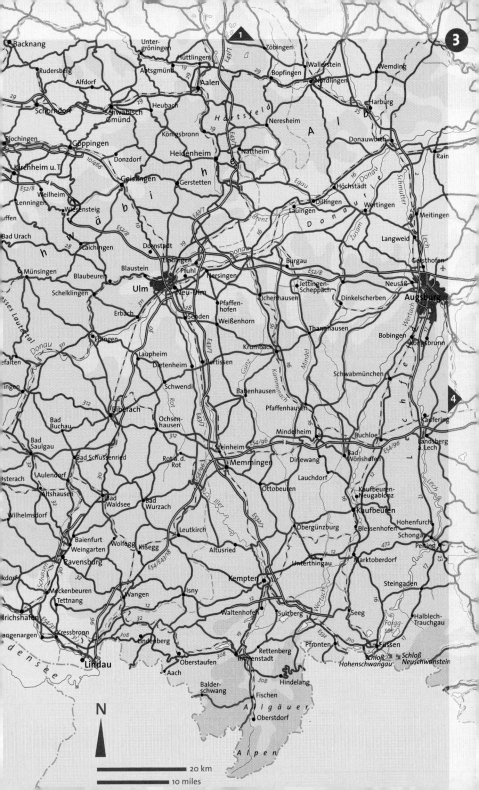

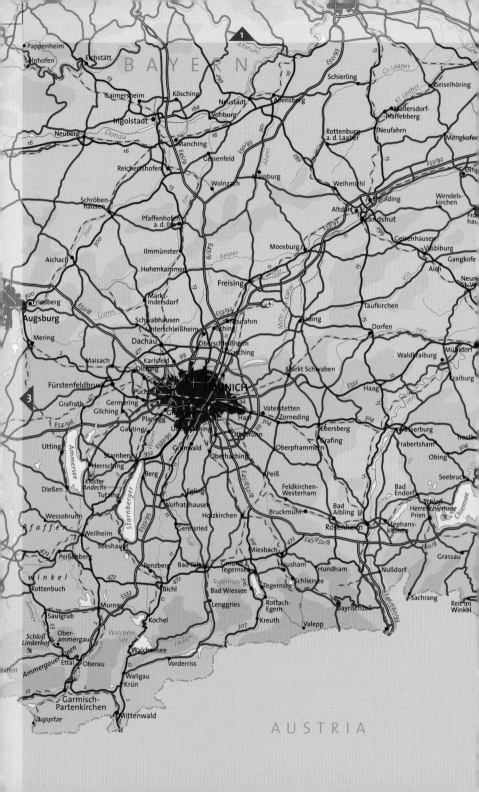

Bögen E56/3
Donau
Deggendorf
Plattling
Hengersberg
Thurmansbang
Osterhofen
Landau an der Isar
Eichendorf
Vilshofen
Vils
Aidenbach
Reisbach
Arnstorf
Malgersdorf
Fürstenzell
Pfarrkirchen
Griesbach im Rottal
Ruhstorf a.d. Rott
Eggenfelden
Rott
Pocking
Rotthalmünster
Bad Füssing
Tann
Malching
Inn
Simbach am Inn
Neuötting
Altötting
Burghausen
Burgkirchen
rching
Traunreut
Laufen
Salzach
Traunstein
Siegsdorf
Inzell
Ruhpolding
Bad Reichenhall
Salzburg
Berchtesgaden
Ramsau

Bayerischer Wald
Grafenau
Philippsreut
Freyung
Tittling
Waldkirchen
Hauzenberg
Untergriesbach
Passau
Donau

AUSTRIA

N

20 km
10 miles

CADOGANguides

For an altogether richer
travel experience...

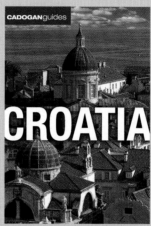